3 50

D0560433

3

2

ONE AT LARGE

31

2   1

30

1 — 14

29

5   1   2

27

4
26   3

3   6

RHODE ISLAND
2 DISTRICTS

NASSAU COUNTY
1—3 DISTRICTS

CONNECTICUT
ALSO 1 AT LARGE

PHILADELPHIA
1—6 DISTRICTS

NEW YORK CITY
4—25 DISTRICTS

BALTIMORE
3,4,5 PT, 7

E AT LARGE

☆ ☆

VOLUME II *of the Report of the Cooperative Research Project
on Convention Delegations* • *Prepared under the auspices of*
THE AMERICAN POLITICAL SCIENCE ASSOCIATION
with the cooperation of
THE BROOKINGS INSTITUTION

Project Director:
PAUL T. DAVID, *The Brookings Institution*

Project Advisory Committee:
ARTHUR N. HOLCOMBE, Chairman, *Harvard University*
LOUIS BROWNLOW, *Public Administration Clearing House*
RICHARD S. CHILDS, *National Municipal League*
ALEXANDER HEARD, *University of North Carolina*
PETER H. ODEGARD, *University of California*
LOUISE OVERACKER, *Wellesley College*
JAMES K. POLLOCK, *University of Michigan*

Project Editors:
PAUL T. DAVID, *The Brookings Institution*
MALCOLM MOOS, *Johns Hopkins University*
RALPH M. GOLDMAN, *The Brookings Institution*

Presidential Nominating Politics in 1952

THE NORTHEAST

☆ ☆

VOLUME TWO

Presidential Nominating Politics
in 1952

THE NORTHEAST

Edited by

PAUL T. DAVID

MALCOLM MOOS

RALPH M. GOLDMAN

BALTIMORE - THE JOHNS HOPKINS PRESS

The project resulting in this report was made possible by funds granted on two occasions by the Edgar B. Stern Family Fund of New Orleans. The American Political Science Association is most grateful for the financial assistance so accorded; however, the Edgar B. Stern Family Fund is not the author, publisher, or proprietor of this publication and is not to be understood as approving or disapproving by virtue of its grants any of the statements and views expressed herein. A similar understanding should be expressed with respect to the financial and other assistance accorded by the Brookings Institution. The Institution's assistance and co-operation in all phases of the project are most appreciated, but it has not assumed administrative or substantive responsibility for the project at any time.

Distributed in Great Britain, India, and Pakistan by Geoffrey Cumberlege: Oxford University Press, London, Bombay, and Karachi. Printed in the United States of America by the Reese Press, Baltimore.

Library of Congress Catalog Card Number: 54-8008

CONTRIBUTORS TO THE VOLUME

The chapters in this volume for the states and other areas listed here were prepared as indicated in the acknowledgments at the end of each chapter. The following contributors provided the reports on which the chapters are primarily based, or otherwise assisted in the preparation of the chapters:

MAINE
Lawrence L. Pelletier, *Bowdoin College*; also, for the Democratic delegation, Herbert H. Wood, *University of Maine*.

NEW HAMPSHIRE
Robert B. Dishman, with the assistance, for the Republican delegation, of John T. Holden, George H. Deming, and Allan A. Kuusisto, all of the *University of New Hampshire*.

VERMONT
Robert S. Babcock, *University of Vermont*; also, for the Democratic delegation, Joan Pauley.

MASSACHUSETTS
Lashley G. Harvey, *Boston University*; Samuel P. Huntington, *Harvard University*; Charles P. Howard, *Middlesex County Government*; John L. Fletcher and Troy R. Westmeyer, *Boston University*.

RHODE ISLAND
Felix Rackow, *Brown University*; also, for the Democratic delegation, John O. Stitely, *University of Rhode Island*.

CONNECTICUT
Mrs. Mary T. Reynolds, Hamden, Connecticut, and Roland

Young, *Northwestern University*, for the Republican delegation.
Bernhard O. J. Linnevold, *University of Connecticut*, for the
Democratic delegation.

NEW YORK
Phillips Bradley, *Syracuse University*, for the Republican delegation.

Mrs. Louise Burr Gerrard, *Barnard College*, and Harold Stein,
Twentieth Century Fund, for the Democratic delegation.

NEW JERSEY
Harry R. Davis, *Beloit College*.

DELAWARE
Paul Dolan, *University of Delaware*.

MARYLAND
Malcolm Moos, *Johns Hopkins University*.

PENNSYLVANIA
G. Edward Janosik, *University of Pennsylvania*.

WEST VIRGINIA
Franklin L. Burdette, *University of Maryland*, for the Republican delegation.

William R. Ross, *West Virginia University*, for the Democratic
delegation.

DISTRICT OF COLUMBIA
H. Rowland Ludden, *George Washington University*.

PUERTO RICO
Henry Wells, *University of Puerto Rico*.

PREFATORY NOTE

In this book, the story is told of how each of the northeastern states participated in the presidential nominating activities of 1952. Similar information for other parts of the United States will be found in Volume III, The South; Volume IV, The Middle West; and Volume V, The West.

Volume I of the series, The National Story, should be read and used in conjunction with the present volume. It contains seven chapters, as follows: Chapter 1, which takes a general view of the presidential nominating process as a subject for analytical study; Chapter 2, an account of the national pre-convention campaigns of 1952; Chapter 3, the Republican National Convention; Chapter 4, The Democratic National Convention; Chapter 5, a review of the varieties of experience in 1952 with the different state systems for participating in the process; Chapter 6, a discussion of the basic issues of nominating procedure; and Chapter 7, an assessment of the record of the two national conventions of 1952, with comment on the possible lines of change in the future. Full details of major roll call votes at the two national conventions will be found in Chapters 3 and 4 of Volume I, and should be consulted in connection with the discussions of individual delegation voting records that appear in the present volume.

TABLE OF CONTENTS

Presidential Nominating Politics in 1952

THE NORTHEAST

☆ ☆

THE

The Northeast

Maine	Rhode Island	Delaware
New Hampshire	Connecticut	Maryland
Vermont	New York	Pennsylvania
Massachusetts	New Jersey	West Virginia
	District of Columbia	
	Puerto Rico (see note)	

Electoral votes, 1952: 153

National convention votes, 1952:
  Democratic, 334
  Republican, 372

Population, 1950: 44,946,802
  Urban, 77%; *rural nonfarm,* 18%; *rural farm,* 5%

Population increase, 1940-50: 4,317,211 (11%)
  Urban, 8%; *rural nonfarm,* 34%; *rural farm,* 23% decline

Presidential vote, 1948:		*1952:*
Democratic,	8,018,334	8,819,582
Republican,	8,235,507	11,375,299
American		
Labor,	509,559	64,211
Liberal,	222,562	416,711
Progressive,	171,810	22,412

Gubernatorial vote (last election before 1952):
Democratic,	7,159,836
Republican,	7,966,371
Liberal,	265,699
American	
Labor,	221,966

U. S. Representatives vote, *all districts, 1950:*		*1952:*
Democratic,	6,974,590	8,871,239
Republican,	7,506,830	10,629,681

U. S. Representatives elected 1950:		*1952:*
Democratic,	60	49
Republican,	73	80

2

NORTHEAST

CHAPTER 1

AMONG THE GREAT REGIONS OF THE UNITED STATES, probably none is more lacking internally in regional consciousness than the Northeast. But only the entire area from Maine to West Virginia can be regarded as a region comparable to the South, from Virginia to Texas; the Middle West, from Ohio to Nebraska; or the West, with all of the Mountain and Pacific states for its compass. Moreover, the northeastern region does have a homogeneity of its own, particularly for political studies, that deserves more study than it has often received. The urban areas from Boston to Washington, D. C., are the greatest agglomeration of nearly continuous metropolitan communities to be found anywhere in the world. There is no sudden breaking-off point just east of New York or between Philadelphia and Baltimore. Certainly other parts of the United States make no such fine distinctions when referring to a large area that has been a center of economic and political power from the earliest days of the Republic.

The present volume includes a chapter for each of the twelve states from Maine to West Virginia. It also includes a chapter for the District of Columbia, which seems to belong in the northeastern region if it is to be assigned to any region of continental United States. Finally, the chapter for Puerto Rico has been assigned to this volume because of the ethnic and economic relationships between the Island and the northeastern part of the mainland. The relative importance of these states and areas in the national conventions is

---

Note: The tabulation on the opposite page includes data for the twelve states listed there and the District of Columbia. It does not include data for Puerto Rico, for which a chapter is included in this volume, and in which similar data will be found. The tabulation also omits data for the Virgin Islands and the Canal Zone, although for convenience those areas were included with the northeastern region in the tabulations on voting at the national conventions in Volume I, and in Table 1 of this chapter.

somewhat indicated by Table 1, which shows the number of votes assigned to each in the national conventions of 1952 under the various provisions of the national party rules.

New York and Pennsylvania are the giant states of the region, with 25 million people between them in 1950, more than half the regional total. New Jersey and Massachusetts are next; both were close to the five million population mark in 1950. Maryland, Connecticut, and West Virginia each stood over two million. Maine was next, with over 900,000; Rhode Island, about 800,000; New Hampshire, over 500,000; Vermont, about 400,000; Delaware, 300,000.

The area as a whole is one of hotly competitive politics, highly organized on a two-party basis. Maine and Vermont are the well-known exceptions, visible islands of perennial Republicanism. Larger one-party areas are buried and almost unheard of among the many congressional districts of New York and Pennsylvania. But the region as a whole is capable of swinging violently from one major party to the other in presidential and congressional elections. In 1952, Eisenhower carried every state in the area but West Virginia; in 1936, Franklin D. Roosevelt had carried all but Maine and Vermont.

In the Republican nominating campaigns of 1952, the Northeast was the earliest center of major Eisenhower support. At the Republican national convention, it provided 301 of the 595 votes that Eisenhower had polled before the Minnesota switch, as shown in Table 4 of Volume I. His nomination probably would not have been possible without a considerable amount of diversified support from all sections of the United States, but it also would have been impossible without the massive support of the Northeast, which gave him 80 per cent of its convention votes.

In the campaigns for the Democratic nomination in 1952, the Northeast played an equally strategic role. It did not begin with a developed enthusiasm for Stevenson, such as it already had for Eisenhower. But the Democrats of the Northeast were certain, far beyond argument, that they did not want Russell; and they were less inclined than the Democrats of other areas to become enthusiastic over Estes Kefauver. In any event, as Table 6 of Volume I shows, the Northeast gave Kefauver only 64½ votes on the first nominating ballot, of whom not many more than half stayed with him to the end.

Table 1

VOTING STRENGTH IN THE NATIONAL CONVENTIONS OF 1952:
THE NORTHEAST

State or Other Area	Congressional District Votes		Votes at Large (Other than Bonus)		Bonus Votes		Total Votes	
	Rep.	Dem.	Rep.	Dem.	Rep.	Dem.	Rep.	Dem.
Maine	6	6	4	4	6	—	16	10
New Hampshire	4	4	4	4	6	—	14	8
Vermont[a]	—	—	6	6	6	—	12	6
Massachusetts	28	28	4	4	6[b]	4	38	36
Rhode Island	4	4	4	4	—	4	8	12
Connecticut[c]	10	10	6	6	6	—	22	16
New York[d]	90	90	—	4	6	—	96	94
New Jersey	28	28	4	4	6	—	38	32
Delaware[a]	—	—	6	6	6	—	12	6
Maryland	14	14	4	4	6	—	24	18
Pennsylvania[e]	60	60	4	10	6	—	70	70
West Virginia	12	12	4	4	—	4	16	20
Dist. of Columbia	—	—	6	6	—	—	6	6
Puerto Rico[f]	—	—	3	6	—	—	3	6
Virgin Islands[f]	—	—	1	2	—	—	1	2
Canal Zone[f]	—	—	—	2	—	—	—	2
Total	256	256	60	76	60	12	376	344

[a] Only one congressman at large, hence all delegates at large.

[b] For electing Republican senator.

[c] Connecticut has five congressional districts and one congressman at large.

[d] New York lost two congressional seats after the 1950 census but had not completed redistricting, hence used its regular Republican delegates-at-large seats for the two disappearing districts; in the Democratic party, special action was taken to prevent loss of delegate seats because of redistricting.

[e] Pennsylvania lost three congressional seats after the 1950 census, and lost delegate strength accordingly in the Republican convention, but not in the Democratic under the rules of that party as applicable in 1952.

[f] Puerto Rico, the Virgin Islands, and the Canal Zone are included in this table for the reasons indicated in Table 3 of Volume I.

On the other hand, on the third ballot it gave Stevenson 287 of the 617½ votes that gave him the nomination, and was thus even more responsible for his nomination than his home area of the Middle

West. The Northeast was thus heavily behind the winner in both major party nominating contests; and its reputation for political power and acumen was maintained.

In the state chapters that follow, we have sought to give as full an account as the space will permit of the manner in which each state participated in the nominating contests of 1952 in both parties. Each chapter includes something on the political background of the state, followed by sections on the state's delegations to the Republican and Democratic national conventions. For each delegation, we have sought information as to how it was picked and on the nature of the contest, if there was one, that controlled the selection of the delegation and its allegiances to national candidates. Details follow on the composition of the delegation, its voting record and other activities at the convention, and the aftermath in the state. Finally, each chapter concludes with a review of the state's experience in the nominating process in 1952.

Presidential primaries were held in almost all of the larger states of the Northeast in 1952, including the primaries held in both parties in Massachusetts, New York, New Jersey, Pennsylvania, and West Virginia. Unpledged delegates were the outcome of these primaries in most of the cases. New Hampshire, on the other hand, was the scene of the first and in many respects the most outstanding presidential primary held in 1952. In Maryland, an unusual type of primary was held for the election of state convention delegates. The other five states of the region—Maine, Vermont, Rhode Island, Connecticut, and Delaware—maintained ancient party processes in full force for the selection of delegates and other activities. Their experience held much of interest, in part because of the skill demonstrated by several of these smaller states in producing delegations that were influential far beyond their numbers at the national conventions.

MAINE

KEY FACTS

Electoral votes, 1952: 5
National convention votes, 1952:
    Democratic, 10
    Republican, 16
Population 1950: 913,774
    Urban, 52%; rural nonfarm, 35%; rural farm, 13%
Population increase, 1940-50: 66,548 (8%)
    Urban, 9%; rural nonfarm, 23%; rural farm, 26% decline

Presidential vote, 1948:			*1952:*
Democratic,	111,916	(42%)	118,806 (34%)
Republican,	150,234	(57%)	232,353 (66%)
Progressive,	1,884	(1%)	

Gubernatorial vote, 1950:		*1952:*
Democratic,	94,304	82,538
Republican,	145,823	128,532
State Rights Democrat,	1,054	—
Republican Independent	—	35,732
Independent	—	1,639

U. S. Representatives vote, all districts, 1950:		*1952:*
Democratic,	100,731	76,708
Republican,	136,901	156,727

U. S. Representatives elected 1950:		*1952:*
Democratic,	0	0
Republican,	3	3

State legislature elected 1953:
    Senate: Democrats, 2;   Republicans, 31
    House: Democrats, 24;   Republicans, 127
Method of selecting national convention delegates:
    Democratic: state convention
    Republican: district and state conventions

8

Based primarily on reports by LAWRENCE L. PELLETIER

——————————————————————————CHAPTER 2

MAINE IS A SAFELY REPUBLICAN STATE. It has not voted for a Democratic presidential candidate since 1912, and the Democrats have elected a governor only four times since 1900. Support for the Republican party is particularly strong in the rural areas, which still dominate Maine politically, but Portland and Bangor are also usually Republican. Democratic strength exists in a few communities in Aroostook and Washington counties, but Democratic majorities are concentrated in industrial communities, such as Biddeford, Lewiston, Sanford, Brunswick, and Rumford. In the 1948 presidential election the Democrats won only two counties, Adroscoggin and York. In 1952, the large vote for Eisenhower resulted in the Republicans' sweeping all sixteen counties.

From 1920 to 1950, the Democrats were able to poll an average of approximately 40 per cent of the gubernatorial and presidential vote. Democratic strength was at its peak during the 1930's when the impact of the depression radically increased the size of the turnout in elections; since 1940 Democratic strength has ebbed with a rise in nonvoting. The Democratic party is not well organized, especially at the local level; in several counties it does not nominate candidates for the state legislature. It is inadequately financed; there are no wealthy local contributors to call upon in Maine, and Maine Democrats receive little assistance from the national party. The unions may possibly spend more money helping Democratic candidates in Maine than the party raises itself. Democratic strength is, however, generally unchallenged in such strongholds as Biddeford and Lewiston. Support on a state-wide basis is sufficient to keep Republicans wary of a possible Democratic coup.

The Democratic party possesses potential leadership of high calibre,

9

but the acute factionalism in the party rarely permits such leadership to emerge. For twenty years, it was often drained off by federal patronage. Democratic politicians have sometimes seemed more interested in self-advancement in the party organization than in winning elections. In this sense, behavior in the minority party is apparently similar to that of its counterpart in some of the southern one-party states. At any rate, even in 1952, when the Republicans were beset by an investigation of the State Liquor Commission and an extremely bitter senatorial primary contest, the Democrats failed to nominate candidates who could be regarded as serious contenders.

Perhaps the ills of the Democratic party can be partially explained by three factors. First, Democratic control of the national government was exercised in a way that made more difficult, rather than facilitated, the building of a strong Democratic party in Maine. Too many Democrats were merely nominal members of the party, seeking rewards from Washington. Even when the intent was otherwise, party leaders frequently had their effectiveness reduced by accepting federal appointments. Second, the Democratic party suffers from a basic cleavage between the French-Canadians and the old-time Democrats. This division may be sublimated, but on occasions it breaks into the open, as it did in the 1952 convention. Visible or not, it is always there and tends to weaken the party. Third, many "presidential Democrats" who vote the ticket nationally register as Republicans because the significant primary contest is usually in that party. This produces a tendency to make the Republican party more liberal than might otherwise be the case.

By Maine Democratic standards, the majority party is well organized and financed. There is, however, no strong state-wide organization, and it would be a mistake to assume that Maine Republicans are bossed or machine controlled. There is no visible Republican organization that can assure the nomination and election of a favored candidate. The two present United States senators are testimony of the weakness of the so-called organization; neither Margaret Chase Smith nor Frederick G. Payne could be called the candidate of the organization. They both have frequently ignored other party leaders and appealed directly to the voters. As governor, Payne was not regarded as an organization man, but this did not prevent him from moving to the United States Senate.

The primary system has apparently dealt a shattering blow to the once proud organization of the Republican party in Maine. The party organization takes little or no part in the primaries; each candidate builds a personal following upon which he continues to rely in the general election. Once the candidate is selected, there is little the party workers can do but go along with the primary choice; but the candidate feels little obligation to the party workers because the general elections often do not constitute a real contest. Many party workers believe that under present conditions the organization has become almost superfluous. It gets out the vote on election day and raises some money, but has no real voice in the selection of candidates or the consideration of public policies. Most party stalwarts blame the primary system for the weakness of the Republican organization.

Republicans enjoy an overwhelming superiority in both houses of the state legislature, but Republican leaders, including the governor, often find it difficult to push through desired legislation. Party lines can be invoked on one or two issues a session, but party caucuses rarely attempt to bind members. The organization of the Republican party is a factor in its continued success in the state, but perhaps even more significant are limited industrialization and a climate of opinion that protect most of the things for which the industrial, financial, and agricultural elements in the Republican party stand. The continued trend toward urbanization will, however, probably strengthen the Democrats.

THE REPUBLICAN DELEGATION

The Republicans select their national convention delegates in district and state conventions. The district conventions are held at the same time as the state convention and are regarded as integral parts of the larger body. The same delegates are usually elected to state and district conventions, although some caucuses customarily make the state convention delegates the alternates for the district convention and vice versa.

In former years, the three district conventions have usually selected the district delegates and the general meeting of the state convention has approved the delegates-at-large. Most of the delegates-at-large were selected in actual practice by the state committee and the national committeeman; it has been frequently charged that this system effectively frustrated any rank-and-file control of the delegates-at-large.

In 1948 the usual procedure was followed. An effort was made to name delegates who would not only attend the national convention but would also represent different segments of the party. Stassen sentiment was strong, but party leaders were included regardless of their stand on presidential candidates. Thus Alan Bird, state committee chairman and a strong Dewey supporter, was named as a delegate even though Stassen supporters realized that his views could not be shaken. The result was a split delegation—7 for Stassen, 4 for Dewey, 1 for Vandenberg, and 1 for Taft. At least four of the delegates were Young Republicans—perhaps the greatest recognition ever given the junior group by the parent organization.

The call for the state convention, which was to elect a state committee, a district committee for each congressional district, and a county committee for each county, as well as formulate a state platform, nominate five presidential electors, and elect 16 delegates and 16 alternates to the national convention, went out on February 4, 1952. All delegates to the state convention, which was to convene in Bangor on March 27, were to be elected after the date of the call, but the caucuses were not required to be held on a fixed day. According to the call, "Each city, town and plantation shall be entitled to one delegate, and for each 100 votes cast for the Republican candidates for Governor in 1948 one additional delegate, provided further, that if after dividing the number of votes so cast in 1948 by 100 the number of votes remaining is 65 or more, said city, town or plantation shall be entitled to one additional delegate." The state convention in 1952 was thus authorized to consist of 1813 delegates and as many alternates. Since attendance was unusually heavy, hotel and eating facilities were strained.

THE SELECTION PROCESS IN 1952

As the struggle between Taft and Eisenhower for convention delegates developed, the state witnessed an unusual amount of pre-convention activity. Taft was brought to Maine as early as August 1951.

The Taft forces were well financed and in the 3d congressional district were well organized. They boasted such political leaders as former Governor Sumner Sewall and Senator Owen Brewster. The latter, as the campaign progressed and as his own struggle for renomination to the United States Senate became more intense, attempted to de-emphasize his Taft sympathies. Finally he decided to take no part in the state convention fight. The Taft organization had as executive-secretary Mrs. Inez Wing, Republican national committeewoman.

Eisenhower supporters were also well organized, except in the 3d district where the support for Eisenhower was primarily from amateurs. The story is told that one important Eisenhower leader in Bangor attended the movies the evening the caucuses were held in that city. The 3d district is Brewster's home and Ralph Masterman, then chairman of the state committee, and state Senator Robert Haskell, strong Taft supporters, were influential in that section of the state. The Eisenhower organization was headed initially by Governor Frederick G. Payne, but after the announcement of his candidacy for the United States Senate, the Governor resigned and his place was taken by a young Portland attorney, Sidney W. Thaxter. The Committee for Eisenhower apparently expended slightly over $4,000 in the pre-convention campaign.

Both sides complained of lack of time to organize, perhaps because Maine was one of the first states to hold its state convention. Although uncertainty concerning the availability of Eisenhower as a candidate may have delayed the organization of his supporters, there is some evidence that with more time the Taft forces, which appeared to get off to an early start, might have made a better showing. One thing is clear: from the beginning Eisenhower showed great grass-roots strength, especially in the southern part of the state.

The delegates to the state convention in Maine are chosen directly at town or, in the cities, voting precinct caucuses; county conventions are not held as an intermediate step. These caucuses are regulated by state law on such matters as notice, participation, etc. In 1952 to an unusual extent the Taft and Eisenhower organizations made a real effort to invade the caucuses, which are usually poorly attended and dominated by a minority group, in some instances by the chairman of the local party committee. The results were interesting. Although some caucuses were packed for a particular candidate, in a remarkable number of instances delegates to the state convention were selected as usual without regard for their preference as to a presidential candidate. They were chosen to go to the state convention primarily in recognition of past services to the party. Proxies are permitted in the state convention. In addition, if the elected delegates and alternates from a locality fail to attend the convention, the delegation or its chairman may fill any vacancy with a Republican voter from that town or city.

Pre-convention maneuvering was not confined to the caucuses. At one point Senator Margaret Chase Smith accused the state committee of circulating anti-Eisenhower literature. The Taft forces apparently hoped to influence the convention by selecting a keynote speaker who would be favorable to their candidate, but it was finally agreed that a neutral speaker would be chosen. Thus, when Governor John Davis Lodge of Connecticut declared himself for Eisenhower, he was permitted to withdraw as keynoter although he had previously accepted.

The Taft-Eisenhower conflict threatened to split the party. As the convention approached, the early confidence of the Taft group was moderated, and on the eve of the convention, Ralph Masterman, state committee chairman, predicted a 50-50 split. The Eisenhower forces, quietly confident, agreed that they would do at least that well, even though the more optimistic Taft supporters still predicted an overwhelming victory for their candidate. In view of the serious division in the party, leaders of both factions were disturbed by the possibility of an extended floor battle. The rules of the convention were of doubtful adequacy for the occasion; one leader expressed a doubt as to whether the rules could be found. Each side, uncertain of its strength and how long its supporters could be held in line, was anxious for an agreement on procedure. In particular, the Eisenhower leaders were disturbed by the fact that the convention was being held in Taft territory. A long fight on the floor would work against their candidate, since it would be difficult to hold some of the Eisenhower delegates from southern Maine. Both sides were well represented in the procedural discussion. The national committeeman leaned toward Eisenhower and the chairman of the state committee was a Taft supporter. The former, in particular, was anxious that the convention be conducted as harmoniously as possible.

An agreement was reached in February at a state committee meeting attended by Payne and Brewster. The agreement gave the selection of all the delegates to the district conventions. Two district delegates were to be elected by each of the three congressional districts. Three delegates-at-large were to be nominated by each of the 1st and 3d district conventions. The 2d district convention was to nominate four delegates-at-large. These nominations were to be submitted to the state convention for approval, which it was assumed would be routine. The decision to award the odd delegate to the 2d district was justified on various grounds, but the fact that the district was still uncertain may have been a factor. The 1st district was clearly for Eisenhower, and the 3d for Taft. It was also agreed that past practice would not be observed by having the state committee include certain party leaders among the delegates-at-large, but it was recommended that the district conventions give careful consideration to the four individuals who would normally be included. In fact, all four were selected, but the two in the 2d district were thought to be for Eisenhower and the two in the 3d district were for Taft. Thus their preferences coincided with those of their district conventions.

There was no general agreement as to how the vote should be taken in the district conventions. A prolonged meeting of party leaders on the eve of the convention failed to produce an understanding in the 2d district. The early hope of the Taft group was to vote on each delegate separately with the hope that they might win one or two of the seats. The Eisenhower leaders desired to present a slate and to select all delegates and alternates on the same ballot, but the Taft supporters were opposed, apparently in part because they had not selected a full slate of alternates. In the end, an Australian ballot was utilized and each delegate was called and cast his ballot individually, which was found to be a lengthy procedure and delayed the adjournment of the convention well beyond that of the other two district meetings. There was less difficulty in reaching an agreement on voting in the 1st and 3d districts. In the 1st, each town and city delegation was polled by secret ballot and the ballots were collected by the chairman of the delegation.

The decisions as to the slates of candidates were apparently fluid until the end. Each side was attempting to enlist prominent individuals, recognize geographical distribution, and in general strengthen its slate. Above all each side wished to be certain that its list of candidates contained only supporters of Eisenhower or Taft, as the case might be. National candidate allegiances were apparently decisive in the contests between opposing slates of would-be delegates. For example, Sumner Sewall, a popular former governor, was unable to overcome the fact that he was a Taft supporter. David Nichols, chairman of the Maine Young Republicans, and Selma Wagg, vice-chairman of the state committee, were elected in the 2d district convention without declaring themselves, but it was widely believed that they were for Eisenhower.

The Eisenhower forces emerged triumphant from two of the three district conventions. They won five delegates in the 1st district and four in the 2d, with two uncommitted who were assumed to lean toward Ike. The Taft supporters controlled the 3d district convention and named all five delegates. As the Eisenhower forces became conscious of their strength, some of the more enthusiastic argued that the fight should be carried to the general session of the state convention, at which the ten delegates-at-large nominated by the district conventions were to be formally approved. It appeared that Eisenhower could thus win 14 of the 16 delegates since his supporters were in the majority. In view of the agreement in February, however, the Eisenhower leadership decided not to risk a floor fight. The decisions of the district conventions were allowed to stand.

Neither Senator Smith nor Senator Brewster took an open part in the convention fight, although they were supposedly on opposite sides. Senator Smith did by implication come out for Eisenhower in a speech made at Orono while the convention was in session; this speech was credited by some as influencing the vote in the 2d district convention. The gubernatorial candidates also refrained from taking sides in the presidential race.

COMPOSITION OF THE DELEGATION

Major officeholders are not ordinarily elected as delegates from Maine to the Republican national convention. The delegation in 1952 was no exception. It included a county attorney and several state legislators; many delegates held or had held party offices. Although the national committeeman was not included, the chairman and vice-chairman of the state committee and the chairman of the Young Republicans were delegates. A conscious effort was made to include women and Young Republicans and to see that every county was represented.

The delegation included three women, and three Young Republicans. The youngest delegate was 34 and the average age of the group was in the forties. Occupationally, the delegation included seven lawyers. No French-Canadians and no representatives of labor were included. Only two of the 16 had attended the 1948 convention as delegates and none had served in the 1944 convention in that capacity. At least two had been elected as alternates to previous conventions. Not more than two or three delegates were widely known in the state, and none had a national reputation. All were expected to pay their own expenses of convention attendance, which in 1952 ran as high as $1,400. This tended to restrict the field from which selections were made.

In 1952 the Republican delegates were chosen first because they were for Eisenhower or Taft and second because they were popular with their respective district conventions. They were left unpledged so that if the situation changed radically before the national convention, the Maine delegation would be able to act freely.

ACTIVITIES AND VOTING RECORD

Shortly after the state convention, the delegates gathered in Augusta. At this meeting Sidney W. Thaxter, the chairman of the Eisenhower committee, was elected to serve as chairman of the delegation by a 10-5 vote. The Taft minority supported Ralph Masterman. The delegation voted to go to Chicago by train and to assess each delegate and alternate $7.50 to pay for a room for delegation headquarters in Chicago. Each delegate and alternate was also requested to raise $100 toward the quota set for Maine by the national committee; and this money was to be sent to the national committee before the convention.

About fifty persons from Maine, including newsmen and radio

representatives, attended the national convention. Only two Taft delegates traveled by train with the group. The remaining Taft delegates flew to Chicago. Senator Owen Brewster was the only member of Congress from Maine present at the convention.

Upon arrival, badges and convention information were distributed. Another meeting was held on Monday morning prior to the opening of the convention at which there was a heated discussion regarding the stand of the national committee on seating contested delegations. It was feared that two of the Eisenhower delegates would vote for the Taft proposals, but the other Eisenhower delegates were able to convince the two doubtful ones that this was a Taft-Eisenhower vote and that they should go along with their choice for president regardless of their opinion on the merits of the specific questions involved.

After this session the delegation held no further caucuses. The procedure for voting on the floor was to pass around a sheet of paper and to let each delegate sign it under a yes or no heading. The major roll call votes, following the Taft-Eisenhower split in the delegation, were 11-5, except that after the first nominating ballot switch and on the final ballot the delegation divided 15-1. Delegate Frank A. Pike refused to make the vote unanimous for Eisenhower. This delegate came from an area where pro-Taft sentiment in the Taft-Eisenhower fight was intense. The decision not to caucus after the first day was apparently made by Thaxter, the delegation chairman, but an amicable agreement as to organization and procedure was reached. For example, it was understood that if a Taft delegate was absent, a Taft alternate would cast his vote and vice versa. An understanding was also worked out as to committee assignments in which the Eisenhower forces placed one of their group on the credentials committee.

Some of the Maine delegates were interested in presenting the name of Margaret Chase Smith for vice-president. Other delegates were cool to the idea. This effort was abandoned when Eisenhower's selection of Richard Nixon as his running mate was made public.

AFTERMATH IN THE STATE

Eisenhower won an overwhelming victory in Maine, and there have been changes in the forces in control of the Republican party. Fred

G. Scribner, national committeeman, who would have lost his post with a Taft victory, has become counsel of the Republican national committee and a more influential figure in the Republican party, both in Maine and the nation. Ralph Masterman, a Taft supporter, was succeeded as chairman of the state committee by Bradford Hutchins, who was for Eisenhower. The earlier defeat of Senator Owen Brewster by Governor Frederick G. Payne in the primary also had an impact on the Republican organization in Maine. The liberal wing of the party has apparently become more important with the victory of the Eisenhower supporters.

THE DEMOCRATIC DELEGATION

Based in part on a report by
HERBERT H. WOOD

In general, the method of selecting a national convention delegation in the Democratic party of Maine is similar to that in the Republican, but district conventions are not used. The personnel of the Democratic state convention is rather strikingly different from that of the Republican. While the latter body includes many business and professional leaders, it lacks substantial representation from elements, such as labor leaders and French-Canadians, that are very evident in the Democratic convention. The selection of convention delegates in the Democratic party suffers from the absence of a state-wide organization. Senator Paul H. Douglas has joked that the Democratic caucus in his home town in Maine could have been held in a phone booth. In many instances attendance is even lower than in the Republican counterpart, if this is possible, and in many municipalities a Democratic caucus is not held at all.

In 1952 the Democrats met without great enthusiasm. They were a party split by factionalism, frustrated by lack of leadership and funds, weakened by such factors as the September election and the tendency of many who voted Democratic to register as Republicans, and divided by ideological and ethnic considerations into Jeffersonian and New Deal Democrats, Yankees and French-Canadians. As usual the party was going through an intra-organization struggle to establish leadership. At first there appeared to be little interest in attending the national convention, but by the time the state convention assembled, twenty-five persons had indicated a desire to go to Chicago. In recent state conventions it has been customary to instruct the delegates. Such was the case in 1936, 1940, 1944, and 1948. It was deemed unwise to attempt to instruct the delegation in 1952. If President Truman had sought re-election, he might have had an instructed delegation, but no other candidate could command sufficient support.

THE SELECTION PROCESS IN 1952

The call for the Democratic state convention went out on January 24, with the meeting to be held in Portland on March 21-22, one of the earliest Democratic state conventions in the entire country. There was no activity in the local caucuses and no real contest in the state for delegates. Thus on convention eve it appeared that the leaders had decided to select an uninstructed delegation and to keep the situation fluid as far as the presidential candidate was concerned. Kefauver supporters were quoted as stating that they did not plan a floor fight for their candidate because "the cards are stacked against us before we start."

Maine was entitled in the 1952 Democratic convention to fourteen delegates, with ten votes. The plan was to select six district delegates, each with a full vote, and eight delegates-at-large, each with one-half vote. The 1st and 2d districts were to have three of these half-vote delegates-at-large, and the 3d district was to have two. According to the rules of the state convention, a nominating committee of 32 members, with two elected by each county delegation, selects a slate of delegates to the national convention. This slate is then approved at a general session of the convention. In 1952, a half-hour floor fight developed over this rule. The opposition, without stating its reasons, attempted to reduce the size of the nominating committee to nine, with three to be chosen from each congressional district. Apparently the proposal, if successful, would have resulted in a delegation somewhat different in complexion from that actually chosen. There was a contest for the fourteen positions on the delegation, and the nominating committee engaged in a long and bitter debate in preparing the slate.

The newspapers reported that fewer than seventy-five persons were present in the convention when the list of delegates to the national convention was presented for approval. Most of the recommendations of the committee were ratified without difficulty. One objection was voiced, however, by Coleman Green, a former chairman of the Democratic city committee of Portland. Green wanted the proposed delegates to be considered district by district rather than as a slate. In the course of his remarks, he said, "We in the First District feel that we have been slighted. The slate is lopsided. Let's divide this thing up among the different religions. The slate is, as I predicted, a packed house, and it sounds to me like a list of delegates to the Knights of Columbus convention." There were violent objections to these comments, but an attempt to strike them from the record failed. The slate was approved.

The convention dates, March 21-22, were before the Truman withdrawal but after the New Hampshire primary. A newspaper poll of the delegates indicated that there was no agreement regarding a presidential candidate if Truman withdrew. Two were for Senator Douglas, who, because of his Maine background, would probably have received unanimous support if he had been a serious contender. Individual delegates were for Sam Rayburn, Adlai Stevenson, Oscar Ewing, Justice William O. Douglas, and Senator Robert S. Kerr. Four delegates were listed as undecided, and nine declared that they would support President Harry Truman if he chose to be a candidate.

Senators Kefauver, Kerr, and Russell later met with Maine Democratic leaders and some members of the national convention delegation, and Franklin D. Roosevelt, Jr., visited the state for Averell Harriman. None of these candidates was able to enlist much support, although rumor has it that at least in one instance a member of the delegation offered his vote to a candidate provided he would pay the delegate's expenses to the convention.

The 1952 Democratic state convention differed rather radically from those of former years because the incumbent President was not seeking re-election. In 1952, deprived of presidential leadership, the party was unable to agree on a candidate. Their willingness to follow national leadership indicated to what extent the Democrats in Maine were a party of patronage and also revealed a rather narrowly based state organization.

COMPOSITION OF THE DELEGATION

The delegation naturally did not contain any major state officials; there were two members of the Maine legislature, a city clerk, and a mayor. It did include the national committeewoman, national committeeman, a former chairman of the state committee, and the present state chairman. One of the delegates was secretary-treasurer of the state Industrial Union Council.

There were ten men and four women. Ages ranged from the late twenties to over 60, and it was probably a younger group than the Republican delegation. Four were lawyers, but the delegation contained fewer well-known lawyers and business men than its Republican counterpart. Five were delegates in the 1948 convention, and one was a delegate in 1944. Several more had served as alternates to previous national conventions. The principal elements were party officials and a few present or former officeholders; delegates were chosen primarily because of their service to the party and because they represented certain factions in the party. As in 1944 and 1948, the CIO had one representative only on the Democratic delegation.

ACTIVITIES AND VOTING RECORD

The delegation met once before it went to Chicago. F. Davis Clark, the national committeeman, was elected chairman without a contest; Miss Lucia Cormier was selected for the platform committee, and Thomas Delahanty for credentials. At Chicago, the delegation was not called together until comparatively late—perhaps because the national committeeman, chairman of the delegation, was not going to be re-elected and knew it. Although he had enjoyed wide support in the party for several years, he had lost influence almost completely in 1950.

The delegation was widely split, when elected, and the voting at the convention continued in the same pattern, although a majority of the delegates were seemingly for a stand on civil rights. On the motion to seat Virginia, the delegation was initially opposed by a margin of 6 to 1, and the final ballot found Maine still against the proposal, 7½ to 2½. A belated and unsuccessful attempt was made to vote in favor of seating Virginia, but the delegation failed to secure recognition from the chairman. This change of heart was brought about by the rumor that an agreement had been reached between the Stevenson and the southern forces.

On the ballots for the presidential nomination, the Maine delegation voted as follows:

	First Ballot	Second Ballot	Third Ballot
Kefauver	1½	1	½
Stevenson	3½	4½	7
Russell	2½	2½	2½
Harriman	1½	1	0
Ewing	1	1	0
	10	10	10

The Russell strength reflected the struggle that was going on in the delegation over the selection of a national committeeman. It was also the result of a previous intra-party fight that had left deep wounds.

With a delegation of only fourteen, it was necessary to poll the delegation twice. The first occasion was for the purpose of securing a parliamentary ruling as to what alternates could vote; the second was to place the names of the supporters of Senator Russell on record.

AFTERMATH IN THE STATE

The Democrats lost decisively in both the September and November elections, but there was some optimism in Democratic quarters for a strengthening of the party organization. But the fight for control of the Democratic party in Maine was not resolved by the election of Edward Muskie as national committeeman. On the contrary, in further meetings of the state committee, his leadership was challenged.

REVIEW AND APPRAISAL

Neither of Maine's delegations in 1952 contained outstanding figures or holders of major appointive or elective offices; both parties gave ample recognition to party officials. The Republican delegation included more individuals of moderate wealth, formal education, and social position. In fact, the delegations reflected the composition of the two parties, except that labor was probably under-represented among the Democratic delegates.

Yet the two delegations were elected under radically different circumstances. The Republicans were chosen after a bitter struggle between supporters of two presidential candidates and their election was controlled by whether they were for Taft or Eisenhower; the Democrats were selected with little consideration for preferences regarding presidential candidates and after a pre-convention period in which no outstanding presidential contenders had attempted to secure delegate support. Apparently past service to the party and present factional affiliation were the major factors influencing the selection of Democratic delegates. There was no contest and little public interest in the Democratic caucuses and convention; on the Republican side there was an unusual amount of popular interest and much pre-convention activity on behalf of two candidates. Yet in both parties, caucuses were often poorly attended, and the selection of convention delegates remained in the hands of local party leaders.

There were no reported flagrant irregularities at the conventions, and while both party assemblies were marked by manipulation and maneuvering for position, there was no evidence of illegal acts or grossly unparliamentary behavior. The Republican convention, moreover, met and survived, without discredit, a head-on conflict between two outstanding national candidates—a conflict all the more serious because it reflected a basic internal division in the state party. The delegates to the Republican national convention were agreed upon in a spirit notable for its restraint and for a desire to reach a decision that would be as satisfactory as possible to both segments of the party. Undoubtedly, the willingness to negotiate that characterized the Republican convention was encouraged by the fact that both Taft and Eisenhower had strong supporters among the convention leaders. If either candidate had been forced to rely on amateur support, a solid delegation for the candidate with professional support would doubtless have been elected—probably amidst cries of steam roller. The Republican organization in Maine, however, will rarely be agreed on one candidate; it is not that closely articulated. Perhaps the loose organization of the party, rather than the convention system, explains the flexibility demonstrated in 1952.

In both parties, the state convention was too far removed from the rank-and-file voter, even though delegates were elected directly in local caucuses. There was no real expression of popular preference among the voters for a presidential candidate in either party. This may have occurred because the caucuses, held in February and March, came so early in the campaign that opinions were not yet crystallized or emotions aroused, notwithstanding the active campaigning that was in progress across the state line in New Hampshire. There is some sentiment among the politicians that local caucuses and the state conventions should be held later in the political year. But with the June primary and September elections, it would be difficult to hold the state conventions later than April or May unless they were held in June after the primary.

The experience in 1952 demonstrates that at least under some circumstances a state convention can undergo great strain and yet operate with reasonable effectiveness. There is no doubt that the division was deep, especially in the Republican convention, and that tempers were short; yet agreement was reached and the decisions of both conventions were probably not far from reflecting popular sentiment in the state. The one exception might be in the support given Estes Kefauver, who was more popular with the rank-and-file voter than his showing in the Democratic convention indicated.

Finally, the observer is impressed by the flexibility of the convention system. While the Democratic and Republican parties operate under the same election laws in Maine, there is a definite difference in the organization and procedure in the two conventions, but each effectively met the particular problems that confronted it in 1952. Those problems were dissimilar because of the different composition, organization, and policies of the two parties.

Maine Chapter Acknowledgments

HERBERT H. WOOD, Assistant Professor of Government, University of Maine, prepared a pre-convention report on the Democratic delegation.

LAWRENCE L. PELLETIER, Director, Bureau of Research in Municipal Government, Bowdoin College, served as a delegate to the 1952 Republican state convention in Maine. He later carried on field work with respect to both delegations and prepared the draft of the chapter, using Professor Wood's report on the Democratic delegation in part.

NEW HAMPSHIRE

KEY FACTS

Electoral votes, 1952:   4

National convention votes, 1952:
Democratic,   8
Republican,   14

Population, 1950:   533,242
Urban, 57%; rural nonfarm, 34%; rural farm, 9%

Population increase, 1940-50:   41,718 (9%)
Urban, 6%; rural nonfarm, 27%; rural farm, 26% decline

Presidential vote, 1948:		*1952:*	
Democratic,	107,995 (47%)	106,663	(39%)
Republican,	121,299 (52%)	166,287	(61%)

Gubernatorial vote, 1950:		*1952:*
Democratic,	82,258	97,924
Republican,	108,907	167,791

U. S. Representatives vote, all districts, 1950:		*1952:*
Democratic,	72,760	95,119
Republican,	112,487	162,550

U. S. Representatives elected 1950:		*1952:*
Democratic,	0	0
Republican,	2	2

State legislature elected 1952:
Senate: Democrats,   6;   Republicans,   18
House: Democrats, 122;   Republicans, 276;   Independents, 2

Method of selecting national convention delegates:
Direct election of delegates, advisory presidential preference poll

26

Based primarily on reports by ROBERT B. DISHMAN

—————————————————————————CHAPTER 3

ALTHOUGH FORTY-THIRD IN AREA AND FORTY-FOURTH in population among the states, New Hampshire figured conspicuously in the presidential nominating process in 1952. Because its primary is the first to be held in presidential election years, the state exerts heavy psychological influence throughout the country, and precipitates a vast amount of speculation and analysis concerning the outcome of the nominating process.

New Hampshire's independent and democratic tradition is reflected in several aspects of her political life. For example, New Hampshire still retains her early provisions for a referendum every seven years to decide whether its constitution, the basic framework of which dates back to 1783, shall be revised. The House of Representatives, the lower chamber of New Hampshire's General Court, is the largest state legislative body in the country, its exact size varying from biennium to biennium but in 1953 consisting of about 400 members representing a total population of only 533,000.

Politically, New Hampshire stands in the middle of the road compared to the other New England states. At the state level, New Hampshire is almost as confirmed in its Republicanism as its northernmost neighbors, Maine and Vermont. Only twice since 1874 have the Democrats elected a governor and only once have they been able to capture control of both houses of the General Court, in 1912 when they were favored by the split in the Republican party. In presidential elections, however, the state has shown much the same independence as Connecticut, Massachusetts, and Rhode Island. Five times in the last half century, New Hampshire has given its electoral vote to the Democratic presidential nominee, twice to Woodrow Wilson, and three times—in 1936, 1940, and 1944—to Franklin D. Roose-

27

velt. Twice in the last four decades the state has sent a Democrat to each house of Congress—a Senator in 1912 and again in 1932 and a Representative in 1922 and again in 1932. Two of the ten counties, Coös and Strafford, have supported the successful presidential candidate in every election since 1896. In practically all elections some Democratic votes are cast in every town and district.

Although the state is predominantly Republican, certain districts are strongly Democratic. At present (1953) seven of the state's even dozen cities have Democratic mayors. In 1950 about 110 of the 399 representatives in the lower house of the state legislature came from districts with so few Democrats that the Republican candidates rarely have opponents on the ballot. On the other hand, in at least 55 cases the reverse was true; the Democrats were so strong that they ran without Republican opposition. Republican strength is drawn primarily from the towns and villages and a few of the larger cities like Concord and Portsmouth. Democratic strongholds are in the larger industrial towns and cities where the labor force is most strongly unionized and largely Irish and French-Canadian in origin. In Manchester, the state's largest city, the Democratic electoral majorities have been so large and so automatic that the Democratic city organization has literally distintegrated for lack of exercise.

Two-party rivalry continues to exist for several reasons. In a state where tradition is so deeply rooted, it is only natural that many voters continue to follow the voting habits of their forefathers. For example, the former Democratic state chairman, Professor Dayton D. McKean, has reported finding "little enclaves of Democrats in New Hampshire who trace their political ancestry back to Andrew Jackson, although individually they may have no clear idea what it was that Jackson stood for." Moreover, there have been no shifts in the population or economy drastic enough to upset the traditional balance between and within the two major parties. Compared with many other states, New Hampshire has had a slow, unspectacular growth in population since 1900. The influx of French-Canadians from neighboring Quebec has slowed down considerably in recent years. The state has not become as urbanized and as industrialized as many other sections of the country. As of 1950 only 56 per cent of the people were living in places classed as urban and only 40 per cent were engaged in industry. In general, persons of English or Scottish descent who are linked together under the name "Yankee" tend to be Protestants and Republicans. The largest non-Yankee groups, the Irish and the French, mostly Catholics, tend to be Democrats.

The balance between the parties is somewhat obscured by registration figures. In New Hampshire, as in other states where one party is predominant, many independents who frequently vote with the minority party in the general election register with the majority party and vote in its primary. This was apparent in the presidential primary of 1952, where 70 per cent of those who cast votes did so on the Republican side, while in the general election only 61 per cent of those voting supported the Republican national ticket.

PRESIDENTIAL PRIMARY LAW AND PROCEDURE

New Hampshire adopted a law in 1913 providing for the direct election of national convention delegates. That measure was supplemented in 1949 with provisions for a presidential preference poll. Thus, in 1952, for the first time, New Hampshire's system had the double feature found in some other states: (1) the "beauty contest," as it was widely referred to, among the presidential hopefuls, and (2) the direct election of convention delegates. Under the original law the election of delegates fell on the third Tuesday in May. The date was soon changed, however, to coincide with town meeting day, the second Tuesday in March. New Hampshire's primary, the first to be held in any presidential year, is particularly significant as a weathervane when there is a genuine contest among presidential aspirants.

Under the 1949 law, a presidential or vice-presidential candidate may be entered in the preference primary upon the filing of petitions carrying signatures of 50 qualified voters in each of the state's two congressional districts. The petition must be filed with the state's secretary of state not earlier than 60 and not later than 40 days before the date of the primary. No filing fee is required. Presidential candidates may withdraw their names within ten days after they have been officially notified of their candidacy. Any petitioner offering the name of a presidential candidate must affirm under the penalties for perjury that he is a "member of the same political party as the proposed candidate," a requirement which proved to be crucial in the early Eisenhower boom of 1952. The statute provides for write-ins.

The candidate for delegate or for alternate may get his name on the ballot by filing with the secretary of state a declaration of candidacy together with either a $10 filing fee or a petition containing the names of 100 legal voters at any time between 30 to 60 days before the primary. Candidates for delegate may be identified on the ballot as "pledged" or as "favorable" to a particular candidate, or they may run without any commitment at all. To run "pledged," the delegate candidate must obtain the written consent of his presidential choice and file it with the secretary of state, and he obligates himself to vote for that candidate as "long as he shall be a candidate before said convention," in effect, until his name is withdrawn. Candidates "favorable" to a particular candidate, while committing themselves and assuming a degree of moral obligation, do not have to submit the affidavit of the presidential candidate nor are they bound until he withdraws. The provision for running as "favorable" was introduced in 1949 by an amendment to the primary laws sponsored by State Representative Charles A. Holden of Hanover, who, as a delegate "pledged" to Dewey in 1944 and again in 1948, objected to the lack of flexibility under that designation.

The procedure appears simple enough. Unlike the system prevailing in Minnesota, South Dakota, and Wisconsin, the presidential preference entries appear together in one block of the ballot, the slates of delegate-candidates in another. It would be possible for New Hampshire voters to express a preference for one presidential candidate while electing delegates legally pledged to another; but this did not happen in 1952. Under certain circumstances the system, and especially the early time schedule, can leave room for difficulties, as the Democratic experience in 1952 demonstrated.

THE REPUBLICAN DELEGATION

Prepared with the assistance of
JOHN T. HOLDEN, GEORGE H. DEMING, AND ALLAN A. KUUSISTO

Prior to the modifications of its presidential primary law in 1949, New Hampshire had failed to take full advantage of the early position of its presidential primary to sound out public sentiment toward the leading presidential candidates when contests were in progress. The difficulty was that few genuine presidential candidates cared to risk a popular contest so early in the campaign, particularly when they were required to give their explicit consent before New Hampshire delegate candidates could run "pledged" in their behalf. This problem was met in 1949, as has been pointed out, by the adoption of the presidential preference poll and by the new provision by which delegates could show their allegiance on the ballot on a "favoring" basis without securing consent.

Nevertheless, New Hampshire played a conspicuous role in 1948 when attempts were made to run a slate of delegates pledged to General Dwight D. Eisenhower in the presidential primary. It was to Leonard V. Finder, publisher of the Manchester *Evening Leader*, that General Eisenhower at that time wrote his famous letter saying he would not accept the nomination for the presidency or for any other "high political office."

Eisenhower's popularity in both parties in New Hampshire was so great that, late in 1951, the vice-chairman of the Grafton County Democratic committee, Roderick L. MacKay, took steps to find out whether Eisenhower would run on the Democratic ticket. MacKay announced he would circulate a petition requesting that the General's name be entered in the Democratic presidential preference primary. Up to this time General Eisenhower had taken pains not to associate himself too closely with the leaders of either party. Since New Hampshire law requires that each Eisenhower petitioner would have to affirm that he was "a member of the same political party as the proposed candidate," the MacKay strategy, if uncontested by Eisenhower's representatives, would have established the General as a Democrat or else put on his unwilling shoulders the blame for a large number of Democrats perjuring themselves. In any event, the strategy, coupled with a similar affair in Oregon, succeeded in "smoking out" the General's Republicanism. MacKay's announcement, which other state Democratic leaders did not endorse, was the spark that precipitated quick action on the part of the Republican leaders.

THE SELECTION PROCESS IN 1952

The Eisenhower slate—Governor Sherman Adams had organized a state draft-Eisenhower committee among Republican leaders late in 1951. On December 17, 1951, Adams wrote Senator Henry Cabot Lodge, then recognized as the unofficial head of the national Eisenhower movement, urging that he get Eisenhower to declare himself a Republican so that he might be properly entered in the New Hampshire primary. The long-awaited word from Eisenhower came on January 6, when Senator Lodge announced at a special press conference in Washington that Eisenhower had personally assured him that he was a Republican and that he was not unwilling to accept the Republican nomination for President if he did not have to campaign actively for it. Lodge indicated that the General's name would be entered in the New Hampshire primary. The next day Eisenhower released a statement from SHAPE headquarters in France which left no doubt that he was a Republican.

On January 11, the first day on which candidates might file for the presidential primary, Governor Adams led a delegation of Eisenhower adherents to the office of Secretary of State Enoch D. Fuller to file formally for the positions as delegates-at-large from New Hampshire, to be listed on the ballot as "favorable" to Eisenhower. On January 17, the governor filed a petition containing 498 names entering the name of General Eisenhower in the presidential preference primary. Between January 17 and January 27, the period in which Eisenhower was allowed, under the law, to withdraw his name from the primary, Governor Adams recruited the strongest possible names to fill out the slate of delegates and alternates. No negative word came from Eisenhower, and, on January 27, the die was cast.

The slate of delegates "favorable" to Eisenhower was by this time oversubscribed. Governor Adams and his party associates had to trim down the list to the exact number to be elected, ten at large and two from each congressional district, so that pro-Eisenhower votes would not be scattered, if serious opposition developed. This was accomplished through the voluntary cooperation of the delegates in the absence of any mandatory legal provision such as exists in Wisconsin. At least two delegate-candidates withdrew before the deadline on February 10.

The Taft and other slates—In the meantime, Taft's candidacy was pushed by William Loeb, publisher of the Manchester *Union Leader* and the New Hampshire *Sunday News*, and Wesley Powell of Hampton Falls, former administrative assistant to New Hampshire's senior United States senator, Styles Bridges. Both Loeb and Powell had been at odds for years with New Hampshire's junior senator, Charles W. Tobey and with Governor Adams, both of whom were identified with the Eisenhower movement. Through his newspapers, Loeb tried to minimize Eisenhower's grass-roots support. He branded the General a pawn of the internationalist "New Dealers" centered in "Wall Street," and ran a series of straw ballots showing that, first, General MacArthur and, later, Senator Taft were overwhelmingly the choice of the Republican voters in the state.

On January 11, Powell met with Taft in Washington and urged the Senator to enter the contest in New Hampshire. On January 14, Taft's eastern campaign manager, John D. M. Hamilton, came to Concord and later to Dover to confer with scores of Taft adherents. That day marked the filing of four delegate candidacies "favorable" to Taft. On January 18, the veteran Republican leader in Manchester, Frederick E. "Ted" Johnston, announced formation of a New Hampshire "Bob Taft for President" Club with headquarters in Manchester. Mayor Shelby O. Walker of Concord was designated chairman, and Johnston himself was executive secretary. On January 29, a few hours before the filing deadline, Taft's name was entered in the presidential preference contest. The petition filed in his name carried 703 signatures, 600 more than were needed and 200 more than had signed for Eisenhower.

Recognizing that there was considerable grass-roots sentiment in the state for General Douglas MacArthur, three out-of-state organizations lent their help to New Hampshire's MacArthur adherents: the National "MacArthur-for-President" organization headed by Ervin Hohensee, Washington, D. C.; the "Fighters-for-MacArthur" group headed by John Chapple, an Ashland, Wisconsin, editor; and the "MacArthur and McCarthy in 1952" Club, headed by Lawrence Daly, its self-styled "director-general." From the beginning these groups fought each other almost as fiercely as they did the Eisenhower movement. State Representative Wayne R. Crosby of Hillsborough, selected as state chairman by the Chapple group, first filed as a delegate-candidate favorable to MacArthur. When he switched to Taft, along with State Representative Holden of Hanover, he was succeeded by Arthur Snell, a Lisbon clothing merchant, who was dropped ten days later when the Chapple group sought a merger (which proved to be short-lived) with the Hohensee followers.

The Hohensee group's chairman, J. Wesley Colburn, a former state senator from Nashua, resigned on February 5, when he received a letter from General MacArthur asking him and the other MacArthur delegate candidates to withdraw and throw their support to some "available" leader of "demonstrated capability in the science of civil government and one whose wisdom is founded upon broad administrative experience," an indirect reference to Taft. Three other delegate candidates withdrew, leaving only six favorable to MacArthur in the field. Hohensee rushed to New Hampshire, as did both Chapple and Daly, to keep the movement from collapsing entirely. MacArthur was not entered in the "beauty contest" part of the primary, inasmuch as this would have required his tacit consent.

The fourth candidate on whose behalf serious efforts were made in New Hampshire was Harold E. Stassen, who had run well in 1948 when he captured two of the eight delegateships in a Dewey-oriented slate. Since then, however, Stassen's star had dimmed. He had never attracted much support among professional politicians, and many of the zealous amateurs who had sparked his campaign in 1948 had gone over to the Eisenhower camp in 1952. The new presidential preference primary in New Hampshire, coming at the moment it did, offered a challenge, however, which Stassen probably felt he must accept if he were not to write off his presidential aspirations completely. On the very eve of the final filing date his name was filed, but no attempt was made to file a supporting slate of delegate candidates.

The ballot—Four presidential aspirants appeared in the preference poll part of the ballot: Eisenhower, Taft, Stassen, and a William R. Schneider, an attorney of St. Louis who was virtually unknown in the state. There were three delegate-candidate slates, respectively supporting Eisenhower, Taft, and MacArthur. Only Eisenhower and Taft had full contingents of delegates and alternates. None of the delegate candidates ran "pledged" to his choice. They all took advantage of the new law to declare themselves merely "favorable" to the particular candidate, but were shown as such on the ballot. Two candidates for delegate-at-large and one candidate for district delegate ran without commitment to any presidential candidate.

An important legal problem arose concerning the order of names on the ballot in the preference poll. Chapter 33 of the Revised Laws of New Hampshire specifies that whenever in a primary election there are two or more candidates for nomination to the same office above the town or ward level, the names of the candidates must be rotated on the ballot so that each will appear an equal number of times at every position in the list. State Attorney General Gordon M. Tiffany ruled on February 17 that the names of the presidential candidates would be listed alphabetically on all ballots and not rotated. Tiffany and Secretary of State Fuller took the position that none of the men whose names were entered in the presidential preference poll could be considered a candidate for *nomination* since the results would be legally only advisory in nature.

This interpretation meant that Senator Taft (and President Truman, on the Democratic side) would have the disadvantage of being last on the list. Before Taft could make a protest, however, a large number of the 350,000 primary ballots had been printed and shipped to the 74 city wards and 223 towns where they were to be used. Taft then decided not to take legal action but declared to the end that the failure to rotate was "clearly in violation of the letter and spirit of the New Hampshire statutes." The Democratic national committeeman also protested, declaring that it was President Truman, not Senator Taft, who was the intended victim of the ruling.

The campaign—The colorful pre-primary campaign, watched by political leaders throughout the country, brought more than three score newspaper and radio reporters from out of the state, including six from London and two from Paris. The galaxy of political stars who participated in the campaign for Eisenhower included Representatives Hugh Scott of Pennsylvania, Patrick J. Hillings of California, Christian A. Herter of Massachusetts, and Walter H. Judd of Minnesota as well as Senators James H. Duff of Pennsylvania, Henry Cabot Lodge, Leverett Saltonstall of Massachusetts, and Frank Carlson of Kansas. In the last few days before the primary, Paul G. Hoffman spoke at the University of New Hampshire at Durham and Connecticut's Governor John Lodge at Laconia. But the brunt of the campaigning was borne by Governor Adams and Senator Lodge, who were assisted in a series of rallies by such professionals of the entertainment world as Fred Waring and his "Pennsylvanians," Jinx Falkenburg, and her husband, "Tex" McCrary.

The Taft forces waged a quiet but strenuous campaign, decrying the synthetic enthusiasm created by "Broadway fanfare." Most of the campaigning fell upon three of the younger, more aggressive delegate candidates, Gardner Turner, Louis Wyman, and Wesley Powell, who began by addressing scattered Taft rallies but later drew greater popular interest through a series of debates sponsored by local Republican organizations in the various towns. So effective were these tactics that Senator Taft was encouraged to undertake a personal swing through the state, making about thirty speeches in three days. Everywhere he was greeted by friendly but not overly enthusiastic crowds. He attacked the Truman administration, blaming it for the Korean war, high prices, high taxes, conscription, and corruption in high places. He compared his own forthright stand with Eisenhower's failure to take vigorous issue with the Democratic administrations which the General had served.

Harold Stassen spent several days in the state, speaking on the few occasions when he was able to find a sponsoring organization. He was well received at the debate-forum held in Concord under the auspices of the Merrimack County Republican Committee on March 3 and at the Durham and Hanover rallies, March 6 and 7, sponsored by the Young Republican Clubs of the University of New Hampshire and Dartmouth College. He was deferential toward Eisenhower and MacArthur but criticized Taft for his isolationist record and for his failure to support federal aid to public schools.

Campaign expenditures of the Eisenhower group ran appreciably higher than those of the other candidates. For newspaper advertising between January 1 and March 11, the Eisenhower camp spent as much as the Taft and MacArthur forces combined. Apparently, the Eisenhower advertisements were also more effective qualitatively. Their emphasis was that only Eisenhower could unify the party and win, and that he was supported by six of New Hampshire's former governors as well as the present governor. According to one estimate in the New York *Times*, the Eisenhower forces spent $65,000 in the campaign and the Taft forces about $50,000. The intensity with which the campaign was waged led to charges and countercharges of "dirty campaign tactics" and "political slush funds." The United States Senate Committee on Privileges and Elections sent a special investigator to New Hampshire but no report of findings has been made public.

The vote—Primary day, March 11, brought out a record-breaking vote in spite of icy roads and a steady, cold downpour, with snow in some parts of the state. This turn-out may in part be explained by the fact that the second Tuesday in March is also the traditional day on which town meetings are held, thus sparing the state the expense of holding a special election except in the cities. Of some 315,000 registered voters, 136,536 cast their ballots: 96,507 of them Republican; 36,652 Democratic. Eisenhower received 46,661 votes; Taft drew 35,838. Eisenhower ran especially well in the larger towns and cities. He carried 71 of the 99 districts classed as "urban" and 118 of the 188 rural districts. Taft carried only 24 of the 78 districts in which he himself had campaigned. Despite MacArthur's request that his supporters vote for Taft, he received 3,227 write-in votes. Stassen polled 6,574 votes; Schneider, 230. Postmortems stressed not only the original popularity of Eisenhower, but voiced the explanation that Taft had appeared stiff and humorless during his campaign tour of the state, comments that may have had some influence on Taft's later campaigning technique in other states.

Preferences for vice president were all write-ins and gave Senator Styles Bridges 6,535 votes; Stassen 5,876; MacArthur 4,722; and scattering votes for Earl Warren, Robert Taft, and Sherman Adams in that order.

The entire Eisenhower slate of delegates and alternates was elected from top to bottom. In the contests for delegate-at-large, the Eisenhower candidates beat the Taft adherents by roughly the same 4-to-3 margin by which the General defeated the Senator in the preference poll. As expected, Wesley Powell topped the Taft slate with 32,562 votes, which was not far below the number polled by Taft himself in the "beauty contest." Under the circumstances, this was a considerable achievement, but even so, Powell's vote fell more than 5,000 votes below that of the lowest Eisenhower candidate. Only one of the races for district delegate was equally close. Thanks to the Johnston organization's tight hold on the Manchester Republican vote, Merrill A. Calkin, one of the organization's stalwart leaders, lost to his nearest Eisenhower opponent by a margin of about 5 to 6, or less than 3,000 votes. In every case the MacArthur candidates for delegate or alternate ran a poor third behind both the Eisenhower and Taft slates. In the contests for delegate-at-large, the largest vote polled by a MacArthur candidate was 6,670 and in the district contests, 3,155 votes.

COMPOSITION OF THE DELEGATION

In spite of the attempt of the Eisenhower organization to insure representation of local party interests, the delegation was criticized by the Taft followers for its top-heavy concentration of "big brass." The delegates-at-large included Governor Sherman Adams; former Governor Robert O. Blood, a Dewey delegate in 1944 and 1948; Foster Stearns of Exeter, a former Congressman and a Stassen delegate in 1948; Robert P. Burroughs, a former national committeeman who had served as a delegate in 1936 and 1944 but had been defeated as a Stassen delegate in 1948; Lane Dwinell, Speaker of the New Hampshire House of Representatives in 1951; E. Harold Young, state representative from Pittsfield and secretary of the New Hampshire Eisenhower-for-President Committee; Basil D. French, prominent AFL labor leader; James T. Colby of Litchfield, a recognized leader in farm groups; and Ralph Langdell, a young Manchester attorney. District delegates, no less well known and no less influential, included William G. Saltonstall, headmaster of Phillips Exeter Academy, and Congressman Norris Cotton, who with Governor Adams and State Representative Joseph Geisel of Manchester was one of the first public figures in the state to work for General Eisenhower's candidacy.

Some of the major political figures, for whom room could have been found on any of the slates, took no active part in the campaign. Most important of these were Senators Styles Bridges and Charles Tobey and Congressman Chester E. Merrow. Bridges took pains to remain outwardly neutral throughout the campaigning, although many of his associates and former assistants were active in the Taft cause. Merrow was also ostensibly neutral, although his personal campaign manager worked for Taft. Senator Tobey indicated in January that he would file for delegate "favorable" to Eisenhower, but failed to do so later.

The delegation included two practicing lawyers, two full-time public officials, two educators, three businessmen, one farmer, one labor representative, one physician, and one writer. Among the alternates were four lawyers, six businessmen, one writer, one housewife, and one farmer. Seven of the delegates and four alternates were holding part-time state or local elective or appointive positions. Nine of the 14 delegates and nine of the alternates had previously served or were then serving as party officials.

The educational background of the delegates was unusually high. Twelve had completed college and six had advanced degrees. Most of the alternates were also college graduates and three of them had advanced degrees. As to religious affiliation, twelve were Protestant and two Roman Catholic. The alternates included nine Protestants and four Catholics. Although women play a considerable role in New Hampshire Republican politics, no women were included among the delegates and only two among the alternates. So far as is known, all delegates and alternates paid their own way to the convention.

Six of the 14 delegates—Governor Adams, former Governor Robert O. Blood, Representative Norris Cotton, former National Committeeman Robert P. Burroughs, former Representative Foster Stearns, and William G. Saltonstall, headmaster of Phillips Exeter Academy—had seen service on one or more previous delegations.

ACTIVITIES AND VOTING RECORD

Once elected, the Eisenhower delegates lost no time in meeting to organize. Governor Adams was named chairman of the delegation. Basil French, the AFL representative, was designated vice-chairman. Former Governor Blood was appointed to the resolutions committee of the national convention, Ralph Langdell to rules, and former National Committeeman Burroughs to credentials. On June 9, in response to an invitation by General Eisenhower himself, thirteen of the fourteen delegates travelled to New York City where they visited the General at his residence at Columbia University. On June 23, the delegates met with Governor Adams and members of the state central committee at the Adams home at Lake Winnepocket. Their next meeting was in Chicago.

New Hampshire delegates were prominent at the convention in more ways than one. They were seated in the front row at the Amphitheatre, and throughout the convention went down the line for Eisenhower. Burroughs consistently supported the Eisenhower position on disputed delegations in the credentials committee. In the debate on July 9 he created considerable stir by accusing the Taft men on the national committee of "conniving" to secure delegations favorable to Taft.

On all issues related to the Eisenhower candidacy the New Hampshire delegates cast their 14 votes unanimously. On only one question was there division within the ranks. Six votes were cast against the resolution to give a "bonus" seat on the national committee to the state chairman of the states going Republican in the presidential election. Back of this was the feeling that the women were not getting a fair "break," inasmuch as the state chairmen have invariably been men.

New Hampshire's greatest influence was exercised primarily through the person of Governor Adams. Weeks before the convention Eisenhower asked Adams to take the stump in his behalf in Massachusetts and on the West Coast. Few, however, anticipated the prominent assignments which Adams would receive at the convention and later. Adams played a leading role in the struggle to adopt the "fair play" amendment; he made the principal seconding speech following Governor Langlie's presentation. On Tuesday, Adams was named convention floor manager for the Eisenhower forces and Senator Lodge's liaison aide to the various state delegations.

AFTERMATH IN THE STATE

Soon after the convention Governor Adams was made Eisenhower's personal "chief of staff." On official leave of absence from his duties in the state, he accompanied Eisenhower in this capacity throughout the campaign. He was credited with having directed much of the national strategy by which the General was elected. Following the election Adams was appointed to the highly influential post of The Assistant to the President and head of the White House secretariat.

In the post-convention campaign, New Hampshire was considered so safe for Eisenhower that neither party made a strenuous effort to win the state's four electoral votes. Eisenhower came into the state only once to address rallies at Nashua and Manchester on October 21. This seems to have been a gesture of courtesy to Governor Adams. Governor Adlai Stevenson penetrated New England no farther than Massachusetts, but on October 16 President Truman made a brief swing through the southeastern corner of the state. The election was further proof of Eisenhower's popularity in the state. The General carried all but one of the state's ten counties and lost that by only a few hundred votes. Moreover, he carried all but four of the state's dozen cities, including Dover, and all but seven of the 223 towns. Percentagewise, he received 61 per cent of the total votes cast, as compared with 52 per cent for Dewey in 1948.

THE DEMOCRATIC DELEGATION

Since the late 1920's the Democratic party in New Hampshire has drawn most of its strength both in votes and in leadership from the Irish and French-Canadian sections of the population. As of 1951, for example, it has been estimated that of the party's 41 top-ranking leaders in the state, 14 were of French or French-Canadian descent, 13 were Irish, 9 were English, Scottish, or native American of many generations, 2 were Jewish, one was mixed French and Irish, one Polish, and one Greek. About three-fourths of these same leaders, it was estimated, were Roman Catholic, approaching the same proportion as the distribution among the Democratic voters throughout the state.

While the support of the Irish and the French-Canadians gives the party its strength in the state, it also is a source of internal weakness. Rivalry between the two groups is traditional and often bitter. According to McKean, "every Democratic primary in New Hampshire is an Irish versus French-Canadian struggle." On the relatively few occasions in which the party has presented a united front at the polls, it has usually been in support of a candidate who was neither French nor Irish. This was notably true in 1922 and again in 1932, when the party succeeded in electing Fred H. Brown of Somersworth, first as governor and later as United States senator. In recent years the party has made its best showing in state elections in backing Yankees like Herbert W. Hill of Hanover.

Until recently the Irish wing of the party has generally been somewhat in the ascendancy. Leadership of the state organization has been shared, not always amicably, by such men as Emmett J. Kelley of Berlin, a veteran state senator and racing commissioner, Charles A. Burke of Manchester, a retired paper manufacturer and a former liquor commissioner, Joseph P. O'Brien of Manchester, the party's chief fund-raiser, and William McCann of Dover, at one time its acting postmaster. In recent years, however, leadership seems to have shifted somewhat to the French-Canadian wing of the party. The present state chairman, Governor's Councillor Romeo J. Champagne, is of French descent, and so are the mayors of four of the seven cities under Democratic control in 1953.

Throughout the New Deal-Fair Deal period the New Hampshire delegations to the Democratic national convention were solidly pledged to support Presidents Roosevelt and Truman. In 1948 one delegate—Harry Carlson of Plainfield—broke his pledge and cast his vote for Henry A. Wallace when the delegation was polled individually. This was the climax to a fight between Carlson and Charles A. Burke, also a delegate, as to which was to be named national committeeman. Both men were finally passed over in favor of Emmett Kelley. At one time or another Burke has been at odds with practically every leader of stature in the party. At present he is a vice-chairman of the state committee and its executive secretary, a position created to make use of his unquestioned ability for raising campaign funds.

THE SELECTION PROCESS IN 1952

Early developments—In 1952, the new presidential preference poll law was in effect, and voters were able to indicate their choice for president as well as for delegates. For the Democrats, the timing requirements could hardly have been worse. The filing deadline was January 30 for presidential preference candidates, February 9 for delegates. New Hampshire's primary fell on March 11. President Truman was not ready to announce his decision not to run again until March 29.

As early as December, however, the leaders of the state Democratic organization had been advised by the national committee to file a slate of candidates favorable to the President. By the time Kefauver announced his candidacy, most of the better known leaders of the state organization were committed to support the President. Their interest in seeking a place on the delegation arose less out of their desire to advance the candidacy of President Truman than from a determination to retain control of the state Democratic organization. In New Hampshire the newly elected delegates to the national convention select the state's national committeeman, through whom federal patronage is dispensed when the party is in control of the national administration.

The state leaders, apparently confident of capturing all of the delegate posts for Truman, decided to enter the President's name in the presidential preference poll as well. Emmett J. Kelley, national committeeman, awaited the President's guidance in vain. He did not wish to file the Truman candidacy against the President's wishes, and Truman himself showed no enthusiasm. Nevertheless, Kelley arranged for a Manchester lumber dealer, James D. McPhail, to file a petition bearing 240 signatures a few hours before the filing deadline on January 30. None of the state leaders was willing to accept personal responsibility for the move.

The Kefauver forces countered later that same afternoon by entering their candidate in the preference poll. This was a more daring move on the Senator's part than his bid to win delegates, for in the presidential preference primary he would be pitted against the one man in the party who, regardless of the outcome of the New Hampshire contest, could almost certainly prevent him from receiving the Democratic nomination. Moreover, under New Hampshire law, he could have won a slate of delegates legally pledged to him without even entering the preference poll. It is probable that he expected to run a close but respectful distance behind the President, especially since the state organization was against him.

In order to put a slate of delegates in the field, Kefauver had to build an organization from scratch. His state chairman was Hugh Waling, a former postmaster in Keene. Eugene S. Daniell, city solicitor of Franklin, state senator in the 1949 session of the General Court, a militant opponent of public utility interests, and an unsuccessful candidate for governor in the 1950 primary, was Kefauver's best known supporter. But his political stature in the state had been achieved as a Republican, not as a Democrat. These two men managed to assemble a full slate of 12 delegate candidates. They were unable, however, to recruit enough candidates for the alternate slate. Only one Kefauver candidate for alternate in each district and none for the state at large appeared on the ballot. At the Senator's request, all but three of the twelve delegate candidates consented to run "pledged" to support him rather than merely "favorable" to his candidacy.

President Truman, queried about the New Hampshire contest at his press conference on January 31, was obviously annoyed at these developments. When and if he made up his mind to seek the Democratic nomination for President, he said, he could have it for the asking, and he would not have to run in any presidential primary to get it. The presidential primaries, he added, were just so much "eye-wash," as the reporters would see for themselves when the convention got around to selecting its presidential nominee. His announcement seemed to be tantamount to withdrawal.

The President's words sounded ungracious to New Hampshire ears. The state leaders feared that if the President withdrew from the preference primary, the organization might lose the contest for delegates, possibly even control of the party organization. They urged the President to change his mind, and on February 5, he wrote the New Hampshire secretary of state that he had decided to stay in the preferential primary after all. He was "most grateful," he wrote, to those who had urged that his name be left on the ballot. He had meant merely to point out, in his remark about the presidential preference primaries, that they did not bind the delegates. He declared that he had "long favored a nation-wide presidential primary, so that the voters could really choose their own candidates."

With this assurance, several additional party leaders favorable to Truman filed as delegate candidates. By February 9, the filing deadline, 16 candidates favorable to Truman had filed for the eight seats as half-vote delegates-at-large and 4 for the two seats in the 1st district. Only in the 2d district was the number of Truman candidates the same as the number of seats to be filled. The organization leaders evidently took the position that they did not have the right or the responsibility to ask candidates to withdraw, though in the Republican ranks both the Eisenhower and Taft organization leaders had trimmed their slates to fit the number of places to be filled. It is probable that the Democratic officials were so confident of a Truman victory that they did not consider it worth the trouble or the risk of ruffled feelings to request particular candidates to withdraw.

The Democratic presidential preference primary was a clear contest between Truman and Kefauver, but the contest for delegates turned out to be more complicated. Charles A. Burke of Manchester put up a slate of five candidates for the delegate-at-large seats and two in the 1st district "favorable" to former Postmaster General James A. Farley. It was not a complete slate but enough to give substance to Burke's feud with the other leaders.

There were also a few scattered individuals who offered as candidates for delegate posts. Walter F. Healey of the editorial staff of the Manchester *Union* filed his candidacy in support of Governor Adlai Stevenson of Illinois. Another person, a district delegate candidate, supported Mayor Josaphat C. Benoit of Manchester.

The Kefauver campaign—Kefauver's campaign tour of New Hampshire in February received national publicity. With his attractive wife, he visited every part of the state, introducing himself to people on the streets, in the market, or at their desks in office buildings. Mrs. Kefauver jotted down their names and, as they sped to the next town, the Senator dictated letters to scores of persons expressing pleasure at having just met them and the hope that they would support his candidacy.

The state organization leaders, backing a reluctant candidate who had no intention of campaigning in his own behalf, became alarmed. Plans to bring such distinguished national officials as Senator Brien McMahon and Congressman John W. McCormack did not work out, and the brunt of the Truman campaigning fell upon former Secretary of the Navy John L. Sullivan, New Hampshire's best known Democrat, who gave three speeches in the last week of the campaign. Among the out-of-state Democrats only former Senator Scott Lucas of Illinois, who was defeated in 1950 partly as a result of the Kefauver crime investigation in Chicago, came in person to help. On March 4 he gave a "pep talk" to the organization leaders in Manchester and later that same day spoke to a rally at Durham sponsored by the Young Democratic Club of the University of New Hampshire. On the eve of the election a recorded speech by Representative McCormack was broadcast over a number of stations in support of the President.

Most of the labor leaders worked actively in the President's behalf. The United Labor Committee, on which the principal AFL and CIO locals were represented along with the United Mine Workers and an independent shoe workers' union, gave its endorsement late in the campaign. Analyzing the campaign a few days later in his syndicated column, Victor Riesel wrote: "The New England labor chiefs hit the airwaves with broadcasts to back up their newspaper pleas. They distributed 65,000 leaflets among the unionized factories in the state, flyers announcing that Mr. Truman is the 'friend of the American workers.' They got their people out via the usual telephoning and carried many of them to the polls for the Democratic machine in union-chauffered cars made available to voters across the bellwether state."

Kefauver returned to the state early in March for six more days of active and widely distributed campaign efforts, ending in Concord, where he awaited the results of the primary. By this time he had won the endorsement of such prominent Democrats as Fred H. Brown, the last Democrat to serve as governor (1923-25) and as United States senator (1933-39), former Mayor Thomas McIntyre of Laconia, and Laurence Whittemore, who, as president of the Brown Company and chairman of the New England Council, is one of the most influential men in the state.

The vote—No one, probably not even Kefauver, was prepared for the magnitude of his victory over the President on March 11. The Senator won the preferential poll 19,800 to 15,927. All his delegate candidates were elected. He carried many of the districts that were considered organization strongholds. He received majorities in nine of the 12 cities, including the largest five. Only Dover, Claremont, and Somersworth stood fast for the organization along with a few of the larger towns such as Lebanon and Littleton and some of the smaller towns and villages. Truman won in only two of the state's ten counties, one of them Strafford, reputedly a "barometer" county in New Hampshire.

For the eight Kefauver candidates for delegate-at-large, 94,940 votes were cast, while the sixteen delegates favorable to Truman received 86,528 altogether. The Kefauver delegates won by large enough margins in every case to have insured victory even if the Truman slate had been trimmed to size. In the 1st district, where only two Truman candidates were running against the two pledged to Kefauver, even National Committeeman Kelley was defeated. Since the Kefauver organization had been unable to muster a full slate of alternates, however, the eight Truman candidates for alternate-at-large, who ran unopposed, and one alternate in each of the two districts were elected.

COMPOSITION OF THE DELEGATION

Among the delegates, Hugh Waling and Eugene S. Daniell, Jr., were probably best known. Of the others, only J. Felix Daniel of Laconia, a former state senator from Manchester, Dr. Daniel J. Hagerty, a Nashua dentist who had attended previous conventions, and two state representatives, Mrs. Amelia Lareau and Gedeon P. Proulx, could claim political experience. The rest were complete novices, politically. One was Mrs. Elizabeth M. Smith of Manchester, wife of the director of the Currier Gallery of Art, making her debut on the political scene. Two others—Gail E. Bower, Jr., a senior at New England College, and George Der Koorkanian, a recent graduate of the University of New Hampshire—were undoubtedly among the youngest delegates at the convention. Still another, Kearn J. P. Devereux, Nashua realtor, was, like Daniell, previously known in politics as a Republican. There were three women in the delegation, two who were delegates and one alternate.

ACTIVITIES AND VOTING RECORD

When the shock of their defeat had worn off, the regular organization leaders made a half-hearted attempt to have two Kefauver delegates, Daniell and Devereux, disqualified on the ground that they were not members of the Democratic party. In 1938, the attorney-general had ruled that the only way in which a voter could shed his affiliation with the party in which he was registered was by registering with another party. Both Daniell and Devereux took the position that by pledging themselves to attend the Democratic national convention, if elected, and to support Kefauver they had in effect become Democrats, but neither had changed his affiliation from Republican to Democratic on the registration lists. When the Democratic chairman of Grafton County asked Attorney-General Tiffany, a Republican, to remove Daniell and Devereux from the delegation, the attorney-general refused to interfere and suggested that the matter be referred to the Democratic national convention.

The delegation met to organize on April 29. Hugh Waling, in recognition of his early services in the Kefauver cause, was chosen chairman. Carlton G. Rayno, a lawyer living in Bartlett, became vice-chairman as well as member of the rules committee of the national convention; Gail Bower, secretary; Mrs. Elizabeth Smith and Eugene Daniell served on the platform committee; and Dr. Daniel Hagerty, on credentials.

The first question of significance before the delegation was the appointment of a new national committeeman. Actually, the overwhelming Kefauver victory did not cause any appreciable and immediate changes in control of the state party machinery. Although the Kefauver delegation had authority to appoint entirely new national committee members, they would subsequently need the full support of the state organization if Kefauver, once nominated, were to make a showing in the general election. The organization made this evident at the annual Jefferson-Jackson Day dinner held in Manchester on May 13. Only one representative of the Kefauver group, Charles J. Griffin, not a member of the delegation, was invited to sit at the head table; and none of the delegates was introduced. State Chairman Dayton D. McKean presided and Emmett Kelley was one of the speakers.

There was general agreement, however, among the delegates that Kelley should be replaced, and four of the leading candidates for the post of national committeeman—Felix Daniel; Mayor Romeo St.

Laurent of Somersworth; Henry P. Sullivan, a former city solicitor of Manchester who directed the Kefauver campaign in that city; and Mayor Laurence Pickett of Keene—were given a chance to meet with the delegation on May 18, each to present his case. The delegation met three times before a decision could be reached, and even then they made their choice only after a telegram from Kefauver's national headquarters cautioned the delegates against creating a rift in the party. Sullivan, who is not related to former Secretary of the Navy John L. Sullivan, was finally chosen on June 8. Mrs. Myrtle McIntyre, wife of the former mayor of Laconia, who had endorsed Kefauver, was made national committeewoman. Sullivan's first move was to call a meeting of the leaders of all factions of the party on July 14, ostensibly to discuss the forthcoming Democratic primary for local, state, and congressional offices. It was also a love-feast for the warring factions. Sullivan named Burke, Thomas Fecteau of Epping, and Mayor Pickett, representing the various factions, to make up a strong slate of candidates for the state and local offices while he himself was attending the national convention. Kelley reciprocated by assuring Sullivan that he would make no attempt to unseat Daniell and Devereux in Chicago.

This newly-found unity lasted only until the delegates reached Chicago. There the Kefauver delegates, suspecting that their alternates were trying to undermine the Senator and were working for Stevenson, barred the alternates from the delegation caucuses. Efforts of some of the alternates to influence a few of the delegates to switch their votes to Stevenson or to absent themselves so that the alternates might vote were not successful. The alternates were permitted to vote only once, on the seating of Virginia; two of them cast a favorable vote, which was contrary to the wishes of the regular delegates.

None of the delegates had sufficient stature within the party to play a significant role at the convention. Eugene Daniell was selected as one of five delegates to speak on the resolution sponsored by the Kefauver forces calling for the creation of a permanent federal crime commission. Convention Chairman Sam Rayburn was uncooperative, however, and none of the Kefauver managers was recognized to introduce the amendment until after the platform had been adopted. The most conspicuous New Hampshire representative at the convention,

Secretary of the Navy John L. Sullivan, was neither a delegate nor an alternate; but he was welcome on the floor of the convention and was considered a person to watch for a clue as to which candidate President Truman planned to support. It soon became evident that he was working for Stevenson. It is reported that when he attempted to talk to the regular New Hampshire delegation, he was angrily ordered to stay away from them.

The delegates held fast to their choice through the three ballots; the defeat of their candidate was a bitter blow. Not only was their candidate's cause lost, but most of them could expect to return to political obscurity.

AFTERMATH IN THE STATE

Despite their disappointment, most of the Kefauver leaders in the state gave the national ticket wholehearted support. But to head off any last-minute defection, the state committee asked Senator Kefauver himself to come into the state to address rallies in Portsmouth, Concord, Berlin, Laconia, and Manchester and to urge support of the Stevenson-Sparkman ticket. President Truman had done likewise, as has been pointed out, in his few "whistle stop" appearances earlier in the campaign.

In the presidential election the national ticket suffered its worst defeat in more than a generation. Stevenson and Sparkman carried only four of the state's dozen cities and only seven of the 223 towns. Candidates for state offices were defeated by equally decisive margins. Only at the local level did the Democratic candidates hold their own and then usually by greatly reduced margins. Following the election, however, the party has shown some signs of rejuvenation. In Laconia and Rochester a Democrat was elected mayor, making a total of seven cities out of twelve under Democratic control.

REVIEW AND APPRAISAL

New Hampshire, through its new preferential primary, wielded an influence in 1952 all out of proportion to its voting strength. The date of the primary, March 11, placed New Hampshire earliest among the primary states indicating a choice for President. The various provisions of the state's primary law, particularly the one allowing a distinction between "pledged" and "favorable" delegate candidates, permitted potential presidential candidates tactical freedom to such an extent as to make it politically embarrassing to fail to be on the ballot in one way or another. Getting on the ballot was easy enough to invite newcomers and to encourage insurgency. Getting off the preference poll part of the ballot, by simple withdrawal within ten days after notice that one's name had been filed, was easy enough to prevent invasion of any public figure's privacy or embarrassment by one's political opponents. In addition, the state's party organizations were sufficiently organized and the factional alignments were sufficiently clear to make the situation at least potentially one of real competition among the local political leaders. The state's electorate was diverse enough to provide a somewhat significant sampling of voter sentiment throughout the nation; the results were inevitably so interpreted. All these attributes combined to make the New Hampshire primary the "kick-off" in the 1952 nomination races, at least insofar as popular participation became a factor.

New Hampshire's role in the presidential nominating process in 1952, moreover, although highlighted by the new preferential primary, was also influenced in a significant way by the personalities who were involved both locally and nationally. The Taft-Eisenhower conflict was brought to a clear issue for the first time in any state, with Taft campaigning in person and Eisenhower unmistakably involved with his own consent. The determination of Governor Adams and his associates to bring about the candidacy of Eisenhower was probably the greatest single contribution of New Hampshire. Given this attitude on the part of the popular state executive and a major segment of the state Republican organization, it is probable that a delegation committed to Eisenhower would have been obtained in any event, whether elected at a primary or chosen in a state convention. But the preference poll dramatized the Eisenhower candidacy at a psychological moment, the law made it easy to run delegates who were publicly committed to the General without having to secure his approval, and the repercussions of the combination were felt across the nation.

The personality of Senator Kefauver and his campaign methods likewise illustrated the importance of the personal element, for which the New Hampshire primary provided a special opportunity. The opportunity was further enhanced by the President's behavior. His unwillingness to state his own future intentions, his annoyance over the Kefauver tactics, and, most of all, his "eye wash" reference to the general worth of presidential primaries, gratuitously confirmed the New Hampshire public's picture of Kefauver as a hard-hitting fighter, battling in a worthy cause with the odds against him.

The combination of preference poll and of delegates who could publicize their preferences on the ballot was probably responsible for the fact that Taft openly entered the campaign and Truman eventually allowed his name to stand. Both were certain to be involved personally in the delegate contests even if they abstained from participating in the preference poll; but neither could do much to help the fortunes of delegate-candidates who were already committed to them unless they ran in the preference contest. The New Hampshire primary was thus distinguished not only as the first, but also as almost the only one in the entire country in which there was something like a balanced contest between leading national candidates in both parties.

There is little doubt that the New Hampshire electorate was challenged by the chance to be first to vote in the pre-convention contests of 1952. Despite snow and icy roads, the turnout broke all records. In both congressional districts and in the state at large, the people of New Hampshire gave unexpected pluralities to both Eisenhower and Kefauver and to the slates of delegates supporting them. The result was a substantial contribution to the formation of national opinion and to the clarification of the pre-convention campaigns in both major parties.

In perspective, the double-headed presidential primary in New Hampshire with its presidential poll and its separate election of "pledged" or "favoring" delegates worked well in 1952. With Florida on the Democratic side, it probably came closer to achieving what has generally been hoped of a presidential primary than any other state.

Several observers have suggested that the New Hampshire law could appropriately be amended to simplify the ballot by bracketing the delegate candidates together under the name of the presidential candidate they favor, as is now the procedure in Wisconsin, Minnesota, and South Dakota, and in California, where delegates names do not even appear on the ballot. Possibly this change would be an improvement if the existing elements of flexibility, or most of them, could at the same time be retained. Several problems would then arise: If the presidential candidate exercises his option to withdraw, what happens to the slate of "pledged" or "favoring" delegates desiring to run under his banner? Would a "no preference" slate of delegates be allowed on the ballot? Would delegate contests be confined entirely to organized slates, trimmed to size? In Wisconsin, Minnesota, and California, and to a lesser degree in South Dakota, these questions were answered when their laws were written in a way that greatly restricts the likelihood that a real contest will be had between the principal national candidates. Among the four states just referred to, only South Dakota permits an organized "no preference" slate to appear on the ballot; and all four states are in agreement in refusing to permit a slate of delegates to appear on the ballot under the name of a national candidate unless he gives his consent. One result, in 1952, was that an Eisenhower slate could not be openly placed on the ballot in any one of the four states.

Any major attempt to simplify the ballot in a presidential primary is likely to introduce elements of rigidity that will sometimes seem undesirable. If New Hampshire can develop acceptable answers to the problems posed above while consolidating the preference poll and the delegate race, it may contribute further to the development of presidential primaries in the United States.

New Hampshire Chapter Acknowledgments

ROBERT B. DISHMAN, Associate Professor of Government, University of New Hampshire, with the assistance of his colleagues, JOHN T. HOLDEN, GEORGE H. DEMING, and ALLAN A. KUUSISTO, prepared a pre-convention report on the New Hampshire Republican delegation and later revised it to include convention developments. After the election, he undertook the preparation of a similar report on the New Hampshire Democratic delegation and also supplied basic material on the political background in the state. He also assisted actively in the revision of the draft chapter.

The initial draft of the material in chapter form was prepared by MRS. ESTHER COLE FRANKLIN of the Washington staff.

VERMONT

Electoral votes, 1952:   3

National convention votes, 1952:
Democratic,   6
Republican,   12

Population 1950:   377,747
Urban, 36%; *rural nonfarm,* 42%; *rural farm,* 22%

Population increase, 1940-50:   18,516 (5%)
Urban, 12%; *rural nonfarm,* 22%; *rural farm,* 23% decline

Presidential vote, 1948:			*1952:*	
Democratic,	45,557	(37%)	43,355	(28%)
Republican,	75,926	(62%)	109,717	(72%)
Progressive,	1,279	(1%)		

Gubernatorial vote, 1950:		*1952:*
Democratic,	22,227	60,051
Republican,	64,834	78,338

U. S. Representatives vote, all districts, 1950:		*1952:*
Democratic,	22,709	43,187
Republican,	65,248	109,871

U. S. Representatives elected 1950:		*1952:*
Democratic,	0	0
Republican,	1 (at-large)	1

State legislature elected 1952:
Senate: Democrats, 3;   Republicans, 27
House: Democrats, 18;   Republicans, 228

Method of selecting national convention delegates:
State conventions (delegates elected in town caucuses)

Based primarily on reports by ROBERT S. BABCOCK

CHAPTER 4

IN VERMONT, NO DEMOCRAT HAS BEEN ELECTED to national or state office, except the state legislature, since 1856. In the state senate, only three of 30 members are Democrats; in the house, 18 out of the 246. Major political contests take place among factions of the Republican party.

Democratic strength is concentrated in the Burlington industrial area, which contains almost one tenth of the state's population. Chittenden County (Burlington and Winooski) has gone Democratic in presidential elections since 1928 by a slight margin. Rutland has voted Democratic in some gubernatorial elections but never in presidential elections. Bennington has an active Democratic minority.

Vermont has a tradition of independence which it maintains with consciousness and vigor. Its rural representation is still overwhelming. Each of the 246 members of the lower house (the third largest in the country) of the legislature is chosen by a "town," without regard to population. The Burlington representative has a constituency of 33,000 people, but he has no more voice than the man who represents the tiniest hamlet. In 1950, the smallest town sending a representative had a population of 49. State senators are apportioned by counties according to population; every county is guaranteed one member in the upper house. With only 30 senators for 14 counties, an equitable apportionment cannot be exactly achieved.

In Vermont, delegates to each of the national conventions are selected at state conventions, composed of delegates selected about three weeks previously in town caucuses. The law provides that the conventions be held the third week in May in each presidential year, but the state committee of each party sets the exact date and hour for both the town caucuses and the state convention. The county has no part in the delegate selection process but often serves as the basic unit for pre-convention campaign groups organized in behalf of the presidential aspirants.

THE REPUBLICAN DELEGATION

Vermont's deep Republican loyalty and the high caliber of its representatives in national official and party councils usually mean an influence at national conventions proportionately greater than the size of its delegation. The 1940 delegation included, for example, Warren Austin, Ralph Flanders, and George Aiken, all of whom have distinguished themselves in the United States Senate.

In each of the recent presidential years, only two presidential possibilities have figured in the state convention proceedings in Vermont, each supported by one of the two wings of the state party. But usually the factional struggle within the state overshadows the concern over the candidates. In 1948, though Vermont Republicans were grouped in either the Dewey or the Stassen camp, the real issue was an effort to oust the national committeeman, James F. Dewey, wealthy manufacturer and an extreme conservative, who was a distant relative of Governor Thomas E. Dewey of New York and a supporter of his presidential aspirations. The leader of the liberal wing was a Stassen supporter, Ernest Gibson, governor of Vermont from 1947 to 1950, when he resigned to accept a federal judgeship.

By custom, the delegation names the national committeeman and committeewoman on the basis of recommendations offered by the state convention. At the 1948 convention there were 18 candidates for the 9 delegate posts; 9 candidates were for James Dewey, 9 for Gibson. Since the conservatives had control of the convention, all 9 of the Dewey delegates were elected, after a bitter floor fight, thus assuring his unanimous reelection as national committeeman over Governor Gibson's candidate. There was no opposition to the reelection of the national committeewoman, Mrs. Consuelo Bailey. At the national convention, despite James Dewey's leaning toward Thomas E. Dewey, three of the delegates voted for Stassen; one of the three was Mortimer Proctor, governor of Vermont from 1945 to 1947.

The custom of electing substantial Republicans from the towns without inquiring definitely into their presidential preferences was partially broken in the selection of state convention delegates in 1952. In part, this break with tradition was engineered by the League of Women Voters, which publicized the importance of the town caucus in presidential nominations and urged that voters be given an opportunity to indicate their preference on national candidates. The break was also induced to some extent by changes within the party.

In 1952, James Dewey prophesied early in February that the Vermont delegation would support Taft. But when Senator Taft came to Vermont to speak at a Washington Birthday dinner, he left the state without having made any great progress in capturing any presidential delegates; for by this time, a vigorous but amateur campaign for Eisenhower was well under way.

Edward G. Janeway, a newcomer to Vermont, who took up dairy farming in the state after the war, sought counsel initially at the Washington, D. C., Eisenhower headquarters in December 1951. By early March 1952, Janeway had made substantial progress in building an Eisenhower organization. He had county chairmen for the seven largest counties and the nucleus of a state committee for Eisenhower. Janeway, with Carleton Howe of the liberal wing of the party, who had served four terms in the state senate, toured the state, talking with political leaders, appraising opinion, and seeking organization workers. Neither was a member of the state central committee; but Frederick P. Smith of Burlington, who was at one time representative of that city in the legislature and who was then chairman of the Republican state committee, soon began to give Janeway assistance while nominally adhering to his neutral position on the committee. Meanwhile, the Eisenhower forces were beginning to find support in unexpected quarters. Mrs. Bailey, national committeewoman, who had received an unfavorable impression of David Ingalls at the January meeting of the Republican national committee in San Francisco, returned to aid the Eisenhower movement. Out of personal respect for her colleague, James Dewey, however, she did not make her presidential preference known for several weeks. Morover, after a talk with Janeway, Mortimer Proctor, presumed leader of the conservatives, caused something of a sensation by announcing his support of Eisenhower and by becoming an active member of the Vermont

Eisenhower committee. Out of all this activity a realignment of the 1948 factions began to emerge, and the Taft-Eisenhower contest began in earnest. There was no longer any appreciable sentiment for Stassen and neither MacArthur nor Warren had any political support in the state.

THE SELECTION PROCESS IN 1952

The date set for the town caucuses in 1952 was April 22. The state convention was called for May 7 in the state capitol, Montpelier. The total number of authorized delegates to the state convention was 921. Of the 246 towns, 61 were allotted the minimum of 2 votes each. Nine cities containing over a third of the state's population were allotted 156 of the 921 delegates. Burlington with more than 33,000 people was allotted 33. Republican state party rules allot convention delegates among the 246 towns on the basis of each town's vote cast in the primary for the Republican candidates for governor in the last presidential year. Each town is entitled to at least two delegates.

The fact that the issue at the caucuses was squarely joined— whether to elect Taft or Eisenhower delegates to the state convention—was tradition-breaking; and the town caucuses drew a larger attendance than ever before. In Burlington, where the Republicans cast 4,317 votes and the Democrats 3,806 in the last gubernatorial election, more than 300 Republican voters attended, three times the usual number. In the South Burlington caucus, which normally draws less than 10 voters, the attendance was 26. Shelburne, with 181 Republican voters, drew 25 as against a normal half dozen. Immediately after the town caucuses, Janeway claimed that more than 600 of the 921 delegates to the state convention were for Eisenhower. A. Luke Crispe, spokesman for the Taft forces, claimed that a majority of the delegates were either unpledged or were pro-Taft. In many caucuses, even the election of the town's members to the county committee, usually a formality or a decision based on local personalities, reflected the Taft-Eisenhower contest. The county committees, so elected, met as usual a week later to choose a man and a woman from each county to serve as a member of the state committee. At this level an important Taft supporter, Gelsie Monti, lost his place on the state committee when the Washington County committee selected an Eisenhower man.

Before the state convention, Frederick P. Smith, chairman of the state central committee, in accordance with custom, appointed the convention committees. The committees heard suggestions the night before the convention from eight in the evening until well after midnight.

The main contest took place in the arrangements committee. Although nominations for delegate-candidates may be made spontaneously on the floor of the convention, in recent years a ballot containing the names of candidates who have announced themselves in the press is printed for use at the convention. The fight in the committee was over the arrangement of the ballot, and on the length of nominating and second speeches. The Eisenhower strategists wanted a ballot designed in columns (Eisenhower, Taft, and unpledged delegate-candidates), so that the state delegates could vote a "straight" ticket for the 12 national convention delegates; the Taft supporters insisted upon a one-column ballot. The Eisenhower group also wanted speech time limits, since they hoped to make their own nominations for the delegates by presenting a single bloc.

Actually, although the Eisenhower forces were in definite numerical command, they felt constrained to make minor concessions lest they be accused of steamroller tactics. Thus, a compromise limited each nominating speech to two minutes, but permitted these two minute periods to run consecutively if more than one candidate was being named. The committee further recommended a single column ballot, with the proviso, however, that the presidential preference of the delegate-candidate be indicated in parentheses after his name. There were 27 names on the ballot: 12 names followed by "Eisenhower"; 5 followed by "Taft"; and 10 names followed by "unpledged," "uncommitted," "unknown," or "none." The order was determined by drawing from a hat.

The state convention opened at 10:30 A.M. on May 7. Out of the potential 921 delegates, 861 appeared or their alternates were seated. Before the balloting, A. Luke Crispe, spokesman for the Taft group, moved that no matter which delegates were elected, they should go unpledged. This motion was countered by a move to table, carried by an affirmative shout, indicating the strength of the Eisenhower group.

In preparation for the balloting, the Eisenhower forces distributed small cards, printed with the list of Eisenhower delegate-candidates on one side and a list of alternate-candidates on the other, to all probable Eisenhower supporters at the opening of the convention. This detail of the planning proved crucial, since the ballot was long and confusing. All twelve Eisenhower delegate-candidates were easily elected. Ex-Governor Proctor, although listed fourth on the official ballot, received the highest number of votes, 679. The next highest, Frederick Smith, received 659 votes; and all the other Eisenhower delegates except one had over 600. The highest Taft supporter, Claude Farr, received 231 votes. Crispe received 211. After the balloting, a Taft supporter moved that the alternates consist of the next highest twelve names among the delegate candidates. This was shouted down, and Crispe magnanimously suggested that in view of the Eisenhower victory all twelve Eisenhower alternate-candidates be elected, a motion carried by voice vote.

A motion to instruct the delegation to vote for Eisenhower as long as there was any reasonable chance of his nomination was then carried by voice vote. The last time this was done in Vermont is reported to have been in 1920, when Vermont alone voted to the end for General Wood. The motion was carried in spite of tradition, partly because the Eisenhower forces wanted to get national attention and partly on a wave of jubilation and sense of power.

Edward Janeway was designated to be national committeeman by voice vote. His term would not begin until the national convention met. Late in June, James Dewey, unable because of illness to continue in the post, appointed Claude Farr, a Taft supporter, as his proxy on the national committee, in spite of the fact that his leadership had been repudiated.

COMPOSITION OF THE DELEGATION

The most prominent member of Vermont's delegation was ex-Governor Mortimer Proctor, president of the Vermont Marble Company, the only one of the twelve who had been a delegate in 1948. Frederick P. Smith of Burlington, a young lawyer with experience in the state legislature and state committee chairman from 1950 to 1952, and Preston Gibson, brother of former Governor Ernest Gibson, leader of the liberal wing of the party, were also well known. John Carbine of Rutland, an attorney active in politics primarily as a lobbyist for the leading public utility in the state, was also influential. Mrs. Dorothy Brown, chairman of the state Women's Republican Clubs, had served in the legislature; and John Swainbank, a young lawyer from St. Johnsbury, was an alternate in 1948. None of the delegates had attended either the 1940 or the 1944 convention.

The other delegates were probably less influential than two of the alternates: Edward Janeway, chairman of Vermont's Eisenhower committee, and Carleton Howe, four-time state senator. John Calhoun, Senator Flanders' administrative assistant, and Robert Babcock of the political science faculty at the state university also were alternates. Neither the governor, the United States senators, nor United States Representative Winston Prouty, were included in the delegation. However, Senator Flanders and Congressman Prouty, both Eisenhower supporters, did attend the national convention; Senator Aiken did not. There were two women among the delegates and one, Mrs. Mortimer Proctor, among the alternates.

ACTIVITIES AND VOTING RECORD

The delegation was formally organized a week after the state convention, although it really existed as a unit before the state convention. Mortimer Proctor was elected chairman. Frederick P. Smith, at the suggestion of the national Eisenhower headquarters, was assigned to the credentials committee, John Carbine to rules, and Mrs. Dorothy Brown to the resolutions committee.

No Vermonter took any prominent part in the proceedings on the floor of the convention, with the exception of Frederick Smith who spoke on the minority report on seating the Texas delegation.

The Vermont delegation, because it was so completely committed, was not subject to the heavy pressures at the convention that were applied to the uncommitted groups, and it faced no serious problems because its candidate's prospects steadily improved. It gave its 12 votes on the Eisenhower side of the early roll calls and on the nominating ballot.

AFTERMATH IN THE STATE

Ordinarily very little election activity takes place in Vermont; everyone anticipates a foregone conclusion. But in 1952, Lee E. Emerson, running for reelection as governor, after having won renomination by only 2,500 votes against an almost political unknown, lost popularity after the primary by virtue of the hearings he conducted in the ousting procedure of a liquor board commissioner. For the first time in years it was feared that the Democratic candidate for governor, Robert W. Larrow, had a chance to be elected. Some Republicans even feared that the antipathy toward Emerson might produce a light vote at the polls giving the Democrats a chance to win the electoral college vote as well.

At the last moment, a state Eisenhower organization was set up under Wayne Sarcka, a political newcomer who had been an Eisenhower alternate at Chicago. The two wings of the party, in so far as they campaigned at all, joined in backing Eisenhower. The earlier fears were groundless; Vermont went for Eisenhower by an unprecedented majority.

THE DEMOCRATIC DELEGATION

Based in part on a report by
JOAN PAULEY

Democratic party activity in Vermont is focused in the Burlington area, including the cities of Winooski and St. Albans. Here the party strength is derived primarily from the Catholic labor vote, partly Irish and partly French-Canadian. In the central part of the state, Rutland has a substantial Democratic minority and has actually cast a majority of votes for the Democratic gubernatorial candidate on several occasions. Bennington, though in a Republican county, maintains a fairly active Democratic organization. Barre, center of the granite industry, has a large labor vote and usually votes Democratic.

In 1948, an attempt to change the nominating procedure in the Democratic state convention did not change the competitive position of the other areas in relation to Burlington. Rutland County, with the second largest delegation, proposed a slate of delegate-nominees in opposition to the slate of the party leaders, so that the delegate candidates were considered one by one instead of as a slate. But the regular leadership demonstrated its strength on the first ballot and its slate was adopted as originally proposed.

Vermont is never entitled to bonus votes in the Democratic national convention and has the minimum allotment of six votes. Ordinarily it sends two full-vote and eight half-vote delegates.

THE SELECTION PROCESS IN 1952

The size of each town's delegation to the Democratic state convention is determined on the basis of the last Democratic vote for governor. Each of the 246 towns automatically has one delegate, plus one for every 100 votes cast in the last gubernatorial race. According to the state committee call, 623 delegates were eligible to attend in 1952. The procedure by which the Democrats select their delegates to the state convention is legally the same as that for the Republicans, but in practice somewhat different. The Republicans hold caucuses in virtually every town; in many towns, however, no one troubles to hold a Democratic caucus, partly because there are not enough interested Democrats and partly because an unknown Democrat has little chance of bucking the Democratic organization at the state convention. While the leaders of the Democratic party do not hand-pick the delegates to the state convention, it is safe to say that they can predict with considerable accuracy who will attend. The grass roots movement that made itself felt in the Republican town caucuses in 1952 was equaled in only one or two of the Democratic caucuses.

In preparation for the state convention, the state committee prepared a slate of national convention delegate-candidates with the co-operation of the leaders of the various county delegations. Robert W. Ready, national committeeman, stated that in 1952 the leaders first decided upon the more obvious choices, among them Mayor Edward Moran of Burlington, who had attended the last four conventions. Following this selection, they included the national committeeman, Ready, and the national committeewoman, Mrs. Beatrice Shurman. Thereafter the state committee held informal discussions with leaders from various parts of the state on the problem of selecting 10 delegates from 14 counties, looking for personalities who would respect the decisions of the established leadership, who wished to make the trip, and who could afford to do so. An individual desiring to go as a delegate to the national convention from sections other than Burlington, needed first to gain the support of his own city committee, and through this committee be recommended in turn to the county members on the state committee. Where a county was not allotted a delegate, dissatisfaction was quieted with promises for the future and with the privilege of supplying one or more alternates.

The Democratic state convention was held in St. Albans on May 14, with 300 delegates in attendance, less than half the number authorized by the state committee. A group representing the more populous cities of Rutland and Burlington attempted to have the delegation chosen by written ballot, but was defeated. Nominations were made from the floor and accepted by voice vote. Before the state convention opened, the slate prepared by the state committee had been given to the chairman of each county delegation. As nominations were made for the ten posts, the first nine on the slate were elected without opposition. The convention also reelected Robert Ready as national committeeman. The only dissension was caused by a delegate from Bennington County, who attempted to make a nomination from the floor that conflicted with plans already agreed upon for sectional representation. What the delegate hoped to accomplish was the nomination of Dr. John D. Lane, also of Bennington, who was opposing the nomination of Mrs. Beatrice Shurman, the national committeewoman. Once a standing vote showed Mrs. Shurman to be the overwhelming choice of the convention, Dr. Lane's backers moved to make Mrs. Shurman's election unanimous.

There was no indication that any group in the delegation was vigorously promoting any particular presidential candidacy. Mayor Moran gave a hesitant nod to Stevenson. Others mentioned Kefauver and Kerr. An uncommitted position seemed to be the general preference. As a small Democratic delegation from a Republican state, the delegation saw its role essentially as one of bargaining and moving with the bandwagon.

COMPOSITION OF THE DELEGATION

All delegates were delegates-at-large, since Vermont has only one congressman, elected from the state at large. The first two delegates chosen were given full votes, the others half votes. Outstanding among the delegates were Mayor J. Edward Moran of Burlington, state chairman; Robert Ready, national committeeman, attorney of St. Albans; and Robert Larrow, city attorney of Burlington and later Democratic candidate for governor. Mayor Moran, besides serving as state chairman, had been chairman of the Chittenden County Democratic committee for 25 years and chairman of the city committee for 28 years, and a member of the last four delegations. Although Ready had been chairman of the delegation in 1948, Moran acted in his place for several sessions and in 1952 was chosen chairman. Ready had been a delegate at the last three conventions. Larrow has always worked closely with Moran and acted as the state convention chairman in 1952. Somewhat less influential were Mrs. Beatrice Shurman, national committeewoman and an alternate on the 1948 delegation, and a long-time leader among Democratic women; Dominic McGary, chairman of the Rutland county committee and member of the state committee; and Matthew Coldbeck, a lawyer from St. Johnsbury.

Other delegates had been chosen primarily to give representation to particular geographical areas. Mrs. Cora Robinson, a milliner of Barre, received the nod of the leaders after her husband mentioned to the county committeewoman that his wife wished to attend the convention. Claude Vellefeuille, farmer of Orange County, where the Democratic vote is negligible, was selected also, no doubt, because this area had not had recent representation, and in order to give some recognition to French-Canadian elements. There were three women among the delegates, none among the alternates. No labor representatives were among the delegates, although two labor union men were chosen as alternates. Four delegates were active members of the Knights of Columbus.

ACTIVITIES AND VOTING RECORD

Following the May 14 state convention, most of the delegates who were selected met with the state committee on May 22. Here they organized, electing Moran chairman, and designating delegates Larrow and Shurman to serve on the national convention platform committee, and Coldbeck to sit on the credentials committee. The delegates had met with Kefauver when he visited the state on June 1, with Russell on June 7, and a few weeks later with Senator Kerr. The first two created favorable impressions. Kefauver's as well as Kerr's pursuit of the Vermont vote backfired, however, at Chicago. The delegates, being Vermonters, felt that the headquarters of the two candidates at the Conrad Hilton Hotel were too elaborate, and that the long telegrams and the distribution of orchids to the ladies each morning were too costly an expression of affection.

Vermont voted unanimously against the seating of Virginia, as might be expected because of its strong faith in civil rights, and did not change its vote. The delegation also voted "yes" on the Douglas motion to adjourn on Thursday night, though it was not voting for Kefauver.

The Vermont Democratic delegation does not follow the unit rule; yet the entire delegation usually votes together. In 1952, it cast 5 of its 6 votes for Stevenson on the first and second ballots and 5½ votes on the third. One half-vote delegate voted for Dever on the first ballot and shifted his vote to Russell on the second and third, refusing to go to Stevenson despite the cajolery of the rest of the delegation. His support of Russell was occasioned by his bitter antipathy for Truman and by a convivial friendship he developed with some members of the Georgia delegation. He was specifically and vehemently warned by at least one of the leaders, without effect, that this would be the last convention he would ever attend. One delegate, an elderly woman with ½ vote, voted for Kefauver on the first and second ballots, shifting to Stevenson on the third. She was personally close to the New Hampshire delegation and reflected their respect for Kefauver. Another delegate, noted for his truculent independence, came to the conclusion that Stevenson would be the best candidate and voted with the majority. His decision apparently happened to coincide with that of the leaders and was taken quite apart from any efforts at persuasion. Others doubtless were influenced by the opinions of the leaders.

The overwhelming vote for Eisenhower in Vermont amounted to more than twice that for Stevenson. Larrow, Democratic candidate for governor, did remarkably well for a Democrat, polling 60,000 votes and running far ahead of Stevenson. He carried the city of Burlington, which is 50 per cent Catholic, against Governor Emerson running for reelection, 6,768 to 5,039. Eisenhower drew 6,861 votes in the city to Stevenson's 5,210, and carried Chittenden County 13,509 to 9,614, while Larrow carried the county by more than 3,000 votes. Ticket-splitting was obviously widespread.

REVIEW AND APPRAISAL

Although Vermont is a small state, exceeding only Nevada, Wyoming, and Delaware in population, its experience in 1952 holds special interest for several reasons. Commonly regarded as the most Republican state in the Union, Vermont naturally invites comparisons with the one-party states in the South. As a small eastern state with an old tradition, Vermont can also be compared usefully with Delaware. Finally, there are the inevitable comparisons with its neighbors, New Hampshire and Maine. With these various comparisons in mind, it can be said that Vermont was outstanding in 1952 as an example of a one-party state that was able to operate the state convention system of selecting delegates successfully in a situation of some strain. The general level of political ethics, democracy, and respect for orderly procedure appeared to be remarkably high.

The procedural details of the system in Vermont were free of many common deficiencies. Caucuses were held throughout the state on the same day. There was no layering of intermediate levels of representation between town caucus and state convention. The apportionment of voting strength in the state convention was generally in accord with party strength throughout the state, although there was an element of rural over-representation. The use of a printed ballot at the Republican state convention facilitated the orderly handling of a complex contest among 27 candidates for 12 posts, assured the legitimacy of the outcome, and probably contributed to the good feeling with which the majority decision was accepted.

Various traditions were broken on the Republican side in 1952. The leader of the Eisenhower organization was a newcomer to Vermont and a newcomer in politics. For the first time in many years, contests in town caucuses were affected or even determined by the national candidate preferences of those who wished to attend the state convention. The latter body, in turn, broke with the tradition of unpledged delegations and elected a delegation pledged to Eisenhower. The Vermont experience thus seems to indicate that under some conditions the caucus and convention system may be more open to insurgency than many primary systems as they exist at the present time.

Representation on the Democratic delegation differed markedly in its composition from the Republican group. Although an attempt was made to bring about a wider geographic representation, the Democratic delegation was dominated by men from the industrial areas of the state. Several of these delegates were men who combined careers of law and politics and a few of them were Catholics. Two delegates represented rural areas; both have accepted their responsibilities as members of a minority party very seriously by running for local offices just to provide some opposition to the party in power. The Republican delegation was a mixed group of partisans under the Eisenhower banner, some conservative, more liberal, and almost all individualists. In general, it represented the older, better established, and moderately conservative elements of communities throughout the state.

Despite the apparently satisfactory working of the convention system, a bill was introduced into the Vermont senate in 1953 that would have provided for both a presidential preference primary and for the election of national convention delegates. This would have taken place at town meeting time in early March, one week earlier than in New Hampshire. The state senate deleted the election of delegates before passage, and the bill died in the lower house on the closing day of the session, largely because of the very early date of the proposed primary.

Both delegations from Vermont were reported to have expressed criticism of the national convention, namely that although it is not a deliberative body, some of the chaos and confusion could be greatly reduced, so that the convention could better go about its business. Yet no delegate suggested that the convention system itself be abandoned.

Vermont Chapter Acknowledgments

ROBERT S. BABCOCK, Associate Professor of Political Science, University of Vermont, and a Vermont state senator, prepared a pre-convention report on the Vermont Republican delegation, attended the Republican national convention as an alternate member of the Vermont Delegation, later prepared an extensive report on presidential nominating politics in both parties in Vermont in 1952, and assisted in the revision of the draft chapter.

JOAN PAULEY, then a student at Bennington College, prepared a pre-convention report on the Vermont Democratic delegation under the direction of Professor Oliver Garceau. Her report was made available to Professor Babcock.

The initial draft in chapter form was condensed from the field reports by MRS. ESTHER COLE FRANKLIN of the Washington staff.

MASSACHUSETTS

Electoral votes, 1952: 16

National convention votes, 1952:
Democratic, 36
Republican, 38

Population, 1950: 4,690,514
Urban, 84%; *rural nonfarm,* 14%; *rural farm,* 2%

Population increase, 1940-50: 373,793 (9%)
Urban, 7%; *rural nonfarm,* 40%; *rural farm,* 36% decline

Presidential vote, 1948:			*1952:*	
Democratic,	1,151,788	(55%)	1,083,525	(46%)
Republican,	909,370	(43%)	1,292,325	(54%)
Progressive,	38,157	(2%)		

Gubernatorial vote, 1948:		*1952:*
Democratic,	1,239,247	1,161,499
Republican,	849,895	1,175,955

U. S. Representatives vote,		
all districts, 1950:		*1952:*
Democratic,	920,990	1,064,454
Republican,	930,280	1,209,742

U. S. Representatives elected 1950:		*1952:*
Democratic,	6	6
Republican,	8	8

State legislature elected 1952:
Senate: Democrats, 15; Republicans, 25
House: Democrats, 117; Republicans, 123

Method of selecting national convention delegates:
Direct election in primary; delegates-at-large usually uncontested; advisory presidential preference poll, write-in only

70

Based primarily on reports by LASHLEY G. HARVEY,
SAMUEL P. HUNTINGTON,
CHARLES P. HOWARD,
JOHN L. FLETCHER,
AND TROY R. WESTMEYER

—————————————————————————CHAPTER 5

IN PRESIDENTIAL POLITICS, Massachusetts and neighboring Rhode Island were the only New England states to go Democratic in every election from 1928 to 1948. This reflected both the influence of the New Deal during the Roosevelt years and the great personal popularity of Alfred E. Smith and Harry S. Truman among the normally Democratic voters of the large industrial cities of Massachusetts: Boston, Worcester, Lowell, Fall River, Cambridge, Lynn, and Somerville. But before 1928 the state had usually gone Republican; and the Republican party has continued to hold great strength in state and local elections.

Seven Republican governors and five Democratic have held office since the end of the First World War in 1918. The Democratic senators from the state during that period have included Marcus Coolidge, David I. Walsh, and John F. Kennedy, now incumbent, but the other senators have been Republicans and the Republican party has usually maintained an edge in the state delegation in the House of Representatives. The struggle for control of the General Court (the state legislature) has been close in recent years, but it was only in 1948 that the Democrats succeeded for the first time in obtaining a majority of the lower chamber, a majority of two. In the same year the senate was evenly divided between the two parties, with twenty senators each. Republican control of the state legislature has facilitated the drawing of congressional district boundaries in a manner unfavorable to the Democrats.

The two parties have been fairly equal in size, but markedly different in their sources of support. Both, moreover, have been forced to cater to a large floating vote; in some years almost 40 per cent of the total voters have registered as independents. The strength

71

of the Democratic party has normally been in the Roman Catholic, particularly the Irish, groups in the large urban centers. The Boston Irish play a crucial role not only in the city's politics but in the state party organization as well. Intra-party conflicts among the Democrats are usually dominated by factionalism within the city of Boston. Democrats from the smaller towns and rural sections of the western part of the state are of a somewhat different stripe. In recent years, organized labor has come to play a growing part in the affairs of the state's Democratic party, although a strong element of conservatism pervades Massachusetts trade unionism. The Republican party, on the other hand, has tended to draw its support from Protestant groups in the rural areas, suburbs, and smaller cities, and from the urban upper classes; all these being summed up as "the Yankee elements." There are notable exceptions to the above. For example, Congressman Joseph W. Martin, Jr., a Republican and a Catholic, has won heavy support from Catholics and industrial workers. But the traditional party alignment has been challenged in recent years by three significant developments: the growth of suburbia; the rise of other ethnic groups to challenge the Yankee-*versus*-Irish polarity in state politics; and the changing patterns of economic activity in the state.

Massachusetts is one of the most highly urbanized areas in the United States; between 1940 and 1950, the farm population of the state declined from 3 per cent to 2 per cent. Meanwhile, the rural nonfarm population, mainly suburban, was growing by 40 per cent. The emigrants to the suburbs frequently come from normally Democratic urban areas. To a large degree the future political control of the state may depend upon the extent to which these new suburbanites adhere to the previous partisan attachments or adjust to their new environment politically by registering as Republicans. Many of them have followed the latter course, and Roman Catholics may become more important in the future in the state's Republican party.

The former Yankee-Irish duality of Massachusetts politics has long been gradually shifting with the rise of other ethnic groups to political maturity. Most important among these new groups are the Italians; both Republicans and Democrats have made serious efforts in the past few years to attract the Italian vote. For example, the passage of a pre-primary convention law in 1953 (Chap. 406, Acts of 1953;

Sec. 54, Chap. 53, General Laws of Massachusetts) was largely moti-
vated by the desire to achieve more "balanced" state tickets. While
the leadership of the Democratic party was divided regarding the
desirability of this law, nearly all Republican leaders favored it. A
similar law had been put on the books in 1932 (Chap. 310, Acts of
1932) but repealed in 1938 (Chap. 473, Acts of 1938). The present
law permits the state committees of the two parties to call pre-primary
conventions in biennial election years. These conventions may adopt
party platforms, elect members-at-large to the state committee, nominate presidential electors in presidential election years, and endorse
candidates for nomination in the party primaries for offices to be
filled by all voters in the Commonwealth. The statement "endorsed
by (Republican or Democratic) convention" will then appear on the
primary ballot after the name of the endorsed candidates. Through
this means some party leaders hope to end Yankee dominance of the
Republican primaries and Irish dominance of the Democratic. In
addition to the Italians, other ethnic groups that may be expected
to play an increasingly important role in state politics are the Jews,
whose strength is concentrated in Brookline and other suburbs of
Boston, the Portuguese, who are particularly strong on Cape Ann
and in southern Massachusetts, the French-Canadians in the textile
cities, and the Poles.

A fundamental element in Massachusetts politics—but one whose
direct influence is almost impossible to measure—is the shift in the
pattern of economic activity within the state. The textile industry,
which has long been of great importance to the state, has tended to
move elsewhere; other significant industries have tended to drop in
relative national importance. This has created a number of significant economic and social problems, particularly in the old "mill
towns" such as Lawrence and Lowell. State administrations of both
parties have devoted considerable discussion to attracting new industry to the state and stimulating capital replenishments in existing
industry. To a certain extent newer industries such as electronics,
as well as the long important tourist trade, have tended to replace the
traditional foundations of the Massachusetts economy. The exact
political consequences of these changes in the state's economic structure are difficult to determine, but some observers in the state are of

the opinion that the Democratic party may be more profoundly affected by the changing pattern of economic activity than the Republican.

PRESIDENTIAL PRIMARY LAW AND PROCEDURE

The Massachusetts presidential primary consists of two elements: (1) the direct election of national convention delegates with provisions permitting the delegate candidate to express his presidential preference on the ballot if the preferred candidate consents; and (2) provisions permitting the voters to write in their presidential preference on the primary ballot. These two sets of provisions are distinct in origin and operation.

The election of delegates—The provisions of the Massachusetts code relating to the election of delegates to the national conventions originated in their present form in 1912 and have not been significantly altered since that date. (Secs. 70A-70H, Chap. 53, General Laws of Massachusetts.) The law provides that delegates shall be elected in party primaries by direct plurality vote. The last Tuesday in April is the legal date for such primaries. The number of district delegates and alternates shall be not less than one from each congressional district, and the number of delegates- and alternates-at-large shall be fixed by the state committee. The nomination of candidates at large requires the signatures of at least 1,000 voters, no more than 250 of whom may be from any single county. Petitions nominating district delegates must contain a number of signatures equal in the aggregate to five voters from each ward and town in the district.

Candidates for delegate may be grouped together as a slate in nominating papers. The names of candidates appearing together in such papers are placed first on the primary ballot and are arranged within the groups in the same order as they appear in the papers. Each group of candidates for alternate delegate immediately follows that group of candidates for delegate with which it is affiliated. The order of the groups is determined by lot. The names of candidates appearing in nomination papers containing nominations for less than all places follow the full groups on the ballot and are arranged in alphabetical order. The effect of these provisions is to benefit organizations which put a full slate of candidates in the field in any given district or in the state at large.

The Massachusetts law further provides that

> The ballot shall also contain a statement of preference, if any, of each candidate for nomination for president, provided that such statement appears in his nomination papers; but no such statement of preference by any candidate for delegate shall appear upon the ballot unless such candidate for nomination for president files his written assent thereto with the state secretary on or before five o'clock in the afternoon of the last day for filing nomination papers. (Sec. 70E, chap. 53)

This provision has remained substantially unchanged since 1912. The statement of preference normally takes the form of "Pledged to John J. Johnson" or "Preference for John J. Johnson." There is no statutory requirement that pledged delegates actually support in any way the candidate of their preference at the national convention.

In general, this provision of the law has not been widely used. The dominant organization in each party normally prefers to run unpledged candidates and to rely upon organizational strength and the personal popularity of the delegate candidates to insure election rather than association with the name of a national presidential candidate. This permits the delegation to go to the convention in a more strategic bargaining position. A further consideration is the requirement that the presidential candidate consent to the appearance of the statement of preference, a consent that is not always available. The net result is that these provisions of the law are used mostly by weaker groups within the state parties in the hope of benefiting from association with a popular presidential candidate who will consent to the use of his name.

The people in Massachusetts have never shown much interest in the presidential primary. There were 2,475,396 registered voters in 1950, yet only a small percentage bothered to vote for delegates to the national conventions in 1952. The number of persons voting in the presidential primaries can be calculated from the election returns for delegates-at-large; and the figures since 1944 are as follows:

Year	Total Vote for National Convention Delegates	Vote by Party Democratic	Republican
1944	109,224	56,714	52,510
1948	123,396	51,207	72,189
1952	537,973	123,739	414,234

Although these statistics indicate a marked increase in interest in 1952, they represent the votes of only a fifth of the registered voters. There were no contests within the parties for delegates-at-large in 1952 but rival factions contested for supremacy in a number of the districts in both parties, and there was a contest throughout the state in the Republican party. The registration figures given above include persons registered as independents as well as those registered as partisans, but under Massachusetts law the registered independents may vote in the primary of either party. By so voting, however, an independent becomes a registered member of the party in which he votes and remains so unless he reregisters as an independent the following year.

The write-in provision—The Massachusetts primary law was amended in November 1951 to provide for a write-in expression of voter preference for the presidential nomination. (Chap. 764, Acts of 1951, amending Sec. 70E, Chap. 53, General Laws of Massachusetts) This was the first time since 1936 that Massachusetts voters were able to make some direct expression of their preferences among presidential candidates. Under the 1951 law, no candidates' names were to appear on the ballot; it was purely a write-in procedure. The ballot included the following statement: "My preference for............ ....candidate for President of the United States is ...." The voter was required to insert the name of the party and the name of the candidate in writing or by sticker. The write-in vote is purely informational and has no binding effect upon the elected delegation.

The bill providing for this expression of preference was introduced into the General Court in the early spring of 1951. It was passed by the lower house on March 26 but was rejected by the state senate the first week in April; in early October the Senate agreed to reconsider. At the end of that month the bill was approved by the upper house by 18 to 17. The final vote on October 25 in the lower house was similarly close: 112 to 94. The bill was signed into law by Governor Paul A. Dever on November 5, 1951.

The principal sponsor of the bill in the General Court was State Senator Charles W. Hedges, a Quincy Republican. The bill was supported by 16 Republicans and 2 Democrats in the state senate and opposed by 5 Republicans and 12 Democrats. One of the opposing Republicans, State Senator Philip G. Bowker, had declared himself for General MacArthur. Another Republican, State Senator George J. Evans, voted against the bill despite his argument that it would benefit his candidate, who had a short name, i.e. Taft. In general, it would appear that the bill received most of its support from Republican Eisenhower supporters although there was some shifting back and forth across party lines and candidate lines. One motive behind the Eisenhower support for the bill was the desire to obtain a clear-cut expression of the preference of Republican voters for Eisenhower and Taft, something that could not be done under existing law if the General was not in a position to assent to the nomination of delegate candidates pledged to his nomination. In addition, the Eisenhower supporters expected that the preferential poll would increase public interest and participation in the primary. So far as the Democrats were concerned, Governor Dever, according to report, was opposed to the bill (although he subsequently signed it), and the Democratic members of the legislature mostly followed his leadership in voting against its enactment, fearing that it might weaken the control of the party organization over the presidential primary process.

THE REPUBLICAN DELEGATION

No clear-cut factional pattern has been apparent in the Republican party of Massachusetts. Political strength seems to have been partly of the personal kind as reflected in the followings of influential leaders like Senator Henry Cabot Lodge, Senator Leverett Saltonstall, and Congressman Joseph W. Martin, Jr. Occasionally in the past local leaders in the western part of the state have resented the preponderant role in the state organization of persons from Boston and the eastern part of the state. There has also been criticism from all ranks in the party of the great influence of the Harvard-educated "Proper Bostonian" leaders. The party leadership has attempted to meet such criticism by presenting slates that would be more representative of the various ethnic and religious groups found in the state. The pre-primary convention in 1952 had this as one of its principal objectives.

THE SELECTION PROCESS IN 1952

The Republican presidential primary campaign in Massachusetts was marked by a hard contest for district delegates between the two skillfully organized groups. Most of the leaders in the state came out for Eisenhower, although in several instances the announcement was delayed until shortly before the national convention. Senator Lodge served as national campaign manager for Eisenhower during the primary; Senator Saltonstall came out for Eisenhower early in the campaign. Congressman Martin did not participate in the primary struggle, although it was understood that General MacArthur was his first choice and Senator Taft his second. A very large number of the local organization leaders had strong Taft leanings. Despite the intensity of the primary contest, it was tempered to some extent by a concern for the forthcoming contest with the Democrats and the need for maintaining as much unity as possible. In an attempt to strengthen the organization for the battle for state offices, the Republican state committee voted in January to hold a pre-primary state convention in June.

Slates for delegates and alternate delegates were entered by both the Eisenhower and Taft forces in each of the 14 districts. In three districts (8th, 9th, 11th) there was an additional group of candidates. Although for a time a contest for delegates-at-large was threatened, this was averted through a compromise arranged by the national committeeman, Sinclair Weeks. Except when a Republican president has been a candidate for re-election, the Massachusetts delegation has been either unpledged or pledged to a favorite son.

The delegate-at-large slate—As a rule, the principal leaders in the party, other distinguished leaders less active in state politics, and at least one representative from the western part of the state have made up the delegate-at-large slate. There had been no contest for the state's delegate-at-large positions since the Bull Moose split of 1912 and the party leadership was anxious to continue the appearance of unity in 1952. Basil Brewer, publisher of the New Bedford *Standard-Times* and the chairman of the Taft forces, originally planned to contest the delegate-at-large posts in 1952, but he eventually accepted a slate on which there were two announced Eisenhower supporters—Senators Lodge and Saltonstall—and two pledged for Taft—Charles Gibbons, minority leader in the lower house of the state legislature, and Clarence A. Barnes, a former state attorney general. The presence on the ticket of another known but unannounced Eisenhower supporter, former Governor Robert Bradford, was compensated for by the expectation that Congressman Joseph W. Martin, Jr., would serve as permanent chairman of the national convention, thus permitting Basil Brewer, as his alternate, to cast a Taft vote.

Others on the list of delegates-at-large were: Sinclair Weeks, Republican national finance committee chairman and national committeeman, who came out for Eisenhower in late June; Mrs. Katherine G. Howard, national committeewoman and secretary of the national committee, who also announced her preference for Eisenhower in late June; Daniel Tyler, chairman of the state committee; and Richard I. Furbush, president of the state senate. Tyler's selection marked the first time in many years that the state committee chairman had been chosen as a delegate-at-large. Tyler and Furbush voted for Eisenhower on the first ballot thus making a total of 7 votes for Eisenhower and 3 for Taft among the delegates-at-large.

Several factors seem to have been responsible for the decision of the Taft group to accept the delegate-at-large slate organized by Weeks. There seems to have been a reasonable basis for anticipating a more evenly divided vote than later occurred. Although W. E. Mullins of the Boston *Herald* stated as early as February 20 that Weeks, Furbush, and Mrs. Howard preferred Eisenhower, his comments appear to have been based on pure surmise, for none of the three had made any statement of preference in public or, as far as can be ascertained, in private. The Taft forces indicated that they wished to avoid, if possible, any further split in Republican ranks, and Basil Brewer's own preference for a single slate for delegates-at-large was buttressed by counsel from Senator Taft. Congressman Martin seems finally to have advised the Taft leadership to modify somewhat its demands for 5 of the 10 delegates-at-large posts. Congressman Martin appears to have indicated to the Taft group that his advice was prompted by a message he had been given by an emissary from the Eisenhower camp. In any case, the Eisenhower management was evidently confident of the result in a contest.

The Eisenhower campaign—The agreement on an official slate for delegates-at-large confined the primary contests to the districts. Both sides organized early and effectively. The Eisenhower-sponsoring group first met in Boston in October 1951. Congressman Christian A. Herter and William Phillips, former Ambassador to Italy, who had also served as a civilian aide to General Eisenhower, were appointed as co-chairmen of the group. Their sons, State Representative Christian A. Herter, Jr., and State Senator Christopher Phillips, were appointed as vice-chairmen. Others in the sponsoring group included Mrs. Henry Cabot Lodge, Mrs. Leverett Saltonstall, former Governor Alvan T. Fuller, and General Robert Cutler, a Boston banker and influential Republican. In December 1951, an executive secretary, Edmund V. Keville, was appointed. The first pro-Eisenhower candidates for district delegates were also announced in December: State Senator Christopher H. Phillips and Frank S. Giles, in the 6th district.

The work of selecting delegates during the early weeks of the campaign was made difficult by the fact that a number of key local political figures desired to run as unpledged delegates. An additional difficulty was the impossibility of specifying on the ballot those delegate-candidates who definitely supported Eisenhower. Under Massachusetts law it was necessary for the presidential candidate to consent in writing before appropriate notation could be made on the ballot; this General Eisenhower would not do. The Taft forces, on the other hand, did have the consent of Senator Taft and the notation "Pledged to Robert A. Taft" was to be on the ballot directly under the name of each Taft candidate.

In three districts, the 8th, 9th, and 11th, the presence of a third slate on the ballot, also undesignated, meant that the Eisenhower organization had the difficult task of educating the Republican voters as to the precise names of the Eisenhower delegates to differentiate them from other "uncommitted" delegate-candidates; two of these slates intended to support MacArthur. The 9th district, in which the only loss of an Eisenhower delegate occurred, presented a special challenge for the Eisenhower forces, arising in part from the fact that the New Bedford *Standard-Times*, published by Basil Brewer, Taft campaign manager in Massachusetts, circulated throughout the major part of the district. Other special problems faced by the Eisenhower organization were confined to single districts. In the 2d district, for example, there was so much support for Eisenhower that at first some fifteen or sixteen persons desired to run as Eisenhower candidates. However, all of these persons did get together and agreed to support the selections of a specially created nominating committee. The group of prospective candidates subsequently served as an effective nucleus for the Eisenhower organization in the district. In one other district, the 11th, a problem of excess candidates occurred in a different manner. In this district, an additional, unofficial, pro-Eisenhower slate also appeared on the ballot, but it did not substantially lessen the vote for the official Eisenhower candidates. The problem of an uncommitted candidate paired with a pro-Eisenhower candidate occurred in the 3d district. The slate was a strong one and the Eisenhower management decided to support it instead of entering another completely pro-Eisenhower slate. This was the only instance in which the Eisenhower management gave its support to an uncommitted candidate. The delegate concerned, Winfield A. Schuster, won his race and eventually cast his vote for Eisenhower at the convention.

Basic to the strategy of the Eisenhower organization was the policy of giving an active role to political amateurs, to independents, and even to persons previously registered as Democrats. By Massachusetts law it is possible to change party enrollment up to 31 days prior to a primary election. The Eisenhower forces did not hesitate to encourage Democrats to change their registration so as to permit voting in the Republican primary. Since their candidate was not available for personal appearances, it seemed important to obtain such speakers as Senators Lodge and Saltonstall and Congressman Herter, Congressman Walter H. Judd of Minnesota, Governor Sherman Adams of New Hampshire, Governor Alfred E. Driscoll of New Jersey, Governor John Davis Lodge of Connecticut, and Senator James H. Duff of Pennsylvania. The Eisenhower success in New Hampshire two months earlier was undoubtedly a great boon to his Massachusetts campaign.

The Taft campaign—Although the top leaders in the Massachusetts Republican organization have usually supported somewhat more internationally-minded presidential aspirants, Senator Taft did not lack supporters in the state prior to the 1952 campaign. The man whom Senator Taft appointed as his Massachusetts manager for 1952, Basil Brewer, publisher and controlling owner of the New Bedford *Standard-Times*, had followed the Senator's activities closely and sympathetically for a number of years. His paper ran several feature stories about the Senator in 1946 and 1947, and in 1948 the newspaper supported Taft's candidacy for the Republican nomination.

Important to the development of high morale in the Taft camp were the Senator's several visits to Massachusetts in the months preceding the primary. On each occasion he met a host of Republicans active in local and state organizations. A large meeting of Republicans held in Plymouth on July 29, 1951, provided a springboard for the 1952 Taft campaign in Massachusetts. Although the Senator's candidacy had not yet been announced, his warm reception at the meeting may have been influential in his later declaration. In any case, by providing an opportunity for him to meet with a large number of state and local Republican leaders, the meeting laid a basis for a statewide Taft organization. The New Bedford *Standard-Times* played an active part in the management and publicizing of this rally which was formally sponsored by the Plymouth County Republican Club. It was billed as a "Pilgrimage to Plymouth," and, according to newspaper reports, was attended by more than 12,000 New England Republicans. Senator Taft's address, which was largely concerned with foreign policy, was telecast nationally and appears to have been well received.

On Labor Day, Brewer reported to Congressman Martin and National Committeeman Sinclair Weeks that he intended to push Senator Taft's candidacy in Massachusetts. Later on the same day, he made arrangements for a pro-Taft delegate slate for the 9th congressional district, the district in which New Bedford is located. George C. P. Olsson, Clerk of Plymouth County Superior Court, and Sheriff Patrick H. Dupuis of New Bedford agreed to run as delegates. Olsson and Dupuis are key Republican leaders in the 9th district. In 1948 they ran as pro-Dewey delegates, and the *Standard-Times* backed a pro-Taft slate which succeeded in upsetting the Olsson-Dupuis team. A similar conflict was averted in the 1952 campaign by their early announcement for Taft. The 9th district slate was the first to be formed in either camp and gave the Taft forces a head start of several months over the Eisenhower group. Thereafter, Brewer traveled throughout the state to build up Taft sentiment and to organize Taft delegate slates for other districts. On December 11, 1951, Senator Taft announced the selection of Brewer as his campaign manager in Massachusetts.

The management of the Taft campaign decided early that all delegate-candidates sponsored by the Taft organization must sign pledges to support Taft's nomination at the convention. The pledged delegates agreed in writing that, if elected, they would vote for Senator Taft on the first ballot and would continue to vote for him until released by Senator Taft himself or his duly accredited agent. The election laws refer to "preference" of the delegate candidates and the ballots for three districts—4th, 12th, 14th—bore the notation "Preference for Robert A. Taft," with the notation "Pledged to Robert A. Taft" appearing on the ballots for the other eleven districts.

During the early weeks of the campaign the Taft organization faced a difficulty also met by the Eisenhower forces: the desire of a number of local political leaders to run as uncommitted candidates. Also, the Taft forces encountered several persons with an original preference for Taft who switched their allegiance to Eisenhower. The policy of pledged delegates only provided the Taft forces with certain advantages over the Eisenhower group, but it did in some cases make it necessary for the Taft management to reject desirable delegate-candidates who preferred Taft but who were not prepared to sign a pledge. The Taft leaders did not seem to think that this weakened their slates appreciably, although they admitted that the pledge requirement made it necessary for them to turn down their first choice for delegate-candidate in a few cases.

In addition to Basil Brewer, the statewide executive board for Taft also included: Charles Gibbons, Republican minority leader in the lower house of the state legislature; Clarence A. Barnes, former attorney-general; Ralph H. Bonnell and Robert A. Welch, delegate candidates from the 5th district; Charles A. Sprague, candidate in the 6th district; and George B. Rowell, candidate in the 11th district. Headquarters for Taft-for-President Clubs was established on February 1 in Boston, and George F. Oakes, candidate for mayor of Boston in 1949, was appointed to head this work.

The leading speaker and campaigner in Massachusetts was Senator Taft himself. Subsequent to his appearance at the "Pilgrimage to Plymouth," the Senator visited Massachusetts on December 11, 1951, when he gave a major address in Brookline, and again for three days in April before the primary, when he visited some twenty cities and towns, including Boston, Worcester, and Springfield. During the nine months preceding the primary, Senator Taft visited each of the fourteen districts in Massachusetts with the exception of the 1st district, which was considered to be fairly secure for the Eisenhower forces.

Primary results—Eisenhower received 254,898 votes and Taft 110,188 in the write-in preference poll. Eisenhower also won overwhelmingly in the district delegate contests, which resulted in the election of 22 district delegates committed to Eisenhower although unpledged on the ballot, 1 uncommitted delegate, and 1 delegate pledged to Taft. The uncontested slate of delegates-at-large was elected, including 2 delegates for Eisenhower, 2 for Taft, and 6 who were still publicly uncommitted. After the primary, more of the uncommitted Republicans among the delegates-at-large swung over to Eisenhower. When Sinclair Weeks, national committeeman and delegate-at-large, announced his decision to support Eisenhower in June he accompanied it with public advice to Senator Taft to drop out of the race for the nomination.

The only loss of a district delegate contest by an Eisenhower supporter occurred in the 9th district where a third slate supported MacArthur. One of the Eisenhower candidates lost by a few hundred votes to a Taft candidate. If the delegate contest results had been in line with the preference balloting for the presidential nominee in

the 9th district, both Eisenhower delegate candidates would have
won. It seems clear that enough votes were won by the MacArthur
delegates as a result of voter mistakes and confusion to account for
the victory of the one Taft-pledged delegate.

The Taft forces, in retrospect, believed that, in addition to the
obvious popularity of the Eisenhower candidacy, certain other factors were instrumental in his victory. The Taft leaders found on a
number of occasions that their requests for help in the campaign
were met with a negative response on the ground that "Taft couldn't
win," in spite of a positive expression of personal liking for Taft.
In comparing the Eisenhower and Taft campaigns, it can be seen
that the Eisenhower forces benefited from the active participation
of many of the top Republican leaders of the state, although the
greater portion of the local leaders were for Taft. With a few exceptions, the managers of the Taft campaign were from the business
and publishing field; political background was somewhat more evident among the Eisenhower managers.

COMPOSITION OF THE DELEGATION

The membership of the delegate-at-large group has been commented upon earlier. It was the Eisenhower group that became,
almost in its entirety, the elected district delegates to the national
convention, but a comparative view of the Eisenhower and the Taft
district slates may be of some interest.

The Eisenhower candidates included many persons with political
experience. At least 17 had held national or state elective public or
political office. Two congressmen, four state senators, one former
state senator, two state representatives, one former state representative, one governor's councillor, two former councillors, a former
assistant attorney-general, and three former state committee chairmen were included. The Eisenhower district slates for delegate and
alternate gave substantial recognition to women and to various racial
groups. They included 16 women, there being at least one for every
district except the 14th. As for ethnic group ancestry, there were
six French-Canadians, four Irish, two Italians, two Jews, two Negroes,
and one Swede.

The district slates for Taft also included a number of persons with political experience. Although there were no congressmen, there were two state senators and four state representatives. Admiral Louis Denfield, candidate in the 4th district, was a former candidate for governor and had been Chief of Naval Operations. Also included on the Taft slates were: a former primary candidate for lieutenant governor, three former assistant attorneys-general, a former chairman of the Republican state committee, three former presidents of the Massachusetts Republican Club, a former candidate for state auditor, and a former chairman of the Massachusetts Industrial Accident Board. In choosing its slates of district delegates and alternates, the Taft leadership gave substantial recognition to women and included 17 of them on their slates. They also gave recognition to ethnic groups: five French-Canadians, three Irish, three Swedes, two Jews, two Negroes, one Italian, one German, and one Greek were among the candidates included.

Delegates were expected to pay the expenses of attendance at the national convention and apparently were well able to do so in almost all cases.

ACTIVITIES AND VOTING RECORD

At the organizing meeting of the delegation, Senator Saltonstall was chosen chairman of the group. The following persons were elected to the national convention committees: Congressman John Heselton to credentials; former Congressman Charles Clason to rules; Congressman Christian A. Herter and Mrs. Nancy Crocker to resolutions.

With very few exceptions, the decisions concerning the vote of the Massachusetts delegation had been made before the convention. All but one of the district delegates were committed and voted accordingly at the convention. The one uncommitted district delegate was supported by the Eisenhower organization during the primary and he cast his vote for Eisenhower at the convention. Two of the delegates-at-large and Basil Brewer, who voted as the alternate for Congressman Martin, had been pledged to Taft. The other 7 at-large votes went to Eisenhower. Senators Lodge and Saltonstall and former Governor Bradford had made known their preference early. Weeks, Mrs. Howard, and Tyler announced their preference in late

June. Furbush seems to have made no public announcement prior to the convention.

The delegation voted with the Eisenhower forces by a 33 to 5 margin on the Brown amendment to the Langlie proposal and on the minority report regarding the seating of Georgia. The initial nominating roll call showed 34 for Eisenhower and 4 for Taft, this became unanimous for Eisenhower on the final count.

AFTERMATH IN THE STATE

Despite the intensity of the primary campaign and the bitterness which it engendered—both sides agree that it was one of the hardest fought Republican primaries in the state's history—there was a joining of forces for the general election. Basil Brewer went to see General Eisenhower in Chicago a day after his nomination and pledged his support. Outward signs since the national convention attest to harmony among Massachusetts Republicans. The present national committeeman, Ralph H. Bonnell, and the present state vice-chairman, Beatrice H. Mullaney, were both defeated Taft candidates for district delegate. However, almost all appointments to important federal posts from Massachusetts have gone to Eisenhower supporters.

THE DEMOCRATIC DELEGATION

Democratic party leadership continues to be concentrated in the Boston metropolitan area and nearly all party leaders have names of Irish derivation. Paul Dever, the late William Foley, John Hynes, John Kennedy, John McCormack, and the late Maurice Tobin have had the kind of support that must be considered in any party decision; the aging James Curley still is a factor because the core of his followers seem never to transfer their allegiance. All of these men have proved their ability in the political arena by winning major elective offices: Tobin and Curley have been both governor and Boston's mayor; Dever was twice elected governor after having served as attorney-general; Hynes was thought to be a fixture as city clerk for Boston until he became mayor by defeating former Mayor-Governor-Congressman Curley. The former majority leader (now minority whip) of the United States House of Representatives, John W. McCormack, has long been one of the key figures in the Democratic party. Apart and perhaps aloof from the others, Senator Kennedy goes his own way to a considerable extent. As state chairman, John C. Carr, former mayor of Medford, coordinates the political activities of these men of political power, although at times his task seems primarily one of arbitration and conciliation. Frequently called a Dever man, he has experienced little difficulty in obtaining support from all the key party figures when such support appeared necessary.

Outside the Boston area, the four Democratic congressmen from other parts of the state represent industrial areas that tend to be strongly Democratic. Upon occasion the mayors from such industrial sections make strong bids for statewide party recognition, but their success has been comparatively meager. Organized labor's chieftains in Massachusetts, AFL and CIO, almost automatically achieve high Democratic party status. The fact that most of the Democratic leaders of the Boston area are of the Roman Catholic faith has been used at times to infer Church participation in political activity, but no evidence that would substantiate such an inference is available.

The Democratic state committee usually initiates the procedure for selecting national convention delegates, or, at least, for drawing up an "organization" slate. Generally the state chairman contacts the congressmen, major state officials, and other leaders of the party in order to obtain their recommendations for delegates. Senators, congressmen, and state elective officials are usually assured places on the ticket as delegates-at-large if they wish. In most instances the congressmen decline in favor of those who do not hold elective office, since there is some feeling that the convention delegate positions should be circulated among the non-elective members of the party. Congressman McCormack is an exception; he has been regularly a delegate for a considerable number of years. James M. Curley insists upon delegate status even if he must represent Puerto Rico, as he did in 1932.

Other members of the slate are usually selected from among the many who have been recommended by the state party leaders, with compromise generally worked out through the state chairman. The criteria used to award or reject persons for the slate include vote-getting ability, geographical distribution, friendliness to organized labor, and the need to have persons representing the important ethnic and national groups.

In 1948, party routines broke down to some extent and there was a wide open contest for places as delegates-at-large, with 44 candidates running for the 16 half-vote seats. The "official" slate headed by Congressman McCormack defeated an opposition slate headed by Thomas P. O'Neill, Jr., of Cambridge, who was then minority leader of the lower house of the state legislature, was later the first Democrat elected speaker of the lower house, and was elected to Congress in 1952. The McCormack slate polled votes ranging from 15,941 to 22,253, while the highest contestant on the O'Neill slate polled 10,762 votes. In addition, 12 other candidates for delegate-at-large who were on neither slate were defeated, with none polling over 2,000 votes.

THE SELECTION PROCESS IN 1952

Under Governor Dever's leadership in 1952, it became a prime objective to avoid another contest over the delegateships between major factions of the state party organization. The Governor decided, in consultation with other party leaders, to extend the half-vote principle to the 28 district positions, although this was contrary to national party rules. It is a matter for speculation just what assurance Dever had that the over-sized delegation would be seated. Nevertheless, arrangements were made to elect 72 half-vote delegates in the primary on April 29: 56 in the congressional districts and 16 at large, with a like number of alternates also to be sent to Chicago. On this basis, slate-making became relatively easy for the organization slate; and the slate for the positions as delegates-at-large, headed by Governor Dever himself, was uncontested. In 6 of the 14 districts, more than one slate was nominated. The contest of greatest interest occurred in the 10th district, where a slate pledged to Kefauver appeared on the ballot; local factional contests of some importance occurred in the 9th and 14th districts.

The Kefauver slate that was run in the 10th district had its origins at the time of the New Hampshire presidential primary, when John P. Mallan of Newton met Kefauver in New Hampshire. Kefauver at that time informed Mallan that he had no delegates from Massachusetts, and Mallan, being impressed by the Senator, then returned home and organized the Kefauver-pledged slate in his home district. At that time, the Kefauver campaign manager in Massachusetts was one Martin Fay, a lawyer and former aid to Governor Hurley. Fay's job was to try to sell Kefauver to the Massachusetts regulars and he did not approve of the running of an opposition Kefauver slate in the 10th district. Nonetheless he did not obstruct the efforts of the Mallan group, although he also did not give them any assistance, financial or otherwise. Kefauver's approval to the 10th district slate was given in conformance to law through John M. Shea, who was a Kefauver supporter running on the state organization slate from the Worcester district. Shea was given a power-of-attorney by Kefauver and filed the formal acquiescence of the Senator with the state election authorities, so that Kefauver's name could go on the ballot as the preference of his delegate-candidates. The 10th district Kefauver slate caused the state organization enough uneasiness so that they expended a significant amount of money in campaigning in the district. The Kefauver people had no money and relied solely on the pulling power of the Senator's name on the ballot.

Only two of the presidential aspirants carried on energetic campaigns in Massachusetts. Senator Kefauver and Averell Harriman opened headquarters in Boston and attempted to rally support. The Senator also had the good fortune of being in Boston at the time of a meeting of the state committee and was invited to meet the committee members informally. The Harriman headquarters was opened with considerable fanfare under the direction of Congressman Franklin D. Roosevelt, Jr., but the activity in behalf of Harriman was far less than that carried on in support of the Kefauver candidacy. Senator Russell did not have formal campaign headquarters in Massachusetts, but he did hold a one day "open house" in a Boston hotel where he met and spoke personally with Democrats who attended. Many of the active political workers expressed favorable impressions of Senator Russell after this meeting.

Primary results—In the April 29 election, all but 2 of the 72 candidates for delegate receiving the support of the state committee were elected. Although approximately one-fourth of the nominees supported by the state committee had publicly indicated their presidential preferences, in no case were these preferences printed with their names on the ballot. This gives an indication of the degree of party organization control in 1952, since several members of the organization slate had worked hard for Kefauver, including Mayor John Hynes of Boston.

The Kefauver slate of four delegate-candidates in the 10th district was defeated. Members of the Kefauver slate polled betwen 1,600 and 1,700 votes each, while members of the organization slate polled from 4,600 to 5,543 votes. The Kefauverites were young, political unknowns; the regulars were well-known party workers who had been successful vote-getters in other elections. Three other candidates, who were not on either slate, polled only 335, 353, and 532 votes respectively, an indication of the vote-getting value of the Kefauver name on the ballot.

In the 9th district, the state committee had omitted a popular New Bedford politician, Edward Dinis, from the slate. He headed an opposition slate that ran well and he himself defeated the trailing member of the organization slate in the district by 3,364 to 2,574. In the 14th district (Fall River), Mayor John F. Kane was omitted from the organization slate and headed an opposition slate that ran well. He himself polled more votes than any other candidate for delegate in the district, 2,680, thus surpassing William P. Grant, 2,650, whom he had dislodged from the mayoralty the previous year by about a dozen votes. Three members of the organization slate were elected, with Kane displacing the other. There was no indication that preferences as to national presidential candidates were of any importance in the 9th and 14th district contests.

The 1951 law, as noted previously, contained a provision that space be provided on the ballot for write-in voting. Such indication of preference was to be exclusively informational and not binding in any manner upon convention delegates. Approximately half of the 123,739 Democrats who voted on April 29 wrote in the name of some preferred presidential candidate. Kefauver made by far the most impressive showing by receiving 29,287 write-ins. Of special concern to state Democratic leaders were the 16,007 preference votes written in for General Eisenhower by enrolled Democrats. President Truman ran a poor third in the balloting with 7,256 votes, but this

was after he had officially withdrawn from the race. Senator Robert
A. Taft received over 6,000 Democratic preference votes while only
1,256 were recorded for Governor Adlai Stevenson. Other write-in
votes included the coincidence of 1,986 for Dever and 1,986 for
Harriman. State Democratic leaders were not wholly successful in
their attempt to minimize the fact that so many of the Democrats
voting in this election voted for leading contenders for the Republican
nomination.

COMPOSITION OF THE DELEGATION

The over-sized delegation of 72 delegates and 72 alternates included
a large measure of political experience and talent: Governor Dever,
who served as temporary chairman of the national convention; Congressman John McCormack, who became chairman of the convention's
platform committee; Secretary of Labor Tobin; and other figures
with reputations reaching beyond the boundaries of Massachusetts.
Most delegates were state party officials or political professionals of
one category or another; a large number had attended one or more
previous national conventions.

Occupationally, most of the delegation seemed to be employed as
public officials at the time of their selection. Among the 144 delegates
and alternates, however, there were 12 labor union officials and 8
active members of Americans for Democratic Action (ADA). Apparently the labor representation was somewhat greater than it had been
in 1948, in part because of representations to the Governor by
William Belanger, the state CIO head, with an assist by Henry Brides
of the AFL. Brides and Belanger both became delegates-at-large.

The delegate roster recorded an overwhelming number of names
of Irish origin, as would be expected. Italian, Jewish, and Polish
members together comprised a small minority of the delegation. It
was customary for each delegate to pay his own way to the national
convention, and this was the case in 1952.

ACTIVITIES AND VOTING RECORD

The delegates met to organize in Boston on June 7. No major
differences of political viewpoints were in evidence. Secretary of
Labor Tobin was elected chairman, and Mrs. H. J. Sullivan, secre-

tary to the state chairman, became secretary-treasurer. Assignments to the national convention committees included: Patrick McDonough to credentials; John Hynes and Mrs. Helen Buckley to resolutions. No appointment to the rules committee was made at this time. It was readily agreed to support Governor Dever on the first ballot at Chicago, and the meeting adjourned. Later on the same day there was a meeting of the state committee which, in contrast to experience of other years, also was without event.

The problem of the oversize delegation from Massachusetts was considered by the national committee at Chicago before the convention opened, along with the cases of five other oversize delegations. At the urging of Chairman Frank E. McKinney, and after the opposing views had been heard, the committee voted to recommend seating, and the convention later agreed. (Official Proceedings, pp. 680-84.)

At Chicago the delegates held an early caucus devoted principally to the position to be taken and the procedure to be followed in regard to the controversial planks of the party platform. Although it was well known that Dever had been favorable to Stevenson's candidacy, he did not take a public stand until the fourth day of the convention. Perhaps his reason was, as he argued on Thursday to the Massachusetts delegation, that at the propitious moment Massachusetts should touch off a swing to Stevenson. Early in the convention Dever was discussed as a possible vice-presidential candidate and this may have prompted his delay in taking any action which might have lessened his chances for the second spot on the ticket.

Others of the delegation were less hesitant in making known their preferences. Under Mayor Hynes' leadership, the mayors of Everett, Somerville, and Springfield, all delegates, announced they would swing their support to Kefauver after their courtesy first ballot vote for Dever. Vice President Barkley received steadfast support from a segment of the delegation, including Maurice Tobin, John McCormack, Boston District Attorney Foley, Council President Piemonte, and John Kerrigan, former mayor of Boston. Some considered it incongruous that Secretary of Labor Tobin should persist in his advocacy of Barkley long after national labor leaders had made it clear that "the Veep" was unacceptable to them. There was some personal admiration in the delegation for Senator Richard Russell, but since he was ruled out by the labor leaders, this came to little more than passing interest.

As temporary chairman of the convention Governor Dever was responsible for delivering the keynote address. In an attempt to improve the effectiveness of his keynote presentation, the Governor had teleprompters placed at either side of the rostrum. Thus, as he read his lengthy speech, he was able to turn from side to side and give the appearance of talking directly to his audience. The idea was perhaps a good one, but during the execution of it the Governor developed a severe case of laryngitis which affected his delivery. The speech itself was considered above average, but the presentation probably reduced rather than added to the Governor's prestige in Massachusetts.

The entire delegation of 72 half-vote delegates was polled with annoying frequency during the convention voting. Results of polling the delegation on one occasion showed a shift of 1½ votes, but for the rest of the time the polling was apparently for purposes of delay or for home consumption. When the vote was taken on the question of seating the Virginia delegation, the delegation was voting 32 to 4 against seating at the time of the Illinois switch, and was eventually recorded as 19 to 16 against seating on the final tally.

As the convention moved to the presidential nominations, Governor Dever made no statement regarding the release of votes pledged to him for the first ballot. Indicative of the divergent views held by delegates, however, was the seconding of the Kefauver nomination by Mayor Hynes and that of Barkley by Congressman McCormack. The first ballot for the presidential nomination showed every one of the delegates fulfilling his caucus pledge by voting for the favorite son.

At the end of the first ballot, according to a published account by Colonel Jacob Arvey of Illinois (*Reporter*, November 24, 1953), Governor Dever joined Arvey and the two went backstage at the convention to telephone Governor Stevenson. Arvey's story follows:

> . . . I told Stevenson: "Governor, all I want you to do is to tell Governor Dever that if you are nominated you will accept."
> Stevenson asked: "Are you sure the Convention can't agree on some other man?"

"If anyone else is nominated," I told him, "he'll split the party wide open."

"Put Governor Dever on the telephone," Stevenson said. I put Dever on the phone and Stevenson told him that he would accept. That was the beginning of the end.

Dever then revealed that his candidate was Stevenson and set about to line up votes for him from Massachusetts. In caucus Dever asked the delegates to vote for him again on the second ballot in order to keep the delegation in a top bargaining position prior to the third ballot which would probably name the presidential candidate. During caucus discussion of Stevenson's candidacy, criticism centered on the points that he was a divorced man and that he had given a deposition which was not unfavorable to Alger Hiss. Much of this was part of a sincere effort to appraise the attractiveness of Stevenson as a candidate. That Dever had delayed too long in letting others know his position was the complaint made by Congressman McCormack. Because of this, the Congressman indicated, he had made commitments that he was honor-bound to fulfill.

Dever's plea for continued support on the second ballot left him with 30½ votes; but there was a shift of 3 votes to Barkley and 2½ votes to Kefauver. The record on the third ballot was first announced as 23½ for Stevenson, but a poll of the delegation totalled 25 votes for Stevenson. Other candidates receiving votes on the third ballot were: Kefauver, 5; Barkley, 4½; Russell, 1; and Dever, ½ vote. Governor's Councillor McDonough voted for Dever on the third ballot.

AFTERMATH IN THE STATE

In the campaign that followed, Stevenson was given the backing of the state Democratic organization, which was firmly under Dever's control. The Kennedy following also provided enthusiastic support, but this group tended to find more congenial associates in the Volunteers for Stevenson movement. Mayor Hynes, who had seconded Kefauver's nomination, accepted the position as chairman of the national "Mayors for Stevenson" group.

While Truman had received a plurality of 242,000 over Dewey in 1948, Eisenhower's 1,292,325 topped Stevenson's vote by 208,800.

Congressman Kennedy proved to be the leading Democrat, heading his ticket and defeating Senator Lodge for the Senate seat. The gubernatorial contest provided the greatest unpleasantness for the Democrats. Dever's re-election had been forecast as "a sure-thing," particularly since two years earlier he had defeated Arthur W. Coolidge by more than 250,000 votes. Contrary to the prognostications of the political experts, Christian A. Herter, former speaker of the lower house of the state legislature and later congressman, won the governor's seat by 14,456 votes over Dever. In the races for congressional seats, eleven of the incumbents were re-elected.

At present Dever continues as nominal head of the state Democratic party. Senator Kennedy has become the ranking Massachusetts Democrat in office. Congressman McCormack and Mayor Hynes are in their usual strong positions. Any early possibility of a bitter, intra-party contest has been all but eliminated by the death of two major leaders since the November election, Maurice Tobin and John Foley. District Attorney Foley—a political power in Boston for many years—in all likelihood would not have been a candidate for another major public office. The unexpected death of Maurice Tobin had far greater effect since he could have been an almost unbeatable candidate for Democratic nomination to any office.

REVIEW AND APPRAISAL

There were marked similarities between the Massachusetts and New Jersey delegate selection procedures in 1952. In both states there was provision for the direct election of delegates and for an advisory expression of presidential preference on the part of the voter. Delegate-candidates could indicate their presidential preferences on the ballot if they so desired but only if they secured the consent of their candidate. Delegate candidates could also run unpledged. In the Massachusetts case, there was sufficient flexibility in the law to permit a distinction among the commitments of the Taft delegates; some appeared on the ballot with "Preference for Robert A. Taft"; others were "Pledged to Robert A. Taft." All delegates were voted on individually, but slates of delegates could be arranged together on the ballot, with or without the name of a presidential candidate to whom pledged. In both states, the regular party organizations were accustomed to taking the initiative in organizing slates of delegates, usually unpledged, but so far as procedural requirements were concerned, it was relatively easy to challenge the regulars in any one of several ways: (1) a national candidate could put a slate of delegates on the ballot with his name attached if he wished to do so; (2) a dissident faction within the state could run a competing slate of unpledged delegates either statewide or in some districts; (3) an individual who wished to run for delegate could do so. Notwithstanding these various possibilities, the ballots in both states were relatively simple.

The Massachusetts statute of 1951 provided for a kind of presidential preference poll; only write-in and sticker voting was possible. There was no way of putting candidate names on the ballot and the candidates were spared any problems of compliance with procedural requirements. The success of the Massachusetts write-in procedure as a valid expression of presidential preference by the voters remains a moot question. The 1952 experience left some doubt. In the Democratic primary, only about half of the Democrats who voted at all troubled to write in a preference. Kefauver won with about 30,000 votes, but over 22,000 votes were cast in the Democratic primary for the leading Republican candidates, General Eisenhower and Senator Taft; around 60,000 Democratic ballots were left blank in the write-in spaces. On the Republican side, the Massachusetts write-in was probably somewhat more indicative of the preferences among the party's voters. Eisenhower received over 250,000 votes to Taft's 110,000; and since all votes were cast by write-in, there was no question as to how the votes cast for one candidate should be appraised in relation to those cast for the other.

In a closely divided state such as Massachusetts, a principal motivation of party leadership is the desire to prevent the presidential nominating process from introducing an uncontrollably divisive element into the state party. If either party were to become seriously divided or caught "off base" in a contest between national candidates for pledged convention delegates, it is likely that its chances of success in the subsequent state elections would be somewhat jeopardized. The opposition in the Massachusetts legislature and in the regular party organizations to any attempt to bind delegate candidates and even to the limited advisory write-in poll that was adopted in 1951 is an indication of this fear of threats to party unity. The leadership of both parties usually seeks to fashion primary laws in such a way as to minimize the likelihood of open factional conflict in the state and to facilitate agreement among various party factions upon delegate candidates. The direct election of delegates without any binding commitment to support any particular presidential candidate is one way of doing this.

Nevertheless, in 1952 there was an organized contest between state-wide slates of district delegates committed respectively to Taft and Eisenhower. The Taft slate was labelled and the Eisenhower slate was not, in that respect much like a similar situation in South Dakota; but the Eisenhower slate nevertheless won a sweeping victory in Massachusetts, losing only one district delegate seat to Taft. Unlabelled third slates were a source of voter confusion in three districts, and contributed to the solitary Taft victory in one district. Had the Taft people actively employed unpledged as well as pledged slates throughout the state, the inroads into the Eisenhower vote might have been greater. On the Democratic side, an openly committed Kefauver slate was entered in only a single district in Massachusetts, where it was defeated by about 3 to 1. There was some question as to whether Kefauver was tactically wise in letting the slate be entered, since no effective campaign could be made for a weak slate in a single district. The result was to antagonize the state party organization without winning any delegate votes.

Both Massachusetts delegations of 1952 were largely made up of party professionals drawn from the ranks of the regular organizations, but they differed strikingly in the extent to which they were committed before arriving at the national conventions. For the Massachusetts Republican delegation, or at least for most of its members, the issue had been settled by the contest in the state; its convention behavior was easily predictable and ran true to form. The Democratic delegation was uncommitted in fact as well as law when it left the state, aside from its *pro forma* commitment of first ballot support for Dever; and for the Democratic delegation the real time of decision came at the convention, as it did for most of the delegations that cast the decisive votes in the Democratic national convention of 1952. On the whole, both delegations performed creditably at the conventions; and both seem to have been representative of their respective party organizations and party constituencies.

Massachusetts Chapter Acknowledgments

LASHLEY G. HARVEY, Chairman of the Department of Government, Boston University, assumed general direction of the preparation of the Massachusetts chapter in June 1953, with the assistance of SAMUEL P. HUNTINGTON, Assistant Professor of Government, Harvard University. MR. CHARLES P. HOWARD, Treasurer of Middlesex County, Massachusetts, directed preparation of the Republican delegation section. He was assisted by JOHN L. FLETCHER, Assistant Professor of Government, Boston University, who wrote the initial draft of the section. TROY R. WESTMEYER, Assistant Professor of Government, Boston University, prepared the initial draft of the section on the Democratic delegation. Professors Harvey and Huntington were largely responsible for the introductory and concluding sections of the chapter, and Professor Huntington took responsibility for assembling and editing the draft materials for the chapter as a whole in cooperation with the national project office.

RHODE ISLAND

Electoral votes, 1952: 4

National convention votes, 1952:
Democratic, 12
Republican, 8

Population, 1950: 791,896
Urban, 84%; *rural nonfarm,* 15%; *rural farm,* 1%

Population increase, 1940-50: 78,550 (11%)
Urban, 7%; *rural nonfarm,* 67%; *rural farm,* 25% decline

Presidential vote, 1948:			*1952:*
Democratic,	188,736	(58%)	203,293 (49%)
Republican,	135,787	(41%)	210,935 (51%)
Progressive,	2,619	(1%)	

Gubernatorial vote, 1950:		*1952:*
Democratic,	176,125	211,953
Republican,	120,684	189,915

U. S. Representatives vote,		
all districts, 1950:		*1952:*
Democratic,	181,502	220,461
Republican,	111,898	186,828

U. S. Representatives elected 1950:		*1952:*
Democratic,	2	2
Republican,	0	0

State legislature elected 1952:
Senate: Democrats, 16; Republicans, 28
House: Democrats, 58; Republicans, 42

Method of selecting national convention delegates:
Democratic: state convention
Republican: district and state conventions

Based primarily on reports by FELIX RACKOW

CHAPTER 6

RHODE ISLAND VOTED FOR EISENHOWER by 51 per cent in 1952; but previously it had been considered safely Democratic in presidential elections ever since 1928 when it was one of the few states that voted for Al Smith. Prior to 1928, however, and going as far back as 1856, the state was just as consistently Republican—the one exception being the 1912 election when Wilson carried the state. The Democratic party has also controlled recent state elections, having won all since 1932 except for that of 1938. Rhode Island Democrats won their first recent United States Senate seat in 1934 and picked up the second in 1936; both have been Democratic since. The two Rhode Island members of the House of Representatives have been Democratic since 1932, except for the debacle of 1938 when both seats were lost to the Republicans.

Rhode Island is the smallest state in area in the nation, being but 1,214 square miles; it is also the most densely populated. The 1950 census lists Rhode Island as being predominantly urban and having a population density of 748.5 persons per square land mile. Although the state is divided into five counties, Providence County alone contains almost 73 per cent of the state's inhabitants, and the cities of Providence, Pawtucket, and Cranston (the last two contiguous to Providence) have 49 per cent. The rural nonfarm population has grown by 67 per cent since 1940, a rate exceeded only by California. Of the nationality background of the population, 14.3 per cent are foreign-born white, with the largest groups emigrating from Italy, French Canada, England and Wales, Ireland, and Portugal. The nonwhite population of the state is only two per cent of the total, but the increase since 1940 was 29 per cent as compared to the white increase of 11 per cent. Fifty-five per cent of the people are Catholic; 3 per cent are Jewish.

Rhode Island is also among the most heavily industrialized states. Manufacturing industries employ 44 per cent of the total employables, a figure almost double the national average of 24 per cent. In contrast, only two per cent of those gainfully employed engage in agriculture, forestry, and fisheries pursuits. Textiles, metal and machinery, jewelry and silverware, and rubber industries are dominant. Faced with increasing competition from the southeast, by 1952 the Rhode Island textile industry had lost some 16,000 "employment opportunities" since 1939. On the other hand, some 17,000 new jobs have developed in the metals industry during the same period, as have some 10,000 in the jewelry and silverware industry. Of the nation's 47,000 jewelry workers, 21,000 are employed in the Providence area.

Those who followed Roger Williams to Rhode Island were largely British. The big period of non-British immigration began in the 1840's when the Irish came to the state by the thousands. The Irish were subject to anti-Catholic attack and, as one student remarks, were "practically driven by the Whigs and the Nativists into the ranks of the Democratic party." The tendency of the later-arriving French Canadians and Italians to associate themselves with the Democratic party was strong, but not to the same extent, partly because the religious attacks were not repeated.

Until passage of an amendment to the state constitution in 1888, naturalized citizens could vote only by meeting the property qualifications of colonial days. It was not until the constitutional amendment of 1928 that suffrage requirements were again liberalized so that any citizen could vote for any office and on all issues, except that the old property qualification is still retained on tax or money questions in the towns. As the party of the "outs" during most of this suffrage history, the Democrats supported the claims and reaped the support of the propertyless foreign born. Economic and religious issues also were important in causing shifts from Republican ranks to the Democratic in the late 1920's and early 1930's. The depression was blamed on the Hoover administration, and the predominantly Catholic citizenry of the state gave unusual support in 1928 to Democratic presidential candidate Alfred E. Smith.

The Republican party first appeared in Rhode Island politics in

1856 and in the 66 gubernatorial races until 1932 it lost the governorship only twelve times. Since 1932, the Republican party had been able to win the governor's office only once; Republican Governor William H. Vanderbilt's victory in 1938 over the Democratic incumbent Governor Robert E. Quinn was the result of a split Democratic vote. In 1940, J. Howard McGrath returned the governorship to the Democrats, where it has since remained.

Except for scattered periods totaling seven years, Providence has had Democratic mayors since 1896; the last Republican mayor to win office was elected in 1938, the same year that the Republicans won the governorship. Yet, because of the property qualification it was not until the election of 1930 that the Democrats were able to win control of the City Council, a feat which they continue to perform at each election.

Again, except for the election of 1938, the Democratic party has easily maintained control of the 100-member lower house of the state legislature since 1934. Not so, however, in the 44-member upper chamber. Except for the election of 1934, there have usually been more Republican than Democratic state senators. In 1948 and 1950, considered unusual, senate seats were equally divided at 22 each between the two parties. The Republicans have been able to maintain a tight hold on the state senate because of rural over-representation in many legislative districts. In the 1950 election, for example, in rural West Greenwich the Republican candidate won his seat by 213 votes to his Democratic opponent's 198; on the other hand, in the 2d Providence senatorial district, the Democratic candidate won 16,006 votes to the Republican's 4,395. The only big city vote the Republicans won was in Cranston where the Republican candidate gathered slightly more than half of the 21,292 votes cast.

THE REPUBLICAN DELEGATION

In 1948, as in 1952, Rhode Island was entitled to 8 votes in the Republican national convention. The 1948 delegation's vote was to be 4 for Senator Taft, 3 for Governor Dewey, and 1 for Congressman Joe Martin. The actual vote on the first ballot, however, was 6 for Martin and 1 each for Dewey and Taft. Members of the delegation, particularly those supporting Dewey, believed that it would be strategically wise to present a united delegation, hence the large vote for the congressman from neighboring Massachusetts, part of whose district falls within the Providence metropolitan area. The second ballot gave Governor Dewey 4 votes, Senator Taft 2, and Congressman Martin and Senator Vandenburg 1 each, and was probably more indicative of the sentiments of the delegation. On the third, all were cast for Dewey.

Although Rhode Island since 1948 requires primaries for the nomination of party candidates for most civil offices, the state does not have a presidential preference primary; state law leaves the selection of national convention delegates almost entirely within the hands of the parties. Each party is required to hold biennial state conventions, but these conventions are usually held in the fall of the even years and come too late to play a direct part in the presidential selection process. Hence, in presidential years each party holds a special state convention early in the spring for the double purpose of electing delegates to the national convention and nominating members for the national committee. The 82-member Republican state convention is made up of delegates from the state's 39 cities and towns: six from the city of Providence and two each from the rest. Thus, the city of Providence, with 31.4 per cent of the state's population, is allotted six seats, which, in turn, represents 7.4 per cent of convention strength. This is to be contrasted to the two seats granted the town of New Shoreham, which, having less than 0.1 per cent of the state's population is nevertheless given 2.4 per cent of the convention seats. State convention delegates are chosen by the various city and town committees. The membership of the city and town committees, in turn, is elected by the party voters at the regular primary to nominate party candidates.

The state chairman and the state central committee usually present a slate of national convention delegates to the state convention; until 1952, this slate was usually chosen by the state convention without much difficulty.

THE SELECTION PROCESS IN 1952

In 1952, the problem was largely one of deciding how the eight-man delegation was to be divided between Eisenhower and Taft supporters. The Eisenhower forces pressed for a 100 per cent Eisenhower delegation. The best that the Taft-men hoped for was an unpledged delegation: as the selection process developed, they reduced their sights to winning three Taft delegates and finally ended their campaign by trying to get two. The nomination of candidates to run for statewide office as well as for one seat in the Senate and two in the House of Representatives was also drawn into the fray. The delegation fight was one manifestation of the struggle for control between a group of "young Turks" and the old state senate leadership.

This intra-party fight came into the open in the fall of 1951 when Vincent C. James started an Eisenhower boom in the state. On November 15, 1951, state representative Bayard Ewing—later to be Republican candidate for the Senate—declared before a meeting of the Pawtucket Men's Republican Club that he was for Eisenhower. Soon afterward at least six chairmen of the city and town committees announced their support of the Eisenhower movement.

Early in January 1952, Vincent C. James, co-chairman with Bayard Ewing of the Citizens for Eisenhower movement, announced that the Eisenhower forces were working to win a pledged delegation, although the state party had never before sent a pledged delegation to the national convention. Steven B. Wilson, leader of the Taft movement, immediately stated that the Taft forces would win at least some places on the delegation. The chairman of the state central committee then declared that, although he would be neutral in the factional dispute, he was opposed to a pledged delegation; on the other hand, he favored the unit rule.

The delegates to the state convention were chosen solely by the city and town committees, whose chairmen were generally quite influential locally. These were the people who had to be convinced. No effort was made by the Eisenhower forces to get the city and town committees to select particular candidates; rather, all efforts were devoted to get agreement on *any* delegate who would vote for an Eisenhower slate at the state convention. The Taft group started its efforts somewhat later, in the apparent belief that the Eisenhower forces were waging an uphill fight in their effort to win the "Old Guard" strongholds in the rural areas and in trying to break the "no pledge" tradition.

There was no formal participation of the rank-and-file of the party other than in the election of the city and town committee in 1950 at the previous primary. However, party members did have some influence in the actual selection process. Both factions placed advertisements in the state's newspapers urging their supporters to phone the city and town chairmen and to indicate their preferences. Surprisingly, many people did, with an overwhelming number supporting the General. The leaders of the Eisenhower movement believed that this action had a tremendous influence on the local committees.

The meetings of the city and town committees to select delegates to the state convention were not all held on the same day, and this permitted a stretch-out of the campaigning. Eisenhower leaders often met with local committees until a few minutes before final selections were made; indeed, on at least one occasion, these leaders were present during the voting process. There were a few contests within the local committees, but these were all settled by majority vote and no violation of party rules was ever charged.

In the meantime, the press reported on March 6th that, at the suggestion of Taft-leader Wilson, the Eisenhower and Taft factions had agreed to poll the members of the state central committee as to their sentiments. The two factions, however, had different purposes in mind. The Eisenhower group, believing that it had a majority of the state central committee, wanted the question posed as to whether the state central committee should endorse a 100 per cent Eisenhower slate. On the other hand, the Taft leadership wanted the results of the poll to be used as a basis for a split of the delegation according to percentage strength.

The Eisenhower men further agreed to having the poll on March 12th. They soon learned, however, that Wilson, as president of the pro-Taft Republican Action Association, organized to interest businessmen in politics, planned to give a dinner for the members of the state central committee on March 10th; the main speaker was to be John D. M. Hamilton, former national committee chairman and a leader in the Taft campaign. Among those present would be David

S. Ingalls and Ben Tate. The Eisenhower faction thereupon proposed March 14th; on that day Senator Leverett Saltonstall of Massachusetts, a leader in the Eisenhower movement, was to speak in Rhode Island. Bayard Ewing then stated that his Eisenhower group had never agreed to a poll, but acknowledged that the state chairman had a right to take one as a guide. Ewing insisted, however, that the state central committee did not have the power to bind the delegates.

State Chairman William J. Thompson did poll the membership of the state central committee at its meeting on April 4 and announced the result as 53 favoring Eisenhower, 29 for Taft, and 1 for Warren. On the basis of these results, he named a three-man committee consisting of himself, Wilson, and Ewing to select a slate of delegates to be presented to the state and district conventions, the slate to be divided five to three in favor of Eisenhower. On May 2nd Thompson announced that the nominating committee, with Ewing absent from its last meeting, had agreed on the following "harmony" slate: five Eisenhower supporters—Bayard Ewing, Mrs. Joan B. Colt, Dean J. Lewis, Fred Colagiovanni, Thomas Casey Greene; two Taft supporters—Steven B. Wilson, Robert B. Dresser; and one neutral—William J. Thompson.

Vincent C. James, however, immediately declared that if the "harmony" slate were put in nomination at the state convention, the Eisenhower forces would nominate a 100 per cent Eisenhower slate from the floor. In the meantime, State Chairman Thompson had written to all city and town chairmen requesting that they select delegates to the state convention who would follow the recommendations of the state central committee. Thompson wrote that "the members of the state central committee are the ones who should recommend to the state convention their choices for delegates to the national convention and also recommend a choice for national committeeman." Just prior to the meeting of the state convention, delegates to the convention and all city and town chairmen were invited to a dinner sponsored by the Eisenhower forces and addressed by Governor Sherman Adams.

The Republican state convention met on May 12 for the major purpose of selecting delegates to the national convention. The Taft leadership appealed to the delegates to recognize the not inconsiderable group of Taft supporters by alloting them some representation on the national delegation. The Eisenhower group claimed a 100 per cent Eisenhower delegation on the strength of the overwhelming Eisenhower support in the state. Thompson, seeking a middle position, claimed that the issue was not merely one of giving two places on the Rhode Island delegation to Taft supporters, but "shall we split the Republican party in this state wide open and run the risk of losing the election next November?"

Right from the outset, however, it was apparent that a decision would be made strictly according to factional lines. The harmony slate was put in nomination, but so was the 100 per cent Eisenhower slate. On a 44-38 roll call vote, with a few proxies, but no abstentions, the state convention rejected the "harmony" slate proposed by the state chairman and elected a solid Eisenhower slate of delegates-at-large: Vincent C. James, Bayard Ewing, Emile A. Pepin, and Mrs. Joan B. Colt. After this unprecedented and dramatic vote, the state convention adjourned and reconvened to form the two congressional district conventions. It was almost anticlimatic when the two district conventions also elected Eisenhower supporters: the 1st district choosing Dean J. Lewis and Fred Colagiovanni; the 2nd, William J. Thompson and Thomas Casey Greene. Thompson was supposedly elected as a "neutral," but many understood him to be in the Eisenhower camp.

The following month, Senator Henry Cabot Lodge noted that it was he who urged the Eisenhower faction to press for a 100 per cent Eisenhower slate. He stated that he came to this decision because in similar situations in both Massachusetts and Colorado the Eisenhower forces gave minority representation to the Taft group, but that Taft refused to allow for minority Eisenhower representation in Utah and Idaho. On this basis, he told the Rhode Island Eisenhower faction to get all they could.

The failures of Wilson and Dresser to win places on the delegation were bitter blows; both were active in Senator Taft's national campaign and both expected to be assigned places on national convention committees. After the state convention, Wilson issued a statement in which he said that "the results indicated quite definitely that I am not in agreement with the group who engineered the convention vote, and if they are to become a dominant factor in the party, I feel I can be of little further service to the party in Rhode Island." He went on to say, however, "this does not mean that I intend to stop fighting for Bob Taft in Rhode Island." Over Wilson's signature as chairman, the Rhode Island Taft-for-President Committee in June sent out hundreds of letters to Republicans within the state urging them to "stand up and be counted for Taft" and to get their friends to do so.

COMPOSITION OF THE DELEGATION

The Rhode Island delegation was composed of the leaders in the Eisenhower faction and in the movement to wrest control of the party organization from the hands of the leaders in the state senate. Only two members of the original delegation as elected by the state and district conventions held public office: Bayard Ewing was one of two Providence Republicans in the lower house of the state legislature, and Dean J. Lewis was mayor of Newport. Most of the delegates, however, held important posts in state party affairs. James was a member of the state central committee and a former state president of the young Republicans. Ewing was chairman of the first ward committee in Providence. Emile A. Pepin, an early Eisenhower supporter, was chairman of the Woonsocket city committee. Mrs. Joan B. Colt was the vice-chairman of the state central committee. Among the district delegates, only Mayor Lewis did not have a statewide party post. Thompson was the state chairman and Colagiovanni was the treasurer of the state central committee. Greene was a former state chairman and a member of the state central committee. Many of the alternates also held party office as members of the state central committee and ward or district committees. Noticeably absent from the delegation were the avowed adherents of Senator Taft. Steven B. Wilson and Robert B. Dresser, although endorsed to the state convention by the state central committee, were not elected. The one change in the delegation as elected was the resignation of Alternate Curran and the appointment by Thompson of Frank Lazarus to take his place; Lazarus was one of those rejected by the state convention. One of four Republicans in the Providence city council,

Lazarus was also secretary to the state central committee and an alternate to the 1948 national convention.

Three of the delegates were lawyers, three were salesmen, one worked in public relations, and one was a housewife. Three were Catholics and five were Protestants. Four were of English extraction, while one was Irish, one French Canadian, one Greek and one Italian. The average age of the delegates was forty-eight; the youngest was thirty-five and the oldest sixty-two. Six of the delegates paid their own expenses in attending the national convention, one had partial assistance, and one had complete assistance. Ewing and Greene were both delegates to the 1948 national convention, and Mrs. Colt and Pepin were alternates the same year; none of the delegates attended any earlier national convention.

ACTIVITIES AND VOTING RECORD

A factional split developed almost immediately among the delegates. Thompson and Greene refused to state that they would vote for Eisenhower in Chicago. Thompson's defection caused a good deal of consternation because it had been the practice in the past to have the state chairman serve as delegation chairman. Some of the state party leaders were of the opinion that Thompson's reticence was sufficient cause to break the tradition. The delegation held several meetings, but no agreement could be reached. The delegation met again on June 16 and finally agreed on its organization. Mayor Lewis was elected delegation chairman; Thompson, vice-chairman; James, honorary vice-chairman; the last two positions had been nonexistent in most previous delegations. Ewing was elected to serve on the credentials committee; Pepin, on the rules committee; Colagiovanni and Mrs. Colt, on the platform committee. Other Rhode Islanders were chosen for other convention posts by the convention management. Henry P. Fletcher of Newport was chosen convention parliamentarian, a position he held in 1948. In view of the battles over the seating of the contested delegations, the post of parliamentarian was of some importance in 1952. Lazarus, the Thompson-appointed alternate in the Rhode Island delegation, was chosen to be the convention's reading clerk.

Relations between the Rhode Island delegation and the national committeeman and committeewoman were quite strained. National committeewoman Mrs. Marian F. Yatman had run unopposed and was unanimously re-nominated by the state convention. National committeeman Felix Hebert intended to retire, and Steven B. Wilson, Thomas J. Paolino, and Edwin H. Arnold all entered this race. Paolino won the endorsement of the full state central committee, the state chairman, and a majority of the city and town committees. Wilson withdrew in favor of Arnold, who in turn withdrew his name one week before the state convention. Paolino, running unopposed, was then unanimously nominated by that body. Under national party rules, Hebert would retain his authority until the newly nominated candidates were elected by the national convention, an election which, as usual, was scheduled to be almost the last official act of the convention. The question arose how Hebert would use his authority, particularly in reference to recognizing contested delegations. The predominant rumor was that he would use his influence to assist the Taft cause, and this proved to be the case.

It was reported as early as February that Hebert intended to give his proxy to Steven B. Wilson. Early in June the press reported that former President Herbert Hoover had asked Hebert to give his proxy to Henry P. Fletcher. Fletcher, one-time Ambassador to Chile under President Taft and a close friend of Hoover, had previously held proxies for Hebert and for former National Committeewoman Mrs. Paul FitzSimons. On June 16, however, Hebert announced that he had given his proxy to Wilson. In the meantime, Fletcher's appointment as convention parliamentarian had been announced. Meeting that same day, the Rhode Island state executive committee recommended that Hebert withdraw his proxy from Wilson and give it to Paolino. State Chairman Thompson, however, noted that "it's entirely up to the [former] Senator to do as he sees fit with his proxy." Eisenhower forces, however, claimed that Hebert's vote belonged not to Hebert but to the Republicans of Rhode Island and that it should be cast in accordance with the latest expression of Republican sentiment within the state. Since the national committee hears contests prior to the national convention, Hebert's proxy vote took on some significance.

Although Rhode Island had only eight votes in the Republican national convention, at least 55 persons went to Chicago. On July 6, Thompson finally announced that he would cast his ballot for Senator Taft. In view of the state convention's rejection of his harmony slate of delegates and the delegation's failure to elect him chairman, Thompson probably thought that a Taft victory in Chicago might help mend his political fences back home. Even after Thompson's announcement, Thomas Casey Greene refused to commit himself. The delegation met Senator Taft on July 7. Chairman Lewis later thought that, although Eisenhower still remained the delegation's first choice, Taft impressed the group to the extent that they might vote for him as a second preference rather than for Warren or Stassen. The same day the delegation split 6 to 2 against the Brown amendment involving the temporary rules. Thompson and Greene cast the two pro-Taft votes in favor of the amendment. The next day the delegation met with General Eisenhower for twenty minutes.

On the following day, a Rhode Islander addressed the convention from the platform for the first time in recent years; Bayard Ewing spoke in favor of seating the Porter-Lane delegation from Texas. The same day the Rhode Island delegation voted 6 to 2 in favor of seating the pro-Eisenhower delegation from Georgia. Again, Thompson and Greene cast their ballots in favor of the Taft faction.

On July 11, the delegates met with Eisenhower a second time; they also saw Warren and Stassen. Later in the day, on the first ballot for the presidential nomination, the delegation cast 6 votes for Eisenhower, with Thompson voting for Taft and Greene for Warren. After the Minnesota switch, all eight votes were given to Eisenhower.

AFTERMATH IN THE STATE

The delegates returned to Rhode Island to consolidate their political victory. The state central committee held a meeting on July 25 and endorsed a state ticket drawn from the "young Turk" faction. At the same meeting, William J. Thompson resigned as state chairman and was replaced by Charles E. Eden. Thomas Casey Greene's political fortunes also took a turn for the worse. On October 19th, Greene announced that, after thirteen years as Warwick city chairman, he was not a candidate for re-election; one week later Herbert B. Carkin was elected to this position.

None of the statewide Republican candidates in Rhode Island won in 1952. In spite of their defeat in the state election, the "young Turk" wing continues its battle with the state senate leadership. Speaking before the Central Republican Club in East Providence early in May, Bayard Ewing stated that "it is not true that the state senate is the Republican party in Rhode Island," stressing that the state party "can no longer be controlled by a small group of bosses from small towns."

THE DEMOCRATIC DELEGATION

Based in part on a report by
JOHN O. STITELY

As in 1948, Rhode Island was entitled to 12 votes in the 1952 Democratic national convention. It has been the custom in recent Democratic conventions for the Rhode Island delegation to support the national leadership of the party. In 1948 it cast its 12 votes for Harry S. Truman. At the time of the 1948 convention, J. Howard McGrath, the former junior senator from Rhode Island, was the Democratic party's national chairman, having been elected in October 1947. McGrath had been one of the few Democrats able to buck the nationwide Republican tide in the 1946 congressional elections.

Like the Republicans, the Democrats hold a state convention in the spring of each presidential election year for the purpose of electing national convention delegates. Unlike the Republicans, who base their apportionment of state convention delegates upon the state's 39 cities and towns, the Democratic apportionment is based upon the 100 districts comprising the lower house of the state legislature. Each representative district is entitled to send one male and one female delegate to the state convention; each district also sends two alternates. Each of the party's three-member representative district committees endorses to the state committee the names of two persons. Where there is no contest, the Democratic state committee promptly issues delegate credentials to the two persons named; where there is a contest, the Democratic state committee first decides between the rival slates. The three members of the representative district committee, in turn, are elected earlier at the state primary election for governor. The representative district is the smallest state-wide election district in Rhode Island, and offers a somewhat better balance between concentration of population and geographic representation than do the cities and towns. Nevertheless, there are inequities: Little Compton, for example, cast only 182 votes for the Democratic party in its 1950 election for state representative, whereas North Providence cast 4,045 votes for its Democratic candidate, yet both representative districts were allowed two delegates to the state convention.

THE SELECTION PROCESS IN 1952

The process of selecting delegates to the Democratic national convention was a relatively harmonious undertaking. State party leaders were in agreement that they favored Adlai Stevenson as their choice to be Democratic presidential candidate. It was only the uncertainty of Stevenson's availability that caused what little disagreement there was. On the assumption that Stevenson might not accept the nomination, it was reported that one or another party leader favored Vice President Alben W. Barkley, Averell Harriman, Senator Estes Kefauver, or Senator Brien McMahon as the second choice of Rhode Island.

In a letter dated April 4, 1952, the chairman of the state committee, Frank Rao, called a meeting of the state executive committee for April 20 for the purpose of issuing a state convention call. On May 2 the call was issued; the state convention was to be held June 2. City and town party chairmen were requested to caucus their representative district committees no later than May 14 for choosing two delegates and two alternates to the state convention. The names of these delegates and alternates were to be sent to the state chairman no later than May 20 so that certificates of appointment could be issued.

Rank-and-file participation in the selection process was almost nil. It was urged in the convention call that the district caucuses be publicized so that Democrats within each district could make known to the representative district committee their desire to serve as delegates to the state convention. But it was the representative district committee alone that endorsed the slate of delegates to the Democratic state committee, with final selections made by the latter committee. In a press release dated the same day as the call, the Democratic state committee declared "that there is no possible method of giving to the people of the various representative districts a full opportunity to vote for candidates to this convention." It was indicated that such elections used to be held under the caucus law, but that the primary law which replaced it in 1948 did not provide for governmental machinery to hold such elections. Local boards and town clerks could not hold such elections, the release continued, because there was neither the legal obligation to conduct such elections nor the funds to finance them. It was stated that local Democratic organizations could not supervise the elections in place of the town boards because "the allegation of unfairness might be raised." The press release ended by stating that "we have, therefore, come to the conclusion very reluctantly that it will be necessary under the present circumstances for the local political committee to make a choice of delegates."

In actual practice, the method by which delegates to the state convention were chosen in 1952 was for individual Democrats to make known to the state chairman that they would like to serve and for the Democratic state committee to make the final selection. The question of an "allegation of unfairness" was not raised. There was one contest in the selection of delegates to the state convention. State Chairman Rao ruled that the West Greenwich Democratic town committee had not organized as required by law and therefore could not designate delegates; Rao, in accordance with party rules, then named the delegates himself. However, the town chairman also named two delegates. The state convention's credentials committee, chaired by state Attorney-General William E. Powers, supported Rao's appointments, and the convention itself followed Power's recommendation.

The state convention met on June 2. Just prior to the convention, the state executive committee met and approved a slate of delegates and alternates to the national convention; this slate was unanimously elected by the state convention. The state convention names the chairman of the delegation sent to the national convention and it has become traditional to select the governor of the state to fill that post. The 1952 state convention followed the custom by electing Governor Dennis J. Roberts to head the delegation. The state convention also decides whether instructions are to be given to the delegation, and, again following tradition, the delegation was sent to Chicago uninstructed.

COMPOSITION OF THE DELEGATION

The 1952 delegation bore a close resemblance to that of 1948; a number of the delegates and alternates had been members of the state's delegation to several previous national conventions. The 1952 delegation included many of the principal party leaders within the state, among them the governor, both United States senators, one of the state's two congressmen (the other was an alternate), mayors of three of the state's seven cities, the state chairman, the national committeewoman (the national committeeman was one of the senators previously mentioned), Democratic leaders in the General Assembly, and the former party national chairman and former Attorney-General of the United States.

Many of the delegates and alternates held public office, and most held important positions within the party. Among the 4 delegates, with a full vote each, Chairman Roberts had been a state senator for two terms, mayor of Providence for ten years; and has been governor since 1950; he had been a former state chairman of the state party, and, at the time of the convention, was a member of the state executive committee. Theodore Francis Green had been a member of the lower house of the state legislature, governor for two terms, and has been a United States senator since 1936; he also serves as national committeeman. John O. Pastore had also been a member of the lower house and governor of the state before being elected to the Senate in 1950; Senator Pastore is also a member of the state executive committee. The fourth delegate with a full vote, John E. Fogarty, has been a member of the House of Representatives since 1940 and is a member of the Democratic town committee in Gloucester. Many of the 16 delegates with half votes also had impressive records of both public and party service. There was J. Howard McGrath, former senator, former national party chairman, and former Attorney-General of the United States. James H. Kiernan has served as speaker of the lower house of the state legislature. John G. Coffey was a member of one or the other houses in the General Assembly since 1945, and secretary to the state committee. Walter H. Reynolds was mayor of Providence; Robert J. Connelly, mayor of Central Falls; Guillaume L. Parent, mayor of Woonsocket.

At the time of their selection, ten of the twenty delegates were members of the Democratic state committee and seven were members of its executive committee. At least thirteen delegates had been either delegates or alternates to previous national conventions; indeed, several of them had attended three, four, and five national gatherings and 1952 was to be the seventh national convention for Kiernan. All the delegates paid their own convention expenses. This relatively stable membership within the delegation may be taken as one indication of the harmony present within the state party. A local newspaper listed John A. McConnell and Victor J. Canzano as being again selected as "representatives of the AFL and CIO."

Of the 20 delegates, 19 were Catholics and one was Protestant. Twelve were of Irish extraction, five Italian, one British, one Portuguese, and one French. Nine were lawyers, two were labor representatives, and two were public servants; among the others were a funeral director, an insurance agent, an engineer, an office worker, a liquor distributor, an automobile agency owner, and a housewife. The average age of the delegation was approximately 46, the oldest being 85, and the youngest 36.

Providence was under-represented in the state convention, but the state executive committee more than made up for this in presenting their choices for national convention delegates. The delegation was heavily weighted in favor of the city of Providence, inasmuch as 13 of the 20 delegates resided in that city. It should be noted that Providence is the Democratic key in the winning of all statewide elections. Conspicuously absent from among the delegates were Democrats from Pawtucket, the second largest city in the state, although four alternates came from Pawtucket. This was in marked contrast to past delegations. The Pawtucket Democratic organization has recently had some difficulty in turning out the Democratic vote: a Republican won the mayoralty election in 1950 and another, in the special election on February 19, 1952, filled the state senate seat from the 1st district, a seat held by the Democratic incumbent since 1932. What was perhaps worse from the standpoint of the state party, the lost 1st district seat caused the loss of control of the state senate.

A number of changes were later made in the delegation elected by the state convention. James H. Kiernan withdrew, and Harry T. Curvin, alternate, was given his place; this action restored to Pawtucket a delegate place. Curvin has been speaker of the lower house of the state legislature since 1941. Mayor Parent of Woonsocket also withdrew as a delegate, and Alternate John F. Doris of Woonsocket was named to take his place. Doris is a member of the state committee. George Paquin took Doris' place as an alternate. In addition, Alternates William A. Borreca, John O. Stitely, Louis J. Lussier, James M. Donovan, and Mrs. Lucy S. Hartigan left the delegation, and, in their places were added H. Clinton Owen, Jr., Nicandro DiSandro, Miss Elvera Ferrari, Julius C. Michaelson, Mrs. Margaret C. Laperche, and John Rao.

ACTIVITIES AND VOTING RECORD

Although the state convention sent the delegation to the national convention uninstructed, the delegates nevertheless had definite predilections: Adlai Stevenson was their choice. However, the uncertainty surrounding Stevenson's availability caused a good deal of speculation about the delegation's second choice. Thus, Senator Green told the state convention that Senator Richard B. Russell of Georgia would not be acceptable because Rhode Island Democrats wanted a man who could stand on the party's 1948 platform. State Chairman Rao and Delegation Chairman Roberts both stated on May 14 that they were waiting for White House direction on the matter of the nomination.

The delegation seemed to split into three groups with respect to a second choice candidate. One group formed around Senator Green and J. Howard McGrath who were said to favor Barkley. A second group, led by Senator Pastore and Congressman Fogarty, seemed to favor Kefauver; Senator Kefauver had sent a man into the state in an attempt to win the delegation to him. A third group thought that the delegation's second choice should be Senator McMahon as an adopted favorite son, at least "until the dust settled." In view of the delegation's avowed intention of supporting a Fair Dealer, it seemed strange that they paid no more attention to Harriman's cause than they did.

Fifty-nine Rhode Islanders journeyed to Chicago. Governor Roberts was their delegation chairman. Senator and National Committeeman Green and National Committeewoman Cullinan were elected to the platform committee. Senator Green had preceded the delegation to Chicago inasmuch as he was also named to the pre-convention preliminary platform drafting committee. Mayor Reynolds served on the credentials committee. Providence City Chairman McElroy was named to work on the rules committee, while House Speaker Curvin of Pawtucket was elected to the Committee on Permanent Organization.

At Chicago, the candidates for the party's top nomination actively wooed the state's small delegation. The candidates presented themselves to the delegates at a dinner given by Senator Green. First to arrive was Senator Russell, who was soon followed by Averell Harriman. When Harriman left, his place was taken by Senator Kefauver. As Kefauver's party was leaving, Senator Kerr came in. Kerr was soon followed by Senator Underwood, who was acting as Vice President Barkley's spokesman.

The next day J. Howard McGrath told the delegation what was supposed to be happening in the back rooms. On the theory that Kerr and Harriman would quickly fade from the picture, McGrath said, President Truman had his top assistants working to produce a deadlock among Stevenson, Barkley, Kefauver, and Russell. After the impasse continued for six or seven ballots, the President's name was to be placed in nomination as the only choice that could produce party harmony. The delegation, however, was not at all convinced by this story, and still believed that if Stevenson were nominated he would carry the day.

The Rhode Island delegation voted for the Moody resolution. Rhode Island made brief national news in this connection when an Associated Press dispatch reported that the state's delegation was one of seven that had not sent signed pledges to the Credentials Committee in conformity with the Moody resolutions; the committee chairman later reported that he had received the pledge. The delegation, however, voted 10 to 2 in favor of seating the Virginia delegation. This vote for the Rhode Island delegation was cast by Delegate-at-large McElroy, inasmuch as most of the other delegates were then five miles away caucusing in the group's headquarters. The delegation was not polled on this issue, and McElroy arrived at the vote he reported through some formula of his own. J. Howard McGrath apparently influenced McElroy to vote as he did.

The balloting for presidential candidates was unusual for Rhode Island in that this marked the first time in more than twenty years that the state's delegation could not agree on one candidate. On the first ballot Stevenson received 5½ votes cast by Roberts, Frank Rao, John Rao, Cullinan, McGrath, Curvin, Feeney, McElroy, Luongo, and Rebello; Kefauver received 3½ votes from Pastore, Fogarty, Reynolds, Connelly, and Arcaro; Harriman received 1½ votes cast by Green and Canzano; Murray and Doris cast one vote for Governor Dever of Massachusetts; while Barkley received ½ vote from McConnell. On the second ballot all the candidates but Stevenson and Kefauver were eliminated from Rhode Island consideration: Stevenson received 8 votes, having added Green, Canzano, McConnell, and Doris among his supporters; Kefauver's vote was increased to 4 by retaining the votes of his original backers and picking up that of Murray. On the third and final ballot, the delegation cast all 12 votes for Stevenson.

AFTERMATH IN THE STATE

Returning home, the delegation set about organizing for the coming election. Rhode Island Democrats supported the party leadership, and, at the state primary, renominated the incumbents for statewide and national office. All the statewide Democratic candidates were re-elected. In winning re-election, Senator Pastore piled up the largest vote—225,228—ever cast for any political office in the state. The Democrats, however, lost 5 of their 21 seats in the state senate, and 10 of their 68 seats in the lower house of the state legislature. The Republicans won control of the state senate. Surprising was the loss of the state's electoral college votes to the Republican party, an event which had not happened in Rhode Island since 1924. General Eisenhower won by a majority of 7,642, in contrast to President Truman's 49,770 majority won in 1948.

REVIEW AND APPRAISAL

Did the delegations act in accordance with the wishes of their parties' membership? This question requires an evaluation of the two state conventions, for it was here that the basic decisions were made.

It seems certain that the apportionment base of the state convention system might well be re-examined. The Republican state convention, basing its apportionment on the state's 39 cities and towns, is almost certainly in violation of the Republican national rules. The Democratic state convention suffers from the same problem to a lesser extent, although its base of apportionment is the 100 representative districts of the lower house; but Rhode Island Democrats are not in violation of the national rules on the point because the Democratic party does not appear to have any rule bearing on the matter. Rhode Island has the unique characteristic of being a city-state, yet the large urban population from which both parties must draw their support is not allotted anything like its proportionate share of the votes in either state convention, in disregard of the usual practice in most states of allocating state convention delegates within a state in accordance with the party vote in a recent election.

Rhode Island has had a primary law since 1948, but this law makes provision only for nomination for statewide public offices, for representatives to Congress, and for certain party officials. The primary law does not provide an opportunity for indicating presidential preferences. A presidential preference primary bill was introduced by Representative Bayard J. Ewing in the lower house of the General Assembly in March 1952, but was killed in committee without discussion. Indeed, well aware of its poor chance of success, Representative Ewing did not bother to submit a complete bill. He introduced only a skeleton measure, intending to complete it by amendment should the proposal find unexpected support.

All this nothwithstanding, both the Republican and Democratic state conventions, and the delegations that each elected to send to the national conventions, did act with their parties' supporters in mind. There is tangible evidence that the Republican state convention and the delegation it sent to support the candidacy of General Eisenhower were voting in accordance with the views of the Republicans within the state. First, when polled, almost two-thirds of the Republican state central committee voted in favor of Eisenhower; second, the Eisenhower faction successfully prevailed on the state convention to break tradition and elect a delegation that was supposed to be committed to the General 100 per cent, a vote probably possible only because of the grass roots popularity of the General; and third, once Eisenhower was chosen to be the candidate, the Republicans were able to carry the state for the first time since 1924. Likewise, the Democratic state convention and its delegation, in supporting the candidacy of Governor Stevenson, were acting in accordance with the views of most Rhode Island Democrats. Even though he lost the state, Stevenson was popular enough to poll 203,293 votes, or 14,557 more votes than the party's previous high in 1948.

Rhode Island Chapter Acknowledgments

The chapter was prepared by FELIX RACKOW, Assistant Professor of Political Science, Brown University, pursuant to an invitation extended in July 1953. One source of data for Professor Rackow's chapter was a preconvention field report on the Democratic delegation that had been submitted by JOHN O. STITELY, Assistant Professor of Political Science, University of Rhode Island.

CONNECTICUT

KEY FACTS

Electoral votes, 1952:   8

National convention votes, 1952:
Democratic, 16
Republican, 22

Population, 1950: 2,007,280
Urban, 78%; *rural nonfarm,* 19%; *rural farm,* 3%

Population increase, 1940-50: 298,038 (17%)
Urban, 11%; *rural nonfarm,* 44%; *rural farm,* 34% decline

Presidential vote, 1948:   *1952:*
Democratic,   423,297 (48%)   481,649 (44%)
Republican,   437,754 (50%)   611,012 (56%)
Progressive,   13,713   (2%)

Gubernatorial vote, 1950:
Democratic,   419,404
Republican,   436,418

U. S. Representatives vote,
all districts, 1950:   *1952:*
Democratic,   435,606   504,257 (district only)
Republican,   425,156   586,922 (district only)

U. S. Representatives elected 1950:   *1952:*
Democratic,   2   1
Republican,   4   5 (1 at-large)

State legislature elected 1952:
Senate: Democrats, 14;   Republicans, 22
House: Democrats, 58;   Republicans, 221

Method of selecting national convention delegates:
Democratic: state convention
Republican: district and state conventions

124

POLITICAL RIVALRY IN CONNECTICUT HAS BEEN highly competitive
for more than twenty years. Franklin D. Roosevelt carried the state
four times but the Republicans have triumphed in the last two presidential elections. At eleven biennial elections for governor from
1930 to 1950, six were won by Democrats and five by Republicans.
In only two of these elections, 1936 and 1946, did the winner's percentage of the two-party vote exceed 55 per cent. During this period,
Democratic chances of electing a governor, a senator, and most of
the Democratic ticket for Congress seemed to be good when voter
turnout was heavy. From 1930 to 1950 the Republicans won the
governorship in a presidential election year only once, in 1944.
Democratic nominees for senator were almost invariably elected in
presidential years, and the Democratic congressional nominees polled
a majority of the vote in presidential election years from 1932 to
1948, and in 1950 as well. In 1952, however, the election produced
a Republican sweep, in which Eisenhower carried the state, two
Democratic senators were replaced by Republican senators, and
Democrats won only one congressional seat, that for the 1st district
(Hartford).

Control over the state senate has fluctuated between the two parties but the Democrats have not held a majority in the lower house
of the state legislature since 1876. Apportionment in the state legislature is weighted in favor of the rural areas. The state is divided
into 36 senatorial districts, each of which elects one senator. Districts are constitutionally required to be as nearly equal in population
as possible, making population the basis of senatorial legislative
apportionment at least in theory. Senatorial districts actually vary
greatly in size, although 25 of the 36 senators come from the urban

counties of Hartford, New Haven and Fairfield. In the lower house of the state legislature, the basis of apportionment is frankly geographical area. Each of the 169 towns into which the entire state is divided (many of them still governed by town meeting in the traditional pattern of New England town government) is entitled to one representative. Each town receives a second representative if its population exceeds 5,000 or if it had two representatives before 1818, but in no case more than two representatives. On this basis, "towns" comprising areas that include over 85 per cent of the population of the state receive less than half of the voting strength in the lower house of the state legislature. Hartford, with a population of more than 177,000 has two representatives; so does the Town of Union, with 261.

The strategic position of the Republican party in the state was improved by a constitutional amendment, the 45th, adopted in 1948, when the party controlled both houses of the state legislature. This extended the governor's term from two years to four, and provided that he should be elected in the even-numbered years when the presidential election is not at stake. The amendment also transferred from the legislature to the governor the effective power to appoint 129 judges in the 67 town and city courts. The amendment became effective in 1949, and Governor John Davis Lodge (R) was elected in 1950 for a four-year term. He approached the 1952 campaign in a position to exert real leadership in the party.

In recent years politics in Connecticut has reflected the urban-rural split and the changing demographic complexion of the state. The urban areas tend to be Democratic and the rural Republican. The movement to the suburbs has more than counterbalanced urban and industrial growth. Democratic strength is concentrated in the four largest cities (New Haven, Hartford, Bridgeport, and Waterbury), which have roughly one-third of the state's population. Even in these cities, however, the two-party vote is closely divided. New Haven and Waterbury have Republican mayors, Bridgeport, a Socialist mayor.

The population of Connecticut is currently about 39 per cent Catholic. Its steadily increasing urban Negro and Italian populations are becoming more politically conscious and active. With party affiliations approximately balanced, neither party is prepared to alienate unavoidably any important segment of the voting population, religious or ethnic.

Organization of the major parties is related to population distribution in the state. The Republican organization is geographically diffuse but politically centralized and strong. The relative isolation of the town organizations is a potential source of strength to the Republican state chairman; for 25 years Boss J. Henry Roraback ruled the state from this position. Since his death in 1937, central power has been exercised only nominally by the state chairman, actually by a fluctuating alliance of "county leaders." The Democratic organization is looser than the Republican because of the Democratic state chairman's dependence on the vote of a few large cities. Each of these cities has a strong local leader at the head of a largely independent local organization.

The town party committees (ward committees in the towns that are also cities) are the basic units of organization in both parties. Governmental and political power focuses on the town and state levels, the county having little significance as a governmental unit. In the nominating process, the state senatorial district is important, and the county leaders in both parties are men—from rural-small town areas in the Republican party, from the big cities in the Democratic party—who are able to control several senatorial districts. In both parties, the members of the state central committee are elected by state senatorial districts.

Connecticut is the last remaining state in which the caucus and the convention are used for all nominations above the local level; and the caucus system is ordinarily used for the nomination of local candidates, although occasionally the local party organizations hold what are called primary elections. Town committees of each party usually prepare a slate, and ordinarily caucuses are brief, unless an opposition slate is filed. In many Connecticut towns caucuses are almost unheard of, they are held so rarely. The nominating process is controlled almost completely by state party rules, state law being limited to some of the fundamentals. Local party organizations have wide discretion in establishing both rules and procedures for the conduct of local caucuses (and primaries in the rare instances when they are held). Procedures thus vary widely, both between the parties and from one locality to another. Above the level of the town caucus (and in the cities, ward caucus), each party's nominees for the general election are selected by a series of conventions.

THE REPUBLICAN DELEGATION

Based primarily on reports by
MARY T. REYNOLDS AND ROLAND YOUNG

In 1948 the Republican party in Connecticut sent a delegation to the national convention led and united by Senator Raymond Baldwin. On the 1st and 2d ballots, the delegation cast its entire vote for the Senator as a favorite son. Dewey received the entire vote on the 3d and final ballot.

Governor John Lodge and State Chairman Clarence Baldwin (no relation to the former senator) were the dominant powers in the Connecticut Republican party in 1952. But the Republican factions that fought for power in Connecticut that spring were not easily defined, for coalitions of party leaders in the state were fluid and unstable. There were three distinct issues over which contests occurred and factional lines were drawn: (1) the contest between Eisenhower and Taft supporters for positions on the delegation to the Republican national convention; (2) the effort to unseat the incumbent state chairman, Baldwin; and (3) the contest for the United States senatorial nomination.

Opposition to the Lodge-Baldwin leadership grew out of criticism of the Governor's legislative leadership, as well as the early and active support given to General Eisenhower. The faction supporting Senator Taft represented the more conservative elements of the party and was led by certain county leaders who resented the active leadership of the state chairman. The focus of opposition to Lodge was in Fairfield County, in the southwest corner of the state, where William Brennan, incumbent national committeeman and the man who gave Lodge his start in politics, was the leader of the wealthiest and most vigorous county Republican machine.

THE SELECTION PROCESS IN 1952

Formal requirements—Both the district delegates and the dele-gates-at-large to the Republican national convention are formally chosen at the state party convention. In practice, however, the machinery for selecting the delegates to the national convention is an undifferentiated part of the machinery which periodically makes decisions on party leadership—whether to ratify or to overthrow the existing leadership—and also chooses the party's nominees for office. This machinery is regulated mainly by party rules, and although very similar is not identical in the two parties.

The selection process for national convention delegates operates in four stages in the Republican party. First comes the holding of town (in the cities, ward) caucuses. In 1952 these were scheduled for Monday, April 28. The date is fixed by the state central committee, and must be announced at least fifteen days in advance. The task of each town caucus in 1952 included the election of two distinct groups of delegates. One group, two from each town, represented the towns at three party conventions held successively in the spring: namely, the state senatorial district convention, the congressional district convention, and the state convention of May 26-27. The other group of delegates was elected to serve at a separate state senatorial district convention, held in July for the sole purpose of making nominations for the state senate. The state central committee has wide discre-tionary authority to call special district or state conventions. It might therefore have called a separate state convention to nominate the national convention delegates. A special state convention was in fact held in September 1952 to nominate the party's candidate for United States senator to succeed the late Brien McMahon.

Some confusion among non-professionals arises from the fact that two different district conventions are held in each state senatorial district within a few months, but for different purposes and with different individuals participating. The later one, in July, is clearly the less important; the delegates are seldom persons of long party experience or influence, and have only one decision, a minor one, to make. The earlier convention, in the spring, is of great importance. Traditionally it is part of the caucus and convention hierarchy leading up to the state convention; it invariably includes the most influential party leaders; and it has a multiple task of great significance within the party.

Before leaving the town caucuses, it should be noted that these caucuses, when held, provide the only point at which the rank-and-file party member acting as a voter can exert any influence on the nominating process in state and nation. All participants must be currently on the books as registered members of the party; lists may be checked before voting in caucus is permitted. Persons chosen as delegates in town caucuses must be legal voters of the town they represent.

At the second stage of the process, the state convention delegates who are elected in the town caucuses meet in separate conventions in the 36 state senatorial districts. As their first act they elect two delegates to the state party convention for each senatorial district. These two delegates-at-large parallel the representation in the state senate. They immediately become voting members of the senatorial district convention in which they are chosen. Then each of these conventions nominates two of its number, one man and one woman, to represent the state senatorial district on the new Republican state central committee. The official party leadership is thus picked for the next two-year period. The senatorial district convention may also bind the senatorial district delegation (which consists of the same persons) to vote as a unit in the forthcoming state convention.

In the third stage of the process, the state convention delegates meet in separate congressional district conventions for the five districts, for the sole purpose of formally electing the district delegates and alternates to the national convention. These meetings take place in conference rooms at the state party convention at 11:00 A.M. of the second day of the convention. Action on national convention delegates in the congressional district conventions is usually no more than a formal ratification of decisions already taken elsewhere by the state central committee members from each congressional district.

The fourth stage is the state convention, where the delegates-at-large to the national convention are formally elected. The state convention also makes nominations for state-wide elective offices and appoints the state central committee. The convention is made up of two delegates for each representative in the lower house of the state legislature and two delegates from each senatorial district. In the 1952 convention this made a total of 626 delegates, 554 representing towns and 72 representing senatorial districts. Rural over-representations, while common to the state conventions of both parties, is especially marked in the Republican convention, in contravention of national Republican rules, because it copies completely the apportionment pattern of representation in the state legislature while doubling the size. The four largest cities, with one-third of the state's population, receive only 6.4 per cent of the convention representation.

National candidate campaigns—The groundwork for campaigning in support of General Eisenhower had been laid as early as 1948. Some scattered organizing occurred in 1951 at the ward club level. The first active organizing of the 1952 campaign came in January, 1952, at a $100-a-plate dinner in Hartford. Soon after, a letter was sent over the signature of state party chairman Clarence Baldwin to each of the 169 town Republican party leaders, asking specifically for support in nominating an Eisenhower delegation to the national convention in July. The letter urged the town chairmen to use their influence to have each town caucus pick state convention delegates who were avowed Eisenhower supporters. It asked for a written report to state party headquarters in Hartford after the town caucuses. This dramatic and unprecedented action was openly resented by Republican leaders in many towns. The principal influence behind the letter was said to have been Meade Alcorn, who took over the chairmanship of the Eisenhower state committee when Mansfield Sprague, the first chairman, opened his campaign for the United States senatorial nomination. Under Alcorn's leadership, Eisenhower clubs had been formed in almost all of the 169 towns before April 28, the date of the town caucuses.

Considerable strength existed for Senator Taft in some localities. Customarily, delegates to the state convention have gone unpledged. Local political leaders, and usually the state leaders also, prefer the freedom of action which this gives them. The backers of Senator Taft had counted on neutrality from the state leadership. They were, at the start of the preconvention campaign, less well organized than the Eisenhower forces. Several of them were the "outs," who had influence locally but had been defeated in earlier factional contests for positions on the state central committee. No solid, aggressive organization was built for Taft on a statewide basis.

Town caucuses—In the town caucuses on April 28, 125 of the 169 towns either instructed their delegates to the state convention or voted some kind of resolution of guidance. At least 20 towns sent delegations definitely committed to General Eisenhower, while only 3 towns sent delegations committed to Senator Taft. Town caucuses were better attended than in previous years, but only a small fraction of the registered Republican voters appeared. From newspaper and eyewitness accounts, it appears that in 1952 contests were frequent; in some cases bitter remarks were made although debate was brief. In the cities, ward caucuses were held to select delegates to a city convention, which met later the same day to choose the delegates and alternates to the state convention. Most ward caucuses were routine affairs even when participation extended beyond the membership of the ward committee.

In several of the larger towns, town Republican committees, under strong pressure from Eisenhower committees, set up presidential preference "primaries," although the delegates to the state convention were elected in the usual fashion. In Hamden, for example, which was then governed by town meeting despite its 16,664 registered voters (about 11,000 of whom are Republicans), an informal presidential preference primary was held on May 20, almost a month after the town caucus had chosen the town's delegation to the state convention. Out of approximately 1500 votes, Eisenhower led Taft by a 300-vote margin. The Hamden town chairman, a strong Taft supporter, said after the poll that he would be "guided" by the result, but that he refused to consider himself bound by it. He continued to support Taft at the state convention. In Stamford, where 18,000 Republicans were eligible to vote, the names of Eisenhower, Taft, and Stassen were printed on one ballot, with space for a write-in. The polls were open for eight hours, and about 5,500 voters expressed a 3-to-2 preference for Eisenhower. Most of these primaries were carried by Eisenhower.

Senatorial district conventions—On Saturday, May 3, when the 36 senatorial district conventions were held, 2 districts replaced both of their members on the state central committee, 12 replaced one each, and 22 made no change. Some of the changes could be laid to normal turnover, but on the new state committee, there were only 12 votes at most that were definitely adverse to Baldwin, in a total of 72. Three of the senatorial district conventions pledged their entire state convention delegations to Eisenhower; four other districts passed resolutions endorsing Eisenhower, but did not undertake to pledge their delegates. The senatorial district conventions were primarily conventions of the professional local party leadership. As a result, almost every meeting was concerned with the factional struggle between the Lodge-Baldwin group and those seeking change in the leadership in state party affairs. The outcome as a whole was an endorsement of the Lodge-Baldwin leadership.

Congressional district conventions—In 1952, with the state leaders driving hard for a delegation completely committed to Eisenhower, the procedure for selecting congressional district delegates to the national convention was under more pressure than usual. Two Eisenhower delegates each were elected in the 1st and 3d districts without incident. The 2d district convention was "prolonged by procedural difficulties," but as previously anticipated, it elected two delegates who were unpledged and uninstructed: Frank C. Parizek and Nelson L. Carpenter. It had been the custom in this district to rotate the national convention delegateships among its four counties; Parizek and Carpenter were the choices, respectively, in Tolland and Windham Counties, which were considered entitled to seats in 1952. The state leaders probably would have preferred a different outcome, particularly as to Carpenter, who was known to favor Taft, but they did not risk a contest and were unable to secure action to bind the delegates who were selected. Shortly after the convention, the Governor favored one of Carpenter's supporters with a major patronage appointment.

In the 4th district, the initially agreed-upon slate carried the names of persons acceptable to William Brennan, national committeeman and leader of the anti-Lodge faction. After the Governor had announced that he would not support Brennan for continuation on the national committee or for a post as delegate-at-large, the 4th district slate was rearranged to include Brennan himself, and he was elected as a district delegate. But the 4th district convention voted to instruct both of its delegates for Eisenhower; and Brennan agreed to accept this outcome.

The 5th district convention named Mayor Snyder of Waterbury, a Taft supporter, as one of its delegates, but also passed a resolution committing the two delegates to Eisenhower. The district conventions thus produced two delegates who were in doubt and eight delegates who were either favorable to Eisenhower or instructed for him, or both.

State convention—Governor Lodge, in consultation with state party leaders and his personal aides, had begun putting together a slate of 12 delegates-at-large by the first week in May in preparation for the state convention on May 26 and 27 at Hartford. The Governor was repeatedly urged by the Taft organization to include in the delegation some representation of the Taft strength in the state. Governor Lodge replied to those requests by invoking the principle of majority rule, stating that in Ohio where Taft controlled the choice of the regular delegation entered in the primary, he had not given any representation to the Eisenhower partisans.

Governor Lodge eventually announced that he would oppose the selection of William Brennan, Fairfield County leader, not only for reelection to his post of national committeeman, but even as a delegate-at-large to the national convention. Brennan replied with statements accusing the Governor of bossism. This exploded into the open the factional split that extended down through the Republican party from top to bottom. The immediate issue was Brennan's identification with the Taft wing of the party. Second, and probably of most importance, was an intra-party fight that began in the 1951 legislative session and which by 1953 was threatening to become a permanent feud with Brennan leading the opposition to the Governor. A third issue was Brennan's alliance with the group who were seeking to remove Clarence Baldwin as state chairman. A fourth came from Brennan's determination to eliminate Prescott Bush from the United States Senate race in favor of William A. Purtell, in the course of which contest Brennan helped to defeat the state organization's men in Hartford County.

As soon as the rift became public, friends of the two men tried to smooth it over. Party leaders from all over the state conferred with Governor Lodge. On one side Clare Booth Luce urged Henry Cabot Lodge, the Governor's brother, "to come down and straighten things out!" On the other Mr. Brennan's friends who were already identified with the anti-organization faction urged him to force the Governor into a showdown battle. Brennan managed his press relations skillfully and won for himself much public and party support. He held and perhaps increased his party following, at least temporarily, even while losing his national committee post and his place as a delegate-at-large.

The only other change in the at-large slate after it was originally chosen was the replacement of Frank M. Lynch, state finance commissioner, by Clare Booth Luce. Even though she came from a part of the state already over-represented on the delegation, no one wished to dispute her announced claim to a place. In consequence, the city of New Haven was deprived of a delegate.

COMPOSITION OF THE DELEGATION

The list of delegates-at-large was composed, for the most part, of state political office holders or of those active in the state political organization. Clare Booth Luce was a principal exception. She had served two terms in Congress, but at the time of her selection held no public office or party office within the Republican state organization. At Chicago, she was active and influential but mixed little with other members of her own delegation.

The district delegates were for the most part county leaders, but of sufficient stature to give them as much statewide prominence as the majority of the delegates-at-large. William Brennan, the national committeeman, and Raymond E. Snyder, mayor of Waterbury, were two such delegates.

To replace Brennan as national committeeman, the delegation chose James C. Shannon, a former governor. Meade Alcorn, the chairman of the state Eisenhower-for-President committee, was Governor Lodge's choice for national committeeman, but party leaders both inside and outside the state convinced the Governor that since Brennan was a Catholic his job should be filled by a person of the same religion. Early in 1953, Governor Lodge appointed Shannon to the state superior court, and Alcorn then became national committeeman.

The inner circle within the delegation included Governor Lodge; Meade Alcorn; National Committeeman Shannon; John Alsop, a delegate from the 1st district; and John Thim, a delegate from the 3d district. Colonel Raymond Watt, the Governor's aide, was a focus of strategic contact both within the delegation and between the delegation and groups from other states. No national legislators were included in the delegation, although four of Connecticut's six representatives in Congress at the time were Republicans.

Three or four delegates were chosen primarily as a reward for their position as financial contributors to the party, as well as other past party work. The remaining delegates were selected mainly as a reward for their work for Eisenhower. There was no effort to balance the delegation with labor or farm representatives, nor to provide special representation for ethnic or religious groups, although certain delegates were members of these groups. Almost all of the delegates were between 40 and 60 years of age and had had a college education. The unusual number of women delegates, seven, was decided not on abstract grounds favoring feminine representation, but by the fact that these women represented real power and influence in Connecticut politics. In general, the delegation was composed of well-to-do or wealthy business and professional people of considerable political experience. Over half of the delegation had had previous national convention experience.

ACTIVITIES AND VOTING RECORD

The delegation met as a group immediately after the close of the state convention on May 27 and elected its officers. Governor Lodge was elected chairman; ex-Governor Shannon was nominated for the national committee; Mrs. Julia Keeney was re-nominated national committeewoman; John Thim, former speaker of the lower house of the state legislature and chairman of the 1952 state convention, was chosen as the credentials committee member; Mayor Snyder was assigned to the rules committee; and Mrs. Julia Keeney and Lewis Dibble, a large financial contributor and chairman of the organizing dinner held in January 1952, were chosen as the delegation's members to the resolutions committee. No sooner had the delegation and its officers been chosen than they began to receive telephone calls and visits from politicians from other states. John Thim had been chosen for the credentials committee only a matter of hours before he received his first out-of-state telephone call, from a Texas woman who wished to give him the Eisenhower faction's story of the split in her state.

The delegation provided competent and willing assistance to the Eisenhower cause. Before the convention, Governor Lodge stumped for Eisenhower delegates in Illinois and elsewhere, and at the governors' conference in Houston he participated in the Republican governors' proposal for changing the convention rules. In Chicago, he was active at all times and spoke from the rostrum in support of the Eisenhower position on the contested delegations. He also attended a conference from which came the selection of Senator Nixon for the vice-presidency. Another Connecticut delegate, Clare Booth Luce, spoke eloquently on radio and television in General Eisenhower's behalf and at one point supported the cause of Senator Margaret Chase Smith for vice-president. Meade Alcorn became one of Governor Sherman Adams' aides during the convention.

The delegation contained only two avowed Taft supporters, one of whom, Brennan, was bound not to vote for him on the nomination. While participating in the pre-convention national committee deliberations as Connecticut's committeeman, Brennan voted to seat the pro-Taft delegations, and indicated that he would continue to vote in the same way on the convention floor. On the morning of Wednesday, July 9, however, he asked that the delegation be convened, and then announced his intention to vote for the pro-Eisenhower delegations. Brennan interpreted the credentials issue as a struggle for delegate strength between Taft and Eisenhower. Since he was pledged to his Fairfield County constituency to support Eisenhower, he had concluded that he could not in conscience vote in any way on the convention floor to weaken the delegate strength of the General.

The other avowed Taft supporter was Nelson Carpenter, a member of the Connecticut House of Representatives and one of the two unpledged 2d district delegates. There were indications previous to his selection that Carpenter would not have received his post as a delegate unless he had promised to vote for Eisenhower. Nevertheless, Carpenter lived apart from and did not associate with the rest of the delegation during the national convention; and he voted with the Taft group on all roll calls.

The Connecticut delegation supported the Eisenhower position with 20 of its 22 votes on the Brown amendment and with 21 votes on the motion to seat Georgia. The initial Connecticut vote on the nominating ballot was 21 for Eisenhower and was later made unanimous. Most of the delegates thus followed the pattern set by the victory of the Lodge-Baldwin faction in the state.

AFTERMATH IN THE STATE

The Eisenhower nomination had the effect of further strengthening Governor Lodge's position in his party in the state. When the death of Brien McMahon (D) opened a second Senate vacancy, the Governor's candidate, Prescott Bush, won it in a contest with Clare Booth Luce.

The outcome of the election in November was a Republican sweep, as noted earlier. Eisenhower received a plurality of 130,000, topped only by Calvin Coolidge's plurality of 136,000 in 1924. Feuds begun in the pre-convention period were discernible in the election results. Ticket-splitting was especially noteworthy in Hartford County, where the Brennan machine had earlier defeated the administration's men, and which produced the lone Democratic winner in the congressional races, Thomas Dodd. In Hartford and Fairfield Counties combined, the narrowness of Prescott Bush's victory over Senator William Benton (D) was emphasized by the fact that the Bush vote trailed well behind that of the (Republican) congressman-at-large. Fortunately for the Republicans, the Fairfield County Democratic vote also showed evidence of factional troubles, some disgruntled Democratic bosses having failed to support Senator Benton and other candidates of the party's liberal wing. Governor Lodge and State Chairman Baldwin appeared to be left in an excellent strategic position from which to face the problems of 1954, when the governorship will again be contested.

THE DEMOCRATIC DELEGATION

Based primarily on reports by
BERNHARD O. J. LINNEVOLD

The Democratic party in Connecticut has been able to compete on equal terms with its opponent in national elections. On the local level it has been less successful. In presidential election years, from 1932 to 1948, the Democrats usually won, although their margin of victory for seats in Congress was a diminishing one. The same trend was also visible in the contests for state elective offices, particularly the state senate. But the national victory of President Truman in 1948 gave a tremendous lift to the state Democratic party, even though Truman did not carry Connecticut. The victory of Chester Bowles in the state elections in 1948 provided a further stimulus.

The state Democratic party leadership was more united in the early months of 1952 than at any time in the past two decades. The leadership included Senator Brien McMahon, the acknowledged leader in national politics, and State Chairman John M. Bailey, his spokesman in state politics. McMahon and Bailey were not on as close terms as Bailey and Bowles had been from 1948 to 1950, but in 1952 they were politically united and headed a strong state organization. In terms of program the party was almost completely New Deal-Fair Deal. Its expressions at the 1948 national convention, the record of the Bowles' administration in the state from 1949 to 1951, the 1950 state platform, and the actions, even if unsuccessful, of its members in the state legislature, all indicated the party's orientation. The fact that Senator Hubert Humphrey was the invited keynote speaker at the state convention, June 13, was additional evidence.

The lack of conflict in the party from 1950 through the 1952 national convention was apparently due in a large part to the skillful management of the state chairman. The defection of the party leader of any one of the four principal cities in the state could almost always mean statewide defeat at the polls. Moreover, as in many states with a large labor vote, party leaders in Connecticut were concerned over the activities of labor leaders in fields usually tilled by professional politicians. The problems of labor politicians versus professional politicians and city bosses versus state organization provided continuing tensions in the party, but the state chairman was adept in balancing these forces up to the death of Senator McMahon, after which new problems began to arise.

In previous years, conflicts over places on the delegation to the Democratic national convention were settled, in some degree, by the expedient of increasing the size of the delegation. In 1940 Connecticut was apportioned 16 votes. To cast these votes the state convention sent an oversize delegation of 48 to the national convention, each delegate with one-third vote. In 1944, 18 votes were cast by the 26 delegates; and in 1948, 20 votes were cast by 30 delegates, both delegations conforming with national party rules.

THE SELECTION PROCESS IN 1952

The method of selecting national convention delegates in the Democratic party in Connecticut has changed a number of times in recent years. Before 1940, county leaders prepared a congressional district delegate slate in a caucus held immediately prior to the state convention; the delegates-at-large were nominated by those who controlled the state central committee. In 1940, the chairman of the state convention appointed a nominating committee of five members, one from each congressional district, and this group nominated the entire slate. All delegates were of "at-large" status. In 1944, a larger committee nominated the entire slate, designating 10 as district delegates and the remainder at-large. In 1948, county leaders and members of the state executive committee met in each of the five congressional districts and nominated two district delegates and four half-vote delegates-at-large from each.

The factors that conditioned ultimate delegation selection in 1952 began to be felt in 1950 with Senator Brien McMahon's re-election to the Senate. A series of conferences in the spring of 1951 with State Chairman John M. Bailey, Senator William Benton, former Governor Chester Bowles, and other leaders, clarified a somewhat muddled leadership situation and enabled Senator McMahon to become the actual leader. It was also decided that McMahon might become Connecticut's "favorite son" candidate for vice-president in 1952, if the situation were favorable, and that McMahon would be chairman of the 1952 delegation.

President Truman's decision at the end of March, 1952, not to be a candidate for re-election changed McMahon's and Bailey's public relations campaign. McMahon became a candidate for president though it was widely assumed in Connecticut that the real objective was another office: vice-president or secretary of state. A group of state leaders met with McMahon and publicly endorsed him. Town committees, led by persons close to the state leadership, followed immediately with endorsements. Middletown, with John Tynan as the actual leader, and Windsor, the home of the state party treasurer, Charles E. Mahoney, were among the first. Hartford followed. The state central committee endorsed him and announced that McMahon would be chairman of the delegation to the national convention.

Thus the major party decisions were already made even before the actual nomination and selection of convention delegates was started. The political situation remained substantially unchanged through the state convention that ratified a seemingly solid pro-McMahon delegation. Neither Senator Kefauver nor any other national candidate entered the state to campaign, perhaps in deference to the favorite-son tradition.

Bailey announced unofficially to a meeting of the state central committee on April 19 that the state committeemen in each congressional district should hold meetings for the nomination of delegates; the first was held on April 28 and the last on June 12. The tardy June 12 date reflected a disagreement over nominees in the 1st congressional district. Attendance at these meetings was formally restricted, in the 2d district at least, to the state central committee members residing in the congressional district, although other "county" leaders attended.

The state central committee consists of one man and one woman for each of the state's 36 senatorial districts. The selection procedures differ only slightly from those employed by the Republicans. Nominations for committeeman made in senatorial district meetings are formally accepted or rejected by the state convention in the even-numbered years. At Bailey's suggestion the congressional district meetings in 1952 were authorized to nominate three national convention delegates for consideration by the state convention: two district delegates and one delegate-at-large. This accounted for 10 district delegates and 5 delegates-at-large. In 1952 the remaining 7 delegates-at-large were nominated by Senator McMahon and the state chairman in consultation with other party leaders.

The Democratic state convention on June 13-14, 1952, consisted of 1,298 delegates, apportioned according to state party rules. Each of the state's 169 towns was entitled to twice its number of representatives in the state legislature, a basic state convention representation of 554. Each town casting a total 1948 presidential vote exceeding 1,000 received a bonus delegate for each 1,000 votes or major fraction thereof. This apportionment plan tended to reward the heavy-vote Democratic urban centers. The delegates to the state convention were selected in town and city caucuses that were held on a date set by the state central committee, May 19. Nine town and city Democratic organizations used conventions; seven used party primaries. Where caucuses were held, they were organized by the town or city party committee and were open to all enrolled party members. Caucuses could endorse presidential candidates. In the party-operated primaries of a very few towns, party members could express presidential preferences, but the vote did not bind the town's delegates to the state convention.

In accordance with the procedures previously outlined the slate of national convention delegates was proposed to the state convention and ratified by it. The convention also bound the delegation with a unit rule, in accordance with the usual practice. There was no formal contest at the state convention involving a complete alternative slate, but there had been contests in some of the pre-convention nominating meetings in the congressional districts. All of the contests were outgrowths of the constant jockeying for position within the state organization and did not result from any preference for a presidenial aspirant. The state convention platform was adopted with relative ease.

COMPOSITION OF THE DELEGATION

The 1952 Democratic delegation included nearly all of the leading active political figures in the state's party. All the Democratic members of Congress—Senators McMahon and Benton, and Representatives Ribicoff and McGuire—were delegates, although Senator McMahon was bedridden with an illness that ended in his death. There was a direct telephone line from Chicago to the bedside of Senator McMahon; at Chicago, he was represented by his administrative assistant, John Lane, and his alternate, former Ambassador Stanton Griffis. While objectives and strategy had been discussed with Senator McMahon, it was State Chairman Bailey who was the delegation's chief at the national convention. The other most influential members of the delegation were: Senator Benton; Representative Ribicoff; Middletown's Assessor, John Tynan, a party leader of long standing; and John Golden, the incoming national committeeman. The outgoing national committeeman was unable to win a seat in the delegation, undoubtedly as the result of a quarrel with Chester Bowles when the latter was governor and also because he had endorsed a Republican candidate for local office. The national committeewoman did not seek a place on the delegation and was not included.

There were last-minute changes in three of the alternate positions. Two union officials, detained by a strike in the Connecticut brass industry, were replaced by two other labor men; and the 1st ward chairman in Hartford was substituted for the wife of the Hartford town chairman. These appointments were made by State Chairman Bailey.

Most of the delegates had had considerable state party experience and many held or had held public office. The two labor delegates had been chosen specifically to represent the labor position and vote. There also were labor people among the alternates. The Young Democrats and the women's group had no special representation. The one woman delegate gained her position through party work and was not selected to represent any special voting group. No delegate was originally chosen as a reward for being a party financial contributor, although Stanton Griffis, who became a delegate when Senator McMahon was unable to attend, was known as a large contributor. The ethnic and religious backgrounds of most of the delegates reflected the large Irish and Italian Catholic population in the state. Most of the delegates came from urban centers of population and as lawyers, public officials, labor leaders, and small businessmen were individuals of middle class incomes. Probably over half of the delegates had had a college education.

The leadership elements had considerable convention experience while the rank-and-file had little or no previous participation in a national convention. Senator McMahon had been a delegate ever since 1936; State Chairman Bailey had been an alternate in 1932, and a delegate since 1936.

ACTIVITIES AND VOTING RECORD

The delegation was bound by the state convention and by its customary unit rule to support Senator McMahon for the presidency. The delegation organized at a meeting on June 19 and confirmed Senator McMahon as chairman. In McMahon's absence, Bailey, as delegation vice chairman, later took over the chairmanship. The delegation ratified the selection of the other delegation officers and those members who were to fill the national convention posts. McMahon and Mrs. Dorothy Satti, the national committeewoman-elect, were assigned to resolutions (platform). Senator Benton was McMahon's platform committee alternate and filled the post throughout the convention. State Chairman Bailey was the representative on credentials; and Michael Blansfield on rules. All these selections had been made well in advance of the organizing meeting of June 19.

Voting always as a unit, the delegation opposed the seating of Virginia and favored tabling Senator Douglas' motion to adjourn. Prior to the vote on Virginia, Bailey explained the criteria for his own actions in the credentials committee; he had voted to seat regular delegations from states that had not bolted the party in 1948 and to seat the challengers from states that had bolted.

Senator Benton placed McMahon's name in nomination for president. The delegation cast its original vote for him as a tribute; but it was withdrawn before the end of the first ballot and upon McMahon's own request. After the tribute to Senator McMahon, there was some uneasiness as to whether, when, and how to shift to Stevenson. In caucus, there was only one dissenting vote; Stanton Griffis was for Harriman. Thomas Dodd, a candidate for congressman, expressed himself in favor of a token demonstration for Senator Russell, but he and the rest voted for Stevenson. The Connecticut delegation was one of the three in the entire convention that supported unanimously the party's nominee on all three ballots.

AFTERMATH IN THE STATE

Senator McMahon, stricken with cancer, died in Washington on July 28, two days after the adjournment of the convention. His death did not give rise to any factional struggles over leadership succession. Leadership passed to State Chairman Bailey without challenge. National Committeeman John Golden was drawn into the inner circle, although engaging in some controversy with Congressman Thomas Dodd. Only Dodd (1st congressional district; Hartford) withstood the Republican sweep in the general election. All others on the Democratic congressional slate, including Senator Benton, were defeated.

REVIEW AND APPRAISAL

Both Connecticut delegations of 1952 were of high quality by almost any reasonable standard. Each contained a strong core of experienced political leadership. Each was prepared to take a responsible attitude toward the problems of its party in state and nation. The Republican delegation undoubtedly ranked higher in wealth, formal education, and social position; it also was unusual for its number of outstanding women. The Democratic delegation underlined its labor affiliations by giving one place each to the AFL and the CIO, but even so, it included only two union men, not counting alternates, in a delegation of 22 from an industrial state. The Governor and other elective and appointive state officials were conspicuous in the Republican delegation; senators and congressmen were prominent in the Democratic delegation.

The processes by which the delegations were constituted were basically similar, although there were significant differences in important details. The authority vested in congressional district conventions, on the Republican side, made possible the election of several delegates with views differing from the majority, even though only one voted for Taft in the end. Slate-making by party leaders was relatively decentralized among the Democrats; but all final action was by the full Democratic state convention, and the tradition of a unit rule was maintained unbroken.

The Republican delegation was the product of a sharp factional fight at every level from town caucus to state convention. The contest demonstrated that the factional opposition within the party organization was not lacking in means for asserting a point of view and making a record for the future. Popular participation at the town caucus and primary level remained limited; nevertheless, a rising level of popular participation was a major factor in consolidating organization support for Eisenhower. There was much evidence that political interest was stimulated both by the multiplicity of contests and by the avocational and middle-class character of the party leadership throughout the state.

In the creation of the Democratic delegation, the factional struggles were minor and local in their origins and consequences. A strong and homogeneous delegation was created and pledged to Brien McMahon with so little trouble that it was almost the incidental result of the continuing organization activities that had to be carried on for other purposes. The ordinary enrolled Democrat had little to do with the process; and no national candidate from outside the state made any significant effort to persuade the voter to intervene. Yet the formal machinery was little different from that through which issues were sharpened and contests prosecuted on the Republican side.

Implicit in the procedures followed by both parties in Connecticut is the concept that a political party is a private organization insofar as its internal management and operations are concerned. The attitudes that have made it possible for a publicly-administered, statewide primary election to be resisted longer in Connecticut than in any other state are also pertinent to the state's methods of participation in the presidential nominating process. Those attitudes have carried over into the intricate machinery in each party by which Connecticut selects its national convention delegates. The attitudes are also perhaps responsible for the extent to which Connecticut often violates Republican national rules, which provide that when national delegates are selected by conventions, representation in the congressional district and state conventions shall be apportioned "among the counties, parishes, and cities of the state or district having regard to the Republican vote therein." Yet the convention system was operated in Connecticut in 1952 by both parties without any public allegations of irregularity, malpractice, or dishonesty. This was all the more notable in view of the sharpness of the factional struggle on the Republican side, and is perhaps a tribute to the political maturity of the state.

Many students will undoubtedly continue to feel that there must be some way by which the electorate could have been drawn more actively and more effectively into the presidential nominating process in Connecticut in 1952. Yet the fact remains that the state was capably represented at both national conventions, that its convention vote was probably cast in a manner broadly consistent with the desires and views of the electorate in each party, and that Connecticut had no special reason to be dissatisfied with the outcome at either convention or its part in securing that outcome. Perhaps the apathy of the Connecticut voter toward suggestions for reform in the nominating process is not unrelated to the fact that he can expect a hot contest and a series of real choices at the general election, whatever the processes through which each party has selected its own leadership and candidates.

Connecticut Chapter Acknowledgments

MARY TRACKETT REYNOLDS (Mrs. Lloyd Reynolds), of Hamden, Connecticut, prepared a pre-convention case study report on the Connecticut Republican delegation, with the assistance of DUANE LOCKHARD, an instructor at Connecticut College. Mrs. Reynolds visited the delegation at Chicago and assisted extensively in the revision of the draft chapter. ROLAND YOUNG, Professor of Political Science, Northwestern University, reported on the activities of the delegation at Chicago and reviewed an early draft of the chapter.

BERNHARD O. J. LINNEVOLD, Assistant Professor of Government and International Relations, University of Connecticut, prepared a pre-convention report on the Democratic delegation with the assistance of two students. Members of the departmental staff gave administrative assistance. Professor Linnevold visited the delegation at Chicago, and has assisted in the revision of the draft chapter.

Dr. Lockhard's unpublished doctoral dissertation, *The Role of Party in the Connecticut General Assembly, 1931-51* (Yale University, 1952), was drawn upon substantially for background information in the preparation of the field reports and the eventual chapter.

The initial draft in chapter form was prepared from the field reports and other sources by ROBERT V. L. WRIGHT, JR., and PAUL T. DAVID of the Washington staff.

NEW

Electoral votes, 1952: 45
National convention votes, 1952:
 Democratic, 94
 Republican, 96
Population, 1950: 14,830,192
 Urban, 85%; rural nonfarm, 11%; rural farm, 4%
Population increase, 1940-50: 1,351,050 (10%)
 Urban, 7%; rural nonfarm, 48%; rural farm, 19% decline
Presidential vote, 1948: 1952:
 Democratic, 2,557,642 (42%) 2,687,890 (38%)
 Republican, 2,841,163 (46%) 3,952,815 (55%)
 American Labor, 509,559 (8%) (Wallace) 64,211 (1%)
 Liberal, 222,562 (4%) (Truman) 416,711 (6%)
Gubernatorial vote, 1950:
 Democratic, 1,981,156
 Republican, 2,819,523
 American Labor, 221,966
 Liberal, 265,699
U. S. Representatives vote,
all districts, 1950: 1952:
 Democratic, 2,162,951 2,779,852
 Republican, 2,384,402 3,618,645
U. S. Representatives elected 1950: 1952:
 Democratic, 23 16
 Republican, 22 27
State legislature elected 1952:
 Senate: Democrats, 19; Republicans, 37
 House: Democrats, 52; Republicans, 98
Method of selecting national convention delegates:
 District delegates, by primary election
 Delegates-at-large, by newly-elected 300-member state
  committee

YORK

CHAPTER 8

IN ANY PRESIDENTIAL ELECTION, the greatest prize among the 48 states is New York, with its 45 electoral votes. It has been political axiom that "he who carries New York carries the nation." There have been only two exceptions: Wilson in 1916 and Truman in 1948. At least one of the major party presidential nominees has been a New Yorker in 15 of the 22 elections since the Civil War; in two elections both major candidates were New Yorkers.

The contest for the electoral vote of New York is intense not only because of the size of the state but also because each major party can hope to win. Both parties are strongly organized in the state, both hold many local centers of power and patronage, both are strongly entrenched in the state legislature, each has often carried the state in presidential and gubernatorial elections, and each has a strong and continuing attraction for a substantial portion of the electorate. Organized politics is carried on in New York state with a vigor and complexity akin to that for the United States as a whole. There are few other states in the Union that can claim so long a record of effectively competitive partisan politics.

New York has had a long line of distinguished and powerful governors, including its present governor, twice nominated for the presidency. The state has a billion-dollar budget, and the governor exercises much discretion in the allocation of funds. This discretion results from: 1) the large amounts appropriated on the basis of lump sum rather than detailed estimates, sums that jumped from $23 millions in 1941, when Herbert Lehman was governor, to around $100 millions under Thomas Dewey; 2) the ease with which funds may be transferred from one budget item to another within each agency through the governor's budget division; 3) the relative secrecy with

149

which the budget is formulated; 4) the governor's power to exercise an item veto. These discretionary powers have contributed to the continuing forcefulness of gubernatorial as contrasted with state legislative leadership.

The governor's job patronage, while limited, can be influential. Over 94,000 employees are under the state's civil service commission, including all the state executive departments as well as the personnel of five counties and one city. More than 267,000 other county and city employees are subject to civil service law but not directly under the civil service commission's jurisdiction. The state's 82,000 teachers are "unclassified," and not under state civil service. New York City's 175,000 employees are not included in these figures. In short, less than one per cent of the state jobs are outside civil service. But the governor does appoint 14 of the 18 state executive department heads, and through them exercises large influence upon the policies and functions carried out by civil servants.

New York politics is a complex jig-saw of ethnic, economic, and geographic factors. Recurring waves of foreign settlers affected the politics first of New York City, spreading later to the upstate area. Dutch, English, German, Polish, Italian, and other nationality groups have long been politically important in upstate areas. More recently, Italians have been filtering into the smaller towns and rural areas, as farmers, artisans, and small-business people. Negroes are heavily concentrated in New York City, as are the rapidly increasing numbers of Puerto Ricans who have migrated to the mainland.

Religious as well as ethnic factors have been influential. The early Protestant pattern of the state has been modified with each wave of immigration. While statistics on religious affiliation are at best unreliable, about two-thirds of the population is normally affiliated with one religious organization or another. Reliable figures for Protestant affiliation are not available. In 1950, there were some 4,248,000 Catholics, many of whom have been active participants in state and local politics. There were about 2,206,000 members of the Jewish faith, fully 90 per cent of this number is in New York City. The balance among religious groups has led to the tradition of "balanced" party tickets.

Since 1932, New York Jews have been voting about 75 per cent

Democratic. Negroes have supported the Democrats in about the same ratio. Until recently, an estimated 500,000 Irish Catholic voters were strongly Democratic, although a sizable defection was under way in 1952. The Poles also have been preponderantly Democratic, although there have been indications of bloc movement between the major parties by the Polish vote in Buffalo. The Puerto Rican vote is just beginning to receive attention as a separate factor and seems to be mainly Democratic. Republicans, on the other hand, have been, geographically, rural and suburbanite. Economically, the farm and the propertied groups have been a main source of Republican strength, although party leaders have actively sought the support of the more than 5,000,000 urban workers. The state leadership of the AFL has traditionally leaned toward the Republicans, that of the CIO toward the Democrats.

At election time the five counties of New York City—coterminous with the five "borough" subdivisions of the New York City government and best known as Manhattan (New York County), Brooklyn (Kings County), Queens (County), Bronx (County), and Staten Island (Richmond County)—with more than half the population of the state, usually roll up a net result that is Democratic. Two of them, however, Queens and Staten Island, are usually Republican in national affairs. The populous suburban areas around the metropolis, including Nassau, Suffolk, and Westchester counties, are usually heavily Republican. The same is true for the entire upstate area, with the exceptions of the Democratic strongholds of Albany and Buffalo.

The hard core of the vote in most areas has been mobilized by a number of "machines": for the Democrats, the Tammany machine in Manhattan, the Kelly and Cashmore organizations in Brooklyn, the Flynn group in the Bronx, the O'Connells in Albany; for the Republicans, the Sprague group in Nassau, the former W. Kingsland Macy influence in Suffolk, the Syracuse law-firm hegemony, the Eastman-Kodak and Bausch & Lomb interests in Rochester, the William Hill group in the "southern tier" counties. The character and the influence of these "machines" have varied. More recently, there has been appreciable change generally in the nature of the relationships between ward captains and voters, with the voters displaying greater inde-

pendence in their election day behavior and the "machines" less able
to predict or "guarantee" delivery of the vote.

Voting participation in New York State is generally thought to be
high. In the 1952 presidential voting, for example, only 606,000 of
the state's 7,822,000 registered voters failed to cast ballots; the proportion was even lower in New York City, where only 54,000 among
the city's 3,515,000 registrants did not vote. Comparisons, however,
do not substantiate the impression of high participation, for New York
actually ranks twenty-seventh in percentage of participation by eligible
as distinguished from registered adults in recent elections.

To the despair of managers in the major parties, the state also
has a large number of ballot-splitters and party bolters, complicated
by the existence of influential minor parties. Any group that has
polled at least 50,000 votes for governor in the most recent gubernatorial election is recognized as an established party, entitled to hold
primary elections at public expense, enroll members, make party
rules that are legally binding, and pick delegates, under recognized
legal auspices, to their own county, state, and national conventions.
The two minor parties that normally meet these requirements are
the American Labor and the Liberal parties. The ALP began its
career in 1936, with the sponsorship of some 250 trade-unions, and,
because of Tammany's coolness toward the New Deal, carried the
burden of Roosevelt's first campaign for re-election that year in New
York. In 1944, the right wing of the ALP opposed the admission
of Communists to party councils, bolted, and became the Liberal
party.

These minor parties greatly complicate New York politics because
the state is so competitive and so evenly balanced between the two
major parties. The ALP gave Roosevelt the margin of victory in
New York in 1940 and 1944, and did the same for Governor Lehman
in 1938 and for Mayor LaGuardia in 1937 and 1941. In 1948, when
the ALP supported Wallace's Progressive party candidacy, it pulled
500,000 votes away from Truman, thus enabling Dewey to carry
the state by 60,000. ALP or Liberal endorsements of either Democratic or Republican candidates have been frequent, and often involve
complex negotiations during which the minor party officials virtually
participate in the major party nominating process. More recently,

both Republicans and Democrats have virtually outlawed all deals with the ALP, but Liberal support is welcomed by both and tends to go to the Democrats nationally, to the Republicans state-wide, and is varied or independent in New York City. In 1952, Liberal party officials were present and in touch with the New York delegation at the Democratic national convention. Subsequently, the Liberals endorsed Stevenson for president but refused to support the Democratic state organization's candidate for the Senate. Instead, they ran Dr. George S. Counts as their own senatorial candidate, a virtual guarantee that the Republican incumbent (Ives) would be re-elected.

Fear of "big city" domination is always important in the politics of the state and in the state legislature. Upstate Democrats frequently distrust the Democratic organizations of New York City. The same situation exists among Republicans. This kind of split often is symbolized in the fact that the two most newsworthy political figures in the state are the Governor in upstate Albany and the mayor in downstate New York City. Republican strength in the state legislature is augmented by districting which results in over-representation of the rural areas, normally Republican. With about 55 per cent of the state's population, New York City has only 45 per cent of the members of the state senate and 41 per cent of the lower house. Between 1900 and 1953, the Democrats have been able to control the state senate for only 8 years and the assembly for only 3 years, although Democratic governors have held office for 26 of the 54 years.

PRESIDENTIAL PRIMARY LAW AND PROCEDURE

The New York direct primary law resulted from the efforts of reformers led by Charles Evans Hughes. The intent was to permit the enrolled voters of each party to challenge the decisions of the "bosses" or even to change the bosses. But in a normal primary the number of enrolled voters who participate may be as few as 10 per cent. In the major parties, the number goes as high as 25 per cent only when there is a real contest. Until recently, the low rate of voter participation made it easy for party organizations in the state to defeat the purpose of the primary system by simply increasing the size of their county committees, which they could do without restriction. In many districts, an insurgent slate would have to muster hundreds of committee candidates to oppose those designated by the regular organizations. County committees in most urban areas formerly had a membership of 200 to 400, numbers expected to drop sharply as a result of the new 1953 law limiting committee members to four per election district. The Manhattan Democratic Committee, as an extreme case, recently had a membership of 11,995, which, under the new law, should be reduced to less than 4,000.

Acquiring party membership in New York is a simple but definite procedure. As voters go to the registration polls each year (except in places of less than 5,000 population and in all unincorporated areas, which have annual non-personal registration, and therefore enroll on election day), they are handed enrollment slips upon which they may check one or the four legal parties. This gives the voter the right to vote in the primary of the party of his choice, and no other, the following year.

At the spring primaries of presidential years only, the enrolled voters of the four established parties may participate in choosing: (a) the delegates to party state and judicial district conventions; (b) a portion of the election district members of their party county committees and the assembly district members of their state committees; and (c) the congressional district delegates to the party national conventions. Rarely does the voter find more than one candidate named for each of these positions, for rarely is the organization's slate challenged.

To run for district delegate to a national political convention in 1952, designating petitions were required to be circulated, signed, and filed not earlier than the sixth Tuesday (in 1952, March 11) and not later than the fifth Tuesday (March 18) before the primary (April 22). Signatures set down earlier than eleven weeks before the primary (February 5, 1952) were not valid and could not be counted. This allowed only six weeks (February 5 to March 18) to secure petition signatures and only five weeks (March 18 to April 22) to conduct a pre-primary campaign where there was a contest. These timing conditions made the process easy only for factions or organizations that were well-established in the community.

The number of signatures necessary for congressional district delegates in New York differed from the requirement elsewhere in the state. All petitions required not less than 5 per cent of the currently enrolled voters in the congressional district who also were enrolled in the party at the preceding enrollment, except that the number of signatures need not exceed 750 in New York City but had an upper limit of 500 in congressional districts elsewhere in the state. The election law is elaborate about the physical details of the preparation of designating petitions; a sworn witness is required for every signature. Few but the party regulars can, in the short time allowed, mobilize the money, effort, and willing signers. The complexities tend to make petitions easy to challenge; those of insurgents are rarely validated. New York election law makes no physical provision on the ballot for the pledging of delegate candidates; there is no prohibition against statements of preference during the primary campaign, but they are rarely made.

THE REPUBLICAN DELEGATION

Based primarily on reports by
PHILLIPS BRADLEY

The New York Republican party suffered lean years during the Al Smith-Franklin D. Roosevelt-Herbert Lehman decades from 1923 to 1943, despite the fact that Republicans were in power in the national administration during the first half of the period. District Attorney Thomas E. Dewey ran for governor for the first time in 1938. Although beaten by Herbert Lehman, Dewey's vote-getting appeal stimulated an unusual Republican turnout in the rural areas. He ran again and was elected in 1942, 1946, and 1950. According to most observers, Governor Dewey has used state patronage and the other facilities available to a governor with rare skill in building a powerful and efficient party organization, from which most of his opponents have been eliminated.

Dewey was the Republican presidential standard-bearer in 1944 and 1948, at which time he and his aides built lasting relationships with party leaders all over the United States. He has been one of the party's most articulate spokesmen as well as one of its most important office-holders. When, on October 15, 1950, he proposed General Eisenhower for the 1952 presidential nomination, it was not certain whether this was a pro-Eisenhower or a pro-Dewey move. This was clarified on June 27, 1951, when Republican State Chairman William L. Pfeiffer virtually pledged the still-to-be-elected New York delegation to Eisenhower. A month later, Dewey himself declared that he would vigorously oppose any moves to have himself become a candidate again.

After Dewey's position became clear, General Eisenhower's candidacy began to take on serious proportions in an organized way. In September 1951, Dewey conferred in Washington with Senators James Duff, Frank Carlson, Irving Ives, and Leverett Saltonstall on a draft-Eisenhower strategy. He also predicted publicly that the General would win and accept the nomination. At the governors' conference at Gatlinburg, Tennessee, on September 30, 1951, Dewey used his own staff to lay the groundwork for a strong interstate pre-convention organization for Eisenhower. At this time, too, Governors Sherman Adams (New Hampshire), Val Peterson (Nebraska), Edward Arn (Kansas), and Walter Kohler (Wisconsin) declared themselves in favor of the General.

THE SELECTION PROCESS IN 1952

Despite Governor Dewey's aim to send a solid Eisenhower delegation to Chicago, there was substantial support among New York Republicans for Senator Taft's candidacy, particularly among certain of the normally Republican business and industrial groups and among "club-house" Republicans. The Taft candidacy also provided a useful and perfectly respectable vehicle for expressing intra-organization discontent with the Dewey leadership, as occurred in Orange County. The national Taft organization made little effort to conduct a pre-primary campaign in New York; local sentiment for Taft was sufficient, however, in some parts of the state to present a problem to the Dewey organization.

The census of 1950 had reduced New York's congressional representation from 45 to 43. At the national committee meeting in San Francisco on January 18, the committee on convention call discussed the meaning of this change with respect to the size of the New York delegation at the national convention. New York Committeeman J. Russel Sprague led a fight to retain his state's allotment at 100 delegates (90 district delegates plus 4 regular delegates-at-large plus 6 bonus delegates-at-large). Harrison Spangler, however, argued that that congressional reapportionment must be used as the basis for delegate apportionment—which would give only 86 district delegates to New York—and his arguments prevailed. The committee on convention call agreed, however, that New York, although it had already been redistricted, could elect district delegates if it wished from the old districts—45 districts, hence 90 district delegates—and choose 6 instead of 10 delegates-at-large.

On January 23, New York's secretary of state asked the state's attorney general for a ruling as to whether the old or the new congressional district lines should be used for the primary on April 22. A few days later the attorney general, in keeping with precedent, ruled in favor of the old district lines. A similar ruling was handed down in 1943, after the 1942 redistricting.

State committee appointment of delegates-at-large—The six delegates-at-large were formally chosen on May 7 by the 300 new members of the Republican state committee elected at the April 22 primary. Two months earlier, however, the six names were made known to the public by the 20-member Republican state executive committee, a more select body consisting of two members from each of the ten judicial districts. In accordance with the usual practice in New York, the six included, practically *ex officio*, the ranking figures in the state organization: Governor Dewey, Senator Ives, National Committeeman Sprague, National Committeewoman Jessica Weis (Mrs. Charles W., Jr.), State Chairman Pfeiffer, and State Vice-chairman Jane Todd.

The position of alternate-at-large permitted inclusion of other major state Republican leaders; for example, Westchester's "boss" William Bleakley; New York County Chairman Thomas J. Curran; the president of the New York State Young Republicans, F. Clifton White; and a long-standing leader of the Women's Republican Clubs, Mrs. Mildred Taylor.

District primaries—In most instances, the names appearing on the primary ballot as candidates for district delegate and alternate were names selected after consultations among county chairmen, county executive committees, and other close associates of the county leaders.

Nowhere were formal nominating meetings conducted; there was not even one instance of a full county committee meeting. Some long-entrenched county chairmen were in a position to practice independence even in dealing with their executive committees. In many rural districts made up of two or more counties, long-standing custom had created a system of rotation of the honor from one county to another; the system is administered by the county chairmen concerned. In upstate metropolitan areas, much attention was also given to two other factors: "recognition" of the suburban or rural areas in otherwise urban districts, and representation of the various ethnic groups.

On February 5, party workers began circulating designating petitions. Open contests developed in only 5 of the state's 45 old congressional districts; in only one district did an avowed pro-Taft delegate win in the April 22 primary. Once the "organization" slates had been composed, state and county leaders coordinated much of their pro-organization primary campaigning through the 300-member state committee. Very often, members of the state committee and candidates for national convention delegates were the same persons; in 9 congressional districts, both persons elected as delegates were also state committeemen; in 13 other districts, one of the two delegates was a state committeeman. The regular organization's primary campaigning was substantially aided by the Federation of Women's Republican Clubs, with 135 locals in 38 counties, and by 140 Young Republican Clubs. Neither of these groups is permitted to endorse candidates at primary elections; however, members of both were active in the 1952 primary, particularly in the contested districts. In most districts, the turnout of primary voters was relatively low. On the other hand, public interest in the contested districts was great, and the turnout in these instances was relatively high.

Eisenhower delegates were chosen without contest in most districts. In the 1st and 2d (Suffolk and Nassau), the leader was National Committeeman Sprague, who had already been announced as a delegate-at-large. Delegates and alternates were apportioned between the two counties, and selections were considered a reward for faithful party service. In the nine congressional districts of Brooklyn, County Chairman John Crews allocated positions primarily among those "regulars" who were members of the state committee. In the four districts of the Bronx, where County Chairman John Knewitz has held sway for about 36 years, every delegate and alternate, with one exception, was a member of the state committee.

In the rural upstate districts, usually made up of from four to six counties, county chairmen and their deputies generally held a meeting to designate delegates according to one or another customary criterion: rotation among counties; some established system for distributing delegates and alternates among all the counties; long party service; one delegate and one alternate from among party workers, the others from among those holding public office; in the 30th district, one delegate and one alternate from each side of the Hudson River. One of the basic criteria of selection everywhere was financial ability to meet the cost of attending the national convention.

Three of the five contests, involving 6 delegates and 6 alternates, took place in Erie and Niagara Counties. These two counties contain the 42d, 43d, and 44th congressional districts. The 42d district covers Niagara County and the northern part of Erie. The 43d and the 44th districts are wholly within Erie County, and mainly in the city of Buffalo.

Erie County Chairman Harry J. Forhead and his county committee refused to accept the state committee's mandate to select a pro-Eisenhower slate. Observers agreed that this refusal resulted more from local-state enmities than from the Taft-Eisenhower struggle, although Forhead declared himself personally for Taft. The slate he and his associates put forward claimed to be the only truly "uninstructed" one, hence the only one able to go to the national convention "with an open mind." It consisted of two delegates and two alternates each for the 43d and 44th districts in Erie, and one delegate candidate and one alternate candidate for the 42d, the district that included Niagara County. Ordinarily, the other 42d district delegate and alternate are selected by the Niagara County committee from its section of the district. In 1952, however, the pro-Eisenhower Niagara County committee not only chose its one delegate and one alternate but also put up Eisenhower candidates to run against the Erie County selections for the remainder of the district. These aggressive pro-Eisenhower tactics were carried further into Erie County itself, where 8 pro-Eisenhower candidates were entered for 43d and 44th district delegates and alternates. The slate in Erie was supported by the Eisenhower-for-President organization, set up at the beginning of 1952 and headed by one of the most prominent younger businessmen of Buffalo, and by the Buffalo *Evening News.* All this had the unofficial approval of the state committee. Many observers believed that the national Eisenhower headquarters and the state committee contributed to the local group; there were substantial expenditures for headquarters, radio, and mailings.

The 10 pro-Taft, or "uninstructed," candidates were representative of the country towns as well as the central cities—Buffalo and Niagara Falls—and were drawn from the major ethnic and religious groups. The Erie County chairman and his associates mainly relied upon the regular organization to mobilize neighborhood support.

The Eisenhower candidates won in the three districts by about three to one. Despite this defeat of all his candidates for the national convention delegation, Erie County Chairman Forhead remained in power and was re-elected on April 30 by the post-primary organizing meeting of the county committee. The Eisenhower organization started too late to attempt to petition and campaign for its own slate of county committeemen.

The fourth contest was in the 29th congressional district: Delaware, Rockland, Orange, and Sullivan counties. In this instance, the state organization controlled the county committees, and the challenge came from the pro-Taft side. The area has been a Republican stronghold for generations. The pro-Eisenhower county leaders put forward an organization slate: the chairmen of Delaware and Orange counties as candidates for delegates; the chairmen of Rockland and Sullivan counties as candidates for alternates. Former Congressman Hamilton Fish then declared himself a candidate in opposition, pledging himself to support Taft, or, in case of a deadlock, MacArthur. His pro-Taft colleagues included the Rockland County Clerk and a Sullivan County dentist long active in Republican politics.

During the heated campaign that ensued, the Dusenberry-Bush organization slate found it necessary to deny that they were for Eisenhower and against Taft. They wished to remain uncommitted, they explained, so that they could be free at Chicago to "pick a winner."

Hamilton Fish charged these organization candidates with disenfranchising the voters by denying them a real choice. Citizens-for-Eisenhower, Fighters-for-MacArthur, and Taft-for-President organizations were active in all four counties. Polls of the county committeemen were taken by both sides. Fish obtained replies from one-third of the 731 committeemen: Taft, 162; Eisenhower, 25; MacArthur, 14; and Stassen, 1. Charles Dusenberry and E. Ogden Bush, the "regular" candidates, polled only 453 committeemen because the Rockland county chairman was reluctant to have his committee polled after he himself had declared for Eisenhower. The Dusenberry-Bush results: Taft, 169; Eisenhower, 93; MacArthur, 14; Warren, 2; no preference, 5; for an uninstructed delegation, 51. Dusenberry and Bush had promised to be "guided" by the outcome of their poll. After its results were made public, they declared only that they would present the figures to the rest of the New York delegation.

The Fish-Coyle ticket carried Orange County by slim pluralities, but was defeated in each of the other three counties. The county breakdown revealed these results:

	Orange	Rockland	Sullivan	Delaware	District Total
Pro-Eisenhower:					
Dusenberry	6,662	2,472	1.448	4,000	14,582
Bush	5,727	2,338	1,413	4,197	13,675
Pro-Taft:					
Fish	8,250	1,922	710	1,189	12,071
Coyle	6,786	2,106	629	1,035	10,765

The size of the total vote in this contest seemed large because the usual turnout was so small. In 1948, when there had been no contest, the total vote in the Republican 29th district primary had been 3,300. After the Delaware County vote in 1952 was announced, ex-Congressman Fish reportedly commented that "the organization" must have "voted the cows," although this county has normally been anti-Fish.

In the fifth contest, the Taft forces concentrated their local New York City efforts in the 16th district, made up of heavily Republican Staten Island and a strip on heavily Democratic lower west-side Manhattan. The Eisenhower sentiment was mobilized behind Congressman and Staten Island Chairman Ellsworth Buck. The Taft support consisted of two elements: (1) the anti-Dewey followers of the former chairman, who had resigned under pressure in 1951; and (2) the middle-and-upper-income groups in the Manhattan section of the district. Congressman Buck (pro-Eisenhower) won his race for delegate by the slender margin of 25 votes. One of the two Taft candidates, Edward J. McCormick, was elected; he received 24 votes more than Buck, and 49 more than the higher of the two defeated candidates. McCormick was the one avowed Taft delegate elected to the New York delegation. The 1950 Republican vote for Congress in this district had been 37,363. Despite the interest in the 1952 delegate primary contest, the turnout in the district was apparently under 7,000.

There were no open contests elsewhere, but this did not mean full accord. The 8-vote delegation from Queens (3d, 4th, 5th, and 6th congressional districts), headed by Frank Kenna, remained in doubt as to its intentions until the national convention met. Thomas Curran's Manhattan delegation (17th, 18th, 19th, 20th, 21st, and 22d districts) started by being almost solidly for Eisenhower, but two Negro delegates from Harlem's 22d district later weakened for a time in their loyalty to the General.

On June 24, an Associated Press poll reported the New York delegation split 79 for Eisenhower, 7 for Taft, and 10 undecided. Taft managers claimed 20 delegates.

COMPOSITION OF THE DELEGATION

Governor Dewey has been a leader of his party in New York during four Republican national conventions, three while governor. In 1952, Governor Dewey for the first time himself headed the list of delegates-at-large. No Republican of top rank in the state party was omitted from the 1952 delegation, with the exception of former Senator John Foster Dulles. There is no adequate explanation of why Dulles was neither a delegate nor an alternate, but this did not prevent him from acting as a principal Eisenhower adviser and from playing a major role in drafting the platform at the national convention; Dulles clearly was not out of favor with Dewey. The list of eminent party figures who were delegates included the Republican United States senator, both members of the party national committee, and the state chairman and vice-chairman.

The incidence of party and public officeholding among the members of the delegation was extremely high. There were 31 state committee members and 24 county chairmen or co-chairmen among the 90 district delegates. A sample of 34 district delegates revealed that 5 were state party officials, 14 county party officers, and 7 leaders at the local level. This same sample showed that the delegation included 6 officials of the state government, 3 county government officials, and 7 local public officers. In the entire delegation, only one delegate was a sitting member of Congress, while two other congressmen were alternates. Two secretaries to congressmen were official members of the delegation. Although not herself a member of the delegation, Congresswoman Katharine St. George of the 29th district was active and influential at the convention.

Six of the 16 public officials in the sample of 34 delegates also pursued private occupations. Among the private occupations in the sample were 11 lawyers, a banker, a manufacturer, a merchant, an automobile dealer, the owner of a laundry enterprise, a real estate agent, and a farmer. One person was retired. Of the 192 delegates and alternates, 33 were women.

All members of the delegation were expected to pay their own expenses for attendance at the national convention, estimated at $300 to $500. The few who were involved in contests probably had additional campaign expenditures. Expenses involved in the circulation and filing of designating petitions were usually met by the regular organization.

Most of the delegates had been active in politics for 15 to 30 years. This experience extended to attendance at national conventions; 77 of the 192 delegates and alternates in 1952 had been members of the 1948 delegation.

ACTIVITIES AND VOTING RECORD

No formal organizing meeting of the delegation was held before it departed for Chicago. The meeting of the state committee on May 7 provided a convenient opportunity for preparatory consultations, as did a dinner early in June, when Governor Dewey invited the other 95 delegates to meet with General Eisenhower in New York. Dewey was reported to have picked up the dinner check ($1,300), but delegates paid for their own transportation.

Dewey arrived in Chicago from Houston, Texas, on July 2, five days before the convention opened. He had been attending the governors' conference there, and apparently used the occasion for far-reaching Eisenhower strategy consultations with the other 22 Republican governors who were present. On July 1, he, Governor Sherman Adams (New Hampshire), and Governor Douglas McKay (Oregon) sent strongly worded telegrams to the Republican national committee urging that the Eisenhower delegates from Texas be seated. On July 3, the manifesto of the 23 Republican governors, asking that contested delegates not be permitted to vote on the seating of other contested delegates, was made public.

A special train carried 146 of the members and friends of the New York delegation. The first delegation caucus took place soon after their arrival at Chicago. It was at this meeting that the delegation officers were formally chosen, although their identity was probably known as long before as February. They included: Governor Dewey as chairman; Speaker of the Assembly Oswald Heck on the credentials committee; Miss Jane Todd and Senator Ives on the resolutions committee; and Stanley Bauer on rules. The public relations director of the state committee rendered some services to the delegation. The state committee met the expenses for the delegation headquarters.

The delegation was basically well organized but showed some signs of disunity after reaching Chicago. The two Harlem delegates made their surprise switch to Taft the day after arrival. Meanwhile, Dewey, as one of the principal Eisenhower convention strategists, was constantly participating in conferences. He called a Sunday, July 6, meeting of his own delegation to prepare for the first test vote of the convention—on the proposal to bar contested delegates from voting on any contest—and to remind the fence-sitters that he would be "Governor for the next two and one-half years, and I mean that." Under this kind of pressure, the few delegates who were potential dissidents began to fall into line. Their vote was 95-to-1 on the roll call vote on Monday on the Brown amendment to the Langlie proposal. The two Harlem delegates read themselves back under the Eisenhower banner in Governor Dewey's presence on Tuesday morning. Just before the afternoon caucus on Wednesday, Frank Kenna announced that the 8 votes of the Queens delegation would be with Eisenhower on the Georgia contest vote. Kenna had told the Taft managers that unless they could rally 17 votes in New York, he would not hold the Queens delegation. This condition was not met.

This left 5 delegates who were still willing on Wednesday to vote with Taft on the Georgia issue. At the caucus that afternoon, Dewey declared that the issue was "who were honest and who were the vote-stealers." Dewey told the caucus that, having himself been called "a thief," his personal integrity was involved in the Georgia seating issue. When the vote was taken in the caucus, 91 supported Dewey, and 5 abstained from voting. Of the 5, Claire Bateman, Livingston County chairman, voted with Dewey on the convention floor. This left only 4 pro-Taft votes on the Georgia roll call: the one pro-Taft delegate from the 16th district (Staten Island); the vice-president of Bausch & Lomb Optical Company (Rochester) who voted "his conscience"; and two dissidents (not the two from Harlem) in the Manhattan delegation, one of whom has since moved to California.

On the nominating ballot, the delegation vote was 92 for Eisenhower to 4 for Taft as initially recorded. One of the Taft delegates— the one from Staten Island—still refused to switch after the outcome was clear.

Dewey and members of the Dewey team were of major importance in the behind-the-scenes operations of the Eisenhower organization at Chicago; but if the New York delegation was conspicuous at the convention, it was only because of its size and known power. The only occasion on which a member of the delegation spoke from the rostrum at the convention hall was when a Manhattan delegate seconded Taft's nomination. No important official of the convention or chairman of any of its committees was a New Yorker. The New York representatives on the rules, credentials, and resolutions committees operated in a competent manner, but there was no special public indication of their activities other than some limited recognition of the service of Senator Ives in drafting the platform.

AFTERMATH IN THE STATE

The 1952 vote for Eisenhower was one of the largest pluralities in the state's history, comparable only to the pluralities for Harding in

1924 and for Roosevelt in 1936. The state Democrats conceded defeat in the unprecedently short time of two hours after the polls closed. All 57 of the upstate counties went for Eisenhower, while New York City remained Democratic by much less than the usual plurality. The only upstate city to remain in the Democratic column was Albany; Albany County went Republican. Governor Dewey's high place in the Eisenhower councils was confirmed by the appointment of Dewey's long-time political associate and campaign manager, Herbert Brownell, to be Attorney General and a chief patronage adviser to the new president.

THE DEMOCRATIC DELEGATION

Based primarily on reports by
Mrs. Louise Burr Gerrard and Harold Stein

Unity is a rarity in the Democratic delegations from New York. In 1932, the Tammany and Brooklyn organizations led the fight for Al Smith and held 63 of New York's convention votes behind him. State Chairman Farley and the late Bronx "boss" Flynn could muster only 31 votes for Franklin D. Roosevelt. In 1936, there was little choice but to join in endorsing the New Deal acclamation. By 1940, however, all too much federal patronage had been given to Fiorello LaGuardia, the third term had become an issue, and Jim Farley's hat was in the ring. At the national convention, New York gave 64½ votes to Roosevelt, 25 to Farley, and 1 to Hull. In 1944, the real fight was over the vice-presidential nomination. Truman polled 69½ votes in the delegation, Wallace 23, and Barkley ½. The year 1948 found Mayor O'Dwyer booming Eisenhower and Justice Douglas, Dan O'Connell of Albany all-out for President Truman, and Ed Flynn assuming that the nomination could not be denied an incumbent president. Queens leader James Roe wanted Eisenhower. When the General declined, Roe was able to have 15 votes cast for himself on the first ballot, but switched these to Truman when the trend became clear.

The party's organization in the five boroughs of New York City, which contain the great bulk of the Democratic vote in the state, has seldom been united in recent years. Tammany has become a toothless cat. There also has been an outburst of competition in recent years among ethnic groups for leadership posts in the party, the Italians contesting the near-monopoly of the Irish.

The Smith-Roosevelt-Lehman tradition of strong state leadership ended with the rupture between Roosevelt and Farley in 1940 and Dewey's election as governor in 1942. Thereafter the most powerful Democratic leader in the state was the late National Committeeman Ed Flynn, who was a staunch Roosevelt supporter and among the first to back Truman in 1944. Paul Fitzpatrick, until his resignation in November 1952 successor to Farley as state chairman, was known as a "Flynn man." Dan O'Connell of Albany has set himself up as a perpetual dissenter, a permanent upstate challenger of the hegemony of the downstaters. O'Connell frequently boycotts state committee meetings, or sometimes shows up to propose that the chairman be removed. He has made common cause with occasional insurgents or dissidents among the New York City organizations. Although he resigned as state chairman in 1944, James Farley remains a well-known and controversial figure in state politics. In the words of one project reporter observing Farley's behavior on the floor of the 1952 convention: "Anyone who watched him . . . must have been impressed by his vigor and by his ability to wrangle with chiefs-of-delegations, successfully or not, as a big shot, not a has-been."

THE SELECTION PROCESS IN 1952

Organization Democrats in New York were for Truman's renomination in 1952 up to the time of the President's withdrawal from the race on March 29. At a press conference on March 30, State Chairman Fitzpatrick announced four "favorite son" possibilities: Senator Herbert Lehman, Mutual Security Administrator Averell Harriman, former National Committee Chairman James Farley, and Congressman Franklin D. Roosevelt, Jr. Fitzpatrick gave this as the order of preference. Lehman's age and religious affiliation, however, made his name little more than honorary mention. Harriman, whose public personality had been considered too undramatic, had up to this time been New York's preference for vice-president. Farley was on the list, according to Fitzpatrick, "to keep peace in the family." Mention of F.D.R., Jr., was intended to prime him for the possibility of a nomination for the Senate in the fall of 1952 or for governor in 1954.

New York Democrats considered the civil rights issue *the* most important one from the point of view of local considerations. They were therefore unable to lend support to any of the avowed national candidates: Russell, Kefauver, or Kerr. Kefauver's position on civil rights improved from the New York standpoint during his pre-convention campaign, but much distrust lingered. This distrust was particularly deep-rooted since it was felt that his Senate crime committee hearings had dealt unfairly with the party organization. These hearings also had produced Rudolph Halley, chief counsel of the committee, who, although a registered Democrat, ran on and was elected on the Liberal ticket for presidency of the New York city council. Many New York Democrats viewed the Kefauver candidacy as part of a Halley "build-up" for the mayoralty. As for the Stevenson candidacy, it could hardly be expected that so influential a delegation as New York's—accustomed to putting forward its own candidates—would go out on a limb in advance for an uncertain possibility from another state.

The discussion of national candidates for the Democratic nomination bore little relation to the selection of delegates to the national convention in 1952. Whatever early sentiment for Kefauver may have existed in the state did not result in timely action to circulate petitions and put Kefauver delegates on the ballot in the districts, mainly rural, where contests might have been promising. The process was already far advanced before the situation as to other national candidates had even begun to clarify; nominating petitions were put in circulation on February 5 and were required to be filed by March 18; the slates for district delegate had been frozen even before the Truman withdrawal. But since the regulars on the ticket who were running for delegate were not officially pledged to Truman, the process was not disrupted in New York as it was in New Hampshire and California.

The number of New York delegates to be selected in 1952 was not the same for the two major parties, mainly because of differences in the national rules. The Democratic national committee had provided that states losing seats in Congress under the census of 1950 would not be penalized at the 1952 national convention. New York therefore retained 90 district delegateships and the usual 8 half-vote posts for delegates-at-large. What it did lose was its four-vote bonus of earlier years, since New York had not gone Democratic in 1948.

State committee appointment of delegates-at-large—Usually, the selection of delegates-at-large and alternates begins when the state chairman asks the leaders in various parts of the state to submit suggestions. In the past, distinguished public and party officials have been put on the at-large slate almost automatically. The new state committee of 300 members, elected at the April 22 primary, met on May 1, re-elected State Chairman Fitzpatrick and other officers, and chose the following half-vote delegates-at-large: Senator Lehman; Averell Harriman, whom 45 of the 62 Democratic county chairmen had named as their "favorite son" at a meeting held just prior to the primaries; New York's Mayor Vincent Impellitteri; Paul Fitzpatrick; National Committeewoman Mrs. William Good; James A. Farley; Congressman Adam Clayton Powell, who, as the first Negro delegate-at-large ever chosen in New York, symbolized the state committee's emphasis on the civil rights issue; and former Senator James Mead, currently a member of the Federal Trade Commission.

The alternates-at-large included the woman vice-chairman of the state committee (who had been dropped as a delegate so as to make room for Farley), a former controller of Kings County, the secretary of the state committee, and others.

District primaries—Unlike the Republican primary in New York, the Democratic primary on the same date, April 22, aroused little interest. In both parties there was some rank-and-file resentment over the lack of opportunity to state a presidential preference. In a few areas, contests for state committee posts elicited some interest in the Democratic party.

Contests over the position of national convention delegate developed in 7 congressional districts, involving four candidates or more in six of the districts. The contests in the 12th and 13th districts of Brooklyn were part of a continuing fight among local factions and were not related to national issues. The contests in the 23d and 25th districts of the Bronx also had mainly local overtones. The Flynn organization was challenged by insurgents who announced for Kefauver but concentrated their attacks upon Flynn. There were contests in the 31st (Schenectady) and 40th (Rochester) districts upstate, and three candidates for the two posts in the 42d district (Niagara and part of Erie county). "Organization" candidates won in all cases. The only delegate-candidate who firmly committed himself to a national candidate not to the liking of New York's Democratic "regulars" was Sharon J. Mauhs of the normally Republican 30th district, a Schoharie County assemblyman in the state legislature. Mauhs was vigorously for Kefauver to the very end, and was unopposed in the primary.

Nominees for delegate were chosen throughout the state by the key party leaders with little discussion among the membership. In a few areas there were attempts to discuss the slate with the various clubs and social groups normally affiliated with the party so that the faithful would have a sense of participation in the choice. Representation of the dominant ethnic groups was sometimes a factor. In one district, the individual chosen had no record of activity in the Democratic party, but "an Italian was needed" and he had offered to pay his own expenses to Chicago. In a letter sent out before the selections were made, the state committee requested that women be given much more than the usual "token" representation; but only 20 women were among the 196 delegates and alternates. Since the expense factor is high, delegates were often chosen for their ability and willingness to pay their own way; at least $300, according to Democratic estimates.

Where a congressional district extends over more than one county, the practice has been—as with the Republicans—to allocate the posts according to residence, rotating delegates and alternates among the counties. The principal party officers—county chairmen, state committeemen—or elected public officials usually decide to attend the convention. Where vacancies occur, the honor is distributed among active party workers, contributors, and other friends of the party. Sometimes custom has been quite specific. Thus, in the 32d district, the mayor of Albany and one of the party leaders from Troy are invariably included.

COMPOSITION OF THE DELEGATION

The delegates-at-large included most of the party leadership group in the state, as previously noted. Traditionally, New York's Democratic delegates-at-large are for all practical purposes an honorary and *ex officio* collection of top party and public officeholders, of whom some are currently in power, some powerful in a previous day. The principal absentee was Ed Flynn, national committeeman, who was at his Putnam County home convalescing from a prolonged illness. Neither Paul Fitzpatrick, the state chairman, nor anyone else on the delegation seemed able to replace Flynn, whose experience and wisdom were sorely missed, according to some of the leading delegates.

The Democratic delegation as a whole consisted chiefly of party professionals, that is, state and county party leaders and past or present public officials. The project reporter's sampling of the district delegations (18 delegates and 14 alternates) revealed 18 county or city chairmen, a mayor, two election commissioners, and an assemblyman. The delegation included 8 incumbent members of Congress. Because of the bruises it received during the Kefauver crime hearings, however, Tammany omitted all district leaders from its Manhattan delegation, selecting instead a "blue ribbon" group including a congressman, the county district attorney, a publisher of an Italian language paper, two bankers, and several businessmen.

It was a middle-aged group. A project reporter observed that "the dominant accent-tone is that of the New York City high schools . . . with only a few accents . . . reflecting Harvard and other alien influences." There was a high percentage of attorneys and real estate people. Five women were delegates; 15 were alternates.

The ethnic composition of the delegation was striking. From a superficial examination of the names of the delegates, it appears that probably one-fourth of the 98 were of Irish descent. The list shows only about a dozen Italian names and perhaps fifteen Jews, mostly from Brooklyn, the Bronx, and Manhattan; and only a handful of Negro delegates and alternates. There were only about thirty white Protestants and German or Slavic Catholics, combined. The delegation distribution reflected in large part a historical survival in Democratic politics that is gradually changing.

Most delegates paid their own transportation and maintenance, and a few were chosen because they could help pay part of the general expenses besides. In the case of the upstate 29th district, however, the county organizations were said to have covered the delegates' expenses.

The most frequent figures given as "years of political activity" were 20 and 25. Most of the delegates and alternates had attended one or two previous national conventions; seventy attended the 1948 convention in Philadelphia.

ACTIVITIES AND VOTING RECORD

In April, 45 of the state's 62 Democratic county chairmen had come out for Harriman, and most of the delegation was thereby committed. But Dan O'Connell's two Albany delegates almost automatically took exception to whatever preference was indicated by the majority in the state organization, and preferred Oscar Ewing. They were joined by a third delegate who supported Ewing, John English of Schenectady. Another early dissident was State Assemblyman Sharon Mauhs. On May 6, Mauhs voiced his protest in strong terms and became the one avowed Kefauver delegate in the state. At about this time, Senator Kefauver set up headquarters in New York City. Previously, he had been reluctant to take on the New York organization in an open fight, but he now adopted an aggressive strategy. On the whole, his supporters were not from among the "regulars," but from among such groups as Americans for Democratic Action (ADA), the Liberal party, and Democrats not yet absorbed into the state party's in-group. Ambitious "grass roots" work was undertaken by the Kefauver adherents. Pro-Harriman activity, on the other hand, was at a minimum, since he already had the endorsement of the state leadership. State Chairman Fitzpatrick did much negotiating outside the state in behalf of the Harriman candidacy, and state committee officers accompanied Harriman on some of his trips over the state. The state committee headquarters, however, took the position of a service agency for all presidential candidates, lending its facilities impartially to all for the distribution of campaign literature.

Over 1,000 persons accompanied the New York delegation to Chicago—delegates, alternates, wives, staff, and so forth. The delegation held three formal caucuses. The first was on Monday morning, the day the convention convened, and disposed of such formalities as electing delegation officers. The group also listened to a talk by Harriman. The delegation officers were chosen by the state chairman and ratified at this first delegation caucus. Senator Lehman was delegation chairman, worked hard with the platform committee, and was active on the convention floor. Chemung County Chairman Richard Heller was vice-chairman. Ed Flynn and Mrs. Good were re-elected to the national committee. The representatives on the resolutions committee were Congressman Emanuel Celler and the state vice-chairman, Miss Angela Parisi. The 1950 gubernatorial candidate, William Lynch, was put on the rules committee. Nassau County chairman Rene Carreau went on the credentials committee. The latter remarked that he had not been consulted in advance about his selection and that the probable reason for his appointment was that he was "available and willing." The second caucus on Monday afternoon continued with formal voting on delegation organizing matters. Franklin D. Roosevelt, Jr., gave an explanation of the strategy of the "loyalty pledge" advocates, and the delegation gave this strategy its formal support.

Of special interest was the behavior of the eight New York Congressmen and the United States senator in the delegation, particularly in connection with the "loyalty pledge" fight. Senator Lehman early expressed doubt about the principles inherent in the initial stringent pledge and worked effectively behind the scenes to have it softened. Meanwhile, some southern leaders, eager to reach a compromise, worked hard to persuade the New York congressmen to support proposals for watering down the pledge or dropping it entirely. Some of the New York delegation leaders were somewhat astonished and not entirely pleased at the evident organizational bonds between the New York and other congressmen. The fact that Congress creates a community, with its own system of favors, obligations, and friendships, seems to have come as a shock to them, and they looked upon the behavior of the New York congressmen as verging on disloyalty to the delegation and to the state party organization.

In keeping with its original support of the "loyalty pledge" advocates, but mostly as a tactical move in behalf of the Harriman candidacy, New York cast its initial vote 90-4 in opposition to the seating of Virginia. Support for seating Virginia came from Farley and "his friends," reportedly including Roy Bush and Anna May Rush of the 40th district, Clifford Ennis of the 41st, Mayor Corning of Albany and Fred Casey of the 32d. After Illinois switched to favor seating Virginia, three New York votes also switched, putting an 87-7 vote on the record. The leaders haggled over the vote, but Senator Lehman, exercising the traditional power of New York delegation chairmen, made the final determination of the vote for the record.

This traditional power to assign delegation votes is worth special comment since it seems to be a practice that is possibly unique to New York Democrats. New York has the largest delegation in the national convention, and the formal polling of some 90 district delegates and 8 delegates-at-large is enough to compel an appreciable delay, usually half an hour, in the convention's floor proceedings. This is a prospect frowned upon by state as well as national leaders, except when the leaders have some reason of their own for wishing a delay. It has therefore become customary for delegation chairmen to consult with conflicting groups in the New York delegation and to estimate the vote without a poll. Occasionally, a chairman will give a stubborn minority an "extra" vote or two to avoid a poll.

After the Virginia vote, Senator Douglas moved to adjourn. This was interpreted as a dilatory maneuver favoring the Kefauver candidacy, and won only 5 New York votes. The 89 other New York votes were against the motion, again largely as a pro-Harriman maneuver.

It was not until the Wednesday caucus that the delegation was formally polled on presidential candidates. The caucus vote was: Harriman, 83½ (including Roe's group from Queens, whose inclinations had been uncertain until then); Kefauver, 1 (Assemblyman Mauhs); Stevenson, 3½ (Farley, Carlebach, Pike, Herman Baruch's alternate, and Sharlette); absent, 3 (2 from Albany); not voting, 3 (all from Buffalo). This was the last formal caucus. All other consultations, including the ones leading to the switch to Stevenson, took place among the leaders, and frequently occurred on the floor of the convention.

Although the rank-and-file delegates seemed willing to follow their district and state leaders, at no time was there complete unity of intent or direction among the New York leaders themselves. O'Connell, as usual, boycotted all the delegation caucuses. Roe of Queens was an uncertain quantity, apparently predisposed to Stevenson but voting for Harriman until the delegation as a whole switched. Franklin D. Roosevelt, Jr., was much occupied elsewhere: in the thick of the loyalty-pledge directorate, and more a Harriman advocate than a New York leader. The character of the Harriman support in the delegation was described in these classic words by the then Coney Island leader Ken Sutherland: "We are pledged with New York State to Harriman, but as a whole the Brooklyn delegates are uncommitted." Tammany leader Carmine DeSapio made a similar statement regarding Manhattan's 16 delegates. Delegate Jim Farley was "for Farley" until the eve of the convention when he gave his preferences as Barkley, Russell, and Stevenson, in that order. Stevenson was an acceptable second choice for most of the delegation from the very beginning. About 16, including some 10 votes controlled by Mayor Impellitteri and Roe of Queens, wanted to vote for Stevenson on the first ballot, but held off out of a sense of personal obligation to certain delegation leaders. The 6½ votes that were cast for Stevenson on the first ballot included Farley's ½ vote; Herman Baruch's alternate; William Carlebach, whom the leaders thought to be entitled to his own course of action; Jesse Sharlette of the 33d district; and the 3 Buffalo votes, demonstrating their independence.

Some delegations act as closely integrated groups, and others as loose collections of individuals. These two types of behavior were typical for different sectors of the New York delegation, but the delegation as a whole did not lend itself to either characterization. Several factors tended toward divisiveness. Such men as O'Connell, Roe, Cashmore, DeSapio, and Impellitteri, to name a few, were powerful, organizationally speaking, in their own local bailiwicks. Other men—Lehman, Farley, Baruch, F.D.R., Jr., Powell, the other six congressmen—were figures of some national renown and personal influence. State Chairman Fitzpatrick had to consult with all of these, yet had no power base of his own: a Buffalo man, he could not control the Buffalo votes. The personal leadership exerted by Ed Flynn for so long was not present.

While Fitzpatrick's leadership task was a difficult one, he was aided by several factors that did make for cohesiveness among most of the delegation. There existed a certain state pride: the delegates had a sense of being New Yorkers, of being viewed by the rest of the country as New Yorkers, and of being required to conduct themselves as "the New York delegation." There were, secondly, the unifying imperatives of mutual respect and obligation, that understanding of personalities and positions that comes with long years of having "fought the good fight" with and often against each other in state politics. Thirdly, the statewide reputation and interests of the delegates-at-large, resulting in part from the manner in which they were chosen, provided a center of reconciliation for an otherwise atomized collection of attitudes. Finally, there was a strongly crystallized conviction among the delegates, overriding the personal preferences of many, that only a certain kind of platform and a certain kind of candidate would be acceptable to the voters of New York. Thus it was that Fitzpatrick consulted much and moved slowly, and that New York's delegates on the convention committees spoke not so much as individuals as representatives of the "sense" of their delegation.

Fitzpatrick's mission was to hold as much of New York for Harriman as possible, even when most of his delegation was eager to switch elsewhere. Both Harriman and Lehman found it necessary to make special appeals during the New York caucuses in order to persuade the delegates to defer their second choice commitments. Liberal party leaders—Berle, Dubinsky, and Rose—also were at Chicago, in frequent consultation with the Brooklyn delegation. New York's official favorite son, however, was low man on their list; Liberals were for a Stevenson-Kefauver or a Kefauver-Harriman ticket. To Fitzpatrick's added discomfiture was the support being given by Jim Farley to the man who looked most like the winner: Stevenson. As soon as Barkley withdrew, according to the New York *Times* and Farley's own statement in *New Republic*, Farley received a favorable reaction from a good part of the Queens delegation, Mayor Impellitteri, and some upstaters in behalf of a pro-Stevenson vote before the second ballot. Fitzpatrick, however, held the delegation for Harriman through the second ballot.

During the recess after the second ballot, several influences converged to bring about forthwith the almost inevitable shift to Stevenson: (1) Farley's implicit threat to poll the delegation; (2) fear that the Russell votes rather than the northern-liberal votes would win credit for pushing Stevenson over the majority mark; and (3) fear, however unwarranted, of a Barkley or Kefauver bandwagon movement. Farley later wrote in the *New Republic:*

> . . . I refrained from polling the New York delegation on the second ballot in deference to the wishes of a number of my personal friends in the delegation, but I served notice I would have the delegation polled on the third ballot.

The threat, if it was one, was intended to speed the switch to Stevenson, but it was not the decisive factor.

Nevertheless, there was a specific urge in the delegation to get the switch accomplished and to do so before the balloting began again. Harriman himself knew that his battle was really over. Actually, a draft of a withdrawal letter had been prepared by him before the first ballot. He redrafted it and immediately made it available during the second ballot for use at the strategic moment. The recess seemed to be the strategic moment. Some New York delegates reported a "real" threat of a Kefauver swing on the third ballot, and there were further rumors about Barkley. More held the view that it was important that Stevenson should "owe" his nomination to northern votes rather than to the southern Russell votes.

It may be noted that the New York leaders saw President Truman at dinner during the recess; but this conversation seems to have been at most confirmatory rather than the cause of their strategy.

New York's position on the ballot presented an awkward obstacle in the way of making the switch in the most impressive manner. Alabama, for example, led the roll and could start the Russell votes moving either to Stevenson or, theoretically, Kefauver long before the clerk called "New York." It was therefore decided to announce the Stevenson switch from the platform before the balloting began. Arrangements were completed just as the recess ended. There was some opposition to Fitzpatrick's maneuver from outside the delegation, but after a delay, Fitzpatrick succeeded in reaching the platform while Franklin D. Roosevelt, Jr., held the fort for him on the floor pending his arrival. The announcement was thus made before any other state had time to speak up and well before Kefauver was able to reach the platform with the object of making his own announcement.

On the final nominating ballot—Stevenson, 86½, Kefauver, 4; Ewing, 3; not voting, ½—the only Kefauver votes came from Assemblyman Mauhs, from Lester Martin of Brooklyn, who had urged Kefauver's case upon Fitzpatrick even before the latter had announced himself for Harriman the previous March, from Charles Simonelli, also of Brooklyn and originally for Harriman, and the fourth came as a bonus vote awarded by delegation chairman Lehman in order to avoid a demand for a poll. The ½ not voting reflected Congressman Powell's disapproval of the national convention's position on civil rights.

AFTERMATH IN THE STATE

The Democratic state convention met in September to nominate candidates for the United States Senate and other offices. Averell Harriman's name was the most prominent under discussion, but Harriman was reluctant to inject himself into a senatorial race, particularly since it seemed likely that he would have a key place in a Stevenson cabinet if the latter were elected. He finally decided to take the plunge but delayed his decision on the matter until it was too late for local leaders to disengage themselves from commitments they had meanwhile made publicly. Ed Flynn, for example, already had come out for John Cashmore's candidacy and could not turn back. There was no Roosevelt or Truman to intervene and unscramble the New York situation in the interest of the national party; a feeble effort by certain of the Stevenson advisers came too late. Brooklyn's Cashmore thus received the nomination. The Liberal party considered this an affront to the voters of the state, and subsequently nominated George S. Counts of Columbia University. Counts received 461,000 votes, but even this did not constitute a balance-of-power bloc in the Republican tidal wave that swept New York. The only bright spot for New York Democrats after election day in 1952 was that the party came out of the campaign without a financial deficit for the first time in years. Apparently, campaign expenditures had been limited to the funds on hand, although financial help did come in from both the national committee and the Volunteers for Stevenson.

Old and new factional struggles broke out with fresh vigor. The three principal fights were over (1) the Brooklyn leadership, (2) the minority leadership post in the state assembly, and (3) the chairmanship of the state committee. The Brooklyn leadership fight ended with Kenneth F. Sutherland defeating the long-incumbent Francis J. Sinnott. This led to the selection of Assemblyman Eugene F. Bannigan, Sutherland's close associate, as minority leader in the state assembly. Paul Fitzpatrick resigned as state chairman in November. On December 10, the state committee chose Richard W. Balch of Utica as its chairman by a vote of 181 to 104. His opponent was William H. Morgan of Cortland. Both had been district delegates at the 1952 national convention, Balch serving in the inner management of the Harriman campaign at Chicago. Morgan had the active support of Jim Farley and a good many anti-Flynn votes. Balch had the support of Senator Lehman, Franklin D. Roosevelt, Jr., Robert Wagner, Jr., and Paul Fitzpatrick.

The fortunes of the Harriman-Roosevelt-Wagner leadership in the state party were further boosted during the 1953 mayoralty race in New York City. Mayor Impellitteri, with the support of county leaders Sutherland of Brooklyn, Roe of Queens, and Sullivan of Staten Island, lost his bid for renomination in the fall primary to Robert Wagner, Jr., who had the backing of Tammany's DeSapio and Buckley of the Bronx. Buckley had become acting Bronx leader shortly after Ed Flynn's death. The political strength revealed by Wagner's overwhelming victory in the primary was again demonstrated by the 2 to 1 vote he received in the general election in November 1953.

REVIEW AND APPRAISAL

Delegates-at-large in New York are selected through the party machinery. District delegates, who make up more than 90 per cent of each delegation, are usually elected without regard to their views on presidential candidates. No presidential candidate is on the New York ballot; no delegate candidate is permitted to indicate his presidential preferences on the ballot. Ordinarily, attention is not focused upon the presidential candidates even in those rare instances when the enrolled voter of either party is given a choice among delegate candidates in the primary. Primary activities occur in March and April, before presidential candidacies are well established.

In 1952, the enrolled Republican voters were called upon to deal with contests between delegate candidates in 5 of the 45 old congressional districts. In only one district, the 16th, was the contest a clear reflection of the national contest between Taft and Eisenhower. In that district the outcome was a draw: one pro-Taft delegate was elected by 49 votes and one pro-Eisenhower delegate by 25. In another district, the 29th, an insurgent slate for Taft, led by Hamilton Fish, was narrowly defeated by an "uninstructed" organization slate that remained unwilling to announce for Eisenhower, although it later voted for him. In three districts of the Buffalo area, a confusing contest occurred in which a pro-Eisenhower slate was elected by a three-to-one vote, with the views of the defeated "uninstructed" slate somewhat in doubt. But in 40 of the 45 districts, there was no contest on the ballot and the enrolled Republican voters were given less opportunity to be influential in the election of April 22 than would have been the case in a series of open precinct meetings or town caucuses, such as were held in many Connecticut towns on April 28. On the Democratic side, contests occurred in 1952 in 7 of the 45 districts, but originated in local factionalism in most cases. The contests did little to direct the attention of the voters to any national candidate, and there is no evidence that they were settled on that basis; regular organization candidates won in each instance.

The New York system thus permits district contests in which the voters of each party may vote and national candidates may intervene; but the system comes into operation earlier than most potential candidates are willing to campaign, is not easily breached by national candidates from outside the state, and is almost wholly immune to attack by voluntary groups of amateurs within the state, whatever the banner under which they assemble. Senator Estes Kefauver, although well-known in the state, was apparently unable to make his candidacy the subject of an effective contest in a single district; and surely there were more than five districts in which the latent strength for Taft might have been expected to produce some sort of a contest. Even the opportunities for local factional in-fighting were relatively little used, much less so than in the similar situations in Pennsylvania and Illinois, apparently because of the burdensome nature of the procedural requirements. A project reporter asked one Manhattan district leader, known to be unfriendly to Tammany Hall, why he did not run his own slate of delegates in the primary since the county committee had named those who were to run in his area. "What's there in it?" he asked. "It's expensive to have a primary fight—circulating petitions, getting your people to canvass, arranging for publicity. And then if you win, what have you got? One or two votes out of 94. Doesn't mean a thing. I'll save my fire for elective offices. Then it pays to fight."

The process as a whole produces delegations from New York that are made up mainly of professional politicians, with an unusually high proportion of delegates who have attended previous national conventions. County chairmen usually predominate among the district delegates, with congressmen often present. There also are generally a considerable number of state legislators and executive officials of state and local government. With the kind of leadership that is usually provided by the outstanding public and party figures who are delegates-at-large, such delegations are strong, influential, and even more effective than their large numbers would suggest.

Partly because of the district election system, New York delegations are seldom completely unified. Even with a governor in office, the Republican delegation of 1952 included its quota of mavericks who represented local centers of power. Forhead of Buffalo, for example, could show his trouble-making potentialities unless given a voice in state patronage matters. On the Democratic side, it was even more apparent that party organization in New York State is a system of local feudalities that never quite become a "state machine." Thus, the O'Connells of Albany were able ostentatiously to display their hostility to the incumbent state leadership.

Yet in both conventions, the bulk of the New York State delegation was always together on every major issue; and its voting record was achieved without benefit of such restricting devices as a unit rule, a statutory instruction, a state-wide slate-making process for getting on the ballot, or a binding pledge to any candidate. The significance of this may become somewhat apparent when contrasted with the California Democratic delegation, the second largest in the country, which had a statutory instruction, had originated as a state-wide slate, and in addition, adopted a unit rule for a time in an effort, not wholly successful, to attain influence comparable to its voting strength. Without a unit rule, the New York delegations recorded one or more splinter votes on every roll-call, but never had any problem in remaining influential.

Consensus was achieved in the New York delegations without such mechanical means through: awareness of the general attitudes of the voters of New York; argument and conviction; the unfolding of the candidate possibilities and strategies through time; and only occasionally by the direct use of sanctions to whip into line a few of the stragglers who happened to waver under outside pressure. Consensus was achieved, moreover, in a situation where there was real representation of the localism of congressional districts. New York had a higher proportion of district delegates than any other state; and in most cases their selection had been controlled at the county level, not at Albany or in city hall. Few other states with as much district autonomy in delegate selection were able to operate with so high a degree of consensus at either convention.

Nearly every session of the New York state legislature witnesses proposals for some change in the delegate selection process. Even more important, perhaps, are the recurring proposals for change in the structure and procedures of the political parties in the state. Manhattan Assemblyman John R. Brook, a Republican not regarded as "regular" by his organization, on October 22, 1951, announced a 7-point program to combat what he calls "political bossism" in the electoral process. Brook was chairman of the Joint Legislative Committee on the Election Law, which expired in 1951. His October 22 statement included these remarks:

> I am convinced that "political bossism" exists because the rank and file enrolled party members in both major parties have no effective means of wresting the party machinery from the bosses. Secure against any attack, some political bosses run their party organizations for the financial and political benefit of themselves and their small coterie of friends. These bosses, who own and control the political organizations, have legally acquired their position under protective statutes incorporated into the Election Law over a period of years.

They have been unwittingly aided by the ignorance of the average enrolled party members of their rights and privileges under the Election Law. . . .

Brook's proposals, although only indirectly related to the selection of national convention delegates, touched at sensitive areas in the system of control that the New York party officials have developed over their parties. Such proposals might be expected to evoke vigorous opposition if pressed. Yet, on March 14, 1953, Governor Dewey endorsed and sent to the state legislature the second in a series of reports by the New York State crime commission in which several proposals quite similar to those of Assemblyman Brook were recommended. The Commission's proposals for legislation were intended to "eliminate the unnecessary obstacles confronting any candidate for district leadership, particularly where he is not sponsored by the party organization" and to achieve a similar result for all persons seeking election to party office or party nomination for public office. The proposals soon became legislative bills, were passed, and, on April 4, 1953, were signed by the Governor.

Broadly speaking, it is probably fair to say that the New York delegations of 1952 were both about as representative and as unrepresentative of the mass of party supporters as the respective party organizations in the state. This reflected the simple fact that the delegations were by-products of the organizations in each case, organizations that have been fairly successful in guessing what the voters want or will accept. Both party organizations are obviously ingrown, subject to the corruptions of long-entrenched power, and at least statistically somewhat unrepresentative of the ethnic, ideological, geographic, and occupational distributions that presently exist within each party in the state. The average age, stability, and length of service of the party leadership, both state and local, in a system where leadership within the parties is not easily challenged, have made this result inevitable. But granting these obvious facts, the voters of New York did not have much reason for discontent with the way in which they were represented at Chicago in 1952. They were given effective representation in the pursuit of aims and in the selection of national candidates that were undoubtedly acceptable to the mass of the electorate in each party in the state.

New York Chapter Acknowledgments

PHILLIPS BRADLEY, Professor of Political Science, Maxwell School of Citizenship and Public Affairs, Syracuse University, conducted field work throughout New York State and prepared a pre-convention case study report on the Republican delegation with the assistance of five graduate students and seven student aides. The graduate students included VINCENT ALOIA; GORDON CLEVELAND, now Assistant Professor, University of North Carolina; PALMER PILCHER, now Assistant Professor, The American University; JOHN OWENS; and NELSON ROBINSON, now Assistant Professor, University of Tennessee. Student aides included ROSWELL DEMPSEY, LESLIE HEILBRONNER, PHILIP HUTTAR, PATRICK KELLY, DONALD LEVITAN, HAROLD LIEBERMAN, and CARL VANN. Professor Bradley did not attend the national convention and the portion of the present chapter on the activities of the delegation at Chicago is drawn mainly from published sources. He later assisted actively in the revision of the draft chapter.

MRS. LOUISE BURR GERRARD, Lecturer in Government, Barnard College, prepared a pre-convention case study report on the Democratic delegation. HAROLD STEIN, Director of the Twentieth Century Fund Study of Civil-Military Relations and Visiting Lecturer, Princeton University, reported on the delegation's activities at Chicago, with the assistance of HENRY BAIN, formerly of the Brookings Institution. Mrs. Gerrard and Mr. Stein assisted in the revision of the draft chapter.

The initial draft of the chapter was prepared from the above reports and other sources by RALPH M. GOLDMAN of the Washington staff.

NEW JERSEY

Electoral votes, 1952: 16

National convention votes, 1952:
Democratic, 32
Republican, 38

Population, 1950: 4,835,329
Urban, 87%; rural nonfarm, 11%; rural farm, 2%

Population increase, 1940-50: 675,164 (16%)
Urban, 13%; rural nonfarm, 39%; rural farm, 17% decline

Presidential vote, 1948:   *1952:*
Democratic,   895,455 (46%)   1,015,902 (42%)
Republican,   981,124 (50%)   1,374,613 (57%)
Progressive,   42,683 (2%)
Other   30,293 (2%)   29,039 (1%)

Gubernatorial vote, 1949:   *1953:*
Democratic,   810,022   959,669
Republican,   885,882   805,750

U. S. Representatives vote,
all districts, 1950:   *1952:*
Democratic,   689,814   977,914
Republican,   859,145   1,317,404

U. S. Representatives elected 1950:   *1952:*
Democratic,   5   5
Republican,   9   9

State legislature elected 1953:
Senate: Democrats, 4;   Republicans, 17
General Assembly: Democrats, 20;   Republicans, 40

Method of selecting national convention delegates:
Direct election at primary; presidential preference poll

Based primarily on reports by HARRY R. DAVIS

NEW JERSEY IS A DENSELY POPULATED STATE. It is highly industrialized and largely urban; nevertheless the agricultural interests are of some importance in the state, and the shore resorts constitute still another factor in New Jersey politics. The state is not simply urban, but increasingly and significantly suburban, with hundreds of thousands of its residents commuting daily to cities outside the state, especially New York and Philadelphia. The people of the state are relatively diverse as to national origin, religion, and race. The proportion of "foreign-born white" population now stands at 13 per cent and is decreasing. The figure for Negroes is 6.6 per cent and increasing. "Civil rights" as a major national political issue is important to many groups.

New Jersey is highly organized for party politics. While the relative strength of the two parties is not far out of balance, a majority of the voters generally vote Republican. The state has given its electoral vote to Democratic candidates for president five times since 1900; on four of these occasions Franklin D. Roosevelt was the candidate, and in 1912 New Jersey's own Woodrow Wilson won only by virtue of the fact that the Bull Moose party split the Republican vote. Traditional Republican preponderance in presidential politics has been clearly re-asserted in the elections of 1948 and 1952, with pluralities of 85,000 for Dewey and 357,000 for Eisenhower. The Democrats have won eight of the eighteen gubernatorial elections since 1900; again, however, three of the eight were won by one man, A. Harry Moore, in large part as a matter of personal popularity. While all congressional seats are normally contested, New Jersey's delegation in Washington has also been preponderantly Republican in recent decades.

The Republican party's control of the state legislature is the most clearly defined pattern of all, its majorities there being almost uninterrupted and usually overwhelming. The Democrats have not controlled the legislature since 1914. Even in the depths of the depression and the heyday of Frank Hague, they were able to capture only the lower house, in 1932 and 1937. The failure of the Democrats to elect more state legislators can be attributed partly to the districting system as it operates in New Jersey. For example, state senators are elected one per county, regardless of whether they represent the 35,000 people of Sussex County or the 905,000 of Essex. Each of the 21 counties must be represented by at least one assemblyman, the total membership of the Assembly being limited to 60; Assembly delegations are elected at large from each county. Such provisions tend to diminish the relative effect of the concentrated urban strength of the Democrats. Further, it is a normally Republican legislature that decides whether or not to reshuffle the constitutionally fixed 60 members among the counties in the light of shifts in population after each census.

The pattern of popular support within the parties is similar to that in other northern urban states. The base of Republican strength is in the upper-middle-class suburban vote in northern counties such as Bergen, Union, and Essex, and in the rural vote of the southern counties, where political allegiances appear to have survived since the Civil War. New Jersey Protestants and the business community tend heavily toward the Republican side. Democratic votes come mostly from the industrial cities of the northeast, centering around the declining Jersey City machine formerly headed by Frank Hague; next to Hudson, probably the most consistently Democratic county is Middlesex (Newark). Camden and Trenton provide significant Democratic support in the central and southwest parts of the state. Most Roman Catholic voters cast Democratic ballots, and in recent years the party has drawn considerable strength from various minority groups and organized labor, particularly the CIO. Support for the two parties is so distributed geographically that on the local level there is real competition between them in relatively few counties. Another political factor is what Woodrow Wilson called New Jersey's "peculiar" location between New York City and Philadelphia; a high proportion of the most influential people in the two great metropolises commute to suburbia in New Jersey but acquire only a secondary interest and little knowledge of New Jersey politics, which they seem willing to leave almost entirely in the hands of the regular party organizations.

Early in 1952, the Republican organization appeared clearly the stronger of the two parties. It was in command at the state house and most court houses. It exhibited vigor and optimism and, despite some opposition to him, was fairly well unified under the leadership of Governor Alfred E. Driscoll. The new constitution of 1947 gave the governor a much strengthened role, bolstering his control over fewer but more important appointive positions. The Democrats, with the old Hague machine weakened by factional fights and impotent as a state organization, with no statewide leader, and with the question of a presidential nominee very much undecided, presented a confused and somewhat dispirited picture.

PRESIDENTIAL PRIMARY LAW AND PROCEDURE

Political parties are required by New Jersey statute to elect their delegates and alternates to the national conventions—and the members of party committees—at the primary election held on the third Tuesday in April: April 15 in 1952. (*Revised Statutes of New Jersey,* 19:3-3) Candidates for election as delegates or alternates must be nominated by petition filed at least 40 days before the primary: March 6 in 1952. One hundred signatures of party members and legal voters resident in a congressional district are required for nominating a district delegate or alternate, and the same number of signatures of such persons resident in the state are required for delegate- or alternate-at-large. Delegate candidates themselves must meet the same residence requirements.

Candidates for delegate may be grouped together on the ballot, and "may also have the name of the candidate for president whom they favor placed opposite their individual names or opposite such groups, if they so request in their petitions and if the written consent of such candidate for president is endorsed upon their petitions, under the caption 'Choice for President.' " The primary election is closed to all except registered party members, registration being accomplished by formal statement or by having voted in the party's primary within the past two years. The candidates for delegate receiving the "highest number of votes" (plurality) are declared elected.

In February 1952, the New Jersey legislature passed a law adding a separate presidential preference poll to its primary election. (*Revised Statutes of New Jersey*, 19:25.) A previous and similar statute was repealed by a Republican administration in 1944, in an effort to head off a primary fight. The present law was passed almost unanimously, with the support of the Democrats, who had been critical of the 1944 repeal, and of Governor Driscoll, who was thought to consider it advantageous for General Eisenhower in any Republican contest. The preference poll permits an expression of popular sentiment but has no legal effect on the delegates, who may continue to vote at the conventions as they choose. Delegates may win election who are recorded on the ballot as favoring a candidate other than the one who wins the preference poll; in that case, the prior obligation of the delegate would presumably be in accordance with his own pledge or preference as recorded on the ballot rather than the popular expression in the preference poll. Names of presidential prospects may be placed on the ballot by petition of 1,000 party voters; positive consent of the prospect is not necessary, but he may withdraw his name within six days after the filing deadline. This latter provision was favorably adapted to the circumstances surrounding the Eisenhower candidacy in the spring of 1952.

THE REPUBLICAN DELEGATION

There appears to be no clear and continuing factional pattern within the Republican party in recent years, except for the configuration of county organizations of which it is comprised. In the early months of 1952, some controversy developed between the supporters of Taft and those of Eisenhower. Support for Taft was in part a reflection of anti-Driscoll sentiment among some county leaders. The selection process for the 1952 convention delegates illustrated clearly the reciprocal nature of the governor-county leader relationship. While the governor's strength depends in part upon his retaining the support of the various county leaders, his powers of patronage and general recognition as party leader put him in good position to keep their favor.

In recent national conventions the New Jersey delegation has stood with the eastern, internationalist wing of the Republican party. In 1940 an original preponderance of Dewey support (20 of the 32 votes on first ballot) gradually shifted to Willkie (all 32 votes on the sixth ballot). In 1944 New Jersey, like the whole convention, was solidly for Dewey. In 1948 the delegation was pledged to Driscoll as a favorite son, a move which held the delegation together and greatly increased its bargaining power. On the second ballot, Driscoll was able to swing 24 of the delegation's 35 votes to Dewey, with Stassen receiving 6, Vandenberg 3, and Taft 2; on the third ballot, all votes went to Dewey.

THE SELECTION PROCESS IN 1952

In New Jersey, party leaders take the initiative in selecting organization-sponsored slates of candidates for national convention delegate. In 1952 almost all organization-endorsed candidates were elected. Thus, the process by which those delegate candidates were nominated generally was decisive. In 1952 New Jersey Republicans were able to claim 38 convention seats. Twenty-eight district delegates and 28 alternates were to be elected in the districts, and the other ten delegates plus alternates were to be elected from the state at large.

The organization slate—On January 9, 1952, Governor Driscoll met with John J. Dickerson, state chairman; Lloyd B. Marsh, secretary of state and former state chairman; and George Becker, Essex County chairman. Prospective delegates-at-large were discussed, but Governor Driscoll announced that no final decisions were made. Evidently it was agreed or assumed that wide geographical representation should be a basic factor. Specifically, each of 20 counties (New Jersey has only 21) was to be represented on the delegate-at-large slate, the more populous and more Republican counties generally being allotted a delegate each, the others only alternates. Considerable consultation with local leaders then began to take place; county chairmen recommended candidates for places on the slate and the state leadership gave the final approval. But the state group appears to have taken the initiative in placing the names of some half-dozen leaders on the ballot. On January 26, a group of ten state leaders met at the Princeton Inn and agreed on candidates for six of the ten delegate-at-large seats.

This slate included the four original conferees of January 9 plus former Governor Walter E. Edge and Senator Robert C. Hendrickson. These six were expected to clear with their county organizations, to give their local leaders at least the appearance of participation in the decision.

County chairmen were more clearly given the initiative in filling the remaining 14 places for delegates and alternates-at-large. Only one case is known in which the recommendation of a county organization was turned down by the state leaders: Amos J. Peaslee of Gloucester County was felt to be too closely identified with the Stassen campaign; instead, Peaslee was accepted as a district candidate. The at-large slate was quickly completed and was officially approved at a meeting of the state committee on February 5. The same meeting voted, not without some expressed misgivings, to recommend Guy Gabrielson for re-election to the national committee. Mrs. Eleanor Todd was named for national committeewoman, succeeding her mother, Mrs. Reeve Schley.

Aside from geographical representation, candidates for delegate were selected on the basis of a combination of such characteristics as party service, financial generosity, and statewide popularity. Leanings toward the right presidential candidate were also advantageous to a would-be delegate. The young Republican leaders and several prominent financial supporters were considered but were omitted. Mrs. Todd was included, particularly in view of her position as president of the Women's State Republican Club of New Jersey and prospective national committeewoman. Some of the disappointed candidates for delegate were selected later as presidential electors.

Both United States senators were omitted from the original tentative list. Senator Smith later withdrew as a prospective delegate, but insisted that Senator Hendrickson be included, which he was. Congressmen and candidates for Congress were apparently not seriously considered by the slatemakers on either state or district level, allegedly because they would be on the ballot in another capacity.

One further decision taken early and confirmed by the state committee was that all delegate-candidates should be entered unpledged and go to Chicago uninstructed. It was pointed out that this would give the delegates opportunity to be guided by the results of the preference poll; also, it permitted the pro-Eisenhower organization leaders to keep the delegation open for a possible full swing to their candidate.

Meanwhile, formation of slates of district candidates was proceeding in all 14 congressional districts. Ordinarily the county chairmen of the counties concerned, sometimes in consultation with their executive committees, selected the candidates to be endorsed as "regular organization" men. Delegates were chosen generally on the basis of party service and regularity, but in a few instances their preference as to presidential nominee was a factor. The party organizations in Bergen and Morris counties declared themselves neutral; in Bergen one candidate leaning toward Taft was named, another favoring Eisenhower. Taft sentiment was strong in several county organizations, but Eisenhower was more generally the preference.

In Essex County, which included all of the 11th and 12th districts and four-fifths of the 10th, the county chairman met with his executive committee in December 1951. The committee voted 15-0 to support a slate of six delegates instructed for Eisenhower. This vote was made public in January after Eisenhower announced his availability. Although the Essex candidates could not be officially pledged on the ballot, they ran openly as "uninstructed for Eisenhower." The six candidates named by the county organization were uncontested in all three districts.

In Hudson County which includes the 13th and 14th districts, the selection process turned basically on local relations with the state leadership. Edmund Stevenson, the county chairman, was under challenge during the pre-convention period by a rival leader, Donald Spence. Both men favored Taft, whether on principle or because each was somewhat upset over his own relationship with the pro-Eisenhower governor. Early in January, Stevenson met with his county executive committee and picked four delegate candidates as the "organization" slate. Later the Spence faction filed a rival slate of 4. These 8 presumably pro-Taft candidates were joined in the contest by two independents filing in the 14th district, who were also supporters of Taft. The Stevenson slate was ultimately elected.

In most of New Jersey's districts, county leaders faced, as usual, the fact that the respective congressional districts are often composed of territory from more than one county, a circumstance necessitating some formula for apportioning the four places (two delegates, two alternates) among the counties concerned. In most cases, some formula had been accepted in previous years and was applied more or less automatically in 1952.

Other delegate candidates—The "organization slate" technique was not entirely successful in avoiding contests. Between February 5, when the statewide slate was announced, and March 6, last date for filing for the April primary, the partisans of the several presidential candidates had to decide whether to contest the organization list or parts of it. Eisenhower supporters were not entirely content with the organization-endorsed candidates, but could not enter candidates officially pledged to Eisenhower in any case, since the General was not in position to give the required written consent. John D. M. Hamilton, Taft's eastern manager, held many conversations with pro-Taft leaders around the state in an effort to decide on how big a scale, if at all, they should contest the organization-backed candidates. Stassen managers announced a full slate of candidates to oppose any Taft-pledged list that might materialize. Stassen's campaign was managed by Bernard M. Shanley, a Newark lawyer later appointed legal adviser to President Eisenhower. State Chairman Dickerson met late in February with representatives of the Taft, Eisenhower, and Stassen forces and all agreed to make every effort to avoid "destructive" primary fights.

In the end the Taft backers decided to enter no candidates against the organization list, but to depend instead upon support already apparent among the organization delegates and upon an impressive showing in the preferential poll. Stassen, however, having only one supporter among the organization endorsed candidates, filed petitions for a complete slate of ten candidates for delegate-at-large, and also for ten district delegates in seven different districts. The ballot was further fattened by twenty candidates who filed independently, either as "volunteers" or representatives of dissident local factions: six for delegate-at-large seats and fourteen in five different districts. Most of these "independents" publicly favored Taft. Several used the ballot slogan "General Return to Morality, Integrity," a thinly veiled preference for MacArthur.

In the districts, a total of 53 candidates sought the 28 delegate seats to be filled, there being contests in nine of the fourteen districts. Organization-endorsed candidates were unopposed in the 1st and 2d districts and in the three Essex County districts (the 10th, 11th, and 12th). They were opposed only by candidates officially pledged to Stassen in four other districts, there being one Stassen candidate in the 4th district, and two each in the 3d, 8th, and 9th. In the 5th, one pro-Stassen, one pro-Taft, and one independent candidate were contesting the two organization men. Eight candidates appeared on the 6th district ballot; two organization, two party rebels favoring Taft, two publicly pro-Eisenhower, one pledged to Stassen, and one other independent. In the 7th, the endorsed candidates were opposed by two factional independents and one Stassen man; and in the 13th and 14th districts there were the ten pro-Taft candidacies described earlier.

Presidential preference campaign—Public interest centered more on the preference poll than on the less spectacular and more complex scramble for delegate seats. Governor Driscoll expressed the opinion that the delegation should be "morally bound" by the decision of the public expressed in the newly-authorized poll. Such questions as "how big a victory is decisive," and whether district delegates should be bound by the statewide vote or the vote in their own districts, were left unanswered and subject to later interpretation.

Early in the year most observers believed that Eisenhower was easily the preferred candidate among New Jersey's Republican voters and even among party leaders. But it soon developed that Taft had strong support among the professionals, especially in the northern counties, and John D. M. Hamilton was in the state periodically from December on, organizing Taft support among the county leaders. Governor Driscoll was generally understood to favor Eisenhower, but he had not publicly committed himself. By the March 6 deadline both Taft and Stassen had decided to join Eisenhower in the popularity poll, and petitions were filed for all three. Governor Driscoll was under increasing pressure to take a public stand. On March 17, at a meeting of the county chairmen and the delegate-at-large slate, he announced his personal preference for Eisenhower. Most county chairmen immediately offered their approval and support; some others gave up their personal preference for Taft in favor of party regularity.

Taft leaders in the state expressed no particular surprise at Driscoll's decision. But on March 20 Taft angrily announced from Wisconsin that he was withdrawing from the contest in New Jersey, declaring that a fair election was no longer possible and charging that Driscoll had violated a promise of neutrality. Driscoll denied any such pledge and issued countercharges. After a confusing political and legal snarl, the courts finally ruled that it was too late for Taft to take his name off the ballot. Nevertheless, Taft cancelled his twenty speaking engagements in the state and his state headquarters was officially closed. Many of his backers continued to campaign for him, and Eisenhower partisans charged that the withdrawal was merely nominal, a ruse to establish grounds for a favorable interpretation of any possible outcome of the poll. In any case, the controversy contributed to a more serious split in the organization than appeared on the surface.

Driscoll's move added professional organization and leadership to the Eisenhower campaign. Taft supporters also continued to work hard. Both campaigns made use of nationally-known speakers, public rallies, and intensive newspaper, radio, and television advertising. The New Jersey air grew heavy with indignant recriminations, particularly as the Taft supporters played on the theme of Driscoll's lack of neutrality and his alleged "double-cross." The Taft campaign appeared to be considerably better financed: some observers estimated that $250,000 was spent on Taft's candidacy, $75,000 on Eisenhower's. (New York *Times*, April 11, 1952.) Stassen was the only candidate to appear personally in the state; he carried out a four-day speaking campaign, aimed mostly at Taft, immediately before the April 15 election day. Except for the 6th district (Union County), where the organization slate was seriously challenged by two rival factions, little or no campaigning was done in the contests for delegate seats as such. As the campaign closed, the outcome appeared uncertain and each of the two leading camps was minimizing its own strength and exaggerating the opposition's.

The ballot—The ballot with which New Jersey Republicans had to come to terms on April 15 provided for the presidential preference poll, the delegate election, the primaries for United States senator and representatives, and primaries for a variety of county and municipal offices. The left-hand column of the ballot listed the various offices to be filled, and the candidates for the respective offices were listed opposite these designations, in further columns, with each identifiable slate in a column by itself. The organization slate of candidates for delegate was carried under the heading "Unpledged" and was generally placed on the ballot or voting machine in as conspicuous a place as possible and in the same column with organization candidates for other offices; as one newsman observed, "County clerks will see to that, or someone will see to the county clerks." Voting machines were used in eight of the more populous counties, paper ballots in the rest; provision for write-in votes was made in both cases. It was necessary for the voter to vote separately for each delegate and alternate even when they were carried on the ballot as a slate. Some voters may perhaps have been mystified by the physical separation of the preference poll from the election of delegates, or by the fact that only the candidates supporting Stassen were clearly labeled on the ballot to show their candidate preference.

The outcome—Election day was rainy, a factor contributing to the relatively light turnout of voters, fewer than 675,000, of whom about 645,000 cast ballots in the preferential poll and apparently only somewhat over 500,000 in the delegate-at-large and district delegate contests. In the preference poll Eisenhower received 390,591 votes, or over 60 per cent of the total; Taft received 228,916, or over 35 per cent; and Stassen trailed with 23,559, about 4 per cent. Eisenhower carried 20 of the 21 counties in the state. Taft's relatively good showing in Hudson County and some other areas was partly a reflection of factional disagreements within the state organization. The result was generally interpreted as a substantial and impressive demonstration of Eisenhower's popular appeal, and a definite setback to the Taft candidacy.

The organization's list of delegate-at-large candidates won easily with an average vote of something over 400,000, carrying the slate of ten alternates-at-large along with them. The Stassen-pledged slate of delegates-at-large polled an average of approximately 55,000 votes each, running well ahead of their candidate's showing on the preference poll. A "cut Driscoll" campaign waged by some Taft supporters had noticeable results, as the Governor ran last among the ten winning delegate candidates by 10,000 votes, although carried on the ballot at the top of the list. Independent delegate candidates polled from 50,000 to 70,000 votes each.

Organization candidates for district delegates won in every district except one: the 6th. The result in that district was a strange and wonderful confusion: Eisenhower won the preference poll by almost two to one; but the same voters turned down the organization-endorsed delegate candidates and four others (two of whom favored Eisenhower, thus splitting the Eisenhower vote) in favor of two open supporters of Taft; then they reversed their field once more and elected two pro-Eisenhower alternates! In one other district, the 5th, the organization candidates were given a fairly close race and an independent appears to have been chosen as one of the alternates. Otherwise the endorsed slates made a clean sweep; in the remaining seven contested districts, their majorities ranged from about 9-to-1 in three of the seven to 2-to-1 in the Hudson County districts.

Taft retained some strength among the organization delegates, to add to his two insurgents from the 6th district. It was expected that he would hold three or possibly all four of the delegates from Hudson County (the county in which he won the preference poll by a narrow margin), plus perhaps two more district delegates. Stassen was supported by one wavering organization delegate, and Eisenhower was favored by the remaining 29 or 30 of the 38 delegates.

COMPOSITION OF THE DELEGATION

The Republican delegation was in general representative of the party's leaders, workers, and contributors. As previously noted, the list of delegates-at-large included several of the most prominent party leaders. The delegation included eight state legislators and several local elective officials, five county chairmen and several state and county committeemen, as well as other local party leaders. An even higher percentage of lesser party officials was found among the alternates.

Some six of the delegates were full-time public officials, state and local; and one other was a retired official. One delegate was a full-time party official; another was prominently identified with veterans' organizations. Agriculture and labor had no discernible representation, except that one banker was also a dairy farmer.

Almost one-half of the 38 delegates could be classified as business-men, including entrepreneurs, industrial executives, realtors, and insurance men, a few of these doubling as part-time public or party officials. Probably the two bankers, two newspaper publishers, one retired businessman as well as the four practicing lawyers should be added to the category of the business community; if so, the proportion would approach the two-thirds mark. As their occupational status indicates, a high proportion of the delegates were men of some wealth and social position; it is estimated that at least three-fourths of the delegates were in the over-$10,000 income group.

A sample of less than one-half of the members indicates that the delegation was overwhelmingly Protestant, with Presbyterians and Episcopalians predominating; Italo-Catholics were represented among the district alternates. Most of the delegates were between 40 and 60 years old, with the average about 54; but several delegates were over 60, and at least one was in his thirties. Three delegates and eleven alternates were women. No Negroes served as delegates, but three or four served as alternates.

The secretary of the delegation estimated that most of the delegates spent $400 or $500 each in attending the convention. All delegates contributed to a fund for such items as dinner meetings and staff work; otherwise, each paid his own expenses, though there appear to be a few instances in which local organizations aided their delegates financially. A former unwritten rule that delegates-at-large make a a political contribution of $1000 is no longer in effect, but most of the delegates are generally expected to contribute to party coffers.

Five of 1952's ten delegates-at-large served in the same capacity at the 1948 convention; two of the same five were delegates-at-large in 1944. Some eleven of the 28 district delegates were delegates in 1948; four of these had also served in 1944.

ACTIVITIES AND VOTING RECORD

Immediately after the primary, Governor Driscoll went to work to organize the delegation and heal the campaign wounds. He called a meeting on April 18, at the Nassau Tavern, Princeton, which 32 dele-gates and 30 alternates attended. Driscoll was unanimously elected chairman of the delegation, and Herbert Holran, secretary of the state committee but not a delegate, was chosen to act as secretary. Driscoll named a committee of seven delegates, with Dickerson as chairman, to suggest assignments to the convention committees. Dickerson later notified the delegates and alternates by letter of the committee's recommendations. Ex-Governor Edge and Mrs. Abbie W. Magee served on the resolutions committee; David Van Alstyne on credentials; and Anthony J. Cafiero on rules. No effort was made to convert the Taft delegates, the preference poll results were not discussed, and no one proposed a unit rule.

The drives for delegate support continued in the period between primary and convention. Delegates were receiving considerable literature by mail, especially from Taft supporters, but it is not apparent that any votes were changed. On June 12 some fifty delegates and alternates (not including Driscoll) journeyed to New York City to visit Taft and Eisenhower. The day before, Eisenhower had met with a much smaller group of New Jersey Republicans, including the more venerable figures in the party, some heavy contributors, and a few delegates. Some days earlier, ten or twelve delegates and alternates who leaned toward Taft had lunch with their candidate at a New York hotel; this group later met at least once with John D. M. Hamilton.

The same period saw other significant activity within the state organization. Driscoll continued his running verbal battle with Taft. The state committee met and heard National Committeeman Gabrielson defend himself against nationally-circulated charges, repeated on this occasion by Driscoll and others, that he was using his position to favor Taft's candidacy. But the vote to recommend Gabrielson's ouster, expected by some, failed to come off. Driscoll held another meeting of the delegation late in June to make final plans for procedure at Chicago. The emphasis again was on reconciliation: Driscoll announced in advance that he opposed any attempt to impose the unit rule—New Jersey Republicans have not used it for many years— nor was there evidence of other types of pressure. The four Hudson County delegates eventually voted for Eisenhower; but Driscoll emphasized that he had made no deal with them.

About two-thirds of the delegation went to Chicago by special train, arriving Sunday morning. The delegation held its first formal caucus Monday morning, and, after hearing the report of a committee studying the question, voted 31 to 7 to support the "fair play" amendment to the rules. Some shifting among delegates and alternates took place before the vote on the Brown amendment Monday afternoon; when the roll was called on that issue, Driscoll announced 6 votes for and 32 against. A Taft delegate requested a poll of the delegation, and the Taft faction lost one more vote, the final division being 33 to 5. The Taft faction had caucused soon after the delegation arrived in Chicago, and State Senator Frank Farley was chosen leader. Farley's attempt to seat his bloc together on the convention floor was unsuccessful.

In the battles over credentials at Chicago, the New Jersey representatives, except for Gabrielson, voted consistently with the Eisenhower faction. In the national committee votes on Georgia and Texas, Gabrielson voted with the pro-Taft majority, Mrs. Schley with the Eisenhower supporters. In the credentials committee, David Van Alstyne voted with the Eisenhower minority on Georgia and again on Texas; he signed the minority report on these two issues, and later spoke to the convention in support of seating the Eisenhower delegation from Texas.

Driscoll was threatened with a minor revolt as the vote on seating Georgia approached. Three prominent delegates not in the Taft camp felt it would be unwise to set a precedent for rejecting credentials committee reports, and some others appeared ready to follow their lead. But Driscoll was able to persuade all but one of these recalcitrants to remain in line, so that New Jersey voted 32 to 6 for the minority report on seating Georgia.

The Monday morning caucus witnessed some confusion and dispute over the question of which alternate should replace an absent delegate. Lacking a convention rule on this point, Driscoll ruled that alternates would be selected in order of their position on the ballot, rather than on the basis of number of votes received; the caucus upheld this ruling.

Governor Driscoll emerged during the convention as one of the leading strategists of the Eisenhower camp. He had been mentioned in pre-convention discussion as a possible vice-presidential nominee, and his effectiveness as an Eisenhower leader renewed and strengthened such speculation. Newspaper reports usually cited him as a "middle-of-the-road liberal" and a champion of civil rights measures. Driscoll was among the first persons publicly to suggest the "fair play" amendment, and was active in getting support for it at the governors' meeting in Houston. At the convention, he was immediately recruited by General Lucius Clay to meet with a number of other governors to plan Eisenhower strategy, and thereafter he served as an effective member of the inner circle. On Monday afternoon he rallied the rather confused Eisenhower forces by mounting the convention rostrum to demand that Chairman Gabrielson give them a fair opportunity in debate. He was a chief Eisenhower strategist in the Georgia case—watching it through committee, supervising research on the legal arguments, supplying Eastvold with material for his speech in convention, speaking himself for the minority report. He was given responsibility for negotiating with Negro delegate-leaders on the ticklish civil rights plank in the platform, and, along with Senator Irving Ives, won agreement from them not to precipitate a floor fight on this issue. He made a warm seconding speech for the nomination of Nixon.

As noted previously, the delegation split 33 to 5 on the Brown amendment, and 32 to 6 on the Georgia seating issue. On the nominating ballot, the division was Eisenhower 33, Taft 5, but the vote was made unanimous for Eisenhower after the Minnesota switch.

AFTERMATH IN THE STATE

During the presidential campaign, most of the Taft dissidents closed ranks and helped the party carry out a vigorous program in support of its candidates. Most observers expected New Jersey to go Republican by a safe margin, but even Republican leaders were not expecting the Eisenhower margin of 350,000 that eventuated. Eisenhower ran at least as strongly as expected in rural and suburban areas, and showed unexpected strength in normally-Democratic industrial areas. The presidential ticket ran ahead of most Republican candidates; for example, about 90,000 ahead of Senator Smith, himself a strong candidate.

In the spring of 1953, the party found itself on the defensive politically and faced with new factional and leadership problems. Gover-

nor Driscoll announced he would not run for re-election; several
Republican counties were the scene of crime and corruption scandals
that threatened to involve the state administration; and Paul Troast,
the gubernatorial candidate backed by the county organizations, was
strongly, though unsuccessfully, challenged in the primary by a young
party rebel, Malcolm Forbes.

THE DEMOCRATIC DELEGATION

For thirty years the Democratic party in New Jersey was run by
one of the most notorious and long-lived of America's "bosses," Frank
Hague. Until his power was broken in 1949, he ruled Jersey City
through a combination of demagoguery, ruthlessness, public service,
and political acumen. He maintained his statewide control by turning
in colossal Hudson County majorities for Democratic candidates and
by influencing gubernatorial patronage. At the height of his power,
even some Republicans found it wise to "co-operate" with him. But
the defeat of Hague's candidate for mayor by John Kenny in May
1949 and of his candidate for governor the following November
signalled his political decline and opened the way for the rise of
new leadership.

At the beginning of 1952, however, Hague still commanded a large
and loyal following on the state committee. It was to circumvent this
group that the National Democratic Club of New Jersey was organized. Until the spring of 1953 the "trustees" of this club exercised
general supervision over party affairs in the state, performing most
of the leadership functions normally performed by the state committee
and its chairman. The group operated as a loose coalition of a half-
dozen county and regional leaders, under the guiding spirit of Thorn
Lord, Mercer County chairman. It included Mayor Kenny; former
Attorney-General David Wilentz; George E. Brunner, mayor of Camden; William Egan, Essex County chairman; Michael U. DeVita,
former mayor of Paterson; and Robert B. Meyner, former state senator and 1953 candidate for governor. The decision-making group
often included also State Chairman Edward J. Hart, who is also a
congressman, and Archibald Alexander, new national committeeman.
New Jersey Democratic delegations voted unanimously for Roose-

velt at the national conventions of 1940 and 1944, and for Truman in 1948, though in 1948 Hague's delegation was initially interested in an Eisenhower nomination on the Democratic ticket.

THE SELECTION PROCESS IN 1952

In 1952 it was clearly assumed that the new alliance of Democratic leaders in the state should and would choose the organization candidates for entry in the primary election. Early in the year these leaders were proceeding quietly and cautiously, sensible of their minority position, hoping that President Truman would decide to run for re-election and that they could persuade Archibald Alexander, then Under Secretary of the Army, to challenge Senator Smith.

Delegates-at-large—The selection of a slate of convention delegates was a part of this decorous process. As in the Republican party, recognition of prominent and faithful party supporters seemed the main basis for selecting candidates for delegates-at-large. But, in contrast with the Republican operation, no great effort was made to secure wide geographical representation; instead, the more strongly Democratic counties dominated the slate and more recognition was given to individual leaders and to minority and interest groups.

On February 20 Mayor Kenny revealed that former Governor A. Harry Moore and Representative Edward J. Hart would appear on the statewide slate. Then on March 3 the executive director of the National Democratic Club made public, along with several congressional candidacies, the names of four more candidates for delegate: Archibald Alexander, who had meanwhile announced his candidacy for the Senate; William J. Egan, Essex County chairman; Mrs. Thelma Parkinson Sharp, vice-chairman of the state committee; and Dwight G. Palmer, a wealthy corporation president. The other two of the eight half-vote delegate-at-large candidates were to be chosen from among the party faithful in Middlesex, Mercer, and Camden Counties. David T. Wilentz and John J. Crean were later selected for these places. Alternates were chosen to represent as nearly as possible other areas of the state, especially Democratic strongholds. All candidates were entered unpledged, and the slate of delegates-at-large had no opposition in the primary. An Associated Press poll of the 16 candidates for delegate- and alternate-at-large early in March, before

Truman withdrew, showed that he was easily their top choice, with Stevenson a strong second. Most delegates made it clear they would abide by general organization policy, and the National Democratic Club pledged its support to Truman.

District delegates—In general, district slates were chosen by the county chairmen, usually in consultation with their executive committees. The chairmen acted singly or in combination, as was appropriate to the district; and, as with the Republicans, the chairmen in multi-county districts were allocated shares of the four positions available on the basis of informal and more or less stable formulas. Again, party service was the prime criterion of selection. The organizations' district candidates were opposed only by three independent candidates entered in two districts (the 1st and 2d), and by two dissident-faction candidates (not Hague's) in each of Hudson County's two districts. The dissidents claimed to favor Senator Kefauver, though Kefauver spokesmen in the state disavowed them. Campaigning, at least on the part of the endorsed candidates, was purely nominal.

Presidential preference poll—Senator Kefauver was the only Democratic presidential candidate showing any interest in entering New Jersey's preference poll; his supporters in the state filed proper petitions for his entry before the March 6 deadline. It had been expected that if his name appeared on the ballot, the party leaders would also enter Truman's; but this move failed to materialize. Under the law Kefauver had until March 12 to decide whether to withdraw his name. After his New Hampshire victory he telephoned his supporters that he would leave his name on the ballot.

President Truman's announcement at the end of March that he would not accept re-nomination stunned the New Jersey leaders and left them without a candidate. Most of the delegates thenceforward seemed to favor Stevenson. Kefauver also had significant support, but many of the leaders, partly because of his apparent independent attitude toward the party organizations, partly because of his relatively unsatisfactory stand on civil rights, generally were inclined to look elsewhere for a candidate. The organization adopted a "wait and see" attitude toward his candidacy in the preference poll. When he campaigned in the state on the day before the primary, he received a cordial but noncommittal welcome from Mayor Kenny and other local leaders.

The outcome—The task of most voters in the Democratic primary was supremely simple, with only one slate of would-be delegates-at-large and one candidate in the preference poll. Even in the four districts where there was competition for district delegate the competition was nominal. On the ballot, the column of endorsed candidates for delegate-at-large bore the heading "Regular Organization Democrat."

About 250,000 Democrats voted in the April 15 primary, a fairly good showing considering the dearth of Democratic contests and the excitement of the Republican races. The whole organization slate of delegates was elected, the delegate-at-large candidates receiving on the average just under 210,000 votes each; apparently the total votes cast in district contests came to a somewhat lower figure. Kefauver received 154,964 preference votes, which was interpreted as an impressive showing, even though he ran 50,000 votes behind many candidates for delegate. Party leaders continued to stress that the organization was uncommitted and still looking about for a candidate.

COMPOSITION OF THE DELEGATION

The Democratic delegation, like the Republican, was in general a selection from the body of the party faithful. Archibald Alexander, former Under Secretary of the Army and candidate for the United States Senate, was probably most influential at the convention and among his fellow-delegates; probably second in influence was Mercer County Chairman Thorn Lord, whose wife was a delegate but who himself preferred to remain off the delegation; David T. Wilentz, former state chairman and former attorney-general, was also a relatively strong leader. Other better known delegates were A. Harry Moore, three-times governor; Edward J. Hart, congressman and state chairman; and Elmer Wene, ex-congressman and 1949 candidate for governor. In addition to Thorn Lord, others present and influential, but not delegates, were Congressman Charles Howell and Joseph McLean, the latter much involved in the "draft Stevenson" movement. Frank Hague, though still national committeeman, had been omitted; and Mrs. Norton, the committeewoman, was ill, as was Mayor Kenny. Besides Hart, one other congressman was an alternate. No state legislators were included, but several city commissioners, mayors, and other local officials appeared among the district delegates. Further party officials included three county chairmen as delegates and two more as alternates, a few members of the state committee, and several city ward leaders.

Almost half the 36 delegates fell into one occupational category: they were lawyers. Approximately another one-fourth of the delegation was composed of full-time local government officials. Some four or five delegates belonged to the business community, only one of them being in the "executive" category. Two delegates were CIO leaders. Two of the lawyers often represent organized labor; one of them was both special counsel to the New Jersey Federation of Labor and a county chairman. One or two delegates appear to have been full-time party workers; most of the delegates—especially the lawyers—are active in this respect. Two housewives, a farmer, an undertaker, and a dentist completed the delegation. An even greater occupational variety was apparent among the alternates. It is estimated that most of the delegates receive annual incomes of from $5,000 to $10,000.

A majority of the delegates were between 45 and 60 years old, the approximate median and average being 51. Two women were delegates, ten were alternates. Probably a slight majority of the total were of Roman Catholic background, mostly Irish. The inclusion of several delegates with Italian and Polish background, and at least two Jews, evidently reflected a conscious attempt to give representation to these ethnic and religious groups. The one Negro delegate was at the same time one of the CIO representatives; at least one other Negro, likewise a CIO official, was an alternate. Organized labor was relatively well represented; besides the two union leaders and two lawyers mentioned as delegates, three alternates were union officials.

Nine of the 36 delegates had also been delegates to the 1948 convention, and four were alternates in that year. At least six of this year's delegates served as delegates in 1944, and at least four in 1940, three of these four persisting as delegates through all four conventions.

The average Democratic delegate apparently spent rather less money in Chicago than did the average Republican. Again, the state organization provided no funds to help with individual convention expenses; but some of the delegates were partly financed by the interest groups with which they were associated.

ACTIVITIES AND VOTING RECORD

The New Jersey delegation entrained for Chicago unpledged, uninstructed, and unbossed for the first time in over twenty years; and its ultimate choice among the presidential candidates was almost as uncertain actually as it was legally. The Jersey delegates assumed that Stevenson would probably not consent to run, and on this assumption they tended to favor either Kefauver or Harriman, Kefauver being relatively more popular with the rank-and-file and Harriman with the leaders.

Several significant actions had occurred before the delegation left for Chicago. On April 24, as the party's state convention met, the state committee voted to recommend Archibald Alexander as new national committeeman, replacing Frank Hague, who had served in that position since 1922. This move signalled the final demise of Hague as a power in the state organization. Hague decided not to attend the national convention, but passed his national committee proxy and the perquisites of office to Charles Quinn, longtime secretary of the state committee. Former Congresswoman Mary T. Norton, despite her illness and relative inactivity, was retained as national committeewoman—partly as a conciliatory gesture toward the remaining Hague forces, partly because no woman prominent in the party cared to contest her for the position.

Early in May the delegates, along with the trustees of the National Democratic Club of New Jersey, met at Princeton and heard speeches by invited presidential candidates or their representatives. Kefauver appealed for support on the basis of his strength in the preference poll. Kerr also spoke in person. Harriman, Russell, and McMahon sent representatives. Afterward the delegates decided in a closed meeting to take no stand on candidates at that time. Harriman and Russell later made personal visits to the state in search of support. Russell spent a day in Jersey City where he talked with some half-dozen delegates. But, although A. Harry Moore did once announce that Russell would get his vote, Russell was the only candidate clearly *not* acceptable to most New Jersey delegates in view of the crucial character of the civil rights issue in the state. Harriman spoke to a large group of delegates at a dinner held in mid-July; he apparently made a favorable impression and improved his already substantial standing with the delegation.

The delegation was formally organized at a meeting held June 15 at a country club near Asbury Park. Representative Hart, the state chairman, was elected chairman and floor leader; Mrs. Elizabeth McBride was chosen as vice-chairman, and Mrs. Nina Lord as secretary. Wilentz and Mrs. Thelma Sharp were designated as members of the resolutions committee, although Alexander substituted for Wilentz when the committee met. Louis Messano represented the state on credentials and John Keenan on rules. A resolution was passed committing the delegates not to express publicly any preference for a candidate before the next meeting of the delegation at Chicago. Other resolutions favored a strong civil rights plank, the Truman foreign policy, revision of the Senate cloture rule, and repeal of the Taft-Hartley Act.

The first caucus at Chicago was held Sunday evening; on a motion by Wilentz the delegates agreed to defer making a choice of presidential nominee for one or two more days. Harriman had made a direct bid to the leaders for New Jersey support; but some Kefauver supporters, notably T. James Tumulty of Jersey City, felt strongly that the delegation should be seriously influenced by the preferential poll. The situation was still flexible, and the likelihood of a Stevenson candidacy seemed to be increasing. This same caucus instructed the state's member of the credentials committee to vote against seating the anti-Truman delegations from Texas and Mississippi unless they agreed to support the convention's nominees.

Archibald Alexander was the state's most active and influential delegate. He had an important role in the "draft Stevenson" movement, having worked vigorously for this candidate from the time Truman took himself out of the race. At Chicago he was in frequent consultation with Stevenson forces and Stevenson himself; he was asked to make the chief seconding speech and actually drafted it, only to have his effort wasted when no such speeches were permitted. Alexander and Chairman Hart maintained close and friendly liaison throughout the convention with National Chairman Frank McKinney and others of the national leadership.

Stevenson sentiment continued to increase among New Jersey delegates as in the whole convention, and at a Tuesday evening caucus the leaders felt the time was right for a poll of the delegation. The result was Stevenson 23½, Kefauver 3, not voting 2, and absent 3½. Thus, even before Pennsylvania, New Jersey was the first large uncommitted state to swing most of its votes behind Stevenson. A poll of the alternates had approximately the same result. Two delegates and one alternate who passed were CIO leaders waiting for the recommendation of that organization. A motion to "suggest" that Kefauver be chosen as vice-presidential candidate was passed. New Jersey's move at this time made it one of the first states to swing its support to Stevenson, and was considered a major blow to the Kefauver-Harriman forces.

On the convention floor, the delegates unanimously supported the Moody resolution by voice vote, though a half dozen of them joined in the unsuccessful request for a roll call on Senator Holland's motion for a substitute. Alexander spoke from the platform in favor of the original resolution. On the later questions involving the seating of southern delegations, the New Jersey delegates voted consistently with the northern liberals. They opposed seating the anti-Truman delegations from Texas and Mississippi, and their delegate on the credentials committee had so voted; but they joined in the convention's voice vote to seat these delegations after they had complied with the Moody resolution. They later voted unanimously not to seat Virginia. Only seven New Jersey delegates could be mustered when the roll call on this issue began; but as other delegates arrived, no dissenters were found, and no one accepted the opportunity to switch his vote when the tide began running to seat Virginia. On the Douglas resolution to adjourn early Friday morning, favored by Kefauver forces, the delegates voted 24 to table, 8 against tabling.

On the first nominating ballot, the delegation gave 28 votes to Stevenson, 3 to Kefauver, and 1 to Harriman. For the second and third ballots, the Harriman vote shifted to Kefauver, and the score read: Stevenson 28, Kefauver 4. On the final ballot, Hart had been authorized to make the delegation's vote unanimous, but failed to obtain the attention of the chair.

The delegates were glad to have been early occupants of the Stevenson bandwagon, and to have made an effective and united showing in exercising their new-found freedom from boss domination. For their own purposes, they would probably have been happier with Kefauver as vice-presidential nominee; but they were quite willing to make some concessions for national party harmony.

The party undertook a vigorous campaign, but Stevenson lost by over 350,000 votes and carried only three counties. Hudson County gave the ticket only a 7,500 plurality—one-tenth of what had been expected. The Hudson fiasco was interpreted as a sign of weakness in the Kenny leadership, but other Democratic strongholds also failed to turn out their accustomed voters.

Democrats comforted themselves by noting that they held all their five seats in Congress and all their county court houses, despite the Eisenhower sweep. Party leaders began immediately to plan a reorganization, a move required by the internal party situation as well as the electoral defeat. The leaders dissolved the National Democratic Club and began efforts to reconstitute the state committee as the actual governing body of the party, preferably with one leader rather than a coalition to speak for New Jersey Democrats. In the spring of 1953, the Kenny-Hague feud was revived in Jersey City and to some extent was reflected in the gubernatorial primary, in which an unknown, Robert Meyner, supported by most of the new leadership, very narrowly defeated Elmer Wene, Hague's candidate against Driscoll in 1949. In doing so, Meyner upset most expectations. He continued to upset expectations when he swept into the governor's office in the fall of 1953 over Republican Paul L. Troast.

REVIEW AND APPRAISAL

The system by which the New Jersey electorate is enabled to participate in the presidential nominating process is remarkable for its flexibility, apparent efficiency, and relative simplicity. Almost any combinations of possibilities can be given expression on the New Jersey ballot. Filing is relatively simple and easy for all classes of candidates. The ballot is also relatively easy to vote, and particularly so if account is taken of the variety of opportunities that it is capable of offering the voter. Organized slates of delegates may be placed on the ballot as such when they exist, either under the name of a candidate if the candidate consents, under a ballot slogan, or as unpledged. Individual candidates for delegate may also run under the same conditions. Presidential candidates may run, complete with a slate of delegates under their name on the ballot; or they may enter the preference contest without entering delegates, thus giving the voter an opportunity to express an enthusiasm without compelling him to enter an instruction.

Yet with all of these possibilities in a year of active contests throughout the country, New Jersey produced two delegations both of which were elected unpledged and each of which had been actually named for the most part by the regular organization of the party in question. Insurgency and factionalism were both given ample opportunities on the ballot, and yet the outcome was apparently not seriously in doubt at any time except in one or two of the district delegate contests.

Senator Taft's vigorous denunciation of Governor Driscoll came in March, and was widely considered an act of bad judgment on the Senator's part. But after Driscoll's announcement for Eisenhower, Taft was in an unenviable position: the probability was that he would be denied the delegate votes of New Jersey even if he won the preference poll, his chances of winning the poll had been gravely prejudiced by the unanticipated mobilization of organization strength against him, and it was too late to enter delegate candidates either at large or in the districts where he might have been able to pick up a few delegate votes even if he lost the preference poll. Presumably Taft thought he had some basis for supposing that the organization would keep itself uncommitted at least until after the primary was over.

Taft had given extensive and careful consideration to the possibility of entering a slate and thus making a direct contest for the New Jersey votes. So far as the record shows, Senator Estes Kefauver did not seriously consider such a possibility, and he did not enter a slate in New Jersey, although he filed contesting slates of pledged delegates in opposition to the regular organization in New Hampshire.

Wisconsin, Ohio, South Dakota, and California. In the other states just named, he won delegates in a series of actual contests for delegate votes, in most cases with little trouble. But in New Jersey, he entered only the preference poll, where in the end his name stood on the ballot unopposed, although the filing conditions in New Jersey for a slate of pledged delegates were relatively simple.

Popular opinions about national candidates might be expected, under New Jersey's present system, to find their most effective expression in the preference poll campaign, even though the poll is not binding. Three Republican candidates were entered in the preference poll; and despite the confusion over Taft's candidacy the campaign and its outcome did demonstrate the real differences of opinion among the electorate and to some degree within the party organization. It happened that the clear expression of pro-Eisenhower sentiment corresponded with the preference of a majority of the successful organization slate of delegates. But under the circumstances it cannot be concluded that there was much evidence showing considerable influence of the preference poll on delegate behavior; and the successful candidates for delegate were selected with much more regard for organizational loyalty than for their preferences among the national candidates.

On the Democratic side, the limited influence of national considerations was simpler and clearer. The slate of delegates was made up by local leaders on the basis of essentially local criteria. The question of presidential choice remained fluid throughout the process from slate-making to the opening of the convention. With only Kefauver entered, the preference poll was almost useless as an indication of public preference or an influence on the delegates. The Democratic delegates were chosen for mainly local reasons and were left free to make their own decisions on national candidates and issues.

One characteristic notable in both delegations, but especially in the Republican, was the absence of most members of Congress. The Democratic delegation included one of its five representatives in Congress, the Republican delegation none of nine. This general lack of serious consideration for congressmen seems to reflect a conviction that a candidate's name should appear only once on the ballot, that party honors should be spread over as wide a field as possible, and that valuable prestige patronage should not be wasted. In any case, it is evident that congressmen are not likely to be chosen as delegates unless they are coincidentally real grass-roots leaders and centers of power in their party. Both delegations split their convention votes, with the great majority in each case voting for the winning candidate and a small minority agreed on another. The Democrats appear to have made their choices largely on the basis of personal preference, whichever candidate they supported; whatever organizational pressures they may have felt were local (county) in origin, and to a lesser degree national, through National Committeeman Alexander. Republican delegates appear to have been more conscious of potential pressure from Governor Driscoll and their county leaders; some of those voting for Eisenhower did so against their personal preferences. On the other hand, some who voted for Taft did so partly out of opposition to Driscoll. It was notable that of the five delegates who voted for Taft, four came from districts heavily favorable to Eisenhower; while the delegates from the only county that Taft carried voted for Eisenhower.

In summary, it may be said of New Jersey's direct election of delegates in 1952 that it did produce delegations that were reasonably representative and effective. Both delegations were able to play important roles at their respective conventions, partly because each was able to provide an early and relatively large bloc of votes to the winning candidate. Eisenhower leaders from the beginning could depend on 30 New Jersey votes, and the state's Democrats were among the first delegations to announce strong support for Stevenson. Both contingents had competent leadership, but neither was "bossed" in anything approaching the old-fashioned sense of the word; and their convention votes reflected to a considerable degree and on a statewide basis the sentiments of the rank-and-file party voters.

New Jersey Chapter Acknowledgments

HARRY R. DAVIS, Assistant Professor of Government, Beloit College, on leave as a Ford Foundation fellow, 1952-53, undertook the necessary field investigations and prepared the draft of the New Jersey chapter pursuant to a request in November 1952. He obtained assistance in reviewing his draft from PROFESSORS ROBERT DARROW and JOSEPH MCLEAN of Princeton University, and from JOHN E. BEBOUT of the National Municipal League.

DANIEL CAREY DAHL prepared an extensive senior thesis at Princeton University on the New Jersey delegations of 1952, completed April 20, 1953. Portions of his information from interviews and questionnaires were incorporated in the chapter by Professor Davis, and a copy of his thesis is included in project files.

DELAWARE

Electoral votes, 1952: 3

National convention votes, 1952:
Democratic, 6
Republican, 12

Population, 1950: 318,085
Urban, 63%; rural nonfarm, 26%; rural farm, 11%

Population increase, 1940-50: 51,580 (19%)
Urban, 6%; rural nonfarm, 67%; rural farm, 25% decline

Presidential vote, 1948:		*1952:*
Democratic,	67,813 (49%)	83,315 (48%)
Republican,	69,588 (50%)	90,059 (52%)
Progressive,	1,050 (1%)	

Gubernatorial vote, 1948:	*1952:*
Democratic,	75,339	81,772
Republican,	64,996	88,977

U. S. Representatives vote, all districts, 1950:	*1952:*
Democratic,	56,091	81,730
Republican,	73,313	88,285

U. S. Representatives elected 1950:	*1952:*
Democratic,	0	0
Republican,	1	1

State legislature elected 1952:
Senate: Democrats, 7; Republicans, 10
House: Democrats, 17; Republicans, 18

Method of selecting national convention delegates:
State conventions

216

Based primarily on reports by PAUL DOLAN

CHAPTER 10

DELAWARE, THE "FIRST STATE" OF THE UNION, ranks second smallest among the states in area and third smallest in population. It
has but one representative in Congress, hence only three votes in
the electoral college. The state has only three counties: New Castle,
in which Wilmington (pop. 110,356) is located and which contains
nearly 67 per cent of the state's population; Kent, the middle county,
containing Dover, the state capital, and about 12 per cent of the
population; and rural Sussex to the south, with 21 per cent of the
state's population. Delaware is technically the home state for many
large corporations with Delaware charters. New Castle County is
the actual home of the main establishment of the Du Pont chemical
industries. Delaware is also a border state and retains some of the
southern tradition, particularly in its rural areas. Fourteen per cent
of the state's population are Negroes, now chiefly concentrated in
Wilmington. There is a Negro representative, a Democrat, in the
state legislature, but racial segregation still prevails generally.

The state is one with special fascination for the political scientist.
So small that other parts of the country often regard it as a museum
piece, it mirrors a remarkable number of facets of the political life
of the country as a whole. The Democratic party in the state includes
an aristocratic gentry in the Jeffersonian tradition, a southern white
yeomanry, a growing industrial union element, and Negroes both
urban and rural who are conscious of the problems of their race.
The Republican party includes families of industrial wealth and long-
established position, rising business and professional groups in an
urban setting, many white collar workers, and a sturdy group of
farmers who value their independence of urban control.

Delaware has become one of the most closely balanced two-party

217

states in the Union. Up to the turn of the century, the state had been predominantly Democratic. Since the early 1900's, Republican strength has grown, and election results are today unpredictable. From 1932 to 1952, the city of Wilmington voted Democratic in national elections but usually Republican in local elections. The suburban and rural areas of New Castle County, where great wealth is centered, are normally Republican, but veered toward the Democratic column in the 1940's. Kent is generally considered Democratic; but Sussex, though it has contributed such important Democratic leaders as former Senator Tunnell and Governor Carvel, more often goes Republican. The state went for Dewey in 1948 but elected a Democratic governor. Members of the duPont family are active in both parties, but most of them are Republicans. The Bayards, who have figured prominently in American history, are still mainly Democratic.

The closeness of the party vote does not necessarily mean that the voter is presented with a real choice of policies. Both parties tend to be conservative. Recently, the Democrats in the northern section of the state have courted the labor and large minority vote located there by declaring for abolition of segregation and for liberal labor laws. They were instrumental in repealing a "little Taft-Hartley" act which the preceding Republican legislature had passed. The fact, however, that the middle county, Kent, tends to be Democratic and at the same time is highly rural prevents the Democratic state machinery from swinging completely to the industrial worker vote and espousing wholeheartedly the interests of the various minorities. The Republicans, on the other hand, realize they also must not disregard the worker and Negro vote in New Castle County, yet their great strength both in numbers and in funds rests with the middle and upper classes. They also have a large following among the conservative rural population of the downstate counties. Contests, therefore, are largely based upon personalities with overtones of appeals to blocs of votes found among the varied interest groups throughout the state. The parties, although county based, serve paradoxically to place the political process on a statewide basis. This perhaps results from the fact that in so small a state the county leaders are aware of the political problems that exist elsewhere in achieving victory throughout the state.

The ordinary citizen rarely participates in party affairs prior to the general election, but does usually exercise the franchise at that time. There is evidence that the party hierarchy when selecting nominees is conscious of the voter's power at the general election.

The county has been the unit for national delegate apportionment, though Wilmington is now acknowledged as a separate unit in both parties, comprising "district one" in the Republican state conventions where national delegates are named, and with separate but less formal treatment in the Democratic conventions. Under the national rules of both parties, all delegate posts allocated to Delaware are considered at-large, because the one congressional district comprises the entire state. The practice in Delaware, however, is to assign all national convention delegates to specific areas in the state.

THE REPUBLICAN DELEGATION

Delaware was entitled to 12 Republican delegates in 1952, including six as a bonus for having gone Republican in 1948. In accordance with past practice, the Republican state committee apportioned the 12 posts equally among the four state convention districts: the city of Wilmington; the remainder of New Castle County; Kent County; and Sussex County. Had the apportionment been based solely on the Republican vote in 1948, Wilmington and New Castle County would each have been given four delegates, while Kent and Sussex would have been given two.

The Republican delegations from Delaware have since the beginning of the present century been made up in large part of well-known public figures. Senators and former senators, governors and former governors have consistently been named to serve. Three or four seats in an average of eight places have been "reserved" for the elder statesmen of the party. The county chairman's task of selecting national delegates is therefore largely *pro forma* because of the outstanding personages in each county who it is assumed "must" be named. In 1940 two former United States senators and the incumbent representative were named as three members in a delegation of six. In 1944, the nine delegates included the same two former senators, the incumbent governor, and the representative in Congress. Five of the nine delegates in 1948 were of this category. Since 1924 each delegation has included the patriarch of the party, John G. Townsend, Jr., former senator and former governor. Mr. C. Douglass Buck, also a former senator and former governor, was a delegate in 1940, 1944, and 1948. It has been the custom to appoint one of the wealthy party members from northern New Castle County. After the outstanding personages are chosen, the other honors are passed around among workers who have given long standing service to the party.

The Delaware delegates to the national convention are chosen by a state convention known as the "little convention," to distinguish it from a later state convention that nominates elective state and congressional officials. To the little convention are sent 160 delegates who are nominally chosen in primaries administered by the parties and held the Saturday preceding the convention. The seats are allocated by the state committee: 38 from rural New Castle County, 40 from Wilmington, 40 from Kent County; and 42 from Sussex County. In 1952 the rural counties made an unsuccessful attempt to secure increased representation. Actually, except in rare cases when contests develop, neither direct primaries nor local meetings of party members are held. The slate of state convention delegates for each county is determined by the executives of the party in the county and local units on an informal basis. The Republican party requires a filing fee of $5, payable to the county committee, of any person who declares his intention to run as a candidate for the post of delegate to the state convention. The names of the persons comprising the slate in each local district are filed with the county chairman and when there are no opposing candidates the primary is *pro forma*, and on primary day, the slate is declared elected with a token vote.

In the meantime the county chairman, after consultation with the district leaders in his county, draws up a list of persons he favors as national convention delegates from his county. If he is in good standing with the state leaders and his list contains no controversial names, the state policy committee gives approval. It is usually known, therefore, well in advance of the little convention who the national delegates will be. Because of the custom of including elder statesmen among the Delaware delegates to the national convention, the county chairman's choice is somewhat limited. Immediately preceding the

meeting of the little convention (usually on the Wednesday of the
last week of April), the state convention delegates from each convention district meet in caucus to formalize the list of national delegates. The little convention then ratifies the choice unless there has
been a contest which the defeated faction wishes to bring to the floor
of the convention. In that case, the entire convention votes on the
nominees. Delegates from other districts usually support the decision
of the district majority; in no instance in recent years has the verdict
of the district caucus been overthrown.

THE SELECTION PROCESS IN 1952

While party harmony is the rule in Delaware, early 1952 saw the
development of several cleavages between young new members of
the party organization and the older leadership. Most of these
cleavages were solved by compromise or agreement among party
leaders. Only seven state convention seats among the 160 in the
state were challenged in the primaries; none at all in Wilmington or
Kent County. In Sussex County, a group of Active Young Republicans
(AYR) challenged the older leadership in the Sussex County caucus
and captured one of the three national delegate posts. There was little
indication that the contest was connected with the support of rival
presidential candidates. In Kent County, however, where the pre-
convention battle was kept undercover, the "young Turks" attached
themselves to the Citizens Committee for Eisenhower and opposed the
oldsters who favored Taft. A compromise gave representation to the
younger group. Serious splits occurred also in the first district, which
comprises the city of Wilmington, where a battle for control within
the city took place between Mayor Hearn and C. J. Killoran, former
state attorney-general and present state chairman. The latter won out
in a spirited caucus fight. Part of this struggle was the result of a
strong Eisenhower movement in the city which was opposed by Hearn
and former Governor Bacon, who was supported by Hearn for the
national delegation. Bacon was a Taft man. In addition, however,
to the Eisenhower-Taft relationship, there was a fight between the
Wilmington politicians and the rising leadership in the northern
rural part of New Castle County. Under party rule, rural New Castle
and Wilmington are divided into two convention districts. Until

recently, the city politicians tended to dominate the activity of the rural district. With the advent of politically active intellectual, professional and business groups associated with the rising industries in that part of the state, the old city leadership has been challenged. In April 1952, after a sharp controversy in the New Castle Republican county committee, the rural district people set up their own leadership and are now completely free from city domination. In two instances, one in rural New Castle and the other in Sussex, there were demands to poll the state convention delegates to obtain their preferences for a national delegate or for a prospective presidential candidate, but no vote was announced.

The 1952 little convention was held on April 30, lasting from about 1:30 P.M. until 5:00 P.M. It had the atmosphere of an orderly and sedate social function, and provided an opportunity for party leaders from over the state to meet each other in Dover. Their ostensible function had already been largely performed. The only question raised in the convention which gave evidence of the pre-convention district cleavages was the allegation of the pro-Bacon men that they had been "steam-rollered" by the Killoran faction in the Wilmington district caucus. The plenary body supported the Killoran, or majority, faction.

COMPOSITION OF THE DELEGATION

The delegation included major Republican personages of the state: state chairman Clair J. Killoran, designated chairman of the delegation; state senator Thomas E. Peeney, chairman of the Department of Elections; and deputy Attorney General Henry J. Ridgely. Also selected were two former United States Senators, John G. Townsend, Jr., dean of the delegation, and Daniel O. Hastings. Former city councilman John O. Hopkins was the only Negro on the delegation. For the first time since 1932 no woman was named as a delegate, but five of the alternates were women. There were two delegates of considerable wealth; two were businessmen. Senator John Williams and the two members of the national committee were not included.

ACTIVITIES AND VOTING RECORD

At the time of their selection, four delegates favored Eisenhower; four were for Taft. Preferences of the others were not known. No delegation since 1940 has been instructed by the state convention. Apparently no commitments had been made. The delegates acted on the theory that they were entitled to exercise their individual rights of judgment and expression. They were not hired hands of the state leaders. They were, severally but not collectively, the leaders.

At its first meeting on May 23 in Wilmington, the delegation appointed Hastings to the credentials committee of the national convention, Ridgely to rules, and Townsend to resolutions. Killoran, an Eisenhower supporter, in the interests of party harmony had stepped aside for Hastings on the credentials committee, thereby giving an apparently unforeseen advantage to the Taft forces. During the convention, Hastings and Townsend were rarely seen at the delegation headquarters at the Palmer House and did not attend the caucuses. There was little opportunity for them to ascertain the views of the other delegates on the important questions coming before their committees, credentials and resolutions.

In the caucuses, there was some discussion of offering the name of Senator John Williams as a vice-presidential candidate, but when word came on Thursday of the choice of Nixon, this plan was abandoned. All the delegates, except John Hopkins, the Negro delegate whose illness prevented his attendance, participated in much of the work of the delegation. Killoran was a conscientious and energetic chairman, but Francis V. duPont, the national committeeman, was a leading force among the liberal-moderate group, and extremely persuasive in terms of victory in November.

On the nominating roll call vote the delegation divided 7 for Eisenhower and 5 for Taft. There had been some indication of a swing toward the General when on the seating of the Georgia delegation Delaware went 8 to 4.

AFTERMATH IN THE STATE

After the Chicago convention, the Republican leaders of both factions closed ranks and worked tirelessly for an Eisenhower victory. A strong slate within the state, particularly the candidacy of Congressman Boggs for governor and of Senator Williams for another Senate term, contributed to unity. As a result of their role in the selection of delegates and their effective campaigning on Eisenhower's

behalf, the Active Young Republicans (AYR) achieved an acknowledged place in the party councils. The older politicians, taking note
of the large vote for the Carvel-Stevenson ticket and the Democratic
bid for young people, will probably accept the AYR as a continuing
voice in the party. This development may signify some continuing
strength of the liberalizing elements as against the rural conservatism
of the southern part of the state and the outspoken individualism of
some of the northern industrialists.

THE DEMOCRATIC DELEGATION

As a state with only delegates-at-large, Delaware has had the option
under the national Democratic rules of splitting all of its national
convention votes and doubling the size of its delegation. Perhaps
because of the aristocratic tradition of the state, this opportunity has
not been used in recent years. Every Delaware delegate since 1912
at least, had had a full vote. In 1952, only the regular 6 votes were
allotted, since the state had voted for Dewey in 1948.

The basic procedure for selecting Democratic national delegates is
almost identical with that previously described for the selection of
Republican delegates. Officials of both parties have similar attitudes
in exercising the discretion permitted by state law. The Democratic
state committee, however, follows a somewhat different pattern in
allotting national convention delegates to the counties. In 1952, it
allotted two delegates and one alternate to Wilmington, one delegate
and one alternate to rural New Castle County, one delegate and two
alternates to Kent, and two delegates and two alternates to Sussex.

The Delaware delegations of 1936, 1940, 1944 were instructed to
vote for Roosevelt, but this does not denote an orientation toward
ultra-liberalism. Most of the delegates have been moderately conservative, especially on matters within the state. In national affairs, they
supported much of the New Deal legislation and have given sponta-
neous allegiance to liberal candidates. There appears to be no simple
explanation for this anomaly.

THE SELECTION PROCESS IN 1952

The Democratic "little convention" consists of 210 members chosen as follows: 60 from each of the southern counties, Kent and Sussex; 60 from rural New Castle; and 30 from the city of Wilmington. The "primaries", usually held early in May, determine the delegates to be sent to the state convention at Dover. The state convention delegates are hand-picked by the local leaders and the county executive committees. The county committee's function is to supervise and to pass on the choice of the local leaders. In 1952, there were no contests in any of the districts. When the "little convention" met on May 24, only one question was raised concerning procedure: whether the national committeeman and national committeewoman were elected for four years or for two. The chairman announced it was the latter.

As with the Republicans, the selection of national convention delegates is carefully prepared in advance. The list is generally known before the little convention meets. There was no contest in 1952 and the business was finished quickly. There was no attempt in 1952 to find out how the convention felt respecting any proposed national candidate. No poll was taken of the national delegates themselves after they were chosen as to whom they would support. They were instructed to vote as a unit.

COMPOSITION OF THE DELEGATION

It was a foregone conclusion that Governor Carvel, who comes from western Sussex County, would be a delegate. For the other post in Sussex, there was a factional contest between state senators Ayres and Cannon, with the result that former United States Senator Tunnell was named as a compromise. In Kent, Vernon Derrickson, county chairman and himself a potential candidate for delegate, announced that if Senator J. Allen Frear wished to go as a delegate, he should have the only post allotted to the county. Frear was named, and Derrickson went as an alternate. In rural New Castle, H. B. McDowell, the Delaware secretary of state and Democratic state chairman, was clearly the logical choice. In Wilmington, Lieutenant Governor A. I. duPont Bayard and Colonel E. Ennalls Berl, the national committeeman, were chosen. Bayard aroused enthusiasm at the little state convention by announcing his availability to run against the incumbent Republican Senator, John Williams. Bayard's family has given the state six United States senators and countless lesser officials. Colonel Berl is a leader in the achievement of Democratic party harmony in the state of Delaware. He is a member of a conservative law firm with many of the state's important corporations among its clients, but gives much of his time to politics.

ACTIVITIES AND VOTING RECORD

In organizing for the national convention, the delegates chose Governor Carvel as chairman and appointed Bayard to the rules committee, Senator Tunnell and Harris McDowell to resolutions, and Colonel Berl to credentials, The first formal caucus of the delegation was held on Tuesday, July 22, as a direct result of the withdrawal of Vice President Barkley from the race. Carvel, Frear, Bayard and Tunnell had favored Barkley, while McDowell and Berl favored Harriman. Governor Carvel spoke in behalf of Stevenson and at the Wednesday morning caucus the delegates voted unanimously to give their 6 votes to Stevenson, as they later did on all three ballots— one of the very few states to do so. In the meantime, Carvel had called a meeting of some thirteen governors on Monday afternoon to discuss the problem of the nomination, and had later volunteered to nominate Stevenson or to make a seconding speech for him.

The loyalty oath problem was viewed with mixed feelings by the Delaware delegation. Delegates concerned with holding the trade union and Negro vote in Wilmington were inclined to hedge, but no one on the delegation was prepared to adopt a militant attitude toward the South. The group was reportedly unanimous in its desire to seat the Virginia delegation and would have so voted even without the unit rule. Delaware's six votes had been recorded for seating before other states began to switch.

The 1952 delegation was not a group of yes-men. Although instructed to vote as a unit, the delegates were all outstanding personalities, not dominated by any one leader.

Stevenson's nomination along with that of Carvel and Bayard presented the voters with an extremely strong slate. Stevenson gained acclaim rapidly throughout the state, especially in Wilmington, which gave him a handsome plurality. He ran ahead of his ticket, with Carvel a good second. Bayard came out a poor third in his fight with Williams, but retained wide popularity in the state. The Democrats failed to organize effectively in the newly populated fringe "hundreds" in rural New Castle county. Here voters split their tickets to a greater extent than elsewhere in the state. The expected record turnout of the Democrats among the industrial workers did not materialize. But in spite of the great personal appeal of Eisenhower and Williams, the Democrats did exceptionally well in other areas, and emerged from the election with sufficient strength to give them encouragement.

REVIEW AND APPRAISAL

Political leaders in Delaware are beginning to express concern over the state's archaic election laws. Certainly the state provides extreme examples of rural over-representation in its legislature and in its state political conventions. It is probably in violation of the national Republican rules, which provide that the voting strength in state conventions electing national convention delegates shall be apportioned with regard for the Republican vote in the state.

The delegations of 1952 reflected the sense of harmony found in the organizations in each party without being subservient to any one leader. But the life of a party, fed by wide participation and frequent contests, generally accepted as a requisite for the democratic process, seems to be lacking in Delaware. The so-called primary consists in fact of the naming of delegates to the "little convention" by the local leaders, not by the rank-and-file of party members. And the little convention itself is an inarticulate body, gathered together to go through a previously arranged routine.

The Delaware pattern as a whole exemplifies in striking fashion the advantages and disadvantages of an aristocratic type of politics in the better sense of the term—a type such as survives in few American

states and in even fewer in which the two major parties are closely
balanced and actively competitive. Some of the disadvantages have
just been indicated; and certainly there were few evidences of democratic control within either party—except as the leaders give consideration to the vote-getting possibilities of alternative candidates and
courses of action, an important exception in a competitive two-party
system. But so far as its participation in the presidential nominating
process was concerned, Delaware could be proud of its record in
1952. In both major parties, it produced delegations that were made
up of its outstanding public men, leaders who took the honor and
responsibility seriously and who had far more influence at the national
conventions than is usually accorded the delegation of any small state.
As to the representative character of the state's delegations at the
national conventions, there is no real indication that the people of
Delaware as a whole are dissatisfied with the method of choosing delegates. In view of the general approval and respect accorded the several delegates throughout the state, it would be difficult to accuse
either delegation of being "unrepresentative" of its constituency. At
least there was accord throughout the state in respect of the final
nominations made by both parties at the national conventions.

Delaware Chapter Acknowledgments

PAUL DOLAN, Associate Professor of Political Science, University of Delaware, prepared pre-convention reports on both delegations, accompanied the
Republican delegation to Chicago, reported later on the activities of both
delegations at Chicago, and assisted in the revision of the draft chapter.

The initial draft in chapter form was prepared by MRS. ESTHER COLE
FRANKLIN of the Washington staff.

MARYLAND

Electoral votes, 1952: 9

National convention votes, 1952:
Democratic, 18
Republican, 24

Population, 1950: 2,343,001
Urban, 69%; *rural nonfarm,* 23%; *rural farm,* 8%

Population increase, 1940-50: 521,757 (29%)
Urban, 18%; *rural nonfarm,* 78%; *rural farm,* 24% decline

Presidential vote, 1948:   *1952:*
Democratic,   286,521 (48%)   395,337 (44%)
Republican,   294,814 (49%)   499,424 (55%)
Progressive,   9,983 (2%)   7,313 (1%)
States Rights,   2,476
Other,   2,941

Gubernatorial vote, 1950:
Democratic,   275,324
Republican,   369,807

U. S. Representatives vote,
all districts, 1950:   *1952:*
Democratic,   283,727   405,135
Republican,   285,957   436,113

U. S. Representatives elected 1950:   *1952:*
Democratic,   3   3
Republican,   3   4

State legislature elected 1952:
Senate: Democrats, 18;   Republicans, 11
House: Democrats, 88;   Republicans, 35

Method of selecting national convention delegates:
Democratic: state convention
Republican: state convention and congressional district caucuses

230

Based primarily on reports by MALCOLM MOOS

———————————————————————CHAPTER 11

IN NATIONAL POLITICS, Maryland likes to be on the winning side. For the eighteenth time in nineteen elections since 1880 her electoral vote went for the presidential winner in 1952. Only in 1948 when Governor Dewey broke the spell did the Free State defect from the victory column, and then only by a plurality of 8,293 votes out of a total of 591,318.

On the registration books, Democrats rate as heavy favorites. Among Maryland's 23 counties, Republican registrants are in the majority in just three counties. Statewide, Democratic registration runs ahead of declared Republican affiliations by a three to one margin; in the City of Baltimore, where approximately half the state's population resides, by the ratio of approximately four to one. But while Maryland voters like to register as Democrats, their behavior at the ballot box indicates they are a perverse lot. The Maryland voter likes to split his ticket, particularly in presidential elections, which are frequently close contests. In 1904 only 51 votes out of 224,224 separated the Democratic and Republican presidential candidates; 1,385 out of 238,533 in 1908; and 8,293 out of close to 600,000 votes in 1948.

Though the Republicans have proved effective challengers in the presidential field, they have been hard-pressed to build strength at other levels. Out of 36 Baltimore members of the Maryland House of Delegates, only one is a Republican; of the six state senators from the city, all are Democrats. Statewide, the Democrats outnumber Republicans in the lower house three to one; in the senate two to one. A Democrat usually occupies the governor's chair, and the same party invariably holds state constitutional offices such as attorney general and comptroller. Since the Civil War, Republicans have elected only four governors. During the same period there have been just six Republican United States senators, two of them taking office since 1950.

A dozen years ago the Republicans acquired a beachhead in the congressional contests that marked the beginning of the strongest bid for power that the minority party has ever made in the Free State. For ten years—1930 to 1940—not one of Maryland's six congressional seats was held by a Republican. Then in 1942, the machine of E. Brooke Lee, the longtime boss of Montgomery County, which borders on the District of Columbia, was overturned and Republican J. Glenn Beall, now a United States senator, was elected to Congress. Since then Maryland's 6th district has been consistently Republican. Four years later the Republicans captured the 1st district, located on the Eastern Shore, which they have held by slim margins; in 1950 they won the 2d, a mixed urban-suburban district; and in 1952 they picked up another congressional seat for a total of four, a majority of the state's seven congressional seats.

Aided by a wide open rift in the Democratic party, Maryland's most effective Republican vote-getter, Theodore R. McKeldin, won the governorship in 1950 by the largest plurality any chief executive has ever received. In the same election John Marshall Butler defeated a Senate veteran, Millard Tydings, to give the Republican party its first Senate seat in more than a quarter of a century. Two years later the Republicans picked up their second senatorial prize by graduating J. Glenn Beall from the House of Representatives to the Senate. Curiously, in this period of Republican ascendancy Democratic superiority in new registrations has continued by about the same ratio. As evidence of brighter days, however, Republicans cite recent successes at the local level in important Prince Georges County, a populous area adjacent to the District of Columbia. Geographically, the Democrats generally look to Baltimore for their heaviest support, the Republicans to the mountainous regions of Western Maryland.

As in many states of the Atlantic seaboard region, certain minority groups are potent factors in Free State politics. Negroes comprise 25 per cent of the population in Baltimore. Two-thirds of the approximately 75,000 Republican registrations in Baltimore are Negroes, though a glance at the 71 precincts where more than 50 per cent of the residents are Negroes quickly reveals that they do not vote Republican in the same ratio. The Catholic population in terms of its proportionate relation to other groups ranks one in five. Baltimore also has a large Jewish population living largely in the 7th congressional district, with part in the 4th. In numbers by national extraction, those of German and Irish descent are dominant in Baltimore, and among other ethnic groups are large numbers of Italians, Poles, Czechs, and Lithuanians.

Neither party has developed a recognized state leader in recent years. Nor has either party had a leader who dominated Baltimore. With the death of William Curran a few years ago his influential following in the Democratic party has receded to an unimportant status and the two principal factional contenders today are the Pollack and the Della-Wyatt forces. A non-officeholder in public or party affairs, James H. (Jack) Pollack is the authoritative voice in the 4th district. In South Baltimore, State Senator George Della and former Magistrate Joseph Wyatt hold the whip hand over Democratic politics. Neither the Pollack nor the Della-Wyatt organizations have been able to extend their influence to citywide control, nor have the efforts of Democratic Mayor Thomas D'Alesandro been successful in this direction, although he retains formidable control in one part of Baltimore City.

In the Republican party, the only figure approaching leadership status in a statewide sense is Theodore R. McKeldin, formerly mayor of Baltimore, and currently chief executive of the state. Not unmindful of his heavy obligation to many Democratic voters, however, Governor McKeldin has not proclaimed his party leadership vigorously in Republican affairs. In Baltimore, the two most influential Republican leaders are Deeley K. Nice and Charles A. Dorsey. Nice, a nephew and secretary to former Governor Harry Nice, was formerly the party's city chairman and is currently chairman of the state tax commission. Though no longer holding party office, Nice still commands the wide support of Negro leaders. Charles Dorsey, president of the Board of Election Supervisors and treasurer of the Republican city committee, has inherited many of the former responsibilities of Nice and has probably been the leading partisan to keep the continuity of the city organization intact.

PRESIDENTIAL PRIMARY LAW AND PROCEDURE

Not the least important in understanding Maryland selection procedure for national convention delegates is a knowledge of its tight relation to the rules regulating the nomination of candidates to statewide offices, and to the election of members of the legislature.

Maryland law provides that major party nominations for statewide offices—governor, attorney general, comptroller, and United States senator—shall be by convention, not by direct primary. This requirement leads to a practice quaint among the states today, whereby state political party conventions in Maryland fulfill a function comparable to that of our electoral college in electing a president. Both parties hold direct primaries in which an expression of popular will is made upon their several candidates. But final determination of the nomination is made not by popular vote in the direct primary, but by the legislative district unit vote in the state convention that follows.

Under Maryland law delegates to a party state convention must be elected in the same manner as members of the state legislature; that is, by popular vote within the same political subdivisions as are members of the legislature. The total number of seats in both houses of the General Assembly, as the Maryland legislature is called, is 152, and this number has been fixed in the practice of both parties as the size of their respective state political conventions. Thus each of Maryland's 23 counties and each of the six state legislative districts in Baltimore is allotted the same number of party convention seats as it holds in the legislature.

Briefly, the procedures followed for electing delegates to the state conventions is as follows: The party voters in each county and city legislative district go to the polls to vote their personal preferences for statewide office in a direct primary. At this same time they also elect the delegates for their respective state conventions which are to follow the popular primary. In theory, the voter is performing two complementary functions: First, he is recording his own personal nominating instructions to the prospective state convention delegates from his district or county, and, secondly, he is electing the delegates to carry out these instructions. Names of the candidates running for delegate to the state convention appear on the ballot and any registered party member may file. By law the delegates so elected must follow the instructions of the political subdivision *as a unit*, that is to say, the six delegates elected in any given county or legislative district must vote as a unit for the candidate receiving the largest number of popular votes.

It is these very same delegates to the state convention who elect the national convention delegates of both parties. Thus a presidential aspirant who hopes to capture the Maryland delegation is up against the same proposition as the candidate seeking nomination for statewide office. He too must win out in state convention unit votes. Moreover, his course is all the more difficult because unlike the statewide office-seeker he must receive a majority of the convention votes, not simply the highest number of votes as in the case of the former. No doubt this requirement has a certain tendency to discourage presidential candidates from filing in the Maryland preference primary unless they are fairly sure of strong local support or feel that an opponent is unlikely. In the event a preference primary is held by either party, it should also be remarked that the voter always has the option of voting for an uninstructed delegation. By law, the designation "uninstructed delegation" must appear on the ballot whenever a presidential preference primary is held. Should the presidential aspirant win a majority of the convention votes, under Maryland law he is assured support from the delegation only so long as the Maryland delegates believe "in their conscientious judgment there is any possibility of his being nominated." In practice this has been taken to mean that after the first ballot, the delegates are no longer bound.

Three factors tend to remove the control of a state convention and hence the selection of national convention delegates in Maryland beyond the reach of the popular will: the inequitable distribution of seats, frequent public indifference to primaries, and certain elements of trickery by various political bosses who handpick the delegates eventually elected to the state convention. Because of the archaic provisions of the 87 year old state constitution, the distribution of legislative seats among the political subdivisions is grossly inequitable, and these same inequities affect the distribution of seats in the party political conventions. How this inequitable representation can undo the popular will can best be illustrated by two recent examples.

In the 1950 Democratic gubernatorial primary, Governor Lane was defeated by George P. Mahoney in the popular vote, but at the subsequent state convention Mahoney failed to receive as many unit votes as his opponent; the nomination went to Lane. At the same time, John Markey defeated John Marshall Butler in the contest for the Republican senatorial nomination in the popular vote, yet lost out by unit votes at the state convention that followed. Thus under the Maryland system it is entirely possible for a candidate who has run up large majorities in some areas and just missed out in others to win a popular victory and still lose the nomination. Usually when this happens—and cases like those of 1950 have occurred before— intense bitterness is stirred up within the political party where the rejection of the popular winner took place.

THE REPUBLICAN DELEGATION

The background for the struggle over who would control the 1952 Maryland delegation to the Republican national convention began in 1946. Theodore R. McKeldin, then completing his first term as mayor of Baltimore, decided to try for the governorship. His decision reputedly ran contrary to the wishes of the national committeeman, Jacob France, and led to a breach between the two men. With the defeat of McKeldin by Governor Preston Lane that fall, Jacob France became the undisputed leader of Republican politics in Maryland. France, president of the Midcontinent Oil Company and chairman of the board of directors of the Equitable Trust Company in Baltimore, has been holder of several other posts of prominence in the industry and finance. He also was identified with the conservative wing of the Republican party nationally. McKeldin's orientation generally has been toward the more progressive wing of the Republican party, and he has been a longtime admirer of Governor Dewey. In 1948, France counselled against the entry of any presidential hopefuls in the preference primary and urged that the state convention send an uninstructed delegation to the national convention. His wishes were obeyed on both counts, but he was not entirely successful in guiding the selection of a delegation that would be solidly for *his* presidential candidate; France was for Taft. At the state convention he had most of the delegates, but McKeldin, who was backing Dewey, also had supporters. After the delegates had met in their district caucuses to select national convention delegates and alternates, McKeldin obtained recognition and moved that two slates for delegates-at-large be approved by the convention and that each delegate-at-large be given a half vote. The motion carried despite the fact that half votes are not permitted under Republican national convention rules. France succeeded in having his candidate for national committeewoman elected—Miss Bertha Adkins, later to become vice-chairman of the Republican national committee—at the same state convention and also in electing his choice for state central chairman.

When both at-large delegations arrived in Philadelphia for the national convention of 1948, a caucus of the district delegates rejected the McKeldin slate. Charles Dorsey, a district delegate, relinquished his seat to McKeldin in a harmony move, but there was little peace between France and McKeldin during the convention and the election campaign that followed. In the balloting at the convention, the delegation gave Dewey a slight edge, with Taft a close second, and Stassen trailing. In the presidential campaign, two separate operations were carried on in Maryland: the official one from France's headquarters, with an unofficial task force under the charge of McKeldin. Dewey carried Maryland, but eight electoral votes in the Republican column failed to bring France and McKeldin together.

At the primary election of September 1950, a state central committee was elected that was a "100 per cent France organization." At the same time McKeldin won the gubernatorial nomination without opposition. Two months later McKeldin won the governorship. As one party leader described it, "overnight the 100 per cent France state central committee became a 100 per cent McKeldin organization." Henceforth no one doubted that McKeldin would dethrone France as national committeeman at the 1952 Republican state convention.

THE SELECTION PROCESS IN 1952

For landing in the Dewey column in 1948 and gaining one House seat under the 1950 census, Maryland was allotted 24 delegates in

1952 instead of 16 as in 1948. Long before the state convention met in May 1952, speculation began regarding the effect the shake-up in Maryland Republican leadership would have on the presidential race. France stood firm in the Taft camp, aided by a vigorous supporter, Brigadier General William Purnell, general counsel for the Western Maryland Railroad. Senator John Marshall Butler, who defeated Tydings in 1950, was also an avowed Taft man and worked with France and Purnell to build a Taft delegation.

Publicly, McKeldin adopted an unhurried stance. Late in 1951 he made an off-the-cuff remark that he disliked the idea of a military man in the presidential office. But on another occasion when asked what presidential candidate he favored he countered by saying that he often took his cues from Governor Dewey in various matters of statecraft. By the time he flew to Palestine for a visit in April 1952, and coming back stopped off to see General Eisenhower at his Paris headquarters, there were signs that McKeldin leaned toward Ike as a candidate. Nonetheless he kept insisting that the Republican party had several strong candidates and made .no positive commitments.

State convention delegate contests—In January and February the county and city legislative district committees, which together comprise the 152-member state central committee, were meeting and discussing how they would select their candidates for delegate to the state convention. Heretofore in some areas it required some effort to find persons who would agree to go to the state convention. Frequently there were no contests, so that the names of delegate candidates never appeared on the ballot. In 1952 the criterion for endorsement by county or city legislative district committees was loyalty to Governor McKeldin. Had the rank-and-file Republican voter known of these party committee meetings, here was the point at which he might have effectively made known, through his district or county representative on the committee, an interest in being a candidate to the state convention. But no publicity was given the meetings, and in many cases agreements on candidacies were arranged by telephone.

The fee for filing as a delegate to the state convention (for Baltimore City and Montgomery County only) is ten dollars, a fee which the McKeldin organization paid when necessary. If there is no contest, no filing fee is required. The last day for filing was moved back two weeks, to March 31, in a last-minute enactment by the state legislature, and this probably caught a few potential non-organization candidates off-guard. Direction of practically all filings was handled by either the state central committee, which was McKeldin's organization, or the organization of Grady Gore, who was a candidate for the Republican senatorial nomination. Gore was a Taft supporter, and it was presumed that the candidates filed by his organization would be for Taft. In Baltimore more than 150 names were filed for the available 42 delegate seats. At midnight of the last day for filing, a member of the state central committee stood by to file as many endorsable candidates as might be necessary to fill out the slate, and a representative of the Gore forces was also on hand.

Maryland election law requires that the names of candidates for the same office must appear on the ballot in alphabetical order. Ordinarily, with far fewer candidates in their primary, the regular Republican organization has not had too much difficulty in getting their endorsed candidate on the strategic top line of the voting machine. But with the unprecedented number of state convention delegate candidates in the May 5 primary of 1952, the regular Republican organization considered itself fortunate to be able to place 29 of the organization candidates on the top line. In the counties there was lively interest, but the scramble was not as intense as in Baltimore and proportionately not nearly as many candidates filed. Both the McKeldin and Gore organizations filed their own slates in the counties as they did in Baltimore.

Between the close of the filing period (March 31) and the primary (May 5), many public-minded citizens despaired at their inability to know just where these delegate candidates stood on the presidential race. As Gore's campaign for the senatorial nomination wore on, he reminded voters that a vote for his slate was a vote for Taft; but all these names were still confusing to the voter. On the McKeldin side, the organization settled down to the serious business of endorsing precisely as many candidates as there were convention seats to be filled, and printing these names on sample ballots. There was no way of judging the presidential desires of McKeldin-endorsed candidates. McKeldin himself made no straight-forward declaration of his own preferences, and had no intention of doing so. Among the McKeldin candidates for delegate were many who preferred Taft to Eisenhower, and they were selected by organization leaders many of whom also liked Taft. But all were confident that they would generally go along with the governor's wishes when the situation jelled. Most of them did.

Taft strategists at the national level apparently decided that it would be a mistake to wage an aggressive state campaign for delegates if McKeldin wished to be a favorite son candidate himself. They also reasoned that there was strong enough support for the Ohio Senator among Maryland leaders so that, in the natural course of events, this would find expression in Taft votes at the national convention. This judgment proved partially correct. The core strength of the Taft support in Maryland centered largely around three figures: Jacob France, General Purnell, and Senator Butler.

Eisenhower was championed in the state by a Citizens for Eisenhower organization headed by a newcomer to local politics, Thomas G. Tinsley, Jr. A heavy contributor to Governor Dewey's 1948 campaign, and a man who apparently knows his way around among national political leaders, Tinsley owns radio stations in Baltimore and Richmond and formerly owned the St. Louis Browns and Baltimore Bullets. The Citizens for Eisenhower kept an active headquarters and organized hundreds of volunteers to compile petitions for Eisenhower. A last minute plan hatched with the idea of circularizing the names of McKeldin delegate candidates under the Eisenhower banner was dropped by Tinsley after consultation with Herbert Brownell. Like the Taft forces, Eisenhower strategists were reluctant to become too noisy in Governor McKeldin's front yard.

The primary—With both Taft and Eisenhower supporters claiming McKeldin as on their side, and the Maryland Governor announcing himself as a favorite son candidate, the state primary was held May 5. It was a record turnout for a Republican primary. Over 80 per cent of the registered Republican voters went to the polls. In Baltimore, virtually every candidate appearing on the top line of the voting machine won. The McKeldin organization lost 14 of 42 delegates selected in Baltimore, and about 20 of the 110 delegates selected by the 23 counties. Following the primary, the Republican state chairman, Joseph L. Carter, sent out the call for the state convention, to be held on May 24 in Baltimore.

Four days before the convention an evening meeting of a few selected leaders was held in the governor's office. In attendance were the three incumbent Republican congressmen—Edward Miller, J. Glenn Beall, and James P. Devereux—and State Chairman Carter, City Chairman W. Rae Dempsey, Stanley Scherr, a magistrate judge and manager of Beall's campaign for the Senate nomination, and Deeley K. Nice, former city chairman. Conspicuously absent were National Committeeman France and National Committeewoman Bertha Adkins. This group selected a slate of officers for the forthcoming state convention: Thomas B. R. Mudd for temporary chairman (Mudd is now commissioner of motor vehicles); Deeley K. Nice, permanent chairman; Stanley Scherr, credentials chairman; and D. K. Rollins, resolutions chairman. In the course of its discussions, the group reputedly went over the names of several delegate candidates.

The state convention—From physical appearances, the surroundings of the state convention on May 24 looked like a Taft pep rally. Hordes of Maryland "Minute-women" sporting Taft campaign headgear crowded the corridors and hung over the balconies of the ballroom chanting: "We want Taft." Eisenhower demonstrators were absent, consciously so, according to Thomas G. Tinsley, who himself remained inconspicuous throughout the day. At 10:30 A.M., each congressional district held its caucus to select its delegates and alternates as well as a representative to serve on the state convention nominating committee that would pick the delegates-at-large. Throughout a large part of the day the convention listened to speeches by various Republican congressional nominees, led by the keynote address of Governor McKeldin.

Late in the day, after formally nominating the winner of the Senate primary, J. Glenn Beall, by 120 unit votes to 32 for Gore, the convention was ready for the report of the nominating committee on the selections for delegate-at-large. This was approved and then a resolution was introduced to instruct the delegates to vote for Governor McKeldin on the first ballot at the national convention. As the resolution was being rushed through, a huge pro-Taft delegate from Montgomery County kept shouting from the floor and wanting to know what was going on. But Chairman Nice rapped him out of order, declared the resolution passed by a voice vote, and then successfully entertained a motion for adjournment—all in a matter of 30 seconds.

COMPOSITION OF THE DELEGATION

Prominent members of the delegation were Governor McKeldin, Senator John Marshall Butler, Mrs. Emmert Bowlus, president of the Federation of Republican Women of Maryland, and Brigadier General William Purnell, head of the Taft forces in Maryland. An interesting aside of Senator Butler's inclusion is that he was left off the list of the state convention committee nominating delegates-at-large. Then at the Governor's insistence, a place was made for him not as a delegate-at-large, but as a district delegate from the 7th congressional district. Except for Senator Butler no other member of Congress or congressional candidates were on the delegation. Important absentees from the delegation were Jacob France, former national committeeman, Bertha Adkins, national committeewoman, and the late Marse Calloway, longtime Negro leader in Baltimore.

Twenty members of the delegation were men; four were women, more than ever before. There were three Negro delegates and two alternates. Among the Negroes were a motion picture operator, a stevedore, and a city councilman from Cambridge. Occupationally, one-fourth were lawyers, and almost as many in the insurance business. One delegate owned a tobacco shop in Baltimore, another ran a small newspaper in Harford County, and one was a steel executive on the Eastern Shore. None were farmers. The delegation was almost solidly Protestant; there was one Jew and one Catholic.

By and large, Maryland's 1952 Republican delegation was quite inexperienced. Only four were delegates in 1948, and only one was a delegate at the 1944 national convention. For the most part this was a new group, although nearly all members of the delegation were party regulars and one-third of them were members of the state central committee.

Meeting immediately after the state convention, the Maryland delegation elected Governor McKeldin as delegation chairman. Deeley K. Nice was assigned to the credentials committee, Charles A. Dorsey and Mrs. Emmert Bowlus to resolutions, and Senator John Butler to rules. At the same caucus, Governor McKeldin was elected national committeeman and Bertha Adkins was re-elected national committeewoman.

Counting noses at the end of the day, Senator Butler claimed 14 of the 24 Maryland delegates as "sure" Taft votes. Those he named were: Wells, Shipley, Fisher, Carlton, Beall, Fletcher, Bowlus, Eierman, Burroughs, Cornish, O'Neill, Purnell, Ray, and himself. Most observers agreed that without a few reminders on the desirability of going along with McKeldin, most of these delegates would have voted for Taft at the convention. Left entirely to their own choice, there were at least two additional delegates who also greatly admired Taft and would have liked to vote for him. While making no claims, Governor McKeldin observed that he felt he could count on 18 of the 24 delegates to follow his lead at the national convention. He also thought he had a chance for the vice-presidency, and felt that Maryland's 24 votes might have some bargaining worth.

Between the state and national conventions, Maryland delegates and their alternates were the subject of continuous conjecture. When asked where they stood, most of them simply said "I'm for McKeldin." On June 10, the delegation was invited to Morningside Heights for a visit with General Eisenhower. Practically all delegates accepted, making the trip together in a special car of the Baltimore and Ohio Railroad. Delegate expenses were paid on this occasion by the Citizens for Eisenhower organization (Senator Butler paid his own). By the time of this trip the Governor's friends were contending that as many as 20 delegates would follow him. Newspaper judgments and careful observers, however, were inclined to believe this was mostly brave talk. Objective estimates gave Taft at least seven or eight votes, and probably more. On June 23, after the date had been changed to meet the Governor's convenience, all delegates and their alternates were invited to a dinner in Baltimore sponsored by the friends of Robert Taft, and in particular, on this occasion, by General Purnell. Taft addressed the delegates and the Governor was present.

Most of the delegates traveled to Chicago by train. The delegation held its first and only real caucus on Monday morning, July 7. Speaking in quiet tones, Governor McKeldin said the very thought of anyone dictating how a delegate should vote was repugnant to him and that he had no such intention. He then said that he would be pleased, of course, to be Maryland's favorite son and that he thought it would be a strategic thing for the Maryland delegation to go along with him for the first few ballots. There were no threatening overtones in McKeldin's speech. On the contrary, some Eisenhower supporters upon learning of his comments felt the Governor had not turned the screws the way he should have and feared that a majority of the delegation might get away from him. On the other hand, Delegates Butler and Purnell were not at all happy over this meeting, and they were not reluctant to say so. Butler in particular made it clear that he disliked reports from some delegates that they were being pressured not to vote for Taft and urged that the delegates be left to do their own thinking. Purnell took much the same line, and the caucus broke up without any poll on individual candidate preferences and without any agreement as to specific instructions. As the meeting adjourned, a telephone call to McKeldin tipped off the news of events to follow. Stomping through the hotel lobby after the call, he kept repeating, "I'm going to nominate Ike." Taft supporters said nothing. Nobody in either the Taft or Eisenhower camps seemed surprised.

That afternoon the first public glimpse of how the Maryland delegation actually stood was revealed by its vote on the Brown amendment to the Langlie "fair play" resolution: 19 delegates against, 5 for passage. When the crucial test over the contesting Georgia delegations reached the floor, however, Eisenhower strength seemed to have declined; Maryland voted 15 to 9 to accept the minority report to seat the pro-Eisenhower Tucker delegation.

The Maryland delegation gave Eisenhower 16 votes on the nominating ballot; Taft 8. In announcing the switch at the end of the roll call after Minnesota started the parade, Maryland gave Eisenhower 20, Taft 4; then all 24 to Eisenhower. This first roll call vote was neither an accurate reflection of progressive-conservative leanings within the Maryland Republican party, nor did it accurately mirror personal preferences.

Curiously, very few on the delegation were strongly pro-Eisenhower. Of those personally favoring Ike, Deeley Nice was clearly the most ardent and articulate. His word was unquestionably effective in giving some Negro delegates confidence that the right course was to go along with McKeldin. A few truculent members of the delegation did a generous amount of carping about accepting the Governor's choice. In holding these in line Nice was assisted loyally by a fellow-delegate who earnestly desired the nomination of Taft, but used his influence faithfully in the interest of making common cause with the Governor as leader of the Republican party in Maryland.

AFTERMATH IN THE STATE

Not since 1928, when Hoover defeated the "Happy Warrior," have Maryland Republicans won as impressive a presidential victory as 1952. Eisenhower carried the state by 104,087 votes, taking 55 per cent of the popular vote whereas Hoover had won 57 per cent. And in a sense, the showing on the congressional side was even more striking; the Republicans won a second Senate seat and four out of seven congressional seats. During the campaign three major efforts were carried on for the national ticket; one operation conducted by the Republican state central committee, two others by nonpartisan organizations. Some friction developed between the nonpartisan Citizens for Eisenhower and Voters for Eisenhower groups during the summer and early fall, and late in the campaign their forces were merged in a harmony move.

There were no reprisals in Maryland following the national convention, though factional strafing continued. Shortly after President Eisenhower took office, Senator Butler sent out a letter to Republican workers in Maryland. The gist of his communications was that, on matters of patronage and other political matters generally, as senior United States senator, he would consequently have the first say. Governor McKeldin, on the other hand, had not taken on the post of national committeeman simply as an additional honor and indicated his intention of acting as the intercessor between Washington and

Maryland on patronage matters. One four-power conference—composed of McKeldin, Senators Butler and Beall, State Chairman D. Eldred Rinehart, and National Committeewoman Bertha Adkins—has been held to reach an understanding. While amicable agreement was publicized, results suggest that the problem is far from resolved.

THE DEMOCRATIC DELEGATION

Factionalism in Maryland's Democratic party has lived riotously in recent years. Four years before the party began selecting presidential delegates for 1952, Democrats held the governorship, both United States Senate seats, and four of the state's six congressional seats. By spring of 1952 they had lost the governorship, one House seat, and one United States senator. Moreover, the announcement of Senator Herbert O'Conor that he would not seek re-election was generally interpreted to mean that he thought defeat in either the 1952 primary or general election was not unlikely.

Back in 1944, the Maryland Democratic delegation played a stellar role in the convention strategy that started the ball rolling for Harry Truman's nomination as vice president. In 1948, Maryland stayed with the "stubborn man from Missouri," who beat down several futile feints to block his renomination. By way of recognition of this loyalty, Governor W. Preston Lane, head of the 1948 delegation, was reputedly offered a chance at the vice-presidency on the Truman ticket. (See New York *Times*, July 13, 1948.) For whatever the reasons, however, Lane turned this offer down. "I am not available because of my obligations to the Maryland voters," said Lane.

In 1950, Governor Lane was challenged in the Democratic primary by a newcomer, George P. Mahoney of Baltimore. Lane lost in the popular vote, but defeated Mahoney with unit votes at the subsequent state convention. This left Mahoney supporters in a bellicose mood. In a last minute harmony move just before the general election, Lane stepped down as national committeeman in favor of Mahoney. This failed to save Lane from defeat. How deep the party rift became is suggested by the returns in the 4th legislative district in Baltimore, led by Democratic boss James H. Pollack. In his home precinct, the 35th of the 15th ward, Pollack delivered a seven to one majority to the Republican gubernatorial nominee. At the same time he carried the vote for the Democratic senatorial nominee, Tydings, by almost the same margin.

The defeat of Senator Tydings by Senator Butler in 1950 deprived the Democratic party of a political figure of national stature. With O'Conor's more recent decision to retire, the remaining person in a top drawer political post is Thomas D'Alesandro, mayor of Baltimore. D'Alesandro has strong organization support in two districts of Baltimore—the 1st and 2nd legislative districts—but has had difficulty in carrying the top of the ticket for the Democratic party. His sometime ally, James Pollack of the 4th district, is probably the leader most consistently able to "deliver" on election day. Pollack, however, has begun to have difficulties as a result of a heavy Negro migration into his district, and to compensate for this change he has begun to concentrate his organizational efforts on the 5th district. The Della-Wyatt leadership operates primarily in the 6th district. Remnants of the late William Curran's following usually make an empty bid for control of the 3d district, but have had practically no success. No one, in short, and no combination has been able to achieve anything approaching a continuous citywide stewardship over Democratic political affairs.

In the counties the picture is much the same. Former Congressman Sasscer, though losing the senatorial nomination in the 1952 Democratic primary (Mahoney won the popular vote contest in the primary, 137,403 to 121,285, and captured the nomination with 84 unit votes as against 64 for Sasscer), still commands support throughout southern Maryland and parts of the Eastern Shore. E. Brooke Lee has shown signs of activity in Montgomery County after a long enforced retirement, while the death of H. Streett Baldwin leaves a large leadership gap in the powerful Democratic organization of Baltimore County.

No one has been able to build statewide control over the Democratic party. Although he has never held elective public or political office, H. C. Byrd, president of the University of Maryland, has long been powerful behind-the-scenes in Democratic politics. Possessing strong support in both the counties and Baltimore, Byrd is a figure with whom Democratic chieftains must often reckon, increasingly so in the light of his university retirement and his candidacy for the Democratic gubernatorial nomination in 1954.

THE SELECTION PROCESS IN 1952

Maryland's quota of votes for the 1952 Democratic national convention was 18. Like the Republicans, Democrats select their national convention delegates by a state convention whose members are elected previously at a party primary. In 1952 the primary election was held on May 5, the state convention, June 3rd.

The storm center in the proceedings leading to the selection of national convention delegates in 1952 was not the presidential rivalries but the contest for the Democratic senatorial nomination. In Baltimore most, if not all, of the Democratic leaders were very quiet about prospective presidential nominees. What the party leaders wanted was to go to the national nominating convention with a free hand. More immediately, however, they were interested in controlling the necessary votes at the state convention to make sure that the national convention delegates eventually selected would in turn choose a national committeeman acceptable to themselves.

The senatorial primary race had two candidates: George P. Mahoney, who lost the 1950 gubernatorial nomination to Lane after winning the primary vote, and Lansdale G. Sasscer, veteran congressman from Maryland's 5th district. In Baltimore, Mayor D'Alesandro took the lead in opposing Mahoney. Accordingly, the state convention candidates in the Mayor's own 1st and 2d legislative districts were left unopposed by the Mahoney organization. Mahoney supporters filed a coalition organization slate of the delegates in just one legislative district in the city, the 5th. Here they later won only two of seven delegate seats, although Mahoney himself carried the district over Sasscer in the senatorial primary. In the 3d district there were just eight candidates for seven convention seats, most of them followers of the old Curran organization, which Charles "Chicken" Carrick has recently been attempting to regroup. Thus for the 42 state convention seats in Baltimore, there was opposition in only half the contests. In the outstate counties there was a greater tendency to have unopposed slates and most of the delegate candidates appeared to be in the Sasscer camp.

On May 5, Mahoney won the senatorial nomination in the primary vote by a substantial margin. Despite the fact that the "regulars" of the Democratic city machine took their worst beating in years at the hands of Mahoney, they won in every legislative district where an opposition slate of delegates was filed. While Mahoney won 70,372 votes to Sasscer's 48,554 in Baltimore, only two out of 42 delegates elected were Mahoney candidates. In the counties, of which Sasscer carried several and made a much better showing than in Baltimore, the great majority of elected state convention delegates were Sasscer supporters.

Senator Estes Kefauver caused a mild flurry of excitement by filing in the preferential primary shortly before the deadline of March 31. No one expected this to make a great deal of difference in Maryland. Running unopposed in the preferential primary, Kefauver ran up a total of 137,833 votes statewide, and actually outdistanced Mahoney's 136,877 votes in the senatorial primary. The vote for an uninstructed delegation in the preferential primary was over 39,000.

The state convention—On May 5, the Democratic state convention met in Baltimore. The Baltimore *Sun* called it the "stormiest, roughest, and most discordant convention in four decades." Delegates were referred to as "Mahoney delegates" or "Sasscer delegates." No delegates were categorized as "Kefauver delegates" or "Douglas delegates" or "Stevenson delegates." Practically none of the 152 delegates made any commitments on their presidential choices between the time they filed as candidates and were elected at the primary.

Right at the outset, Mahoney's announced choice for state convention chairman, Joseph H. George, was roundly defeated by a coalition of Democratic old-line regulars who put forward E. Brooke Lee of Montgomery County as their candidate. It was the first contested election of a state convention chairman since 1915. On the roll call, the vote was 105 for Lee, 45 for George. With Lee in the chair, events moved more or less to the cadence that the regulars desired, despite the catcalls and boos from the well organized convoy of Mahoney supporters, who took up much of the space in the Emerson ballroom.

One incident introduced an explosive element into the carefully directed program of the organization coalition. In some of the pre-convention planning meetings between Mayor D'Alesandro and various Democratic leaders, prospective candidates for delegate to the national convention were discussed. Among those scheduled for election as a delegate was Jack Pollack, boss of Baltimore's 4th district. Pollack supported Sasscer during the primary and carried his district for him, but his usual associates in the 5th and 6th districts worked for Mahoney. Moreover, the latter districts were carried by Mahoney. Following the primary, Pollack made a gesture to moderate these differences. His efforts were eyed with misgivings by some organization leaders who felt that he was nudging too close to Mahoney; he was soon charged with trying to take over control of the state in alliance with Mahoney. At a fruitless harmony meeting the night before the convention Joseph Wyatt, leader of the 6th district, called Pollack a Republican and the two almost came to blows.

The organization leaders contended that Pollack had made a commitment to be on their side in opposition to Mahoney and that in return it was agreed he should be on the list of national convention delegates. Pollack denied making such a commitment. In any case a place was made for Pollack and he remained on the list until the time came for the roll call on the permanent chairman of the state convention. When the Pollack-controlled 4th district split 4-3 for Mahoney's candidate, George, then switched to a unanimous vote for George, the incensed coalition leaders, shouting "double-cross," immediately scratched Pollack's name from the delegate list. State Senator Melnicove, ranking officeholder of the 4th district, said this "action violated all rules of decency and fair play," and constituted "an affront to the Democratic voters of my district." But Pollack was out as a delegate and his name was not on the list sent down by the resolutions committee.

In the Democratic state convention, the resolutions committee prepares the list of recommended names for national convention delegate. The resolutions committee is composed of one delegate from each of the 23 counties and each of the six state legislative districts in Baltimore. Each county and city district holds a caucus at the state convention to determine which member of their delegation shall serve on the resolutions committee. Following this, the resolutions committee holds its own meeting to prepare a list of delegates to submit to the convention. Senator Della was chairman of this committee in 1952.

Following Lee's election as permanent chairman, the list of national convention delegates, as amended to delete Pollack's name, was sent to the floor of the convention. After Senator Della finished reading the list, a Pollack man tried to get the floor, but before recognizing this man, Chairman Lee calmly called for a voice vote and declared all the delegates elected. In contravention of national party rules, 36 delegates were elected to cast 18 votes at the convention. All but a comparative few of the 36 delegates and their alternates had opposed Mahoney in the Democratic primary.

Without discussion or a roll call the convention then instructed the delegates to the national convention to vote for Senator Estes Kefauver in accordance with the provision of Maryland law, "as long as in their conscientious judgment" there would be any possibility of his being nominated. Thereafter Mahoney was nominated for United States senator in conformity with the unit vote system. Curiously, not a Kefauver placard, button, or card appeared at the convention all day. Two Harriman representatives were on hand hoping to line up rank-and-file support for later ballots; James Lanigan, director of Harriman's Washington headquarters, and Oliver Quayle, 3d, of Bethesda, former treasurer of the Democratic national party.

COMPOSITION OF THE DELEGATION

Among the delegates-at-large were several prominent political figures: Senator Herbert O'Conor; George P. Mahoney, the nominee for the Senate; Representative Sasscer; Philip B. Perlman, Solicitor General of the United States; J. Millard Tawes, state comptroller; former Senator Millard Tydings; E. Brooke Lee; and Mayor Thomas D'Alesandro. Standing out among the congressional district delegates were: Robert B. Ennis, chairman of the state central committee; George Della, president of the state senate; John C. Luber, speaker of the state's lower house; Mrs. Alice Canoles, national committeewoman; J. Neil McCardell, Baltimore city comptroller; and Arthur B. Price, president of the Baltimore city council. Others of important standing in the state included: Christian H. Kahl, a leader

in Baltimore County; Joseph H. Wyatt; the late State Senator Omar
D. Crothers of Cecil County; and the late Baltimore County leader,
H. Streett Baldwin.

Eighty per cent of the 1952 delegation had held public office
sometime during their lives; 20 per cent at the time of the convention.
Three of the delegates held federal posts, and three held top drawer
positions in Baltimore.

Thirty-three on the delegation were men, three were women. One
woman, Angela Bambace, is secretary of a labor union. The great
majority of the delegation was in the 50-59 age bracket, and it was
predominantly Protestant in its religious affiliation. Catholics were
well represented, however, and there were a few Jews. No Negroes
were named either as delegates or alternates, and it might be added
that there were no Negroes among the 1952 delegates to the state
convention. Occupationally, one-third had their own businesses, one-
fifth were practicing lawyers, and one-fifth were professional men of
some kind. About one-fifth were employed by various industrial
concerns and commercial organizations. One-fifth of the delegation
held party offices at the time of the convention and over half of them
were members of business, fraternal, social, and veterans organizations. Geographically, 21 of the delegates represented the counties
and 15 the City of Baltimore.

Three delegates bear special mention: Samuel Hoffberger, James
Bruce, and Philip B. Perlman. Hoffberger, an industrialist with interests in realty, fuel, and brewing businesses, is reputedly the largest
single contributor to the Democratic party in Maryland. James Bruce,
wealthy industrialist, was former Ambassador to Argentina and at the
time of the convention was a North Atlantic Treaty Organization official. Bruce was close to the leaders of the Truman administration
and also a person who helped substantially to raise funds for the
Democratic campaign chest. Perlman, then United States Solicitor
General, was close to President Truman, an effective spokesman for
many minority groups, and a key figure in the 1952 Democratic national platform drafting operations.

Twenty-one delegates had attended the 1948 convention as delegates and at least a dozen of this group were on the 1944 delegation.
Nonetheless, many important faces were missing in 1952, among

them former Governor W. Preston Lane, Jr. (Lane was offered a seat but declined); Attorney General Hall Hammond; Judge Joseph R. Byrnes; former City Council President C. Markland Kelly; and James H. Pollack. In all, 15 who helped nominate Harry Truman in 1948 were missing from the Maryland delegation of 1952.

ACTIVITIES AND VOTING RECORD

Following the state convention a special office was set up in Baltimore at the Emerson Hotel to handle the special business of the delegation. The factotum for this office was William Bishop, who formerly handled many Democratic campaigns in Baltimore and who was closely allied with Mayor D'Alesandro.

Meeting immediately after the state convention, the delegation chose Representative Lansdale Sasscer, the defeated candidate for the senatorial nomination, as its chairman. Mayor D'Alesandro was elected national committeeman, ending George Mahoney's hopes of re-election to this post as well as the hopes of many Democrats that some peace offering would be extended to Mahoney. The national convention committee assignments were: E. Brooke Lee to the credentials committee; Samuel H. Hoffberger to the rules committee; and Philip B. Perlman and Mrs. M. Alice Canoles to the resolutions committee.

While Sasscer was chairman of the delegation, it was D'Alesandro, the driving force behind the coalition organization that controlled the state convention, who made many of the important early decisions affecting the delegation. As representative from the 3d congressional district, D'Alesandro had been a loyal supporter of Franklin Roosevelt, and later became a sturdy friend of Harry Truman. D'Alesandro was close to the Truman management at the Chicago convention in 1952.

The highpoint of the delegation's Chicago experience was on Thursday evening, July 24, when Representative Sasscer moved that a statement by Governor John S. Battle of Virginia be accepted by the convention as substantial compliance with the Moody resolution. National Chairman McKinney and Convention Chairman Rayburn have been credited with developing this strategy to keep Louisiana, South Carolina, and Virginia in the national convention. Precise reasons for Sasscer's selection to present the motion are not known, but these reasons probably took account of D'Alesandro's and Sasscer's close ties with the convention officers as well as Maryland's almost immediate position after Louisiana on the roll call. Louisiana yielded to Virginia so that Governor Battle could make his statement. Chairman Rayburn then ruled that Louisiana, South Carolina, and Virginia had not complied with the rules of the convention. Maine passed. Maryland was called next, and Sasscer made the motion to seat Virginia, leading to the convention's first test ballot. Maryland's 18 votes were all cast in favor of seating Virginia.

On the first nominating ballot, the delegation complied with the dictates of state law and cast its entire vote for Kefauver, who had won the preferential primary. On the second ballot, 15½ stayed with Kefauver, 2 moved to Russell, and ½ to Barkley. The third ballot showed Maryland's vote distributed 8½ to Kefauver, 6 for Stevenson, 2½ for Russell, ½ for Barkley, and ½ not voting.

AFTERMATH IN THE STATE

Some of the hurts and stings of the state convention were painfully evident during the course of the subsequent campaign, but there were no open explosions as in the case of the Democratic general election campaign of 1950. Mahoney failed to win the Senate seat he was seeking. Critics of Mahoney resented his failure to identify himself more prominently with the head of the national ticket. In the presidential campaign two groups performed the real yeoman work in Maryland as elsewhere: regular Democratic party leaders, and the Volunteers for Stevenson. Governor Stevenson's major campaign address at the Baltimore Armory was sponsored by the Volunteers for Stevenson.

REVIEW AND APPRAISAL

Maryland was the only state classed as having a presidential primary in 1952 in which there was no provision for the direct election of national convention delegates. The national convention delegates are elected in state party conventions. But the delegates to the state conventions are elected in a public primary in which the law offers an opportunity—little used—for a presidential preference vote. The choice made in the preference election in the various localities is binding upon their delegates to the respective state conventions . . .

. . . as long as in their conscientious judgment there is any possibility
of said choice obtaining a majority of the votes of the state convention and as long as said choice is voted for by delegates of any
nine counties of Maryland in said convention, any legislative district
of Baltimore City to be taken and considered for such a purpose as
the equivalent of a county.

Through this indirect means, a national convention delegation may
come into existence that is instructed by law to vote for a national
candidate who has won the preference election if one was held.

In 1952, Kefauver entered the preference primary on the Democratic side and defeated the alternative of an "uninstructed delegation" by about 3 to 1. In accordance with the law, the delegation
selected by the Democratic state convention was

. . . instructed and bound to vote as a unit in the national convention for such candidate for President so selected as the choice of
the State of Maryland as aforesaid, and such delegates shall continue
to vote in such national convention for the choice of the State of
Maryland, as aforesaid, for President as long as in their conscientious
judgment there is any possibility of his being nominated.

The Kefauver-instructed delegation gave him a solid vote on the first
ballot, after having voted contrary to the Kefauver position on the
issue of seating Virginia. In fact, it was Maryland's Representative
Sasscer who offered the crucial motion to seat the Virginia delegation
on the basis of Governor Battle's statement in regard to the Virginia
ballot. The "conscientious judgment" of delegates controlling 15½
votes remained with Kefauver on the second ballot, and gave him
about half of the delegation's vote on the third.

On the Republican side in 1952, there was no presidential preference vote. The last preference vote conducted by the Republicans was
in 1940 when the instruction was for Dewey. Governor McKeldin was
the state's favorite son in 1952 by state convention action, but at
Chicago, after McKeldin was chosen to place Eisenhower in nomination, the delegation gave 16 votes to Eisenhower and 8 to Taft.

Conspicuous among the frailties of Maryland's system for selecting
national convention delegates are three: (1) the inequitable distribution of seats in the state convention which selects the national convention delegates; (2) frequent popular indifference to the selection

of state convention delegates because other statewide primary contests overshadow it; and (3) the inability of the voter to determine what the presidential preference of a candidate for state convention delegate really is.

Geared to legislative apportionment which is ordained by an 87-year-old constitutional provision, each county and each of six legislative districts in Baltimore is allocated the same number of seats as it holds in the legislature. Thus Baltimore County, with a population of 270,273, has seven seats: one for each 38,612. By contrast, Calvert County, with a population of 12,100, has three seats: one seat for each 4,033. Elsewhere, Baltimore City has one seat for each 22,802 residents, while Dorchester County has one seat for each 8,954. This inequitable distribution of seats in a state convention can defeat, and has defeated, the popular will as reflected in the popular vote at the primaries. The presidential candidate who piles up heavy majorities in some areas and loses by a shadow in others can win the popular vote in a primary yet go down to defeat at the state convention. He can lose simply because an inequitable distribution of seats blocks him from getting the right combination of unit votes.

Widespread public indifference to primaries is obviously not peculiar to Maryland alone. But there is a dual nature in the Free State's procedure whereby nominations for statewide offices have a tendency to sidetrack and confuse the expression of popular attitudes on the presidential candidacies. In 1952 the sharp primary fight for the senatorial nomination encouraged a large turnout, but hard fought contests in other years have rarely produced large primary participation. In 1950 only 59 per cent of the registered Democrats went to the polls, barely 23 per cent of the registered Republicans. In 1948 —a presidential year—the primary turnout for both Democrats and Republicans was poor. But quite apart from turnout, the tendency for statewide candidacies to take the stage center has a way of discouraging and frustrating the party rank-and-file from taking greater interest in the election of state convention delegates, who in turn must chose the national convention delegates.

Some apathy toward the election of state convention delegates is a consequence of the feeling that the political bosses have predetermined the results. For the Republicans, the role of the 152-member state central committee in advancing delegate candidates for the state convention gave some semblance of broad rank-and-file representation in the process. But even here the meetings of the various county and city components of the central committee were scantily publicized, if at all. In the Democratic party the situation is altogether comparable, with the single exception that the state central committee took very little part in the selection of candidates for delegate to the state convention. This left the matter of selecting delegates very much in the hands of district or county leaders, often persons without any official party position.

But the chief difficulty of national convention delegate selection in Maryland for the rank-and-file party voter is that his party leaders make it uncommonly difficult for him to vote a state convention delegate preference that is clearly related to his own presidential choice. Confronted with a handful of strange delegate-candidate names, the voter is at a loss to know who thinks alike with him on presidential candidacies and will work at the state convention for the selection of national delegates favorable to that candidate. There is little or no campaigning by the delegates, other than the distribution of flyers by the political organizations. And the latter simply urge election of the slate, almost always omitting any mention of presidential preferences. In the Republican primary of 1952, the newspapers attempted some elucidation. Presumably, election of the McKeldin organization's delegate-candidates to the state convention would yield a national delegation favorable to Eisenhower; election of the Gore organization's candidates, a delegation favorable to Taft. The McKeldin delegate candidates to the state convention won hands down. Yet the national convention delegation gave Taft 8 of its 24 votes, and, except for some genuflection to the state party leadership, might easily have given him several more votes. No attempt was made in the Democratic party to identify state convention delegate-candidates with national presidential candidacies. In this case, the contest for the Senate seat and the coalition of party bosses led by Mayor D'Alesandro to unseat Mahoney as national committeeman completely sidetracked presidential interest.

Though complaints were strenuous about the inadequacies of the Maryland system for delegate selection during the presidential pre-convention period, the hubbub has not led to any clarion call for action. Newspapers, particularly the Baltimore *Sun*, have campaigned steadily for specific refinements in Maryland law and procedures on the presidential nominating process. Yet, as in the case of most reforms, improvements must apparently flow at a leisurely pace. Clearly one of the foremost impediments to improvement is constitutional—an obstacle rarely hurried.

Maryland Chapter Acknowledgments

MALCOLM MOOS, Professor of Political Science, Johns Hopkins University, and an alternate delegate-at-large to the 1952 Republican national convention, originally undertook to prepare a pre-convention report on the Democratic delegation. Professor Moos attended both national conventions, and subsequently wrote reports on both the Republican and Democratic delegations. After the general format for state chapters had been established, he prepared the present chapter.

PENNSYLVANIA

Electoral votes, 1952: 32

National convention votes, 1952:
Democratic, 70
Republican, 70

Population, 1950: 10,498,012
Urban, 70%; *rural nonfarm,* 23%; *rural farm,* 7%

Population increase, 1940-50: 597,832 (6%)
Urban, 5%; *rural nonfarm,* 20%; *rural farm,* 22% decline

Presidential vote, 1948:		*1952:*
Democratic,	1,752,426 (47%)	2,146,269 (47%)
Republican,	1,902,197 (51%)	2,415,789 (53%)
Progressive,	55,161 (1%)	
Other,	25,365 (1%)	

Gubernatorial vote, 1950:
Democratic, 1,710,355
Republican, 1,796,119

U. S. Representatives vote,		
all districts, 1950:		*1952:*
Democratic,	1,672,788	2,151,247
Republican,	1,834,128	2,353,167

U. S. Representatives elected 1950:		*1952:*
Democratic,	13	11
Republican,	20	19

State legislature elected 1952:
Senate: Democrats, 18; Republicans, 32
House: Democrats, 98; Republicans, 110

Method of selecting national convention delegates:
Delegates-at-large by state committee
District delegates by direct election
Advisory presidential preference poll

Based primarily on reports by G. EDWARD JANOSIK

—————————————————————————CHAPTER 12

PENNSYLVANIA HAS BEEN MORE CONSISTENTLY REPUBLICAN than
other seaboard-industrial states. Since the Civil War, it has supported
the Republican candidate for president in all elections except in 1936,
1940, and 1944; and it has chosen Republicans for the Senate except
in 1874, 1934, 1940, and 1944. On only three occasions since the
Civil War has it chosen Democratic governors: 1882, 1890, and 1934.
The strength of the two parties from 1896 to 1940 varied in Pennsylvania much as it varied in the nation, but the Republicans were
generally 6 to 8 per cent stronger than they were nationally. During
the last several years, eastern Pennsylvania has run counter to the
national trend and shown increasing Democratic strength.

The consistent Republicanism of the state has been in large part
due to the fact that the political machine in the largest city, Philadelphia, remained Republican, whereas big city machines elsewhere in
the nation were mostly Democratic. Pennsylvania's Republicanism
has also been attributed to the skill and ability of a dynasty of bosses:
Simon Cameron, Lincoln's Secretary of War; his son, Donald Cameron; Matthew Quay; and Boies Penrose.

Pennsylvania resembles California and differs from the majority of
northern metropolitan states in that it has two large metropolitan areas
that have become sufficiently equal in size and industrial strength so
that neither can dominate the other. In the 1920's, after the death of
Senator Boies Penrose, the Pittsburgh industrial leaders, represented
by Secretary of the Treasury Mellon, fought with Senator William
Vare, Penrose's successor in Philadelphia, for control of the Republican party. This destroyed the unity of the Republican party in the
state; and ever since it has been subject to severe factional conflicts.
One or more factions have had their base primarily in the Philadel-

261

phia Republican organization; another faction is based on the Pennsylvania Manufacturers Association; still a third advances and recedes under the progressive banner.

More than most large cities, Pittsburgh is a center of industrial labor, largely populated by the more recent immigrant groups, the Poles, Italians, Hungarians, and Slavs, as well as by Irish, Germans, and Negroes. Although Philadelphia remained Republican throughout the 1930's and the 1940's, Pittsburgh went Democratic in 1934, and has remained Democratic since, except in 1946 when Governor James Duff carried the city by 1,500 votes. Democratic majorities in Pittsburgh, however, have been steadily decreasing in recent years. Philadelphia finally elected Democrats to county and city offices in 1949 and 1951, just at the time when Republicans were gaining strength elsewhere. Philadelphia Republicans had been in power for 64 years. Besides Pittsburgh and Philadelphia, there are nine other metropolitan districts in Pennsylvania, each with a population of 85,000 people or more, including such cities as Scranton, Wilkes-Barre, and Bethlehem.

The owners of the industries and mines of Pennsylvania have been the main support of the Republican party organization in the state, often so clearly so that Pennsylvania is frequently alluded to as an example of class-conscious or class-based politics in America. Joseph Pew of the Sun Oil Company of Chester is today probably one of the largest financial supporters of conservative Republicanism in the country. After the death of Penrose in 1922, Joseph Grundy, for many years president of the Pennsylvania Manufacturers Association, led Pennsylvania Republicans in fighting for high tariffs and against child labor laws. His successor as president of the association, G. Mason Owlett, is now one of the leading personalities in Pennsylvania politics.

The influence of trade-unions in state politics is also considerable. Prior to 1932 most union officials and local business agents were registered Republicans; more recently most of the labor leadership moves in Democratic circles. There is evidence to suggest that more trade union members have run for public office in recent years in Pennsylvania—most of them as Democrats—than in any other state. The most influential union has been the United Mine Workers; but it is hard to obtain agreement on the direction, extent, and form of its influence. In the Pittsburgh area, the influence of the Steelworkers, CIO, is particularly great.

The governor of Pennsylvania has at his disposal considerable patronage power, perhaps more than any other state executive in the country. In addition, the governor has primary responsibility for an executive budget which at present runs to about three-quarters of a billion dollars. He has the right to hire and fire for about 26,000 salaried positions. By custom, an application for one of these positions is signed by a "sponsor" before appointment is made. The sponsor is generally the county chairman in the county where the applicant resides. In addition, the governor has the power to hire and fire about 19,000 per diem workers, chiefly on highway construction. There are also about 13,000 state positions "under civil service" but the act setting up the civil service system provides that "notwithstanding any other provisions of the act" the governor may discharge any of the persons selected by civil service. So far as known, no governor has done much firing under this provision; but the knowledge of the possibility may affect the political actions of the state employees.

There were 3,129,700 registered Republicans in 1952 as compared with 2,136,800 registered Democrats; in more than half the counties the Republican registration is at least twice that of the Democrats; in one county, it is seven times as great. But in 1952 the statewide vote for Eisenhower was 750,000 less than the Republican registration whereas the statewide vote for Stevenson was approximately the same as the Democratic registration. It is probable that this registration arises in part from the superior financial and organizing resources available to the Republicans; it is known that in some counties Democrats have been hard put to persuade anyone to undertake continuing party work.

Registration in Pennsylvania is personal and permanent. The county registration commission is supposed to cancel the registration of anyone who has not voted for two years. It is possible to register at any time of the year with the exception of the fifty days before and the five days after primary elections and fifty days before and thirty days after general elections. It is possible to change one's party affiliation only between a general election in the fall and the following primary election. Party affiliation may be changed by appearing personally before a registration official and completing an affidavit which authorizes the registration officials to change the party designation as it appears on the voter's permanent registration card.

PRESIDENTIAL PRIMARY LAW AND PROCEDURE

Pennsylvania is allegedly the "mother of the direct primary": party organizations in some counties are said to have conducted primaries as early as 1841, and the state made provision by statute for party primaries in some counties in the 1870's. A statewide direct primary law was passed in 1913. The election laws were recodified in 1937; and, with one exception discussed below, there has since been no material change in the state statutes affecting delegate primaries or presidential preference polls. A political party is defined by state law as a body one of whose candidates in the preceding general election has received at least 2 per cent of the statewide vote for the office for which he was running. It is also required that in each of 10 of the 67 counties a candidate of the group shall have received at least 2 per cent of the vote.

Political parties—normally the Republican and Democratic—hold primaries every year. The majority of the candidates for statewide office are selected in May of the even-numbered years between presidential elections; the primary in presidential years takes place on the fourth Tuesday in April, April 22 in 1952. A presidential preference as described below may be expressed at this primary; in addition, delegates and alternates to the national convention, members of state and city or county committees, and a variety of nominees for state and national offices are chosen. The presidential preferences of the delegate candidates cannot be indicated on the ballot. The burden placed upon Pennsylvania voters does not appear to be light. In odd years, a substantial number of county and municipal officials are elected. All together during a four-year period, for example, the Philadelphia voter—until 1951, when the city adopted a new charter—was supposed to vote for at least 113 officials, the Pittsburgh voter at least 83, and voters in less populous second-class townships at least 56, usually with several candidates for each office at the primary.

Little emphasis has been placed upon the presidential preference feature of the primary. Republican leaders have usually wished to use Pennsylvania's big bloc of votes at the convention for bargaining purposes and have therefore sought to avoid prior commitments; but in 1952 the names of Eisenhower and Stassen appeared in the presidential preference row of the ballot. No one was filed for the Democratic presidential preference. However, 175,000 persons expressed a presidential choice by write-in. This compares with 460,000 votes cast statewide for Democratic candidate for United States senator. According to the Committee of Seventy, a civic reform group, a write-in campaign is encumbered by either of the most commonly used types of voting machine; the voter may be forced to ask for a pencil and has some problem in inserting a name because of the physical structure of the machine. For a presidential candidate's name to appear on the ballot, 100 registered, enrolled voters of his party in each of 10 counties must sign petitions for him. The petitions must be filed at least 64 days before the primary, or, in 1952, by February 16. The candidate's consent to filing his name is not required. There is a filing fee of $50. The first row on the primary ballot is assigned to aspirants for the party's presidential nomination; write-ins are also permitted.

The "promise to support" provision—A provision of the election code allows a candidate for delegate to the national convention to promise to support the popular choice of the party in his congressional district. Beneath the name of the candidate for delegate or alternate is written in parenthesis either "does not promise" or "promise to support." There have been some years in which no elected candidate for delegate promised to support the popular choice. No more than three Republican candidates for delegate who "promised to support" were elected in 1952, whereas ten who promised to support were defeated. Four Republican candidates for alternate who "promised to support" were opposed; only one of these was elected. Nine unopposed candidates for alternate "promised to support." No plausible reason why more candidates for alternate "promised to support" than for delegate is apparent.

Although no Democrat was filed for the presidential preference, 41 candidates for delegate and 24 candidates for alternate "promised to support" the popular choice in their district. Just what they meant by this is not clear. Apparently the "promise" has become somewhat of a tradition in the Democratic party, the precedent having been set in 1932. In recent years, contests for the Democratic presidential nomination have not been of a nature which would cause candidates for delegates to reflect upon the "promise to support" pledge one way or the other. Twenty of the 41 Democratic candidates for delegate who "promised to support" and 19 of the 24 candidates for alternate who "promised to support" were unopposed, or were opposed by candidates who had also promised to support. Where there were straight-out contests for delegate between promisers and non-promisers, eight of the promisers were elected and thirteen were beaten; but all five of those engaged in contests for alternate who had "promised to support" were elected.

Evidently delegates who promised to support did not feel themselves obligated by write-in votes for presidential candidates. Kefauver carried the districts of all 28 delegates who promised to support; yet he failed to receive most of their votes on the first ballot, and 16 of the delegates who might have been considered obligated to support Kefauver did not in fact cast their votes for him on any ballot.

Delegate elections—Designating petitions, under an amendment to the election code adopted in 1949, must be filed at least 64 days before the primary; in 1952, this was February 16. Signatures may be counted only if they bear a date not more than 20 days before the filing date. This allows only 20 days to secure petition signatures and only seven weeks to conduct a preprimary campaign if there is a contest. These timing conditions probably make the process easier for well-established factions and organizations, especially in contests which are generally as little noticed as those for delegate. The number of signatures required on a petition for delegate or alternate to the national convention is 200. The filing fee is $10. Provisions of the law governing the physical form of petitions appear reasonably simple. Names of candidates for delegates and alternate usually appear on the seventh to tenth row of the ballot.

Until 1951, delegates-at-large were elected at the presidential preference primary, essentially by the same process as district delegates. In 1951, the legislature amended the election code to permit any political party whose rules provided for the appointment of delegates-at-large by the party's state committee to make its selection in this manner. Both the Republican and Democratic parties had such provisions in their rules, and delegates-at-large were appointed rather than elected in 1952. Actually, this change only legalized the political practice which had prevailed for many years. The Committee of Seventy, a Philadelphia "good government" organization, advised that throughout the last three decades the only names that appeared on the ballot for election as delegate-at-large in both parties were those supported by the state committees. Rarely did an independent file, and the Committee of Seventy could not recall any occasion upon which two competing slates for delegate-at-large were filed.

Under the law, the state committee, when it selects the delegates-at-large, shall do so not later than April 1, more than three weeks before the primary. This means that the selection of the delegates-at-large is left to the outgoing state committee. Two members of the state committee are elected from each state senatorial district biennially. State committee members and district national convention delegates are elected at the same time, the fourth Tuesday in April. If a factional conflict for control of the state committee should arise, there would be an obvious tendency for it to correlate with factional contests for district delegates, but it would be too late for the outcome to have any effect on the selection of delegates-at-large.

THE REPUBLICAN DELEGATION

In 1940, Governor Arthur James of Pennsylvania apparently regarded himself as having a better chance than the ordinary favorite son; he held 53 of the 72 delegates until the fourth ballot. On the fifth, his supporters switched to Taft; and on the sixth, the Pennsylvania group provided Willkie with the winning votes by shifting unanimously to him.

In 1944, the Pennsylvania delegation unanimously and harmoniously supported Dewey. In 1948, on the other hand, the Pennsylvania delegation showed serious signs of disunity. Prior to the convention the 72 delegates had been pledged to Senator Edward Martin, according to the custom of favoring a native son. Senator Martin dismayed the delegation by announcing on the second day of the convention that he was withdrawing as a candidate and releas-

ing the members pledged to him. Compounding the mischief, he
added that he would place in nomination the name of Thomas E.
Dewey. This proposal was upheld by that wing of the party controlled by former Senator Joseph Grundy of the Pennsylvania Manufacturers Association. Chairman M. Harvey Taylor sided with Governor James Duff, along with a number of appointive state officials
and delegates from counties with leaders friendly to the governor,
in opposing Dewey. On the first ballot 41 of Pennsylvania's delegates voted for Dewey, 28 for Taft, and 3 scattering. The lines held
on the second ballot. Governor Duff moved that the convention be
recessed until that evening. The Pennsylvania delegation then held
a caucus. The paramount issue appeared to be not Dewey or Taft
but control of the Republican party in Pennsylvania. The dispute
was temporarily settled when the caucus voted 42 to 30 for Dewey,
despite the strenuous efforts of Governor Duff. Thereupon Duff cast
the votes of all 72 delegates on the third ballot for Thomas E. Dewey.

Since then, factional contests have continued among Republican
leaders in Pennsylvania. In 1950, the Pennsylvania Manufacturers
Association, led by Grundy and G. Mason Owlett, bitterly opposed
Duff's candidate for governor, John S. Fine. Coolness has since developed between Senator Duff and Governor Fine, ostensibly because
of Fine's generally independent course after Duff's exertions to win
the gubernatorial candidacy for him.

THE SELECTION PROCESS IN 1952

Pennsylvania was reduced from 33 seats to 30 in the House of
Representatives under the 1950 census. Thus it was entitled to 60
district delegates to the Republican national convention. The lines
of the newly apportioned districts were used in 1952, apparently
without challenge.

Delegates-at-large—The ten delegates-at-large were chosen (under
the 1951 amendment to the election code) by the outgoing state
committee on January 12, 1952. This action occurred in advance
of the issuance of the national call on January 18, but was apparently
valid under the national rules since the action was by a state committee rather than a convention. In effect, the selections were made
ex officio and included: the governor, lieutenant governor, the two

United States senators, chairman and vice-chairman of the state committee, the national committeeman, the national committeewoman, the president of the state federation of Republican women's clubs, and a deputy attorney-general. Since the selection of these delegates was not according to factional criteria, it was not surprising to find that, according to an Associated Press report of February 1, three delegates-at-large supported Taft and Owlett, two Eisenhower and Duff, two MacArthur, and three were on the fence. While Pennsylvania politics is fought vigorously, there is rarely any desire on the part of factional leaders to create ineradicable scars or totally to exclude their opponents from representation in party affairs.

District delegates—Unofficial caucuses were held in most of the congressional districts during January and February. These caucuses consisted of ward leaders or county leaders or of the key figures in the county organization. In 11 of the 30 districts, there was no contest for the office of Republican district delegate in the primary elections on April 22. In 6 districts, there were 3 candidates for the 2 positions; in 5, there were 4; in 4, 5; in 2, 7; in 1, 8; and in 1, 9. The last four districts are all in Alleghany County.

In the 3rd and 6th districts (Philadelphia) the defeated candidates were independents without strong organization or backing; the organization candidates received over 80 per cent of the vote. In the 2nd district a successful merchandiser, William Sylk, allegedly an independent, and basically pro-Eisenhower, won one of the posts while a supporter of William F. Meade, former city chairman, was elected to the other. Sylk, often treasurer of special funds for the city committee, received Meade's support in preference to the two other candidates, who were supporters of former Sheriff Austin Meehan. Meehan and Meade have for some time led opposing factions in Philadelphia Republican politics. Meehan and an associate received over 80 per cent of the vote in Meehan's own 5th district running against Meade supporters.

In the 10th district, including Lackawanna County, which is closely associated with Luzerne where Governor Fine has been an organization leader for some years, three independents received about 9,500 votes each compared with the 30,500 each of the two winners. In the 12th district (Schuylkill and Northumberland) an independent, without organization support, received 18,410 votes compared to 29,127 and 37,536 for the winners. In the 13th district (Montgomery County) a non-organization candidate, pledged to support Eisenhower, received 21,412 votes. One of the winners, Russell Crawford, uncommitted when he ran, received 54,534 votes; he later followed his county leader, Peters, in supporting Duff and Eisenhower. However, the other winner with 50,022 votes, was Joseph Pew, a very prominent Republican figure, who was considered a Taft man at the time. In the 14th district (Berks) all five candidates were Taft supporters. The winners received 32 per cent and 22 per cent of the total vote, respectively. In the 17th district (eight counties around Williamsport), there was an upset. Thomas Finn, a Taft man, was expected to win the second delegate position but was beaten by 3,500 votes by a Williamsport city councilman, Richard Merrell, who was pledged to Eisenhower. In the 20th district (Blair, Center, and Clearfield Counties) there were four candidates, two pledged to Eisenhower, two to Taft. One winner, D. Emmett Brumbaugh, had been state secretary of banking under Duff, but the other winner was Elmer J. Miller, a Taft man. The vote was Brumbaugh, 19,916; Miller, 15,955; Benjamin Jones (for Eisenhower) 14,185; William Sieg (Taft) 13,684.

Contests in the 21st, 22nd, and 23rd were difficult to evaluate. In the 23rd (seven counties around Oil City), George V. Potts ran last with 10,274 votes, and although unknown to the politicians, nevertheless came within 2,705 votes of L. Merle Campbell, the second highest. In the 24th (Erie, Crawford, and Mercer Counties) Gordon Ward, an "independent" auto dealer, who resolutely refused to commit himself to any presidential candidate, ran 514 votes ahead of the third man, an organization-backed candidate. In the 25th district (Beaver, Butler and Lawrence) all four candidates favored Taft, but the result was regarded as an upset because a principal Owlett lieutenant, Roger Rowland, was defeated by 507 votes, running a very close third.

In the four Allegheny County (Greater Pittsburgh) districts, there were 31 candidates altogether for eight positions. Twelve favored Taft, 11 Eisenhower, 1 MacArthur; 5 "promised to support" the popular choice for the nomination. Two Taft candidates were victorious, one in the 29th and one in the 30th. Six Eisenhower candidates were elected, but two of them (James Snee in the 27th and Laird in the 30th) had margins of less than 725 votes.

The reasons for the contests, and the results of them, were so disparate as to make classification difficult. In some cases, seasoned political workers had neither heard of nor could identify some of the candidates in their districts. In each of at least three districts— the 17th, 29th and 30th—one Taft and one Eisenhower delegate were chosen.

Presidential preference vote—Eisenhower and Stassen were the only candidate names appearing on the presidential preference portion of the ballot. The returns showed 863,785 for Eisenhower and 120,305 for Stassen; Taft received a write-in vote of 178,629, and MacArthur, about 6,000. Apparently, Taft votes were proportionally most numerous in those counties where the county organization made some effort for him. In Governor Fine's own home county, Luzerne, Eisenhower received 37,000, Taft 4,000.

COMPOSITION OF THE DELEGATION

The chairman of the Pennsylvania delegation, Governor Fine, probably provoked more columns of newspaper speculation than any other single Republican delegate. He had made his start in the two-fisted politics of the hard coal country in Luzerne County, later becoming county leader and county judge. In 1947 he was appointed superior court judge, but resigned this comfortable position, which carries long tenure, to run for governor in 1950.

Governor Fine appeared to enjoy his ostensibly strategic role in the preconvention bargaining in 1952 and was quoted as saying with evident relish, "I'm being kinda wooed." It was believed that his real devotion was to General MacArthur and that he hoped to be able to swing the Pennsylvania delegation to the General. As late as July 3, the Governor gave a newspaper interview in which he was reported as stating that General MacArthur could beat the Democrats and that he felt General MacArthur to be "above" the bitterness engendered by the Eisenhower-Taft nomination fight in a way that would work to his advantage in the campaign.

Senators Martin and Duff were both delegates-at-large. Because the chairman of the delegation has, in recent years, always been the governor, Martin was chairman in 1944, also a favorite son in 1948. Duff was chairman in 1948. Duff apparently won the ill-will of the Pennsylvania Manufacturers Association by his support of several state measures that they opposed. Thus, the preconvention maneuvering in the Pennsylvania delegation had an ironic twist. Martin had reportedly selected Duff to be his successor as governor, and Duff had selected Fine. But in 1952 Duff and Fine led two of the three opposing groups of Pennsylvania delegates, and Martin was a prominent member of the third.

Joseph N. Pew, Jr., chairman of the board of the Sun Oil Company, was elected one of the vice-chairmen of the delegation. Pew's influence has been mainly that of a contributor; his political influence in his own county organization is limited. Other prominent delegates were: Mrs. Gaynelle Dixon, president of the Pennsylvania State Council of Republican Women, who was also elected vice-chairman of the delegation; the attorney-general; and the secretary of forests and water.

Sixty-nine of the delegates were interviewed by field reporters; partial information on the remaining delegate was obtained. Twenty-five of them were public officials, ten of whom occupied state positions, and 15 held county or municipal posts. Two had held national party offices previously, 14 state party offices, 38 local party offices. Fifteen headed their own business, 6 were employed as executives in other businesses, and 8 were lawyers in private practice. Thirteen had attended the 1948 convention, 9 the 1944 convention, 7 the 1940 convention, 6 the 1936 convention.

Sixty-five delegates were men, 5 were women. Seven were over seventy, 2 under 40. Sixty were Protestant, 7 Catholic, 3 Jewish. Although names may be sometimes misleading when used as an index of ethnic origin, it appears that 45 of the delegates were of English descent, 12 of German, 6 Irish, and at least one Negro.

It appears that the delegates paid their own way to Chicago but did not have to contribute to delegation expenses otherwise.

ACTIVITIES AND VOTING RECORD

Much of the preconvention maneuvering can be explained as a three-way competition among the groups identified respectively with

Governor Fine, Senator Duff, and G. Mason Owlett. Governor Fine, according to newspapers and periodicals, controlled some 30 votes at the convention, and a good deal of national attention focused on him as a potential king maker. Three delegates who were interviewed, two of them in relatively informed positions, denied this. According to them, the number of delegates controlled by Fine was actually not more than 15. Governor Fine's alleged leanings toward Mac-Arthur have already been noted. Senator Duff was early identified with the Eisenhower movement. He was one of the small group of senators who conferred with Governor Dewey in September 1951 on "draft-Eisenhower" strategy. He was prominent among Eisenhower Republicans from then on. A good deal of Senator Duff's state-wide support came from ten Republican county leaders in the southeastern part of the state, seven of which are normally and currently Republican. The pro-Taft leader of the third faction, G. Mason Owlett, was chairman of the arrangements committee for the 1952 convention and in this capacity was responsible for arranging for Douglas MacArthur to keynote the convention. Senator Martin was a prominent member of this group. Owlett and the Pennsylvania Manufacturers Association were active in arranging for delegates. Immediately after General Eisenhower had received over 860,000 votes in the Republican primary, Owlett commented that the primary was "mostly shadow-boxing" and had not changed the situation. M. Harvey Taylor, Republican state chairman, was notably neutral.

About three weeks before the primary, John D. M. Hamilton, manager for the Taft-for-President campaign in Pennsylvania, had announced that his organization would not sponsor any Taft write-in at the primary. Hamilton observed: "The state's too big and we don't have the money. A write-in campaign doesn't take place overnight. . . . It takes much planning, much money and much time." Nevertheless, Taft did receive 178,629 write-in votes in the primary, presumably with the help of the Owlett-Grundy-Martin forces.

The delegation first assumed identity when it met concurrently with the state committee on May 24. Officers were selected for the delegation in a most informal fashion. A project observer was present on May 24 at the organizational meeting, along with a number of other guests without official status. After Governor Fine had been elected chairman of the delegation, the meeting took on a somewhat humorous aspect. On one occasion the Governor recognized a delegate, obviously so that he could place a name in nomination. The delegate rose and declared that he was "present but uninformed." Fine proceeded to instruct him as to his duties, whereupon the compliant delegate made the proper nomination. This performance was repeated several times amid general merriment and banter. The process of choosing officers went on to the accompaniment of much hubbub. One delegate was nominated for the wrong office, but the error was easily corrected.

Informal and unofficial estimates during June showed from 20 to 25 Pennsylvania delegates leaning to Eisenhower, 18 to Taft, and the remaining 27 to 32 inclined to follow Governor Fine's lead. On June 8, Governor Fine conferred with General Eisenhower in New York City for three hours, and afterwards declared that he personally had no preference of his own. Governor Fine said, according to the New York *Times*, that the three-hour conference had been devoted to "practical politics—I never discuss anything else but." A moment later, he modified his statement to say they had talked about matters of principle, adding, "I am primarily interested in principles . . .," then, after a pause, "at this time." One of the purposes of Governor Fine's meeting with Eisenhower was to discuss plans for the meeting between the General and the entire Pennsylvania delegation at the General's Gettysburg farm the following week. Of the 70 delegates, 57 made their appearance at the farm. Governor Fine commented after the conference that "the chasm between myself and the General is daily becoming less" but refused to say that he was more for the General than he had been the day before.

Senator Taft met the delegates at Hershey, Pennsylvania, June 24. At this meeting, as a matter of courtesy, Senator Duff, the Eisenhower leader, sat along with the other state leaders at the speakers' table. When all the men at the speakers' table were introduced, "Big Red" Duff received such sustained applause that the entire press commented on it. One of the delegates commented on the difference in atmosphere between the Gettysburg and the Hershey meetings. His first reaction to the Gettysburg meeting was that it was too informal, and that it was not too well planned. However, after the

Hershey meeting, he felt this was a virtue rather than a vice. His reaction to the Taft effort was that it was over-organized, with too much emphasis on punctuality and dead-lines. He objected to the planted questions asked of Taft, and was particularly dubious when the delegates were subtly asked not to raise certain questions with Taft concerning foreign policy.

Governor Fine arrived in Chicago on July 2 still silent on his presidential preference. He promptly conferred with Arthur E. Summerfield, leader of the large uncommitted portion of Michigan's delegation. On July 5, the Pittsburgh *Press* quoted "an unimpeachable source" as saying that Governor Fine "told top state GOP leaders he favors General Dwight D. Eisenhower." On this same day, Fine announced his own support of the rules change sponsored by the Eisenhower forces, and predicted that "50 to 55" members of the Pennsylvania delegation would probably go along with him. On July 8, the syndicated column of Joseph and Stewart Alsop reported that Fine and Summerfield, meeting in the latter's hotel room, had reached a firm agreement to throw their combined support to Eisenhower "at the psychological moment." "Among the delegates, among the Pennsylvania county leaders, among the members of the Pennsylvania legislature, Fine found the great majority convinced that General Eisenhower was the most likely man to win nationally and to help the ticket locally in Pennsylvania," wrote the Alsops. On July 9, Governor Fine publicly announced his support of Eisenhower at a delegation caucus.

On the convention's first critical roll call—the Brown amendment to the Langlie proposal—Pennsylvania voted 57 to 13 with the Eisenhower forces. The delegation voted 52 to 18 to seat the pro-Eisenhower Georgia delegation; and on the nominating ballot divided 53 for Eisenhower, 15 for Taft, and 2 for MacArthur. This became a unanimous Eisenhower vote after the first ballot switches.

AFTERMATH IN THE STATE

During the campaign, none of the principal Republican leaders of Pennsylvania played a key role in the management of the national campaign. Senator Duff received no further assignments despite his early work for the Eisenhower candidacy, nor did Governor Fine.

In the late summer G. Mason Owlett was dropped from the executive committee of the Republican national committee. However, there is no evidence that the factionalism within the state party in any way impeded campaign efforts in the state for the national ticket.

After the election, newspaper commentators noted a growing affinity between Duff and Owlett arising out of their mutual antagonism for Governor Fine. The Governor's influence, on the other hand, appeared to diminish markedly, perhaps in part as a result of his pre-convention activities. He cannot succeed himself in the state's chief executive office. Pennsylvania Republicans have been at some disadvantage in obtaining federal positions from the Eisenhower administration, according to press commentators, because of the number of factions that must be conciliated, although there is evidence that Senator Duff has principal control of federal patronage in Pennsylvania. More recently, however, the Republican factional leaders were exploring the grounds for unity in avoiding a 1954 gubernatorial primary fight. Fine and Owlett conferred and agreed to support a single candidate. Shortly thereafter, Fine and Owlett met with John McClure, Fred Peters, and Graybill Diehm, the latter three close associates of Senator Duff, but the outcome of this meeting was not immediately evident.

THE DEMOCRATIC DELEGATION

The Democratic strength in the state is of relatively recent vintage. In 1928, only two counties, Lackawanna and Luzerne, went Democratic. In 1932, a total of 25 counties supported Roosevelt. Two counties in the state, Greene and York, are like many southern ones in their Jeffersonian Democratic tradition. The others that now show consistent Democratic strength are either industrial or mining counties, and their adherence to the Democratic party dates back only to 1932. An active Democratic leader in the state has said that although the party is organized on paper in every county, there are many voting districts where the party is not strong enough to man the polls on election day. Of the fourteen counties in which the Democrats had a preponderance of registration, only half went Democratic. All except two of the counties that went Democratic in 1952 were located in the southwest part of the state. The exceptions were Philadelphia and Lackawanna (Scranton) Counties.

Neither the Philadelphia nor the Allegheny County Democratic organizations can be considered unified. Congressman William Green of Philadelphia was a competitor of James Finnegan, later president of the city council, for the chairmanship of the Philadelphia city committee in 1948. Finnegan had the backing of most party leaders. In February 1953, however, Finnegan's doctor ordered him to drop some of his activities. He chose to retain the city council presidency, and informed Mayor Clark of his intention to resign the chairmanship of the party's city committee. Congressman Green was elected city chairman without opposition on February 17, an outcome that may have been unwelcome at the time to the supporters of Mayor Clark and District Attorney Dilworth.

The state-wide Democratic party was almost devoid of leadership in former years. The story is told that Woodrow Wilson could hardly find the Democrats in Pennsylvania to appoint to patronage positions. During the 1930's, Senator Joseph Guffey was the leader of Pennsylvania Democracy, a leadership which he in part exercised through his sister, Emma Guffey Miller, later national committeewoman. Guffey's successor as state leader was Mayor David Lawrence of Pittsburgh, who first became mayor of that city in 1945. Guffey and Lawrence have had their differences, and others have differed with them. Nonetheless, in the period after 1932, one or the other, as recognized leader, could always depend upon the support of a delegation majority at the national conventions. Some of the disagreement among Pennsylvania Democrats in 1952 may be regarded as a challenge to Lawrence's leadership, although these challenges were not pushed to extremes. Within Philadelphia itself there has been much disagreement between the party's professionals and the reform wing.

The only occasions during the preceding four conventions that found the Pennsylvania contingent at odds internally occurred when the incumbent Democratic president did not specifically indicate what action he desired. In 1940, Senator Joseph Guffey and State Chairman David Lawrence disagreed over the issue of the vice-presidential candidate. Guffey supported Wallace before the opening of the convention, while Lawrence favored either Governor Lloyd Stark of Missouri or Paul McNutt of Indiana. Prior to Roosevelt's having chosen Wallace, a caucus showed that Wallace had but 39 votes. When Roosevelt expressed a preference, however, Wallace received 68 votes from Pennsylvania on the first ballot, including that of David Lawrence, while only 4 votes went to unsuccessful candidates.

The absence of unequivocal directions by Roosevelt again in 1944 led to similar friction between Lawrence and Guffey. Aiding Guffey this time in his support of Wallace was Philip Murray of the CIO and Attorney General Francis Biddle. Lawrence, who was strongly anti-Wallace, was joined in his efforts by Postmaster General Frank Walker and by Matthew McCloskey, a generous financial contributor from Philadelphia. On the first ballot Pennsylvania gave 46 votes to Wallace and 23½ to Truman, thus following the lead of Senator Guffey and adhering to the principle of party regularity. On the second ballot the vote from Pennsylvania was 46 for Wallace to 24 for Truman with Guffey holding his delegates firmly until the third ballot on which Truman's nomination was made.

The Pennsylvania delegation gave its unanimous support to Franklin D. Roosevelt in both 1940 and 1944. In 1948, the Pennsylvania Democrats withheld their support until efforts to find a man to supplant President Truman failed. They came out strongly for the Truman nomination two days before the balloting began and on the first ballot gave him the 74 votes of the entire delegation. Even after the anti-Truman rebellion had spent itself, the 1948 convention was not without dramatic moments for the state party. Pennsylvania's Francis J. Myers was chairman of the resolutions committee that reported a mild civil rights plank to the convention. Under the leadership of Mayor Hubert Humphrey of Minneapolis and Representative Andrew Biemiller of Wisconsin, an amendment to strengthen the plank had been offered by a minority of the committee. When the clerk called Pennsylvania, it voted 74 votes in favor of the Biemiller amendment; among those voting for the amendment was Senator Myers. Since the amendment passed by a vote of 657½ to 582½, Pennsylvania's unanimous vote was decisive.

THE SELECTION PROCESS IN 1952

Delegates-at-large—The meeting on January 26 at which the delegates-at-large were selected was conducted in accordance with established organization methods. Pennsylvania had been allotted 70 votes and 80 delegates at the Democratic convention. The list of 20 names for delegate-at-large, each with half-vote, and 20 for alternate was submitted by State Chairman Maurice Splain, Jr., to the state committee, which unanimously approved the selections. Qualifications for the position of delegate-at-large consisted of past or present service to the party or related interest groups. There were 5 delegates whose principal contribution was money, 8 who had held elective office on either state or national levels, 6 who held important positions in the party hierarchy at the state level, and 5 members of minority economic, racial, or religious groups. Several delegates could be assigned to more than one category. There was no overt attempt to limit selections to those who would be likely to accept the decisions of delegation leaders; in the actual event, 8 of the delegates-at-large voted on the first nominating ballot against the expressed desires of Mayor David Lawrence and his associates, and 6 did so on the second ballot.

The issue of whom these delegates would support at the convention did not arise when they were selected. President Truman had not yet withdrawn himself from consideration, Governor Stevenson's intentions were still a mystery, and the importance of the Kefauver campaign had not yet become apparent. The uncertain conditions prevailing at the time of the selection were borne out by Richardson Dilworth, district attorney of Philadelphia, who recently remarked that he had become a Kefauver supporter in January only after Governor Stevenson had issued his denial of candidacy.

District delegates—In the absence of a crystallization of sentiment in the state, no names were entered on the Democratic ballot for presidential preference before the close of filing on February 16. Candidates for district delegate made little effort to associate themselves with any of the presidential candidates, even though 37 delegates promised to support the popular choice for president in their district. The strategy followed by partisans of the various presidential candidates apparently was to accept the choice of the voters for district delegates, and then to make an attempt to attract these delegates to their particular candidates.

In 16 of the 30 districts in the state there was no contest for delegate in the primary on April 22. Of the 14 contested districts, 8 had three candidates for the two places as delegate, and 6 had four candidates. The issues at stake in these contests were personal or factional rather than the desire to support specific presidential candidates at the convention. The contests would probably have taken place even if all the candidates for delegate were supporting the same man for the nomination.

With only 80 candidates filed for 60 district delegate positions, it seems clear that there was not much activity by organized groups attempting to obtain control of the party in their districts. The majority of the candidates who filed for a place on the ballot were chosen by the party organizations within their districts. Of the 20 candidates who filed without organization support, only one was elected. The regular candidates were selected by their organizations at formal caucuses or informal meetings of important leaders within the district. There is no standard practice in Pennsylvania on this point. It is not covered by the state election code, nor by the rules of the state Democratic party. Custom and tradition which vary from district to district seem to be the only guides.

Presidential preference vote—All the preference votes cast for Democratic presidential candidates in the primary on April 22 were write-ins, about 175,000 write-ins in all. Senator Kefauver received 93,160; General Eisenhower placed second with 28,660 Democratic write-ins; President Truman was third with 26,504; Senator Taft was fourth with something over 8,000 votes; Stevenson and Harriman were close together with between 3,000 and 4,000 votes; scattered votes went to other candidates such as Russell, Barkley, Kerr, and Mrs. Roosevelt. Forty-nine thousand of Kefauver's votes came from four counties in the southwestern part of the state: Allegheny, Washington, Beaver, and Cambria. In one of them, Washington, Kefauver received twice as many votes as he did in Philadelphia County—where Dilworth, the most prominent of the state leaders working for him, was active—although Washington County has only 10 per cent as many registered Democrats. In these same four counties, Truman received 17,000 of his 26,504 votes.

COMPOSITION OF THE DELEGATION

There was a distinct difference in political achievement between the delegates-at-large and the district delegates. The former included the national committeeman and committeewoman, the mayor and district attorney of Philadelphia, the chairman and vice chairman of the state committee, a former senator, a congressman with 20 years in the House of Representatives. Four large contributors to the Democratic party and representatives of the CIO and AFL were also included. Among the district delegates, the 12 from Philadelphia and five of the eight from Allegheny County were intimately connected with the political organizations in their areas. The 40 district delegates from the remainder of the state included at least 15 who could be classed as professional political leaders, but almost all the delegates had had some connection with politics. There were four congressmen in the delegation. Four women were delegates.

The delegation included a number of representatives of minority groups. From the Philadelphia area alone, there were 2 Negroes, 7 Jews, and 12 Catholics. Generally there appeared to be greater representation of these groups in the Democratic than in the Republican delegation.

The delegates paid their own convention expenses. In fact, their ability to do so was a factor in the choice of some candidates for district delegate. Many of the delegates had attended previous conventions as either delegates or visitors. This was especially true of the delegates-at-large, 16 of whom had attended conventions between 1940 and 1948. The location of the Democratic convention in Philadelphia in 1940 and 1948 was undoubtedly a factor in the convention experience of the delegation.

ACTIVITIES AND VOTING RECORD

The announcement that the President did not intend to run complicated matters in Pennsylvania, and the enigmatic actions of Adlai Stevenson were not considered helpful. A personal friend of Mayor Clark, Stevenson presumably could have had the support of all those from Philadelphia who finally decided upon Kefauver as the most available choice. District Attorney Richardson Dilworth was one of the most active Kefauver men in the state. He publicly and without qualification came out for the Tennessee Senator. Not having had the time or resources to file a slate of Kefauver delegates, he engaged in a campaign to pledge as many delegates for his man as he could. Senator Kefauver visited the state in June, and a dinner was held in Harrisburg in his honor. Although all the Pennsylvania delegates were invited, only about half of them appeared. The only delegates-at-large in attendance were Dilworth, Mayor Joseph Clark, Matt McCloskey, Albert Greenfield, Philadelphia civic and business leader, and George Rhodes, congressman from Berks County and the city of Reading.

Senator Kerr was guest at a dinner held in Reading by Clarence Bowers, a delegate-at-large and storage battery manufacturer. This affair had even fewer delegates in attendance, although a number of invited county chairmen swelled the crowd. The policy of the state leadership was to ignore both Kefauver and Kerr and take an uncommitted delegation to the convention.

As late as July 19, Mayor Lawrence of Pittsburgh, Philadelphia City Chairman James A. Finnegan, and ex-Senator Myers were reported watching Stevenson and Truman closely for clues to their convention wishes. James Finnegan was among those making early financial contributions to the Stevenson cause. During the days just prior to the convention in Chicago, however, the principal pro-Stevenson activity in the Pennsylvania delegation apparently originated with James P. Clark, delegate from the 3rd district in Philadelphia, but no relative of Mayor Clark. Later there was disagreement as to the distribution of honors for the earlier initiatives, but several disinterested sources agree in giving major credit to James Clark. Clark is a former chairman of the party's city committee, and, prior to a recent illness, was considered by many to be the most active and skillful politician in Philadelphia. He arrived in Chicago some days before any of the other delegates and became converted to the Stevenson candidacy. Reportedly with the assistance of Philadelphia City Councilman Lewis Stevens, who was also in contact with James Finnegan, Clark's efforts among the Pennsylvania delegation leaders soon bore fruit. On Sunday morning, July 20, the leaders of the Pennsylvania delegation met in James Clark's suite in the Blackstone. Present, besides James Clark, were Lawrence, Finnegan, Myers,

State Senator Joe Barr from Allegheny County, Genevieve Blatt, secretary of the state committee, Michael Lawler from Scranton, and Bill Teefy, treasurer of the Philadelphia city committee. All candidates for the nomination were discussed but, with the exception of Stevenson, none generated any enthusiasm. The only question about Stevenson was his apparent unwillingness to try for the nomination. In discussing the possibility that Stevenson might "pull the rug" out from under his supporters by refusing the nomination, Finnegan argued that if he really did not want the nomination, he would probably have stated his withdrawal in such unequivocal terms that all efforts in his behalf would end.

The first delegation caucus took place in Chicago on Sunday evening, July 20. At that time, ex-Senator Francis J. Myers was formally elected chairman of the delegation. He was also elected, along with National Committeewoman Emma Guffey Miller, to the resolutions committee. John J. Kane, Allegheny County Commissioner, was elected to the credentials committee and Mayor Joseph S. Clark of Philadelphia to the rules committee. These officials had been in Chicago performing their duties several days prior to their election, but this did not seem unusual to the Pennsylvania delegates.

The second major item of business at the Sunday evening caucus was a surprise for the Kefauver forces. It came when Lawrence, Myers, and Finnegan asked for an "expression of sentiment" by the delegates as to their preference for the nomination, Finnegan making it known that he would be voting for Stevenson. The caucus voted 32 for Stevenson, 14 for Kefauver, 7 for Truman, and 2 for Harriman. Most of the missing votes were those of Kefauver delegates whose leaders had apparently assumed that nominations would not be discussed at the first caucus.

The vote in the caucus indicated other cross-currents than the one between the Dilworth-Clark group and the Lawrence-Myers-Finnegan entente. The Truman votes came from Congressman William Green of Philadelphia, formerly the chief competitor of James Finnegan for the city chairmanship and eager to stand apart. Since he did not wish to appear to associate himself with either group, Green was forced to find himself another candidate. The Harriman votes came from Allegheny County Commissioner John Kane. This elderly man broke a friendship of 18 years with Lawrence over the latter's support of Stevenson.

As the convention opened, the drive to draft Stevenson received renewed impetus when he formally greeted the delegates as the governor of the host state. Late on Monday, word was given the press that Francis J. Myers, well known for his former activities as majority whip in the Senate, had been selected by the "draft-Stevenson" group as floor manager for the Stevenson drive. At about the same time Dilworth and Clark attended a meeting of Kefauver supporters at which they reaffirmed their support, partly on the grounds that they did not think Stevenson would allow himself to be candidate.

The Pennsylvania delegation furnished other fuel for the political fires at this time. The late Philip Murray, preoccupied in Pittsburgh with the steel industry controversy, had declared for Truman, but with small expectation that the President could be drafted. This was primarily a gesture of confidence in an incumbent president and party leader. Because Stevenson seemed unavailable, top CIO leaders around Murray were split between Kefauver and Harriman. David McDonald, secretary-treasurer in Murray's steel workers union and delegate from the 27th district of Pennsylvania, was for Truman first but actively for Harriman second. Murray, in his own absence, deputized a group of CIO vice-presidents to observe events at Chicago and counsel the labor delegates. Jack Kroll was in charge, but Walter Reuther was probably the most compelling force in this group and soon threw his weight to Stevenson.

By Wednesday the Pennsylvania delegation was beginning to rebel against its leaders. The chief cause for complaint was the lack of communication between the leaders and the rank-and-file. Led by district delegates from suburban Philadelphia and state senator Samuel Neff of Lawrence County, about 20 delegates signed a petition requesting information from the leaders and reminding them that, if no information was to be made available, it might be difficult for uninformed delegates to conform. The next morning a breakfast was held to which the entire delegation had been invited several days earlier. Lawrence, Finnegan, and Myers took the opportunity to try to placate the rebels, explaining that Myers' responsibilities as floor manager for the Stevenson drive made it difficult for him to keep in close touch with the delegates.

The most important opportunity for a vote prior to the balloting on the nomination was furnished by the motion to seat the Virginia delegates after they had refused to sign the loyalty pledge. The Pennsylvania delegation was not polled on this issue. The vote of 57 in favor of the motion and 13 against was arrived at by mutual agreement between Senator Myers and Richardson Dilworth, the Kefauver leader, on the floor of the convention. According to John Calpin of the Philadelphia *Bulletin,* this agreement came after Mayor Lawrence brought back to the delegation information that most of the key national party leaders wished to arrive at a compromise with the South. Dilworth had not been able to keep his group of supporters in line on the Virginia vote and was amenable to compromise, while, to most of the other party professionals, reared in Pennsylvania's tradition of factional accommodation, this was a logical step toward healing the wounds of the convention's loyalty pledge fight.

The Pennsylvania vote to seat Virginia is reported to have caught the Illinois delegation by surprise. When the Illinois leaders returned to the floor of the convention in response to an emergency call, they took note of the Pennsylvania action and eventually switched to favor seating Virginia, a move decisive to the outcome. When Senator Douglas of Illinois, a strong backer of Senator Kefauver, moved to adjourn the convention at a very late hour, the tactic was recognized as an effort by the Kefauver forces to delay and divert the growing Stevenson drive. In order to avoid embarrassing any of the Pennsylvania delegates who had at that particular time retired for refreshment, Richardson Dilworth and Senator Myers mutually agreed that the delegation should be voted 35 against the motion and 35 for, without polling the group.

The factional pattern of the Pennsylvania Democratic party exhibited itself on the first two ballots for the presidential nomination. On the first nominating ballot the vote was 36 for Stevenson, 22½ for Kefauver, 6 for Truman, 4½ for Harriman, ½ for Kerr, and ½ for Justice Douglas; on the second ballot, 40 for Stevenson, 21½ for Kefauver, 6 for Truman, and 2½ for Harriman. At this point, the rival factions within the Pittsburgh and Philadelphia groups were still at odds, while the other delegates were split between the two major candidates. Kefauver's 22½ votes came primarily from the southeast and southwest areas of the state and from some of the central counties. On the third ballot, Pennsylvania cast 70 votes for Stevenson.

The Kefauver people had consented to a unanimous vote on the condition that the vice-presidential candidate would not be selected from the ranks of the Dixiecrats. Apparently a number of them felt Sparkman was sufficiently associated with this group to justify a protest. Senator Myers assured Dilworth that he knew nothing of the plans to nominate Sparkman when the final vote for Stevenson had been cast. Dilworth, along with representatives from California, New York, and Minnesota, called upon National Chairman Frank McKinney the next day to protest the Sparkman selection. McKinney questioned Dilworth's right to object, saying that since the arrangement had the approval of Senator Myers, Dilworth was not entitled to represent Pennsylvania opinion.

AFTERMATH IN THE STATE

The end of the convention was not the end of factionalism in the Democratic party in Pennsylvania, not even for the duration of the campaign. Immediately upon his return to Philadelphia, Richardson Dilworth, who at that time had a proclivity for washing political linen in public, criticized City Chairman James Finnegan for his part in "steam-rolling" the Pennsylvania delegation to Stevenson. Finnegan's leadership in the city was already being questioned by Congressman William Green. The personal pique of ex-city chairman James Clark, who felt his contribution to the Stevenson nomination was being ignored and all public credit going to Finnegan and Myers, aggravated the situation. Thus, in mid-August, a revolt against Finnegan was impending, but Finnegan called a meeting of the city committee on ten days' notice and succeeded in obtaining a vote of confidence.

The Democratic ticket in Philadelphia enjoyed a phenomenal success on election day. Finnegan had publicly stated on numerous occasions that the plurality in the city would be 150,000 in favor of the Democrats. Privately, it was rumored that he was willing to wager on a 75,000 plurality. It was 162,000. Major credit for the sweep is given to the work of Americans for Democratic Action (ADA) and to the eagerness with which many independent and "respectable" elements sought a change from prolonged Republican control of the city.

On February 17, 1953, Congressman William Green was elected chairman of the city committee to succeed James Finnegan, who had resigned for reasons of health. To many, Green represented the older party organization in Philadelphia. Under the new city charter, Mayor Clark and District Attorney Dilworth had been attempting to hold the patronage line against the professionals. In February 1954 Green sponsored charter amendments that were intended to enable city employees to engage in political activity and also to subject the mayor to greater control by the city council. A two-thirds vote in the 17-member city council was needed to place the amendments on the referendum ballot. Mayor Clark was able to muster seven votes and defeated the move.

REVIEW AND APPRAISAL

Pennsylvania is like New York and Illinois in having a presidential primary that is mainly a system for the direct election of district delegates who, for practical purposes, are unpledged. Like Illinois and unlike New York, Pennsylvania does provide opportunity for a presidential preference poll; and unlike either, it has a unique procedure by which the would-be delegates may declare on the ballot whether or not they "promise to support" the winner of the preference poll. But the promises to support, when given, seem to be honored in the breach about as much as in the observance. In either party, the presence or absence of the promise seems to have almost no effect upon the fortunes of a candidate for delegate. A busy electorate, confronting a long ballot under frequently congested voting conditions, pays little attention to the "promise" when voting and applies no later sanction if it is violated. The presidential preference poll could have more meaning in Pennsylvania than in Illinois, New Jersey, or a number of other states with similar preference polls if the "promise to support" feature of the system were effective in practice. But since it is not, the Pennsylvania preference poll is in actuality no more than advisory, and becomes merely an incident in the flow of events given consideration by leaders and delegates in deciding how to vote at the conventions.

As a system for the direct election of district delegates, the Pennsylvania primary works smoothly. As in Illinois, the filing requirements are less onerous than in New York, and opposing candidates for the delegateships appear on the ballot more frequently. But even so, there was no contest over the Republican delegateships in 11 of the 30 districts, and none over the Democratic in 16. Most of the defeated candidates were independents who ran without organized support. Only four Republican candidates for delegate and one Democratic were successful against the opposition of the regular party organizations in their districts, and all of these had the support of organized groups of independents. Candidates who ran as individuals without organized backing of any sort did not carry a race and usually polled only a negligible number of votes. On the other hand, at least three of the defeated Republican candidates were professionals. This was probably a reflection of the sharply drawn lines between the Taft and Eisenhower forces in some areas, which operated to split the professionals and produced local factional contests in a few instances that bore some visible relationship to the national contests. But the contests reflecting national candidate preferences were the exception rather than the rule; and even in those cases it was not clear that national candidate preferences were decisive of the outcome. Several districts gave one Republican delegate to Taft and the other to Eisenhower.

Neither party faced a situation in which organized competing slates of candidates were presented for the major presidential aspirants. It seems to be the political tradition in Pennsylvania for county leaders to choose their own candidates for convention delegates, with presidential aspirants and their managers then negotiating with the county leaders for support. This usually means that the county leaders actually select the district delegates except in those rare cases when an independent is successful. In 1952, at least half of the 60 district delegates in each delegation could be considered professionals in politics; the contingents from Philadelphia and Pittsburgh were almost completely so. As such, they were prepared to apply the usual tests of availability in the consideration of national candidacies.

The selection of delegates-at-large in Pennsylvania is a process that gives both parties freedom to recognize individuals and interest groups that are important in their respective parties. As a result of recent amendments to the electoral code, the free choice of both state committees was legalized, since delegates-at-large are now elected by the state committees rather than by the party electorates at the primary election. The institution of delegate-at-large in Pennsylvania also has served to give state party leaders an opportunity to bolster their strength by choosing delegates sympathetic to their views. But Pennsylvania political leaders are cooperative enough to avoid using their power to "pack" the at-large delegation, and all party factions are usually represented. Thus in 1952 the Republican delegates-at-large were split 7-3 in favor of Eisenhower. The Democratic delegates-at-large split their 20 votes on the first ballot among five different candidates for the nomination and on the second ballot among three.

Both Pennsylvania delegations occupied positions of critical importance at the national conventions. As the third largest state, Pennsylvania would have been important for its size alone, if for no other reason; but in both conventions, Pennsylvania was much more uncommitted in the earlier stages than either New York or California, the two larger states. In the Republican convention, Governor Fine pursued tactics presumably intended to enhance the bargaining position of his delegation. In the end, he was found on the winning side with a substantial number of votes; but there is no evidence that either he or his delegation profited by the tactics that had attracted so much national attention. In the Democratic convention, the delegation arrived with some of its members pledged to Kefauver, but with most of them not only uncommitted, but actively on the search for a candidate. Nearly half of them decided that Stevenson was the man the evening before the convention opened; and the chairman of the Pennsylvania delegation, ex-Senator Francis J. Myers, became the floor manager of the draft-Stevenson movement.

Split voting was characteristic of both delegations in 1952, although both gave their votes unanimously to the winner while the tally could still be revised. The split voting reflected the factionalism that has existed in both parties in the state in recent years. It also reflected national factional alignments in part: Taft and Eisenhower each attracted bands of early adherents in the Republican delegation, and so did Kefauver in the Democratic. Such a voting pattern might be expected from a large state with several metropolitan centers, in which the district delegates, unlike those in California, are separately elected in their own districts. But the Pennsylvania voting pattern in both conventions was strikingly different from that of New York, where the system for electing district delegates is much the same. Governor Fine was less effective than Governor Dewey in unifying his delegation, perhaps in part because of his own reluctance to accept the visible evidences of popular sentiment in his state party; and on the Democratic side, Pennsylvania had no Averell Harriman of its own and was not prepared to support New York's.

The voting record supports one significant conclusion, that Pennsylvania did not have an effective state-wide political boss in either party in 1952. Even with the powers of the gubernatorial office, Governor Fine left observers in doubt as to whether he was leading his delegation; some thought that the delegation was leading him. In the Democratic party, out of power in the state government, probably only Mayor Lawrence held some kind of veto power, and probably only with respect to the actions of the party's state committee.

The traditional concept of a national convention delegation is an aggregation of party bosses and party hacks, more interested in candidate "availability" than in qualifications for the highest public office, prepared to enter actively into trading operations in the political market place, and hoping to leave the convention with a firm patronage commitment from the winner. The professionalism of both Pennsylvania delegations, the attitudes and behavior of many delegates, and the somewhat sordid history of Pennsylvania politics would tend to justify the suspicion that both Pennsylvania delegations of 1952 were close to the stereotype. Yet there was the impressive record of split voting in both delegations; and there is no evidence that any substantial portion of either delegation was able to swing its votes on the basis of a "deal."

Perhaps this is merely a tribute to the high-mindedness of the winning candidates in both conventions; but it also suggests that both Pennsylvania delegations found themselves under strong compulsions to seek the best available candidate. It would be difficult to argue that either delegation was unrepresentative of its constituency. Eisenhower was clearly the choice of the Pennsylvania Republicans; and while Kefauver probably would have been acceptable to many Pennsylvania Democrats, Stevenson was apparently no less acceptable and far more capable of unifying the party effort in the state.

In general, the Pennsylvania procedures for electing delegates and otherwise participating in the presidential nominating process seem to be workable and in accord with the political habits of the state. The experiment with the optional "promise to support," however, seems to be a failure. There is little apparent reason why this complicating feature should not be repealed. The optional features of the New Jersey ballot, by which the candidate for delegate may indicate a preference among the presidential candidates as a guide to the voter, would seem more useful if any new feature is to be added.

Relatively simple types of direct election system for delegates, particularly district delegates, seem to be favored by the experience of many of the metropolitan states. In the absence of some strong national impulse toward uniformity, it would be difficult to argue that Pennsylvania should abandon procedures that have been found satisfactory by other comparable states. It is probably not accidental that the systems in New York, Pennsylvania, and Illinois have all evolved along such similar lines. All three states resemble each other in the competitiveness of their parties, in their pivotal leadership role, and in the nature of their politics. The procedural decisions that each have reached in the light of experience should not and cannot be lightly disregarded.

Pennsylvania Chapter Acknowledgments

G. EDWARD JANOSIK, Assistant Professor of Political Science, University of Pennsylvania, prepared pre-convention and post-convention case study reports on the Republican delegation, with the assistance of DR. HENRY ABRAHAM, University of Pennsylvania, DR. ALBERT B. MARTIN, University of Pittsburgh, MARY FRANCES HARVEY, and MARTIN REAM. Dr. Janosik later prepared a report on the Democratic delegation and assisted in the preparation and revision of the draft chapter.

The initial draft in chapter form was prepared from the field reports and other sources by LEWIS A. DEXTER, Research Associate, Bureau of Social Science Research, American University, whose services were temporarily available to the Washington staff.

WEST

————————————————————————

Electoral votes, 1952: 8

National convention votes, 1952:
    Democratic, 20
    Republican, 16

Population, 1950: 2,005,552
    Urban, 35%; *rural nonfarm,* 45%; *rural farm,* 20%

Population increase, 1940-50: 103,578 (5%)
    Urban, 20%; *rural nonfarm,* 14%; *rural farm,* 23% decline

Presidential vote, 1948:		*1952:*
Democratic,	429,188 (57%)	453,578 (52%)
Republican,	316,251 (42%)	419,970 (48%)
Others,	3,311 (1%)	

Gubernatorial vote, 1948:		*1952:*
Democratic,	438,752	454,898
Republican,	329,309	427,629

U. S. Representatives vote, all districts, 1950:		*1952:*
Democratic,	374,921	471,175
Republican,	287,915	403,427

U. S. Representatives elected 1950:		*1952:*
Democratic,	6	5
Republican,	0	1

State legislature elected 1952:
    Senate: Democrats, 22;   Republicans, 10
    House: Democrats, 67;   Republicans, 33

Method of selecting national convention delegates:
    Direct election in primary, first Tuesday in May
    Advisory presidential preference poll

VIRGINIA

CHAPTER 13

West Virginia is often classed with the solid south as Democratic, but elections in the state are always marked by intense campaigning. The heavy Democratic registration margins are not always reflected in the vote. An analysis of the period since 1863 when the state was admitted to the Union shows that control of state affairs has been almost evenly divided between the two parties. Up to 1952, the Democrats had elected two more governors than the Republicans; the state's presidential electors were won by each of the parties exactly the same number of times. The same two-party distribution of strength is reflected in the election of members of Congress from West Virginia; it is not uncommon to find a split delegation at the nation's capital.

Democratic control since 1932, however, has been almost complete in statewide elections. The only major Republican successes have been the election of a few Republican congressmen and a Republican senator. The 1952 election saw the state remain in the Democratic column, as had been expected, but the Republican vote was impressive. Stevenson's margin over Eisenhower was only 33,608, while the Democratic candidate for governor won by only 27,269 in a state with a registered Democratic majority of approximately 245,000. The Republican electors won a majority of the presidential vote in 27 of the 55 counties, but the Republican party managed to win only one congressional seat.

Intra-party conflict is not unusual within both parties. Primary elections are frequently as bitter as general election campaigns. Currently, there are struggles for leadership in both parties. Some independent Democrats, operating without any well-defined leadership, are struggling to overthrow the present Democratic administration;

this struggle apparently had little effect on the selection of national convention delegates in 1952. The split in the Republican party is drawn between the supporters of National Committeeman Walter S. Hallanan and those opposing his leadership; this disagreement has been so severe as to render practically impossible the distribution of patronage which would normally accrue during a Republican administration on the national level.

West Virginia is primarily rural, and relies economically upon the coal industry. Because so many of its citizens are employed in the coal industry or are directly dependent upon it for a livelihood, the political role of organized labor has been a dominant factor. The CIO and AFL are well organized in the state, but it is the large United Mine Workers Union that wields the telling power. United Mine Workers President John L. Lewis frequently comes into the state to participate in its campaigns although there is no certainty that the miners vote as he asks. Labor has usually thrown its support to the Democratic party in recent years and has been one of the large factors in that party's success.

PRESIDENTIAL PRIMARY LAW AND PROCEDURE

Delegate selection—The selection of West Virginia's delegates and alternate delegates to the national conventions is governed by a 1915 statute that has undergone little modification since its passage. So brief is the relevant section of the statute that much is left to the rules of the parties. Delegates and alternate delegates are popularly elected by their respective parties at the primary elections held on the second Tuesday of May of presidential election years. In each party two delegates and two alternates are selected from each of the state's six congressional districts and, normally, four delegates and four alternates are elected from the state at large. Operation of the bonus system in the Democratic party has increased the at-large delegation by two votes in 1944 and four votes in 1948 and 1952. The Democrats, with fractional voting in 1952, selected 16 delegates-at-large, each with one-half vote.

Candidates for delegate and alternate file certificates of candidacy as generally prescribed for candidates for public office or party committee, although, according to an attorney-general's opinion, delegateships are not classed in either category. These certificates need not be accompanied by petitions. Candidates must certify that they are legally qualified voters, members of the party they seek to represent, and that they are *bona fide* candidates for election to the position. Certificates of candidacy are filed with the secretary of state and must be accompanied by the prescribed filing fee. The filing fees are as follows: delegate-at-large, $20; alternate delegate-at-large, $10; district delegate, $10; and, alternate delegates from districts, $5. Names of all candidates properly filed are printed on the primary election ballots of their respective parties along with their permanent home addresses. No indication appears on the ballots as to which aspirant for president the candidate favors.

The preference primary—Since 1915, it has been possible for any presidential candidate to have his name printed on the official ballot of his party to be voted upon in the primary election. The results of this vote are not binding on convention delegates, and there is little incentive for a national candidate to file. During the 37 years in which the presidential preference primary statute has been in effect, covering ten presidential campaigns, there has been no outstanding contest in the state among presidential aspirants in either party. Usually not more than one national pre-convention favorite has entered the primary of either party and quite often no candidate has entered. In 1928, Senator James A. Reed and Governor Alfred E. Smith engaged in a preference contest in the Democratic primary. In 1932 and 1936, Franklin D. Roosevelt was entered as the sole favorite. Since 1936, no Democratic candidate has announced in the state. The record of Republican candidacies has been about the same, although in 1952 both Senator Robert A. Taft and Harold Stassen had their names entered. Local candidates, ostensibly seeking publicity, have run at times against national candidates if any of the latter chose to enter the state primaries. No provision is made for write-in votes. Thus, delegates have generally received no clear-cut instructions from the voters of their respective parties as to whom they should support at the national conventions. This resulted in the repeal in 1939 of the 1915 requirement that candidates for convention delegate announce prior to the primary whether or not they would support the popular preference.

Two 1951 amendments to the primary election laws made it even more difficult for convention delegate candidates to ascertain the preference of the voters. One amendment established a $1,000 filing fee for presidential candidates, intended to discourage frivolous candidacies. The other amendment advanced the date for the filing of candidacies. To facilitate voting by the large number of persons serving in the armed forces, the deadline for filing announcements of candidacy was moved forward from the fifth Saturday to the fourteenth Saturday next preceding primary election day. In 1952, certificates of candidacy had to be filed before midnight of February 9, or postmarked prior to that time. At that time, Senator Estes Kefauver was the only Democrat who had formally announced for president, and President Truman had not indicated that he would not run again; had the filing deadline remained unchanged in West Virginia it would have fallen on April 12. Many more Democrats, including leading political figures within the state, might have joined the race for the delegate positions. On the Republican side, supporters of General Eisenhower could not encourage a full slate of candidates to enter because the General had not announced by the February 9 deadline whether he would accept the nomination if offered, although he had allowed his name to stand in the New Hampshire primary and the deadline for withdrawal in that state had passed.

THE REPUBLICAN DELEGATION

Prepared in consultation with
FRANKLIN L. BURDETTE

Delegations to the Republican national conventions since 1940 have, with the exception of 1944, been split in their preferences for presidential nominee. No one in the state party has been in a position fully to control the delegations. In 1940, the delegation divided its 16 votes on the first ballot, giving Dewey 8, Taft 5, and Willkie 3. By the fifth ballot, Dewey had lost all support and the delegation was divided 9 to 6 between Taft and Willkie. The delegation finally united on the sixth ballot to cast 15 votes for Willkie, with one absentee. The 1944 delegation was solidly in the Dewey camp. At the 1948 convention, the West Virginians split between Dewey and Stassen for the first two ballots but finally unified behind Dewey on the third. The split in the delegations of recent years bears little clear relation to current party factionalism; in 1952, when the party split was most extreme, most of the party members on both sides were Taft supporters.

THE SELECTION PROCESS IN 1952

The 1952 primary campaign was one of the most vitriolic in the annals of the state party. The race for governor was a principal one and featured a contest between Rush D. Holt of Weston, a former Democratic United States senator, and three other candidates, the strongest of whom was John T. Copenhaver, the mayor of Charleston. After serving as a Democratic member of the state legislature and of the United States Senate, Holt most recently has served in the state legislature. He transferred his allegiance to the Republican party in 1950 and was successful in winning the nomination to Congress from the 3d congressional district, although he shared the defeat of all Republican nominees in the general election. His campaign for the gubernatorial nomination was a dynamic one and, despite his record as a former Democrat, he polled more votes than his two leading opponents combined.

The selection of the state's 16 national convention delegates created as much if not more controversy. Because the delegates to the national convention select the national committeeman and committeewoman from the state, and because of the traditional importance of the national committeeman in the state party's leadership, this contest had other facets than the determination of the state's vote at the national convention. It was a struggle for the control of the Republican party in the state between supporters of National Committeeman Walter S. Hallanan and those desiring new party leadership. Hallanan had served on the Republican national committee for 24 years. Having achieved marked success in the business world, serving for many years as president of the Plymouth Oil Company, Hallanan first came to political prominence as secretary to Governor Henry D. Hatfield prior to World War I. He later served a term in the state senate from 1926 to 1930. Since that time he has not been a candidate for public office, but his political influence has been greater than that of any other Republican in the state.

Hallanan occupied the center of the 1952 political controversy over state party control. His supporters wanted to see him re-elected national committeeman; his opponents wanted him replaced. His critics said that the party had been unsuccessful too long under his leadership. They accused him of circulating slates in behalf of his own supporters throughout the state and of using his position as national committeeman to thwart the rise of a younger leadership. Many felt that his unrelenting conservatism lacked popular appeal. Hallanan supporters cited his long service to the party in the lean years, his considerable contributions of time, talent, and money, his influence nationally, and his substantial political acumen.

Hallanan advocates started early in their efforts to re-elect him to the national committee. Pro-Hallanan slates of candidates for delegate, four at large and two in each of the six congressional districts, were given wide circulation. These candidates were favorable to Senator Taft. Hallanan was a candidate for the position of delegate-at-large. While the presidential and the party control campaigns were separate, the Hallanan campaign theme varied with local interests, here pushing the Hallanan candidacy, there emphasizing the Taft candidacy. Support of the pro-Hallanan slate had the strong backing of county chairmen and precinct workers in many areas.

The opposition to Hallanan was never as fully organized or as homogeneous as his support. Differences in emphasis and strategy developed, impairing the effectiveness of the campaign to unseat Hallanan. The presidential preferences of the anti-Hallanan delegate candidates also were largely for Taft, but some were for Eisenhower, and at least one seemed to favor MacArthur. The opposition delegate candidates agreed early in the campaign that, in the event they succeeded in electing half of the convention delegation, a free caucus would be held to discuss the selection of a national committeeman, anticipating the replacement of Hallanan.

Observers outside the state have generally discussed the West Virginia Republican split as a cleavage between Taft and Eisenhower forces. This was not the case, for Republicans in the state were preponderantly for Taft. Efforts to win Eisenhower delegates were exerted with much less intensity. Stassen's name appeared on the presidential preference ballot, but he made almost no personal campaign in the state. The West Virginia Republican voter was nonetheless confronted with a confusing situation and had difficulty separating presidential preferences from state factional allegiances. Phil Hill, General Eisenhower's pre-convention manager in the state, was the only Eisenhower candidate for delegate-at-large to give full support to the move to unseat Hallanan. Some of the Eisenhower district delegate candidates were associated with the movement, but, in many instances, anti-Hallanan candidates were also Taft supporters. Among the most vigorous and open leaders of the anti-Hallanan campaign were Thomas E. Millsop of Weirton and R. J. Funkhouser of Charles Town. Millsop, president of the Weirton Steel Company and mayor of Weirton, was an ardent supporter of General Eisenhower and outspoken in his criticism of Hallanan. He was also running for the position of district delegate in the 1st congressional district, where he enjoys tremendous prestige. Funkhouser, candidate for delegate-at-large, published the most vituperative attacks on Hallanan in his newspaper, the *Jefferson Republican*, originating in Ranson and distributed to Republican leaders throughout the state.

The campaigns—No difficulties were encountered in creating enthusiasm in West Virginia for Senator Taft. The majority of the party workers and those whose influence was felt in Republican councils were by conviction supporters of the Senator from neighboring Ohio. Phil Conley of Charleston managed the Taft campaign. Conley's name also was carried on the Hallanan slate for delegate-at-large. The official Taft slate and the Hallanan slate were the same for delegates-at-large and contained substantially the same names in the districts.

Harold Stassen's was the only name to appear on the presidential preference primary ballot in opposition to Taft, but Stassen made no attempt to carry the state. Taft's campaign received approbation from the press and from party members generally, but no all-out campaign to win delegates for him seemed necessary. Modest funds were spent in his behalf, and automobile tags, buttons, and literature were distributed. The Senator himself appeared in the state during early May and received an enthusiastic welcome.

Supporters of General Eisenhower were beset with difficulties from the outset in promoting his campaign. First, public sentiment in West Virginia was clearly for Senator Taft, although the support for Eisenhower was never negligible. Secondly, the February 9 deadline for filing delegate candidacies created some difficulty in the organization of an Eisenhower slate. Complete Eisenhower slates were possible in only three of the six districts and in the state at large. The early filing date also operated to prevent his name from being placed on the presidential preference ballot.

Some consideration was given to the idea of urging Eisenhower supporters to vote for Stassen in the presidential preference primary since the General's name would not be on the ballot. This was abandoned and voters were urged to write-in the General's own name and to vote for favorable delegates. Write-in votes are not counted in the West Virginia primary, but backers felt that any effort here would serve as a protest and reduce the size of the Taft vote.

Considerable support was rendered by the state Eisenhower headquarters to those candidates for delegate who indicated a preference for the General. Since West Virginia has no law permitting presidential preferences to be indicated beside the name of delegate candidates on the ballot, this assistance to some who were not themselves too well known was of significant proportions. Several outstanding West Virginians were among the early Eisenhower advocates: Arthur M. Hill of Charleston, chairman of the board of the Greyhound Corporation; Thomas E. Millsop of Weirton; F. Paul Chambers, Logan attorney; former State Auditor Edgar C. Lawson; and Phil Hill of Charleston, who also became a candidate for delegate-at-large. The Millsop campaign for delegate in the 1st congressional district was by far the principal one waged in Eisenhower's behalf.

The primary election—The results of the primary election gave Senator Taft an overwhelming victory in the advisory presidential preference poll, officially reported as 139,812 for Taft to 38,251 for Stassen. (According to a study by Franklin L. Burdette, cited in the note at the end of the chapter, the official returns reflect a copying error in Grant County which reversed the Taft-Stassen returns in that county, and the official returns for the state should therefore have been 141,533 for Taft and 36,530 for Stassen.) The write-in votes for Eisenhower were not counted but they were numerous and sometimes indicated organized effort. Only one pro-Eisenhower delegate was elected, Thomas E. Millsop of Weirton.

The primary election was also considered an overwhelming victory for Walter S. Hallanan. Of the 16 delegates to be chosen, 13 supporting Hallanan were elected. Hallanan led the ticket in the contest for delegates-at-large and the other at-large candidates elected were on his slate. The three successful anti-Hallanan delegates, all of whom campaigned vigorously, included Thomas E. Millsop who led the ticket for 1st district delegate by more than 3,000 votes. In the 2d district, Mrs. Davis Elkins, wife of a former United States senator, received the highest vote, defeating a Hallanan candidate by 2,800 votes. Andrew E. Douglass, Parkersburg insurance man, outdistanced a Hallanan candidate by almost 1,000 votes to win second place in the 4th district delegate race.

Several prominent political leaders shared defeat in the delegate contests: Thomas Sweeney of Wheeling, who had been Republican nominee for the United States Senate in 1940 and 1946 and a delegate-at-large in 1948, ran fifth in the delegate-at-large contest; Phil Hill, state Eisenhower chairman, ran sixth; R. J. Funkhouser, a 1948 delegate-at-large, ran ninth. The only Negro in the state filing for delegate, James F. Wade, an Eisenhower backer, finished seventh.

COMPOSITION OF THE DELEGATION

Most of the members of the West Virginia delegation to the national convention were well known to the public. Of the delegates-at-large, Henry D. Hatfield had served as governor of the state and as United States senator, Walter S. Hallanan was national committeeman, Carl Bachmann was formerly Republican whip in the national House of Representatives and mayor of Wheeling from 1947 to 1951, and Phil Conley was chairman of the Taft campaign. Probably Thomas E. Millsop, Weirton industrialist and mayor, and Robert B. McDougle, retiring chairman of the state executive committee, were the best known of the district delegates, among whom were: Austin V. Wood, prominent editor of the Wheeling *Intelligencer;* Robert H. C. Kay, Charleston attorney, counsel to the state executive committee; and Ezra Hamstead of Morgantown, who held the position of chairman of the Monongalia County executive committee. The others were prominent locally, but not on a statewide basis.

Occupationally, lawyers dominated the 1952 delegation. Seven of the sixteen members of the delegation were practicing attorneys. No other occupation was represented by more than one delegate. With the exception of Mrs. Elkins, those not lawyers represented business and professional groups.

While seven of the delegates had never had previous convention experience, the other nine had served as delegate at least once and six had been elected as many as three times. In each district, one of the delegates had never served before while the other was invariably a veteran. Only one of the delegates-at-large, Phil Conley, had not served previously.

ACTIVITIES AND VOTING RECORD

Walter S. Hallanan and Mrs. Frances Ogden Stubblefield, newspaper publisher, were endorsed at the organization meeting held in Charleston on May 24 for re-election to their positions on the national committee. Since almost all the delegates favored Taft and most were Hallanan supporters, no friction developed. Robert B. McDougle, 4th district delegate and chairman of the state executive committee, was elected chairman of the delegation despite the fact that this honor usually goes to the delegate-at-large receiving the highest vote. The delegates named Robert H. C. Kay for vice-chairman, and for secretary, Hardin R. Harmer, Shinnston attorney. The following convention committee assignments were made: Walter S. Hallanan, committee on credentials; Phil Conley, rules; and Austin V. Wood and Mrs. Davis Elkins, resolutions. When Hallanan was selected by the Republican national committee to be temporary chairman of the national convention, he was replaced on the credentials committee by Robert H. C. Kay. The designation of Hallanan as temporary chairman did not conform to Republican precedent. The convention keynoter usually serves as temporary chairman until the permanent chairman is chosen. General MacArthur's unusual position prevented him from being considered seriously as presiding officer of a political convention, although he served as keynoter. The selection of Hallanan evoked sharp protest from Senator Henry Cabot Lodge, Jr., the Eisenhower manager at the convention.

All West Virginia delegates and all but one of the alternates attended the convention. The votes were all cast by the delegates and none of the alternates had an opportunity to function as a delegate. Thomas E. Millsop was the single delegate voting against the Taft point of view on the Brown amendment relating to the modification of the rules, and on the minority report on the seating of the Georgia delegates.

Millsop also cast the single vote for Eisenhower in the roll call for presidential nomination. Fourteen of the delegates voted for Taft and McGinnis Hatfield of Welch voted for MacArthur. When it became obvious that Eisenhower would be nominated, Hatfield and Andrew E. Douglass of Parkersburg switched their votes to him. The final vote of the delegation was: Taft 13, Eisenhower 3.

AFTERMATH IN THE STATE

Following the national convention, Walter S. Hallanan was named vice-chairman of the Republican national committee despite his pre-convention adherence to the Taft cause. The 1952 election, however, did not settle the controversy within the Republican party in the state. To date, party leaders have been unable to agree on patronage recommendations, or even on the methods of making them, resulting in an impasse in this connection.

THE DEMOCRATIC DELEGATION

Based primarily on reports by
WILLIAM R. ROSS

The Democratic party in West Virginia has been a consistent victor at the polls since 1932. Its most intense intra-party battle during its period of control occurred in 1940 when one faction, headed by United States Senator Matthew M. Neely, collided head-on with another under the leadership of Governor Homer Holt. The struggle for state party control became so intense that Senator Neely resigned his seat in the United States Senate to seek and win the governorship. Since that time, persons favorable to Neely have been responsible for the direction of the state party.

Considerable discontent has evidenced itself from time to time over the party leadership. Those opposed to the present direction, however, have not been well organized. This discontent came to a head in the 1952 Democratic primary when opposition candidates for governor polled 206,923 votes to 140,688 for the organization candidate. Senator Neely had backed William C. Marland for the Democratic nomination for governor. Some of the leaders of the United Mine Workers, although usually in agreement with Neely, opposed Marland and threw their weight to then Representative E. H. Hedrick. A third principal contender was Cyrus S. Kump, running as an independent Democrat; two other candidates appeared on the ballot. Senator Harley M. Kilgore, seeking his third six-year term, faced a less serious challenge for renomination.

Recent West Virginia delegations to the Democratic national convention have reflected greater unity, probably resulting from the fact that, with the exception of 1952, presidential incumbents were up for renomination in each instance.

THE SELECTION PROCESS IN 1952

Forty-eight persons sought election as delegates, 18 as delegates-at-large and 30 as district delegates. Twenty-three candidates filed for alternate delegate, 13 of this number in the statewide contest.

No outstanding contest occurred among candidates for delegate other than in the 3d and 4th districts. In the 4th district, four of the five candidates resided in Huntington, the fifth in Parkersburg. The residence factor alone was almost sufficient to assure the election of Dorr Cato, a prominent Parkersburg attorney. Among the four Huntington residents, the race narrowed down between Charles A. Adkins and Thomas W. Harvey, both practicing attorneys and both publicly endorsing the candidacy of Senator Estes Kefauver for president. Adkins established and directed the Kefauver-for-President headquarters in West Virginia. By a slim margin of 214 votes, Harvey was elected. In the 3d district, eight persons filed for election as delegate. Former Congressman Andrew Edmiston was elected easily to one of the delegate positions. The contest for the other seat was won by a Glenville State College professor, Miss Bessie Boyd Bell, by the very slim margin of 90 votes. She received only 14 per cent of the total primary vote cast and this represented only 11 per cent of the registered Democratic party voters of the district.

Among the 18 persons filing candidacies for delegate-at-large positions were many who were relatively unknown to party regulars. But on the day after the filing deadline, National Committeeman Arthur B. Koontz announced that the half-vote privilege would be operative in the selection of West Virginia delegates-at-large. Thus, 16 of the 18 candidates would have to be selected to cast the state's 8 at-large votes at the national convention. This avoided the possibility of a lively contest among the 18 candidates, but it also caused some consternation among persons who might otherwise have filed. It had been generally expected that the West Virginia delegate-at-large positions would be filled by full-vote incumbents, as in 1944 and 1948.

Very little interest was evidenced in either the district delegate or the delegate-at-large contests. No formal slates appeared on the part of any labor, business, farm, veteran, or political group. Few political announcements appeared in the newspapers and almost no literature was circulated. It appeared likely even before the election that the two candidates for delegate-at-large whose names had little voter appeal, Ed Jude and Nathan Tickle, would be defeated; final returns backed up this expectation. These contests were considerably overshadowed by spirited campaigns on the part of candidates for governor, United States senator, and representative in three congressional districts.

On the basis of the 1952 Democratic party registration, there were 683,566 registered Democratic voters at the time of the primary. The candidate for delegate-at-large polling the largest vote received only 191,471 votes or 28 per cent of the number of registered Democratic voters. The largest percentage vote cast for any district candidate was 26 per cent of the registered voters of the district, and this occurred in the 6th district where only three candidates were entered. In the 4th district, where five candidates competed, the candidate receiving the greatest number of votes had only 12 per cent of the registered Democratic vote.

COMPOSITION OF THE DELEGATION

Several prominent party leaders were among those representing the state in Chicago: Governor Okey L. Patteson and former Governor Clarence W. Meadows, United States Senator Matthew M. Neely, and former United States Representatives Andrew Edmiston and Jennings Randolph. Four of the delegates were members of the state executive committee. Three of the alternate delegates were also members of the state committee. Two prominent newspapermen, Frank A. Knight of the Charleston *Gazette* and Clarence E. "Ned" Smith of the Fairmont *Times* served as delegates. Absent from the list of those in the delegation were such prominent persons as former Governor John J. Cornwell and United States Senator Harley M. Kilgore, both of whom had served in previous conventions. Neither sought election in 1952. The retiring party chairman, Ernest L. Bailey, did not attend the convention.

The delegation was predominantly male, 25 men and 3 women. Two women served as alternate delegates, only one of whom was elected in the primary election; the other was appointed to fill a vacancy. Twenty-one of the delegates either had held public offices or were currently serving in public office, state or county. Two others had served as presidential electors.

Eleven of the delegates were or had been members of state or county party executive committees. Nine delegates were lawyers, two were medical doctors, one was a college professor, one was a practicing dentist, and one was a civil engineer. Most of the alternate delegates were business or professional men and women and approximately one-half of them held or had held some public office. As a whole, the delegation consisted mainly of business and professional men. Only one delegate was a member of a labor organization and none was actively engaged in agriculture. In neither the Republican nor Democratic delegation was there anyone who might be said to represent organized labor by virtue of his full-time occupation, and only one person, Laurence E. Tierney, Jr., of the Democratic delegation, was directly associated with the coal industry, unless the Republican's Thomas E. Millsop of Weirton Steel Company might be classed in this category.

No Negroes were elected as delegates, although three were elected as alternate delegates. In the matter of religious belief, 25 of the delegates were Protestant, two were Catholic, and one agnostic. The delegation was composed of persons of middle-age, only two being over 70 and three in their late thirties.

Of the 28 delegates elected to the 1952 convention, 13 had attended one or more previous conventions as delegate and 3 had attended as alternate delegate. Three delegates had been elected to as many as five conventions; 10 were serving for the second time. Five of the delegates had sought election to a previous convention and had been defeated. Thirteen of the delegates had never before attended a national convention as either delegate or alternate delegate. One delegate, Dr. Chester R. Ogden, disclosed that he had missed only one convention since 1912, but he had attended only two as a delegate and one as alternate delegate.

ACTIVITIES AND VOTING RECORD

Traditionally, the Democratic party delegation does not caucus for any purpose until the delegates assemble in the convention city. Since the West Virginia representatives on the Democratic national committee are designated by the state executive committee, rather than by the convention delegation as is the case in the Republican party, there is no need to convene for this particular function. The newly elected state executive committee in 1952 designated Mrs. Lynn S. Horner as national committeewoman and re-elected Arthur B. Koontz as committeeman.

The organizational caucus was held on Sunday evening at the LaSalle Hotel at which time Governor Okey Patteson was named chairman of the delegation. This was in keeping with the tradition of bestowing this honor upon the governor if he is a member of the delegation. Mrs. Mary Hart Davisson was named vice-chairman. The following were named to the principal national convention committees: Jennings Randolph to credentials, Carl B. Galbraith to rules, and Senator Matthew M. Neely and Mrs. Mary Vinson Clark to resolutions. National Committeeman Arthur B. Koontz served on the national committee's subcommittee on credentials, which dealt with the difficult Texas, Mississippi, and loyalty pledge issues.

The other main business of the caucus, which was presided over throughout by National Committeeman Koontz was, first, to confirm the appointment of persons designated by the state executive committee to fill three vacancies and one absence in the alternate delegate positions and, second, to assign alternates to delegates on the basis of votes polled in the primary election. After the caucus adjourned, Senator Richard B. Russell was introduced and spoke briefly.

The West Virginia delegation divided on the first test vote of the convention. As the roll call on seating the Virginia delegation proceeded, West Virginia voted 10 in favor of seating Virginia, 6 against, 4 absent. This was soon changed to 11½ in favor and 6½ against. After the Illinois switch, the results read: 13½ for seating Virginia, 5 against, 1½ not voting. In the vote on the motion to table the Douglas resolution, the delegation favored tabling by 10 to 9.

In the absence of overriding pressure from the delegation leadership, no candidate for president received a majority of the West Virginia delegation vote on any of the three ballots. The votes were divided as follows:

	First Ballot	Second Ballot	Third Ballot
Kefauver	5½	7½	7½
Stevenson	1	5½	9
Russell	7	6½	3½
Barkley	6½	½	0
	20	20	20

Only one West Virginia delegate had committed himself openly in the primary campaign. On the eve of the national convention, it was generally assumed that most of the delegates would follow the leadership of Senator Neely and Governor Patteson. It had been presumed that both would support Vice President Barkley on at least the first ballot. To most West Virginia delegates, the withdrawal of Vice President Barkley from the race on Monday fell like a bombshell. On the first ballot, however, those who were inclined toward the Vice President chose to give him a token vote. On the second ballot, only the one-half vote of Senator Neely was cast for Barkley. Nearly all of Barkley's supporters switched to Stevenson except Neely, who remained with the Vice President, and Delegates R. C. Curry and Mrs. Clark, each with one-half vote, who voted for Senator Kefauver. Only two delegates consistently voted for Stevenson on all three ballots: former Governor Clarence Meadows and the sheriff of Mercer County, Clarence C. Elmore. The support of Senator Russell came mostly from the southern part of the state. Both delegates from each of the 5th and 6th districts supported the Georgia senator on the first two ballots, but, on the third ballot, the delegates from the 6th district switched to Stevenson. The most loyal supporters were those of Senator Kefauver. All West Virginia delegates who voted for him on the first ballot did likewise on the second and third ballots.

Prior to the announcement of the West Virginia delegation's vote on the first ballot, Governor Patteson, as chairman of the delegation, personally had polled each delegate and had in writing each delegate's announced vote. Upon request that the delegation be polled, however, Barkley lost 1½ votes to Kefauver. This loss came as a result of vote-changing by one full-vote district delegate, Minter L. Wilson of Morgantown, and one half-vote alternate-at-large, A. James Manchin of Farmington voting for Ernest Bailey. Delegate Wilson's explanation was that he recognized the Governor's announcement to be in error and that he had been a supporter of Senator Kefauver from the beginning and had so informed the Governor. Manchin explained that he was of the opinion that the votes of the entire delegation from West Virginia were to be cast for Barkley on the first ballot. When, however, the results on the first ballot were announced and Barkley had failed to receive even a majority, he felt free to vote his own convictions. On the second ballot there was no challenge of the announced vote. On the third ballot, Delegate Wilson once again challenged the accuracy of the announced vote and requested that the delegation be polled. At the completion of the poll, the result was as originally announced.

AFTERMATH IN THE STATE

West Virginia was not caught in the landslide which swept General Eisenhower and Senator Nixon into office but remained once again in the Democratic fold, although by a margin somewhat smaller than normally. Governor Stevenson polled a majority of some 33,000 votes, whereas the normal Democratic majority hovers around 100,-000. The gubernatorial race brought out a somewhat larger vote than the presidential. William C. Marland defeated Rush D. Holt for governor by a margin of 27,269 votes. Senator Harley M. Kilgore was re-elected by a margin of 63,465 over his Republican opponent. All the Democratic candidates for statewide offices were elected. Republican voting strength rose in both the cities and the agricultural counties, whereas the coal-mining counties maintained their position as Democratic strongholds.

REVIEW AND APPRAISAL

West Virginia is closely akin to New York, Pennsylvania, Illinois, and Nebraska in its practices for participating in the presidential nominating process. The similarities and differences among these five states also can be viewed in the light of their varying degrees of political party organization. Parties are highly organized and competitive in New York, Pennsylvania, and Illinois. Nebraska has a strong tradition of nonpartisanship, has weakly organized parties, and tends to be Republican in its electoral behavior. West Virginia is somewhat like Nebraska in having a relatively loose type of party organization, but is Democratic on election day.

All five states elect congressional district delegates to the national conventions by direct primary. Delegates-at-large are chosen by party state committees in New York and Pennsylvania, by state convention in Illinois, and by statewide primary voting in West Virginia and Nebraska. In none of these states does the presidential preference of the delegate candidate appear on the primary ballot. In all but New York, however, presidential aspirants may be entered in preference polls. If their favorite is not on the preference ballot, voters in Nebraska, Illinois, and Pennsylvania may use a write-in procedure. Write-ins in West Virginia, however, are not counted. Nevertheless, the Eisenhower supporters did encourage write-ins in 1952, undoubtedly to demonstrate the irrepressible character of the popular demand for the General, and many voters did vote in this way.

Another aspect of the presidential preference provisions in these states may be compared. It requires petitions with the signatures of 100 party voters in each congressional district to put the name of a presidential candidate on the ballot in Nebraska; it takes from 3,000 to 5,000 signatures in Illinois, and 100 names from each of 10 counties in Pennsylvania. In West Virginia, however, self-declaration and a filing fee of $1,000 are the requirements, with no petitioning involved. West Virginia's preference for filing fees rather than petitions is again reflected in connection with the declarations of candidacies for delegates: self-declaration suffices in West Virginia whereas petitions must be signed in the other four states; a $10 to $20 filing fee is required in West Virginia, with Pennsylvania the only other among these five states having a similar requirement. Apropos of the use of petitions, it should be noted that delegate slate-making, particularly by party "regulars," is a regular practice in the strong party states of New York, Illinois, and Pennsylvania, but a relatively unimportant feature of delegate selection in Nebraska and West Virginia.

West Virginia also has an early filing date compared to the others, but not earlier than that of Illinois, January 21 in 1952. In West Virginia the date was February 9; in Pennsylvania, February 16; in Nebraska, February 20; and in New York, March 18. Thus, West Virginians share with others the problems arising from having to express themselves on presidential candidacies before these candidacies have become organized public movements.

West Virginia in 1952 provided illustration for two minor procedural aspects of national party politics. The practice of having the convention delegation select the national committeeman and committeewoman led to a sharp factional contest on the Republican side in this state between the Hallanan and anti-Hallanan forces, a contest that overshadowed the Taft-Eisenhower struggle in the state even though it was oriented in part along similar lines. The winning Hallanan faction was clearly pro-Taft; the anti-Hallanan faction was partly pro-Eisenhower and partly pro-Taft.

The second procedural development arose on the Democratic side when National Committeeman Koontz made a belated announcement just after the filing deadline that the delegates-at-large would be 16 in number with a half-vote each under the national party rules instead of 8 with a full vote each. Although technically permissible, the tardiness of this announcement in effect prevented many potential delegate candidates from filing and amounted to a changing of the rules in the middle of the game.

West Virginia Chapter Acknowledgments

WILLIAM R. ROSS, Assistant Professor of Political Science, West Virginia University, prepared a pre-convention report on the Democratic delegation, attended the national convention as a West Virginia alternate-at-large, and later amplified his earlier statement in a mimeographed report issued by the Department of Political Science, West Virginia University.

FRANKLIN L. BURDETTE, Professor and Head of the Department of Government and Politics, University of Maryland, acting in response to a project request in the spring of 1953, prepared a report on the Republican delegation, which was issued in mimeographed form under his personal deposit for copyright by the Department of Government and Politics, University of Maryland, under the title "The West Virginia Delegation to the Republican National Convention, 1952."

The initial draft in chapter form was prepared from the field reports and other sources at the Washington staff office in November 1953 by DR. MAVIS A. MANN, Assistant Professor of Political Science, West Virginia University, on leave as a Congressional Interne of The American Political Science Association, 1953-54.

DISTRICT OF COLUMBIA

Electoral votes: none

National convention votes, 1952:
Democratic, 6
Republican, 6

Population, 1950: 802,178
Urban, 100%; *rural,* none

Population increase, 1940-50: 139,087 (21%)

Presidential vote: none

Congressional representation: none

Local elected officials: none

Method of selecting national convention delegates:
Democratic: primary election (by party rules)
Republican: "state" convention (by party rules)

Based primarily on reports by H. Rowland Ludden

---CHAPTER 14

The district of columbia has been recognized in the assignment
of national convention votes for most of a century. The recognition
has been somewhat similiar to that accorded the territories that were
expected to become states, and in part on the basis of a similar
rationale. But regardless of the arguments that were used at the
national conventions during the period from 1860 to 1884, when the
matter was intermittently controversial, the real explanation seems to
be that both political parties have found it convenient to have delegateships available at the national capital. The 6-vote District quota is
equivalent to the minimum allotment for the smallest states, although
the population of the District exceeds that of 13 states. The District
would be entitled to two members of the House of Representatives if
given representation in that body on the same basis as other parts of
continental United States.

In addition to being the seat of the government of the United States,
the District of Columbia is the central city of a metropolitan area
with a population in 1950 of 1,464,089. There is a continuing migration of middle and upper income white population out of the District
into the nearby residential areas of Virginia and Maryland. The
population of the District in 1950 was 35 per cent Negro. In the
decade 1940-1950, the white population increased 9 per cent, the
Negro population 49 per cent. Within the District, problems of traffic
stagnation and developing slum areas attract an increasing amount
of attention. Action to solve these problems is progressing but is
handicapped by the jurisdictional fragmentation of the over-all metropolitan area. Because of land holdings of the Federal Government,
foreign governments, and tax-exempt institutions, less than half of
the land area of the District is taxable for local government purposes.

The District of Columbia has no vote in national or local elections at the present time. From 1802 to 1874 residents of the District were enfranchised for some purposes of local government; from 1871 to 1874 they had a "territorial" delegate in the House of Representatives. Since 1874 the District government has been administered by a three-member commission appointed by the President. Congress serves directly as the "city council," passing all local tax and other laws and appropriating funds derived from local taxes.

In recent years, a considerable portion of the population has supported agitation for home rule and the suffrage, but home rule bills have usually been defeated in committee in the House after passage by the Senate. Both major parties espoused the cause in their platforms in 1948 and 1952. President Truman took a favorable stand early in his Administration. This local political situation is complicated by the race issue. Some opponents of home rule and suffrage admit that they are influenced by "fear" of the large Negro population. An economic facet of the situation is seen in the opposition of the local board of trade to proposals for effective home rule.

Political life is made atypical in part by the high percentage of the population engaged in federal employment. The real or imagined transitory nature of this portion of the population is a factor retarding the development of normal types of community activity. The political neutralization of civil service employees through the various laws limiting their political activity is another factor. The general effect is to decrease participation in the few available local channels of political action. Of the 583,000 persons of voting age living in the District, only an estimated 100,000 maintain legal residences elsewhere and are able to vote absentee. Such absentee voting has only indirect effect upon the government of the District of Columbia.

The political party organizations in the District of Columbia cannot, by their own efforts, gain control of any elective or appointive office. This gives them an appendant, almost parasitic, nature. Their position is further complicated by their nearness to national party and pressure group headquarters. These offices contain personnel upon whose resources, time, and counsel the local parties may draw through a variety of informal channels. More generally, in the absence of the normal objectives and constituencies of local parties, the party managers in the District find that their "constituency" consists of party and pressure group officials in and from the rest of the nation who have congregated in Washington. This tends to make District party leaders especially sensitive to those factional developments within the national parties that will determine control of the presidency, Congress, and the congressional committees that deal with District affairs.

There seems to be no continuing factional pattern within either major party in the District. From time to time, usually during presidential election years and for purposes connected with the nomination, individuals or newly-organized groups will challenge the control of the persons who dominate the local party organizations. The challengers, however, either pass rapidly from the scene after defeat or join with and are assimilated into the regular organizations, depending on the circumstances. In recent years there have been no challenging groups that continued to act as an opposition more than a few months after the events of the campaign that brought them into existence.

There are no laws regulating party primary elections in the District of Columbia. In 1952 an unsuccessful attempt was made to secure enactment of a law by Congress to provide a preferential primary for choosing delegates to the national conventions. In the absence of laws on the subject, both parties utilize methods of choosing party officials that were first adopted 30 or 40 years ago and which have been modified only slightly from time to time.

The party organizations in the District of Columbia played important roles in national party affairs during the formative years of the two major parties. In 1844 a separation of function between the "Democratic Association of the District of Columbia" and the evolving Democratic national committee began to appear. The separation was complete by 1848 when the Democrats first formed their national committee and assigned it the task of conducting presidential campaigns, a function previously performed in part by the District Association. The "Republican Association of the District of Columbia" was one of the groups sponsoring the formation of a Republican party and national committee in 1856, and it has been accorded membership on the national committee since that time.

Voting representation in a national convention was first accorded the District of Columbia in the Republican convention of 1860. Though no distinction was made between the District of Columbia and the territories of Kansas and Nebraska in the convention debate on the subject, the District was allotted 2 votes and the territories 6 votes each. The District of Columbia rode in on the coattails of the territories in the debate, which emphasized the importance of the party struggle in "Bleeding Kansas." The existence of good Republicans in the territories and the District of Columbia, it was also argued, should have some weight in the convention. In 1864, delegates from the District and the territories were seated, but they were not allowed to vote or sit on the main convention committees. No reasons were given in the convention for this action, which was reversed in 1868 when the District and the territories were given 2 votes apiece on recommendation of the credentials committee. Thereafter, the District was allotted voting delegates at all Republican conventions, except in 1916 when a three-way contest among District delegates prevented the seating of any of them. The District delegation was increased to 3 for the 1936 convention and to 6 for the 1952 convention.

In the Democratic convention voting privileges were not extended to delegates from the District of Columbia until 1884. Prior to that time delegates from the District and the territories were seated, but without voting rights, whenever they attended a convention. In 1884 broad support for extension of voting privileges to the territories and the District of Columbia existed in the national committee, which included in the call an invitation to them to send 2 delegates each subject to the decision of the convention as to their admission. Opposition to the seating of delegates with voting privileges from the territories and the District arose on the floor of the convention when it was argued that "the Delegates from these Territories have no votes at home and they should have no votes here; and . . . this is a poor year to follow Republican precedent." The rejoinder to this argument was presented by a delegate from Oregon who maintained, "It seems to me that every Democrat in this broad land . . . has a living, vital interest in the proceedings of this convention, and it would be unjust to the people who are struggling to build up the Territories into prosperous States to adopt this amendment (seating the delegates without voting rights) and silence the voices of the Delegates that have been invited to attend, and came here with the understanding that they would participate fully and freely in the deliberations of this body."

Though this argument failed to state the basis of the understanding as to "full and free" participation and though the District of Columbia was not engaged in a struggle to become a prosperous state, the convention extended voting privileges to the delegates in question by a voice vote. After several roll calls had been taken, during which the territories and the District were apparently overlooked, they were included in the roll call to name the national committee. They were then called on subsequent roll calls, including the nominating ballots. No clear factional pressure was apparent behind this extension of voting privileges in the Democratic national convention of 1884; most of the territorial, though not the District delegates, gave strong support to Cleveland's nomination. This move can be explained as simply a part of the general revision of Democratic party national organization and procedure at this time, during which the District of Columbia was included without reference to the fundamental distinctions that differentiated it from the territories.

Allotment of 2 votes each to the territories and the District of Columbia became standard practice in Democratic national conventions until 1892 when New Mexico and Arizona were given 6 votes each after the House of Representatives had passed their enabling acts. In 1896 the national committee recommended that all territories be treated alike, and the convention, without floor debate, granted 6 votes to all territories and the District of Columbia, which voting strength has continued to the present in Democratic national conventions.

THE REPUBLICAN DELEGATION

During the past decade the Republican party of the District of Columbia has come to speak through the voice of Joseph C. McGarraghy, chairman of the "Republican State Committee in and for the District of Columbia." The previous chairman was McGarraghy's law partner, James C. Wilkes. Before becoming committee chairman in 1949, McGarraghy had served as chairman of the District of

Columbia campaign committees for the Willkie-McNary and the Dewey-Bricker campaigns. Until 1952, he and an inner core of conservative Republicans, mostly lawyers, had been able to maintain their leadership position through control of party machinery without having to defeat significant opposition.

A traditional policy of paving the way for compatible relations with whichever presidential candidate became the nominee was reflected in the voting of the District delegation at the 1940 and 1944 conventions, and, with modifications, at the 1948 convention. The unpledged, three-vote delegation divided evenly among Taft, Dewey, and Willkie on the first ballot in 1940 with all three votes switching to Willkie on the final ballot. In 1944, the votes were initially divided one for Taft and two for Dewey, but were three for Dewey before the tally closed on the first ballot. On the first ballot in 1948 Everett Dirksen received one "favorite son" vote and Dewey received the other two, but Dewey received all three on the second ballot.

The state committee's policy of choosing delegates on the basis of past service to the party in the District has resulted in a "seniority rule" which places hard-working party leaders at the top of the list of possible delegates. Influential leaders of the party frequently attend the conventions as visitors. This makes it possible to pass the positions of delegates and alternates around among other members of the organization. (The members of the executive committee of the state committee are voting members, along with the delegates and national committeeman and woman, of the caucus that controls the delegation's actions at the convention.) In recent years no person has been a delegate twice in succession.

The 6 delegates and the 6 alternates of 1952 were to be chosen by a "state" convention that usually meets early in June of presidential election years. The membership of the state convention is identical with that of the state committee and is chosen in three stages: (1) Republican voters are registered by party officials; (2) registered Republican voters assemble in precinct meetings and elect single delegates from each of the 43 precincts, into which the city is divided by the state committee; and, (3) this group of 43 persons selects, by majority vote, an additional 43 "delegates-at-large" to complete the membership of the committee and convention. By this method, the leadership of the state committee insures self-perpetuation since a majority of the precincts (22) could control a voting strength of 65 of the total 86 delegates in the state convention and state committee.

THE SELECTION PROCESS IN 1952

State committee chairman McGarraghy announced the rules, registration dates, and election dates decided upon by the state committee at a meeting on April 9, 1952. Qualified Republicans could register at one central location or with their precinct chairman on April 24-26 and 28-30. Registration at the one central location was open to public view but a precinct chairman could register a voter at his and the voter's convenience at any place, even the voter's own home. This procedure allowed the precinct chairmen a certain freedom in communicating with the specific persons they preferred to register. Only registered voters could participate in precinct meetings, held between May 16 and 22, at which one delegate from each of the 43 precincts was chosen to attend the state convention. The 43 delegates so chosen met on June 2 and elected the 43 delegates-at-large to the state convention. The 86-member state convention then met on June 5 and selected the 6 delegates and 6 alternates to the national convention.

The Republican party in the District of Columbia during the 1952 delegate selection process consisted of three different forces: Eisenhower supporters organized under an Eisenhower-for-President Club; Taft boosters with a Citizens Committee for Taft; and the officially neutral state committee. The neutrality of the state committee was questioned by the Eisenhower forces who claimed that the majority of the committee's members were in favor of Taft and that the committee was actively pro-Taft in spite of its announced neutrality. In view of certain events during the delegate selection process and the voting record of the state-committee-controlled delegation at the national convention it appears that this claim was substantially true.

The battle between Eisenhower and Taft supporters was joined in February when the former attempted, together with the Democratic party in the District, to secure a city-wide primary for both parties under city auspices. This proposal was defeated when McGarraghy publicly refused to participate. Another attempt to establish a presidential primary system for the District, this time by Congressional action, was also supported by Eisenhower adherents and District Democrats. This was defeated when the bill was bypassed in the Senate at the request of Everett M. Dirksen, Taft's campaign manager in Illinois and in 1948 the "favorite son" candidate of the District Republican delegation at the national convention. With the elimination of these possible alternative methods for selecting national convention delegates, the Taft-Eisenhower battle took place within the framework of the usual procedure.

Controversy over the rules governing registration and conduct of precinct meetings resulted in some modifications of the previous rules. Eisenhower adherents failed in four of their objectives: (1) to end "private registration" by precinct chairmen; (2) to obtain permission for watchers at registration places to copy registration lists; (3) to gain access to the 1948 registration list of some 2,000 names; and (4) to have several public registration places in various parts of the city. The state committee adopted modifications of previous procedure, including: (1) provision for secret balloting at contested precinct meetings; (2) publication of precinct boundaries in advance of registration day; (3) establishment of one central, public registration place; (4) publication of registration lists after completion of registration; (5) designation of a uniform cut-off time for registration in the precincts by the precinct chairmen, eliminating a previous practice of allowing precinct chairmen to register persons up until the time balloting started; (6) a 15-day period between closing of registration and voting in precinct meetings; (7) reduction from two to one year of District residence required of registrants; and (8) realignment of precinct boundaries so as to give each precinct about 18,000 persons.

Charges and denials of gerrymandering in the drawing of precinct boundaries were made but not supported with substantial evidence by either side. A delay in the composition and publication of the precinct chairmen list, finally announced five days before the start of registration, was interpreted by Eisenhower forces as "another restriction imposed by the Old Guard." There is no evidence to indicate that this delay was occasioned by any consideration other than the desire to find a person living within each precinct who would be willing to serve as chairmen and who would support the "neutral" position of the state committee. No chairmen were chosen from the pro-Eisenhower group.

The registration proceedings, a most crucial stage in the delegate selection process, were marked by lively competition between Taft and Eisenhower forces. Eisenhower supporters utilized standard publicity methods, car pools, telephone campaigns, and a hastily assembled and spottily effective system of block workers. Taft workers used similar tactics and in addition were assisted by a Taft rally the night before registration opened. The rally, at which Taft and Dirksen spoke to a crowd of approximately 3,000, had been arranged by the Republican club of the District of Columbia, which McGarraghy described as an "agency" of the state committee. Chairman McGarraghy, however, denied any connection between the timing of registration and the rally. At the rally Taft announced that his supporters, if registered, could vote for Taft delegates at precinct meetings. However, no persons identified as Taft candidates had been or ever were announced to run in the precinct meetings. The voters' choice was restricted to Eisenhower-pledged delegate candidates and the officially-neutral state committee candidates.

The state committee played a quieter and less frantic role in the registration drive than did the adherents of the two leading contenders. Important advantages were inherent in its control over the precinct chairmen and its monopoly of past registration lists. Some precinct chairmen had served in the same capacity for several years and could be expected to be familiar with, and to assure registration of, persons who were in sympathy with the state committee's position. New chairmen lacking familiarity with Republicans in their districts could be provided with the names of "interested" persons from the old registration lists or other sources. For example, in one precinct, in which 129 persons registered and 79 voted, the names of approximately 40 persons were sent to the precinct chairman by McGarraghy.

Total registration was 11,879, of which 4,690 were registered by the precinct chairmen and the remainder—more than half—at the single public registration place. Though rainy weather cut down on registration during the first three days, the total was more than six times the number of registrants in 1948, when almost 2000 registrants had established a registration record. Registration in individual precincts varied from 1,188 in one precinct to 33 in another, though all precincts included approximately the same total population.

Following release of registration lists by precincts the campaign to influence voting at precinct meetings began. The Eisenhower-for-President Club sent out stock political literature plus the names of the Eisenhower candidates in the respective precincts. The Citizens Committee for Taft sent a personal letter from Taft on his Senate stationery requesting the voter to support the state committee candidate in each precinct meeting as ". . . the only effective way to help my nomination at Chicago in July." The state committee itself sent letters explaining its traditionally neutral stand and the value of having non-pledged delegates who could exercise maximum flexibility at the national convention.

Detailed rules governing the conduct of precinct meetings had been established by the state committee and sent to the precinct chairmen in May. Only registered voters resident of the District of Columbia, accredited members of the press, representatives of the state committee, and one duly accredited representative each from the Eisenhower-for-President Club and the Taft Washington Committee could be admitted to meetings. Each precinct chairman could appoint a secretary and as many election officials as he deemed necessary. Election tellers representing each candidate were required and each candidate was to have equal representation among the election officials. Time limitations were placed on the one nominating and four seconding speeches that were to be allowed for each candidate. In case the precinct chairman were nominated he was required to designate some other registered voter to preside over the meeting. Provisions were made for run-off balloting in case no candidate received a majority of all votes cast on the first ballot. Ballot counting and election certification procedures were established. Distribution of campaign literature at the precinct meetings was prohibited.

Balloting at the May 16-22 precinct meetings, preceded by nominating speeches, was generally orderly and marked by only a few complaints about some advance voting and one or two rules fights.

There was no indication whatsoever of any significant irregularities that might have influenced the results in these meetings. They ranged from small gatherings with a folksy, neighborhood touch to mass meetings with much cheering and evidences of strong partisanship. Of the 11,879 registered Republicans, 7,569 voted in the precinct meetings. The state committee candidates received 4,597 votes and the Eisenhower candidates 2,972. Eisenhower candidates won in 4 precincts and the Taft-supported state committee candidates in the other 39.

The 43 precinct victors met on June 2 and chose 43 other persons to serve both as delegates-at-large to the District of Columbia "state convention" and as members of the state committee. The pro-Taft state committee slate of 43 delegates-at-large, selected by the incumbent national committee members and a member of the state committee from a longer list of 100 names compiled by the state committee and its friends, contained only one Eisenhower supporter. The 4 pro-Eisenhower precinct victors nominated 8 candidates for delegates-at-large from the floor at the June 2 meeting, none of whom received more than 6 of the 43 votes in the meeting. Twenty-four members of the previous state committee were among the victorious delegates-at-large.

At a meeting of the new state committee on June 4, Joseph C. McGarraghy was re-elected chairman; George L. Hart, Jr., lawyer, continued as secretary; and Bruce Baird, bank president, defeated in his precinct meeting but chosen a delegate-at-large, was re-elected treasurer. Miss Mildred E. Reeves, a practicing attorney, was elected vice-chairman.

The state convention on June 5 was a distinct anti-climax to the excitement of the registration drive and precinct meetings. Clyde D. Garrett, lawyer, was overwhelmingly re-elected national committeeman and the incumbent Mrs. Howard Coffin, housewife, was unopposed as national committeewoman. Attempts by both Taft and Eisenhower supporters to the contrary, an uninstructed delegation was chosen to go to Chicago. The traditional position of the state committee was maintained when a motion to instruct the delegation for Taft died for lack of a second. Two resolutions, referred to the attention of the national convention delegation, called for inclusion in the platform of a plank supporting national representation and local self-government for the District and put District Republicans ". . . on record in favor of pending legislation to regulate District primaries."

COMPOSITION OF THE DELEGATION

All 6 delegates were prominent Republicans in the District of Columbia. All were members of the state committee; five were members of the executive committee of the state committee, and four were on the executive subcommittee of the state committee including chairman McGarraghy and Secretary Hart. None held or had held public office except for one person who was a member of the Selective Service Appeal Board. The group was drawn predominantly from high income professional and business groups. There were three lawyers, one bank president, and two housewives. Of the latter, one was the treasurer of the District of Columbia Taft Committee, and the other was the wife of one of McGarraghy's law partners. In the absence of any information to the contrary it is assumed that all delegates paid their own expenses; they all came from occupational groups that would be expected to be able to afford the sums involved.

Of the four men, two were white, one Catholic and one Protestant; two were colored, both Protestant. Of the two women, both were white, one Catholic and one Protestant. Four of the delegates completed law school and two completed high school only. The delegates were all over 40 years old; two between 40 and 49, two between 50 and 59, one 65 and one over 70.

One delegate had never previously attended a national convention, even as a visitor. The other five had been present at earlier conventions as delegates, alternates, or visitors and had probably participated in the caucuses controlling the delegations. They neither lacked experience of conventions nor were they newcomers into the inner circle of District of Columbia Republicanism.

ACTIVITIES AND VOTING RECORD

The caucus, consisting of the delegates, alternates, national committee members, and the executive committee of the state committee, met in Chicago on the Sunday before the convention and informally bound the entire delegation to Taft. With a few exceptions the delegation and the caucus group worked as a harmonious and well-controlled unit. Three or four persons were opposed to taking the early stand in favor of Taft but went along with the big majority at the first caucus. After the two convention floor defeats for the Taft forces, another caucus decided to hold the line for Taft through the first nominating ballot but to leave each delegate free to vote as he pleased thereafter. The delegation voted unanimously on all roll calls with the Taft side, but, on the nominating ballot, after first casting its 6 votes for Taft, switched to Eisenhower after the Minnesota switch and before the final tally.

State committee chairman McGarraghy, who also served as delegation chairman, cast the District of Columbia vote in the credentials committee for the Taft side of all questions. George L. Hart, Jr., serving on the resolutions committee, was successful in securing District of Columbia home rule and suffrage planks in the platform. He was a member of the subcommittee on the FEPC plank and a leader in the fight against a plank favoring compulsory FEPC.

AFTERMATH IN THE DISTRICT

Chairman McGarraghy stated that District of Columbia Republicans had not been hurt by their delegation's actions at the convention. That was apparently the case since McGarraghy was chosen to be chairman of the presidential inaugural committee. The pre-convention Taft and Eisenhower forces worked side-by-side on campaign and inaugural committees. However, the future position of the 5 pre-convention Eisenhower supporters on the state committee is not clear.

THE DEMOCRATIC DELEGATION

The Democratic party of the District of Columbia has in recent years been a tightly-knit organization under the direction of a "state central committee." Melvin D. Hildreth, national committeeman, and A. L. Wheeler, attorney and central committee chairman, usually serve as the formal spokesmen for the 26-member central committee which is chosen at the party primary in presidential election years. F. Joseph Donohue, chairman of the District of Columbia commission government under President Truman, was the leading public figure of the District Democratic party after his appointment by Truman in 1951. Since 1948 members of Americans for Democratic Action (ADA) and labor leaders in the CIO and AFL have been influential in District Democratic councils; and there are some indications that suggest that the ADA has become the controlling influence within the District Democratic organization.

In 1940, a short-lived "Independent Democratic Association of the District of Columbia" made demands for an "open, fair, and competitive election." This appeal was received "unsympathetically" by the central committee, whose position was supported by the national committee. The District of Columbia delegation cast unanimous ballots at the national convention in 1940 for Roosevelt and Wallace. In 1944, the central committee met no competition in the primary. The delegation gave its 6 votes to Roosevelt, but was split 4-to-2 between Truman and Wallace on the first vice-presidential ballot, and 5-to-1 for Truman on the final vote.

In 1948, an open primary movement backed by the ADA and a "Veterans for Eisenhower" organization resulted in a court order that delayed the primary until these organizations and the central committee arranged a compromise. The central committee had provided a ballot containing only the names of its own slate of delegates, and listing only Truman though providing space for write-ins, on the preferential portion. The compromise caused the striking of the names of four of the central committee delegate candidates and the substitution of four ADA members. After this compromise, and in spite of a lively campaign, only 471 votes were cast in the primary. The delegation was bound by the unit rule and cast all 6 votes for Truman, who had beaten Eisenhower in the preference vote by 236 to 181.

The established method of delegate selection, which has followed the same general pattern since 1916 and was approved by the national committee in 1940 when it was questioned by a group opposing the central committee, is determined by the central committee. Delegates and alternates are chosen in a "preference primary" held early in June of convention years. The central committee meets at least 60 days prior to the national convention to issue the call for this primary in which the national committeeman and committeewoman and members of the central committee are also chosen.

No pre-election registration is required. Voters simply appear at any one of several polling places provided, indicate that they have resided in the District for the required length of time, that they are Democrats, and that they have not voted elsewhere. They then are allowed to vote for the candidates for the various party positions and to register their opinions on the several propositions that are usually included on the ballot. These propositions usually include an opportunity to express an opinion on some of the leading aspirants for the presidential nomination, various potential platform planks, and the question of binding the delegation by a unit rule. The candidates for the various party offices, including delegation membership, put their names on the ballot by filing and posting the required filing fee according to rules set by the central committee.

On several recent occasions there have been more candidates competing for positions on the delegation than there were positions to be filled, but rarely have there been full slates of delegate candidates competing with the slate backed by the central committee. The central committee has not attempted to maintain a position of neutrality with respect to possible presidential nominees, since in recent years, until 1952, there was little question as to who the nominee would be with an incumbent president seeking renomination.

THE SELECTION PROCESS IN 1952

The central committee, having endorsed President Truman in the fall of 1951 as its candidate for the 1952 Democratic nomination, was forced to reconsider its stand after Truman's announcement of non-candidacy. The committee met on April 1, 1952, set the primary for June 17, and announced its unanimous support of Estes Kefauver for the nomination. Candidates for the various party positions to be filled by the primary were to file between May 1 and 15. The filing fee for delegate candidates was $200, which had to be paid in cash or by certified check. Though there were no precincts or any boundary lines dividing the District, a total of 45 polling places well-scattered throughout the District were designated for the balloting. Voters in the primary were required to sign a statement affirming that they were citizens, at least 21 years of age, had one year residence in the District, had not voted in any other presidential primary in 1952, would support Democratic candidates and principles, and had not already voted in the District primary.

The central committee, attempting to give as wide a choice as possible in the preferential vote for candidates for the presidential nomination, sent letters to all prospective presidential candidates stating that their names would be placed on the ballot unless the committee was informed otherwise. During the first week in June, Barkley, Kerr, McMahon, and Russell withdrew from the primary, leaving only the names of Kefauver and Harriman on the ballot. The major referendum questions on the ballot dealt with control of the delegation by the unit rule, pledging delegates to vote for the winner of the preference poll, and home rule for the District. The primary campaign was thus waged between Kefauver and Harriman supporters. In addition, a running fight, involving litigation and some comic opera sequences, was waged between different elements of the ostensibly pro-Kefauver group.

The central committee, which had announced for Kefauver in April, apparently began to doubt the wisdom of that early declaration and named a slate (12 delegates with ½ vote each) of delegate candidates that included Joseph L. Rauh, Jr., Averell Harriman's local campaign manager, and Tilford E. Dudley of the CIO-PAC, who had not announced his choice in the presidential contest. In opposition to this slate, a group of strong Kefauver supporters filed a partial slate of candidates.

When it was discovered that "bullet voting" was prohibited by rules laid down by the central committee under Chairman A. L. Wheeler's leadership, attorney William A. Roberts, on behalf of himself and several other Kefauver supporters, brought suit against a majority of the central committee. "Bullet voting" was the name used in the press to describe voting for less than a full slate of delegates. District Court Judge Walter M. Bastian denied the request for an injunction, the Court of Appeals supported his decision at 11:30 P.M. on the evening before the primary, and there was no postponement.

Merged with the court action against the central committee and the split among pro-Kefauver ranks was a contest for the position of national committeeman. Melvin D. Hildreth, incumbent supported by the central committee, was opposed by Major General Albert L. Cox (Retired), who was claimed by Kefauver supporters as one of their own though he had issued no public statement as to his choice for presidential nominee and was believed by some elements in the party to be a Russell admirer. Key figures in the complex opposition to the central committee included several former delegates to previous conventions who were considered to be conservatives. They were disturbed by the strong position that ADA adherents had gained in the District Democratic party following the 1948 compromise.

The intensive Kefauver-Harriman battle for votes followed normal patterns of speeches, rallies, and personal appearances. The Kefauver campaign pointed up the Tennessee Senator's long record of support for home rule for the District of Columbia, while the Harriman appeal was based primarily on a New Deal-Fair Deal line with emphasis on civil liberties.

The anti-central-committee Kefauver group circulated a green sample ballot with their candidates indicated by check marks. The central committee Kefauver group circulated a yellow sample ballot which supported the same candidates listed on the sample ballot being distributed by the Harriman supporters. Senator Estes Kefauver himself arrived at a Kefauver picnic two days before the primary and was asked by both sides to announce which candidates for delegates he would support. He took copies of both ballots with him, remarking, "How can anyone make head or tail out of this thing?"

On election day, June 17, both Kefauver and Harriman made campaign appearances while the balloting was in progress. The congregation of a Negro church, marching under Harriman banners, was led to the polls by its minister. Kefauver visited various polling places accompanied by a parade and a sound truck. A few minor incidents required police attention near some polling places, though there were no serious interferences or interruptions in the balloting. There is no way of gaining an accurate estimate as to the amount of "repeating" that was done by voters going from one polling place to another, but apparently some did occur.

There was a record vote for a Democratic primary in the District of Columbia and a decisive victory for Harriman. Of 18,781 votes cast, Harriman received 14,075, and Kefauver 3,377. Stevenson, with 176, led thirty other write-in candidates. Harriman carried 40 of the 45 polling places. The final tally for delegates and central committee members showed a total victory for the slate endorsed by Harriman headquarters. This slate, with but one exception among the candidates for membership on the central committee, was identical with the slate supported by the central committee. The incumbent national committee members, Melvin D. Hildreth and Mrs. J. Borden Harriman (unopposed), were overwhelmingly re-elected. Very one-sided votes were cast in favor of all referendum questions which: (1) favored home rule for the District of Columbia; (2) required the delegates to continue voting for Harriman until a majority of the delegation decided otherwise; (3) bound the delegation to a unit rule; and (4) gave the central committee permission to fill any vacancies that might occur in the convention delegation.

COMPOSITION OF THE DELEGATION

Six members of the 12-member delegation had never held any public office of any kind. Two had at one time held various appointive positions with the Federal government, but were no longer so employed. The 4 delegates who held public office at the time they were delegates were: F. Joseph Donohue, District of Columbia Commissioner and former special assistant to the Attorney General; Francis Biddle, member of the Permanent Court of Arbitration, who had held many top level governmental positions, including attorney general; J. C. Turner, labor member on the District of Columbia Minimum Wage and Industrial Safety Board; and Miss Lucy Waters Lonergan, a congressional secretary. Four of the delegates had never held any party office other than that of delegate or alternate, though at least two of them, Donohue and Biddle, were important persons in national party affairs. The other 8 were members of the central committee, including its chairman, A. L. Wheeler, and vice-chairman Joseph L. Rauh, Jr., lawyer and ADA member. Also included in this group were the alternate national committeeman, Tilford E. Dudley, and alternate national committeewoman, Mrs. Katie Louch-heim.

Ten of the delegates were men, 9 white and 1 Negro; 2 were women, both white. There were 6 Protestants, 2 Catholics, 2 Jews, 1 who "attended all faiths," and 1 who claimed no religion. In age the delegation ranged from below 30 to over 60: 1 between 20 and 29, 2 between 30 and 39, 4 between 40 and 49, 2 between 50 and 59, 2 between 60 and 69, and 1 who did not list any age.

Four of the delegates were practicing lawyers. Two ran their own businesses, a taxi fleet and a wholesale liquor firm. Three were engaged in professional labor organization work—AFL Building Trades, AFL Operating Engineers, and the assistant director of CIO-PAC. One listed her occupation as a writer; her husband is employed by the federal government; the other woman was the congressional secretary mentioned above. The twelfth person was Commissioner Donohue. Five delegates were ADA members; 3 were members of national labor organizations; 2 of the American Bar Association; and 1 was an official of a business association. In the absence of any information to the contrary, it is assumed that all delegates paid their own expenses.

Of the 12 delegates, 5 had been delegates in 1948, and 1 of these had been a delegate in 1944 as well. Two of the delegates had been visitors at the 1948 convention. Four had never attended any previous convention in any capacity.

ACTIVITIES AND VOTING RECORD

The delegation organized in Washington late in June and chose the following officers: chairman, Commissioner Donohue; vice-chairman, Francis Biddle; secretary, Miss Lucy Waters Lonergan. Representatives on major committees were: credentials, Tilford E. Dudley; resolutions, Joseph L. Rauh, Jr., and Mrs. Katie Louchheim; and rules, J. C. Turner.

On all controversial matters the delegation caucus supported the New Deal-Fair Deal "liberal" position, and this was reflected by its committee representatives. In the credentials committee Dudley sided with the "liberal" factions in the struggle with Dixiecrat groups over the Texas and Mississippi delegate contests. In the rules fight on the floor of the convention the delegation voted unanimously against the Holland substitute and for the Moody rules change. It continued this stand by voting solidly against the motion to seat Virginia. It also voted with the minority favoring the Douglas resolution to adjourn. After the fire on the newspaper-strewn convention floor, Rauh made a further unsuccessful motion to adjourn, emphasizing his move with the preface, "I am willing to give my life for my country, but not tonight!"

The delegation was successful in pressing for a home rule and an "eventual national representation" plank. The delegation soft-pedaled the national representation issue because it might endanger or delay the gaining of home rule and because this was the policy line followed by strong opponents of home rule. On home rule, Dudley served as the spokesman for the Central Suffrage Conference of the District of Columbia before the preliminary platform drafting committee. The delegation supported a strong civil rights plank, but acquiesced in, though opposing, elimination of a plank calling for an end to segregation in the District of Columbia.

Commissioner Donohue and Francis Biddle participated influentially in non-delegation affairs. Donohue was interested in welding all the territorial delegates into a formidable unit that would cast its vote at the end of the convention roll calls. This arrangement failed to materialize when the rules were changed to permit Alaska to vote immediately after Alabama and when it was discovered that some of the territorial delegations were pledged to different candidates.

Biddle's efforts were concerned mainly with the management of the ADA caucus of delegates and alternates, over which he presided as national chairman. The first meeting of the caucus took place on Saturday just prior to the convention, and was attended by approximately 100 persons.

Following the first nominating ballot, when all 6 votes were cast for Harriman as required by the primary, a caucus was held. There was no majority to switch to another candidate, and the 6 votes were cast for Harriman on the second ballot. Following the second ballot, the delegation caucused and split: 7 for Stevenson and 5 for Kefauver. Under its unit rule, therefore, all 6 votes went to Stevenson on the third ballot.

AFTERMATH IN THE DISTRICT

Members of the delegation participated actively in the Stevenson campaign. Their efforts were spent primarily in fund-raising and programs to influence absentee voters resident in the District of Columbia. Donohue stated that he planned to work for "a permanent political organization of territories" after leaving his position with the government of the District of Columbia.

REVIEW AND APPRAISAL

In 1952, each major party organization in the District found itself taking part in a significant contest for the presidential nomination. Each found itself in the limelight on the national stage to an extent that was quite unusual and not wholly welcome. In both cases, the result was a turnout of the electorate which, while small for a major city, was nonetheless of record proportions by comparison with prior experience. The Republican registration in preparation for precinct meetings was nearly 12,000, more than six times the figure in 1948; the actual vote in the meetings was 7,569. In the Democratic primary, the vote was 18,781, as compared with 471 in 1948. In both cases, the accustomed routines were put to a severe strain.

On the Republican side, the contest between Taft and Eisenhower supporters took the form mainly of an argument over procedure, in which the local Eisenhower supporters favored all measures that seemed likely to facilitate broader participation by Republican "voters" and more openness to observation by the press, while the local Taft supporters and the local organization tended to take a more restrictive view. The resulting arrangements were a compromise in which the local organization gave ground to a remarkable degree, presumably because of the effect of the publicity to which it was being subjected in the showcase situation of the nation's capital. Yet, a sufficient number of procedural advantages were retained to make the outcome almost certain; and the total process remained one well calculated to assure retention of control in the hands of persons already dominant in the "state" committee.

The process on the Republican side is basically a state convention system for electing delegates to the national convention. It starts with the problem of precinct meetings, and of who shall participate in them. In an effort to establish a base of legitimacy on which to erect the remainder of the structure, the Republican party in the District of Columbia has established its own registration system, there being none under public auspices. The rules for the registration system were a focus of argument in 1952, and will undoubtedly continue to be a point of argument and criticism. Within the framework of the party rules as amended, the contest was carried forward in an orderly manner and without notable irregularities. A capable delegation was selected, and apparently gave effective representation in securing District of Columbia home rule and suffrage planks in the Republican platform. There is no way of knowing whether the delegation was truly representative of its constituency in voting for Taft, particularly since it would seem difficult to define the constituency of the delegation in the absence of an electorate that votes. The delegation was undoubtedly drawn from a self-perpetuating group that continues to retain control of the local party machinery. The system as it exists has evolved in an abnormal situation; in that situation it has served to maintain a cohesive party organization with enough stability and flexibility to survive in the swift political currents of the nation's capital.

On the Democratic side, the District of Columbia came into national prominence in 1952 because it was the scene, on June 17, of the last of the presidential primaries in which Estes Kefauver was entered and one of the few in which he had a serious contest. His defeat by Averell Harriman, 14,075 to 3,377, did much to deflate the claim of Kefauver invincibility, particularly since Harriman had started so late that he had not been entered in the other presidential primaries. The Kefauver defeat, moreover, was not the result of opposition by a local machine, although it may have been in part the result of opposition from the national administration. The Democratic committee for the District had announced for Kefauver shortly after the Truman withdrawal, but later weakened in its support.

Fortunately or unfortunately, the significance of the outcome was open to grave question because of the procedural weaknesses of the election that was actually held. There was no formal system of registration prior to the election. This made it possible to get out an unprecedentedly large vote, but left room for many election irregularities; some undoubtedly occurred. Electioneering at the polls was neither prohibited nor seriously restricted. The campaign emphasis upon civil rights and the group marching of Negro voters to the polls brought accusations of "bloc voting," although little evidence was available as to the extent or the effects of this tactic. The ballot itself was difficult to vote, in view of the number of candidates for delegate posts and the confusion of overlapping slates, none of which was segregated or separately identified on the ballot.

The result, nevertheless, was a competent delegation that gave active support to the winner of the preference poll, Averell Harriman, until his candidacy could no longer be maintained. The Democratic delegation, moreover, was probably more broadly representative of different occupational and age groups than the Republican, which was almost a one-class delegation of upper-income group lawyers and businessmen.

The Republican state committee placed great emphasis during the selection process on the desirability of delegation flexibility at the convention, though at Chicago the delegates did not evidence this characteristic. The Democrats were controlled by the primary results and a unit rule and conducted themselves accordingly at Chicago. However, Commissioner Donohue later expressed himself as opposing the technique of binding a delegation by inflexible, primary-imposed commitments to specific candidates. In different ways, therefore, both delegations gave support to the proposition that uncommitted delegations with a maximum of bargaining flexibility are most adapted to successful participation in the convention process.

The lack of a statutory basis for the choosing of delegates and for the regulation of party activities is a weakness that afflicts both major parties. The weakness is compounded by the disfranchisement of the local population in national elections and the complete absence of local self-government. Local racial tension complicates the situation and is magnified by the attention paid to it by the Congress, which acts as the local city council for the District.

The experience of McGarraghy and the Republican delegation in 1952 lends support to the contention that the congressional contacts, with their continuing importance for the District, are more important than presidential relations, since the President's impact on the District decreases appreciably after he makes his initial appointment of District commissioners. Thus, the pro-Taft stand at the convention probably strengthened the position of the Republican state committee since much of the key Congressional committee membership is from the "Taft wing" of the Republican party.

Since neither party has need of popular support in elections, both parties in the District take on aspects of "rotten borough" patronage machines, without much patronage to sustain them. Both tend to promote the interests of District residents as interpreted by the groups that are dominant in the respective parties at any given time. Introduction of local self-government or any popularly chosen representation in Congress, even a non-voting delegate in the House of Representatives, would so change the basic political environment that both local party organizations would have to adapt their organizations and procedures markedly to the changed situation or face the danger of extinction.

Meanwhile, if voting for national convention delegates continues to be the only voting that is permitted to citizens resident in the District, some regulation of the process by law seems clearly desirable. Almost any public system of voter registration and of direct election of delegates would probably be an improvement over the procedures of 1952 in either party. In the absence of legislation, the legitimacy of existing procedures will almost certainly remain under constant attack.

District of Columbia Chapter Acknowledgments

H. Rowland Ludden, Assistant Professor of Political Science, The George Washington University, prepared pre-convention reports on both delegations with the assistance of five of his students, George Emory, Gaylord Hoftiezer, Raymond J. Malloy, Norman Schwartz, and Daniel Sullivan. He carried on further research and prepared the draft chapter in consultation with the Washington staff during the winter of 1952-53.

PUERTO RICO

Electoral votes: none

National convention votes, 1952:
Democratic, 6
Republican, 3

Population 1950: 2,210,703
Urban, 40%; *rural,* 60%

Population increase, 1940-50: 341,448 (18%)
Urban, 58%; *rural,* 1%

Presidential vote: none

U. S. Representative
(Resident Commissioner) vote, 1948:

	1948	1952
Popular Democratic	392,033	430,296
Independence	66,141	126,208
Statehood *(Estadista)*	88,189	85,788
Socialist	64,121	21,719
Reform	28,203	—

U. S. Representatives
(Resident Commissioner) elected 1948:   *1952:*

	1948	1952
Popular Democratic	1	1

Commonwealth legislature elected 1952:
Senate: Popular Democrats 23; Independentists, 5; *Estadistas,* 4
House: Popular Democrats 47; Independentists, 10; *Estadistas,* 7

Method of selecting national convention delegates:
Democratic: state central committee
Republican: state convention

Based primarily on reports by HENRY WELLS

—————————————————————————————CHAPTER 15

FROM 1899 TO 1952 PUERTO RICO, a Caribbean island about three-fourths the size of Connecticut and with a population now somewhat larger, was an unincorporated territory of the United States. On July 25, 1952, the island became the Commonwealth of Puerto Rico, having achieved this new status as a result of a compact between the United States and the people of Puerto Rico initiated in 1950 by Public Law 600 of the 81st Congress.

Commonwealth status means that the Puerto Rican people are now locally self-governing. They elect or otherwise choose all of their own local officials under a constitution of their own adoption. They remain citizens of the United States, however, and are still subject to applicable laws of Congress and to applicable provisions of the federal Constitution. They do not have the right to vote in presidential elections or to send senators and representatives to Congress, but on the other hand they pay no federal taxes. Every four years they elect a non-voting resident commissioner to represent them in Congress and before the executive branch of the federal government. The governor of Puerto Rico is Luis Muñoz Marín, founder and president of the Popular Democratic party, the majority party in the island since the elections of 1940.

During the thirteen years of Popular Democratic control the government has undertaken a bold program to reform and revitalize the island's economy, political life, and social outlook. The results already visible are impressive. In the past ten years the national income has more than doubled and the standard of living has risen 70 per cent. A start has been made toward the diversification of agriculture and the introduction of industry, thus modifying the previous pattern of almost exclusive dependence on a single crop, sugar. Unemployment

341

has been reduced, slums have been cleared, and public health and welfare programs have been expanded. Acute population pressures have to some extent diminished as the result of the migration of Puerto Ricans to continental United States and the recent decline in the birth rate.

Political reforms have included reorganization of the executive branch of the government, extension of the merit system, elimination of vote-buying and other prevalent electoral frauds, popular election of the governor (achieved by act of Congress in 1947), and achievement of home rule through the adoption of a constitution and the establishment of the Commonwealth in 1952. As a result of these advances and of the personal popularity of Governor Muñoz, the government is stable and the Popular Democratic party is firmly entrenched. In the elections of 1944, 1948, and 1952 its candidates received more votes than all their opponents combined.

Puerto Rico does not have a two-party system. The Puerto Rican party system, in fact, bears little relation to that of the United States. Comparatively few "continentals" established residence in Puerto Rico after 1899, and those who did were confronted with an indigenous party system that dated back to Spanish times. Puerto Rico, moreover, has never been an incorporated territory, and statehood is controversial even as a remote possibility. Hence the two national parties have had little reason to encourage the development of territorial branches against the day when congressional majorities and even electoral college majorities might turn on the outcome in Puerto Rico. The Puerto Rican party system thus has followed its own evolutionary course, arising out of the political groups active in the island prior to the Spanish-American War and later developing new forms and principles in response to changing circumstances. The most important determinant of change has been the fact of American control, an essentially alien force which has had a pervasive effect on the political, social, and economic life of the island. The Puerto Rican parties for the most part have taken this potentially "disruptive" development in their stride.

At the time of the 1952 national conventions four organizations were active in insular politics; in order of importance, the Popular Democratic, Independence, Statehood, and Socialist parties. As their names suggest, the insular parties are considerably more ideological in character than the national parties. Each of the first three was committed to a different version of what Puerto Rico's political status should be *vis à vis* the United States. Puerto Rican parties also differ from the two national parties in that the influence of personalities is normally much greater in Puerto Rico. The ideological commitments of party leaders, especially on the status issue, are persistent sources of inter-party competition because of the customary loyalty of the rank-and-file to the established leaderships. Another difference is the fact that party discipline is much more strict and effective in Puerto Rico than it is in most parts of the United States. This is a consequence both of the *personalismo* pattern of leader-follower relations and of the parties' ideological differences, and it tends to exist on all levels of the party hierarchy. The personal ascendancy of the *barrio* leader over his followers is normally matched by his own loyalty to the municipal leader of his party, who in turn recognizes the ascendancy of a district leader, and so on to the top of the party pyramid.

Both national parties have long been represented on the island, but their influence has been limited mainly to dispensing the small amount of available federal patronage. The jobs that normally change hands when a new national administration comes in at present include only the following: the collector of customs, the United States attorney for the District of Puerto Rico, two assistant United States attorneys, the federal marshal, and the director of the Caribbean area office of the Production and Marketing Administration. In the past all of these posts were awarded to continentals, either political appointees sent down from the mainland or residents of Puerto Rico who had been active in the local branch of the party in power. Of late, however, Puerto Ricans have been named to some of these jobs. When vacancies occur in the offices of postmaster and federal district judge, they too tend to be filled on the basis of rewards to the party faithful.

The insular branch of the Republican party, however, has since its founding in 1899 been primarily a Puerto Rican party, active in island politics. It has in fact been so much more insular than national in character that it can scarcely be said to bear any resemblance to the Republican party in the United States. Known as "the Republican party of Puerto Rico" until 1924, the party has since undergone several changes of name. From the beginning, statehood for Puerto Rico has been the chief if not the only plank in its platform, and from 1948 to 1953 it was known simply as "the Statehood party" (*Partido Estadista Puertorriqueño*).

Until recently the Democratic party of Puerto Rico (*not* the indigenous Popular Democratic party) was composed of a handful of continentals, formerly Democrats in the United States, and a few Puerto Ricans with business, educational, or professional ties with the mainland. The Democrats have not identified themselves with any of the insular parties and have never endorsed candidates for local elective office. Early in 1952, however, a new and younger group, mainly Puerto Ricans, many of them active members of the Popular Democratic party, won control of the organization and have changed its character to some extent.

THE REPUBLICAN DELEGATION

From 1940 to 1952 the chairman of the Statehood party (then called the Union Republican Party) was Celestino Iriarte, a conservative San Juan lawyer who had been active in politics and a member of the legislature for many years. Between 1948 and 1952 his influence within the party began to wane. Inasmuch as the party had been out of power since 1940, Iriarte was deprived of patronage as an instrument of control. What few positions he could fill, he received from the Popular Democratic leadership in return for cooperation with its program. His willingness to cooperate, especially his failure to oppose Puerto Rican ratification of the Muñoz-sponsored compact of 1950, which led to the creation of the Commonwealth, and his active participation in the drafting of the new constitution, alienated a number of his followers who felt that he had betrayed the historic statehood ideal. Others, who believed that the party was losing ground under his leadership, desired to replace him with a more aggressive chairman.

THE SELECTION PROCESS IN 1952

The 1952 call of the Republican national committee entitled Puerto Rico to an allotment of three votes in the convention. The credentials of its delegates and alternates were to be filed with the national committee at least twenty days prior to July 7, the opening day of the convention. The regulations of the Statehood party prescribed that delegates and alternates be chosen by a party convention held not less than six months prior to the November elections; in this instance, on or before May 4, 1952. Because of the factional fight within the Statehood party, the names were not certified to the national committee until the last week in June, and the delegates finally seated at Chicago were not the ones who had been elected by the Statehood convention.

In keeping with the basically insular rather than national complexion of the party, the growing sentiment against Iriarte had little to do with the fact that he had long been closely identified with the Taft wing of the national Republican party. The leaders of the anti-Iriarte group—Miguel A. García Méndez, a vigorous young lawyer from Mayaguez, and Luis A. Ferré, a Ponce industrialist—were also Taft men. Although there was some support for Eisenhower within the party, most of the leaders as well as the rank-and-file were in favor of Taft, who had been a good friend of Puerto Rico in Congress.

Apparently sensing the "time for a change" mood within the party and hoping to forestall a show-down, Iriarte put off calling the party convention for 1952. He was finally prevailed upon to set the date for June 22, less than twenty days before the opening of the national convention and well after the deadline set by the local rules of the Statehood party. When the convention assembled in Ponce, it was clear that Iriarte would not be reelected to the chairmanship and that his slate of delegates to the national convention would not be accepted. After being interrupted by boos and heckling during a speech in which he attempted to give an account of his stewardship since 1940, Iriarte and some sixty of his followers walked out of the convention hall.

The remaining 480 delegates then proceeded, with only two dissenting votes, to elect García Méndez as chairman and Ferré as vice-chairman. They also elected an uninstructed delegation to represent

Puerto Rico at the Republican national convention. The list included Marcelino Romany, Charles H. Juliá, and Ramiro L. Colón as delegates and Guillermo Chiesa, Earle T. Fiddler, and Mrs. Providencia R. Villamil as alternates. Juliá was known to be an Eisenhower supporter, Colón was a Taft man, and Romany, a loyal alumnus of the University of Pennsylvania, was expected to cast at least his first ballot for Stassen. These delegates were instructed by the convention to nominate Luis Ferré as national committeeman and Mrs. Rosa M. González as national committeewoman for the forthcoming four-year terms.

Meanwhile the Iriarte faction was holding a rump convention in a nearby theater. It selected a delegation pledged to Taft and composed of Héctor González Blanes (chairman), Iriarte, and Ramiro Colón as delegates and José G. Salgado, Francisco López Domínguez, and Mrs. Providencia Villamil as alternates. The presence of Colón and Mrs. Villamil on both lists is explained by the fact that the Iriarte group erroneously supposed them to be on their side. Colón had accompanied the Iriarte faction out of the convention hall in an effort to persuade them to return, but failing in this he went back and later nominated Ferré for the post of national committeeman. The rump convention meantime selected Norman E. Parkhurst and Mrs. Iriarte as its candidates for membership on the national committee.

COMPOSITION OF THE DELEGATION

The leading members of the Statehood contingent, García Méndez and Ferré, were not delegates. The former was a prosperous lawyer and the latter the leading Puerto Rican industrialist. They were also brothers-in-law, having married sisters belonging to a wealthy landowning family. All of the delegates and alternates paid their own way to the convention, a substantial item from Puerto Rico. Three were lawyers and one of them, Romany, had been a judge. The latter's chief claim to fame prior to the convention was the fact that during his service on the insular bench in the early forties he had caused the members of the Executive Council (Governor Tugwell's cabinet) to be put in jail for failing to obey an injunction which he had issued against them.

The chairman of the Iriarte delegation, Héctor González Blanes, was Iriarte's law partner. Ramiro L. Colón, the delegate common to both lists, was president of the Coffee Growers' Cooperative, a producers' association. He and González Blanes had been delegates to the 1948 convention. Celestino Iriarte had been state chairman and his wife national committeewoman since 1940.

ACTIVITIES AND VOTING RECORD

Neither of the delegations had official standing before the convention since neither list had been submitted to the national committee before the prescribed deadline. Hence their respective leaders arrived in Chicago several days before the convention opened, each determined to seat his delegation. On July 3 García Méndez and Ferré, representing the Statehood delegation, and González Blanes and Parkhurst, representing the Iriarte delegation, met with National Chairman Guy Gabrielson, each side presenting its claims.

The Statehood leaders rested their case on their own party rules, adopted under the chairmanship of Iriarte himself, which in effect declared the Statehood party to be the only party in Puerto Rico affiliated with the national Republican party and provided that delegates to the national convention be elected by the Statehood party convention. González Blanes, for the Iriarte group, appealed to paragraph (i) of Rule 2 of the rules adopted by the 1948 convention, which held that "the election of delegates and alternates from Alaska, Hawaii, Puerto Rico, Virgin Islands and the District of Columbia shall be held under the direction of the respective recognized Republican Governing Committee therein in conformity with the Rules of the Republican National Committee." González Blanes contended that the election of delegates by the Statehood convention was invalid because not authorized by the "recognized Republican Governing Committee" of Puerto Rico, which he claimed was precisely the group that had withdrawn from the Ponce convention.

Chairman Gabrielson refused to decide the controversy and said that it would have to be brought before the national committee on the following day. Fearing that the Taft majority on the national committee would decide against the Statehood delegation since at least one of its members was an Eisenhower man, García Méndez and

Ferré approached González Blanes with a proposal that the two delegations be merged on the basis of the two members they already had in common, each side selecting one additional delegate and alternate. González Blanes fell in with the plan, and it was agreed that the delegation should consist of Colón, Romany, and González Blanes as delegates, and Mrs. Villamil, Fiddler, and Salgado as alternates. On July 4 the national committee unanimously approved this compromise list and enrolled the names on the temporary roster, it being understood—though later denied by the Statehood party negotiators—that the delegation was pledged to Taft.

This arrangement was soon upset by two unexpected developments. The first came on the following day, when the duly elected Statehood delegate and Eisenhower supporter, Charles H. Juliá, arrived in Chicago. Since he had not been in the city when the leaders of the two delegations reached their understanding, they had not consulted him before dropping his name from the list. When he discovered what had happened, he immediately challenged the agreement by filing a protest with the credentials committee. The second development came on Monday, July 7, when the convention voted on the Brown amendment, which, if it had carried, would have favored the Taft forces. When Puerto Rico's turn came, González Blanes asked that the delegation be polled. This revealed two votes in favor (González Blanes and Colón) and one (Romany) opposed, thus indicating that the compromise delegation was not solidly in the Taft camp after all. This same 2 to 1 preference for the Taft position appeared again in the Puerto Rico vote on seating the Georgia delegation.

The credentials committee, on which the Taft supporters also had a majority, took up the Juliá case on July 8 and, after a bitter controversy, repudiated the temporary roster based on the compromise between the two delegations, and approved for the permanent roll the list of delegates and alternates originally drawn up by the Iriarte group. Thus Iriarte replaced Romany and the delegation consisted of none but ardent Taft supporters. The Statehood leaders' only hope lay in getting the Eisenhower headquarters to bring the matter before the convention and ask that it overturn the credentials committee's ruling. Otherwise, they would lose not only their seats in the convention but also their representation on the national committee. The

Eisenhower forces agreed to help; the plan was to have Sherman Adams present the Puerto Rican case after the convention had disposed of the Georgia and Texas contests.

This plan was never carried out. The contests over the seating of the Georgia and Texas delegations, though won by the Eisenhower forces, produced so much rancor and lasted so late into the night that the Eisenhower managers feared losing some of their support if they kept the convention in session any longer. Hence they decided not to raise the Puerto Rican issue and let the three votes involved go to the Taft forces by default.

It was during this hectic evening that Romany rose to national fame by virtue of his unintentionally amusing exchange with the temporary chairman over the polling of the Puerto Rican delegation on the Georgia contest. (Official Proceedings, pp. 193-95.) Still a member of the delegation because listed on the temporary roster, Romany unwittingly voiced the swan song of the Statehood group when he cast his widely televised vote for the Eisenhower delegates. He may have saved the convention and the party by dissolving some of its tensions in laughter, as certain commentators later suggested, but he was not able to save his own Statehood delegation.

González Blanes cast Puerto Rico's three votes for Taft on the nominating ballot but during the changes after the roll call reported one vote changed to Eisenhower. The convention later elected Parkhurst and Mrs. Iriarte to the national committee.

AFTERMATH IN THE COMMONWEALTH

The split between the García Méndez and Iriarte groups widened after the convention. The Statehood party put up a full slate of candidates for the November election, none of whom represented the Iriarte faction. The party fell from second to third place in the total vote, but it is doubtful whether defections on the part of Iriarte supporters had much to do with this decline. The Iriarte forces organized the Boricua Party in two municipalities, but its candidates received only a handful of votes. Neither Iriarte nor González Blanes now holds public office, whereas García Méndez is a senator-at-large and Ferré a representative-at-large in the Commonwealth legislature.

Prior to the January 1953 meeting of the Republican national committee the Statehood leaders discussed with national officers the question of setting aside the election of Parkhurst and Mrs. Iriarte so that Ferré and Mrs. González could take their places. They were advised not to request such action by the committee on the ground that it did not have the power to overrule a decision of the convention. In a maneuver obviously designed to prevent a repetition of the 1952 fiasco at the 1956 convention, the Statehood leaders announced on July 27, 1953, that the name of the party in Spanish, *Partido Estadista*, had been changed to *Partido Estadista Republicano*, and that in English it would henceforth be known as "the Republican party of Puerto Rico." In November 1953 it was announced that the national committee had effected a rapprochement between the two factions and was prepared to award patronage to members of both groups on a basis mutually agreed upon.

THE DEMOCRATIC DELEGATION

The Democratic party of Puero Rico was founded in 1904 by Henry W. Dooley, a product of "Kings County Democracy." Dooley ruled it with an iron hand until his death in 1932. Since the Republicans were in power nationally during most of the Dooley regime, the party remained small and consisted mostly of loyal Democrats who had been born in the United States.

With the advent of the New Deal, more Puerto Ricans joined the party and a scramble for power and patronage ensued. The party split into two factions, each dominated, however, by continentals. Contested delegations from Puerto Rico presented themselves at the national conventions of 1936 and 1940. In the latter year one delegation was pledged to Roosevelt and the other to James A. Farley. As it had done in 1936, the convention seated both groups, dividing Puerto Rico's six votes equally between them. During the administration of Rexford G. Tugwell, governor of Puerto Rico from 1941 to 1946, some of the Puerto Rican Farley supporters did their best to discredit Tugwell among influential Democrats in the United States but were unsuccessful in their efforts to have him removed from office. The two factions got together in time for the 1944 convention, and sent a delegation composed of members of both groups. During the next seven or eight years deaths and departures removed from the scene a number of continentals whose factional squabbles had done much to keep the party alive. As control fell more completely into the hands of Puerto Ricans, the party's militancy declined to a point where a member of the Statehood party was elected vice-chairman and members of the Independence party held other posts. Its chairman from 1948 to 1952 could not speak English.

During the winter of 1951-52, however, the organization took a new lease on life. In November 1951 José A. Benítez, an energetic young Popular Democrat and executive assistant to the attorney general, joined the party, and by February 1952 had captured it. With the backing of National Committeeman Frank Antonsanti, he launched a bold attack on the chairman, forcing him and his supporters on the executive committee to resign. The remaining members of the committee, safely within the Benítez camp, then called a party convention.

THE SELECTION PROCESS IN 1952

The convention met in San Juan on February 24 with more than five hundred delegates in attendance, much the largest assembly in the history of the party. Every legislative district in the island sent delegates, most of whom were more or less closely identified with the Popular Democratic party and all of whom supported the Benítez *coup.* The convention elected a new executive committee which included Bernardo Segura as chairman and Benítez as executive secretary. It chose Mrs. Richard C. Durham as its nominee for national committeewoman for 1952-56, and it recommended the reelection of National Committeeman Antonsanti for another four-year term.

The convention then instructed the executive committee to select the six delegates and six alternates to represent the party at the national convention. This procedure was adopted because the members of the delegation would have to pay their own expenses, and it was felt that a delegation willing and able to do so could be organized more easily by the executive committee than by the convention.

By July 9 the executive committee drew up a list of delegates and alternates, but last-minute substitutions had to be made in several instances. Those actually present at the national convention were the following: as delegates, José A. Benítez (chairman), Frank Antonsanti, his son Orlando Antonsanti, Eulogio Riera, and Mr. and Mrs. Richard Durham; as alternates, Mrs. Henry W. Dooley, Ruben Gaztambide, Modesto Velázquez, Mrs. Haydée Antonsanti de Feliciano, Mrs. Orlando Antonsanti, and Mrs. Eulogio Riera.

COMPOSITION OF THE DELEGATION

All but two of the twelve delegates and alternates were long-time Democrats or members of their families rather than Popular Democratic "come latelies." Five of the seven men in the delegation were lawyers, and of these four were wealthy and conservative. One of the two non-lawyers was a government official and the other owned and operated a small factory.

Benítez, 30 years old, was the youngest delegation chairman at the national convention, and Mrs. Durham the youngest national committeewoman. Mrs. Dooley was attending her eighth convention; National Committeeman Antonsanti was attending his fifth, and his second as committeeman. Durham, originally from Virginia, had served for a time as acting secretary of the Democratic national committee and was attending his fourth convention. Velázquez had served as a Puerto Rican delegate at the 1944 convention.

ACTIVITIES AND VOTING RECORD

National Committeeman Antonsanti, a member of the credentials committee, joined the majority of that committee in voting to seat the states rights delegations from Texas and Louisiana. The delegation, through its spokesman Benítez, indignantly declined an invitation to join a proposed "territorial bloc," on the ground that Puerto Rico, having achieved Commonwealth status, was not a territory. (See District of Columbia chapter.) Before the nominations began, the Puerto Rican delegates went through the motions of visiting the headquarters of the principal candidates in order to ascertain their views on (a) the proposed appointment of Puerto Ricans to posts in American embassies and (b) the proposed establishment of a resident commissionership for Puerto Rico in the United States Senate in addition to the existing one in the House of Representatives. On July 19 Chairman Benítez presented the latter proposal before the platform committee. The question of including it in the platform came to a vote on July 23 but failed of adoption by a narrow margin, 37 to 34.

The San Juan convention of February 24 had instructed the delegation to follow the unit rule and to cast its first ballot for Harry S. Truman if he were nominated. In view of the announcement of his unavailability and of his support for Stevenson, the Puerto Rican delegation cast its six votes for Stevenson on all three ballots.

AFTERMATH IN THE COMMONWEALTH

On August 28, 1952, the executive committee of the Democratic party of Puerto Rico elected José A. Benítez as its chairman to replace Bernardo Segura who had recently resigned. Benítez then launched an energetic campaign to arouse local interest in the national election and to secure contributions through the sale of "Ruml plan" certificates. Finance Chairman Richard Durham raised about four-fifths of the total amount by organizing a "Hundred Dollar Club." Altogether, more than $40,000 was collected, a considerably larger sum than Puerto Rico had ever contributed to national campaign chests in the past.

During October Benítez campaigned for the national and state tickets in New York City, where he worked among the very numerous Spanish-speaking voters there.

REVIEW AND APPRAISAL

Back in 1904 when Puerto Rican delegates made their debut at national party conventions, it was presumed that the island might eventually became a state. The Republican group in Puerto Rico has clung to this belief, and indeed has made it the chief article of faith in its insular party creed, despite the national party's lack of enthusiasm for the notion. It was not until 1940 that the Republican national platform contained a statehood plank, and then, as in 1952, it committed the party to only a cautious recommendation of "eventual" statehood.

The national Democratic party has been even less receptive to the idea of statehood for Puerto Rico, which in any case has not been pushed very strongly by the local branch of the party since the death of Dooley in 1932. On the other hand, most of Puerto Rico's advances toward self-government have occurred during Democratic administrations, and the national party has not neglected to take credit for this. The 1952 Democratic platform congratulates the party and the people of Puerto Rico on the establishment of the Commonwealth and pledges support for its continued development. But statehood is not a dead issue in Puerto Rico. No insular party regards Commonwealth status as necessarily the end of the line.

It is unlikely that Commonwealth status will have much effect either on Puerto Rican participation in the national nominating conventions or on the methods by which its delegations are chosen. Although the basis on which Puerto Rico was first given recognition is less valid today than it seemed to be fifty years ago, it still has some merit. Moreover, quite aside from the still flickering possibility of future statehood, there are other reasons why both national parties are likely to continue to grant recognition to Puerto Rico in their nominating conventions, on their national committees, and in other party activities. One is the fact that there is a certain amount of federal patronage to be dispensed in the island and that traditionally most of the jobs go to residents of the island—and increasingly to Puerto Ricans rather than to continentals—who have been active in the local branch of the party in power. It is not in the nature of American political parties to upset such traditions once they are firmly established.

A second factor that tends to bind the Puerto Rican organizations to the national parties is the amount of money for campaign funds and other national political purposes that can be raised in the island. Although the amounts have been small by comparison with the contributions from many states, they have been increasing in recent years. Hard-pressed national committees are not likely to jeopardize this source of revenue by questioning Puerto Rico's right to send delegates to the national conventions.

A final factor is the increasing number of Puerto Ricans who have migrated to the United States in recent years. Since 1950 more than a thousand a week, on the average, have left the island to take up residence on the mainland, where, being American citizens, they soon become eligible to vote in national elections. Until recently the overwhelming majority of them have settled within the confines of metropolitan New York, where today one person in every twenty is a Puerto Rican. More recently, however, large Puerto Rican communities have been building up in other parts of the country. "The Puerto Rican vote" is gradually becoming a vital element in the calculations of New York politicians, city and state, and hence of national political strategists as well. Politically speaking, the land from which so many voters spring is not likely to be rebuffed by denying it recognition in the national conclaves of either party.

Puerto Rico Chapter Acknowledgments

HENRY WELLS, Visiting Professor in the School of Public Administration, University of Puerto Rico, prepared the original chapter draft in response to an invitation extended in July 1953. Professor Wells is currently preparing a study of the government of Puerto Rico.

NAME INDEX

357

SUBJECT INDEX

Illinois: 45, 46, 94, 137, 174, 181, 285, 287, 288, 291, 308, 310, 311

Kansas: 36, 156

Kefauver, Estes: 4, 21, 51-52, 180; appearances, 45, 46, 66, 205, 208, 282, 331; entered in pres. preference poll, 43, 205, 249, 330; entered in primary for delegates, 43-44, 89-90; instructions for, 251; post-convention activities, 50; support for candidacy, 25, 64, 89-90, 93, 114, 118, 172, 205, 280, 281, 329; visits R. I. delegation, 119; votes for at national convention, 4, 23, 50, 66, 95, 120, 178, 210, 254, 285, 308

Kefauver-for-President: 304

Kerr, Robert S.: appearances, 208, 282; support for candidacy, 21, 64; visits R. I. delegation, 119; votes for at national convention, 285

Key facts: the Northeast, 2; Conn., 124; Del., 216; D. C., 314; Maine, 8; Md., 230; Mass., 70; N. H., 26; N. J., 186; N. Y., 148; Pa., 260; P. R., 340; R. I., 100; Vt., 54; W. Va., 292

Legal opinions and decisions: attorney-general rulings, 35, 48, 157, 294; state court rulings, 196; federal court rulings, 330

Legislation on delegate selection: Conn., 127; Maine, 13; Mass., 74-77; N. H., 29-30; N. J., 189-90; N. Y., 154-55; R. I., 104; Vt., 55; see also Presidential primary law and procedure

Louisiana: 253, 254, 352

Loyalty oath: 22, 49, 66, 94, 119-20, 144, 173-74, 209, 210, 226, 253-54, 285, 308, 333-34

MacArthur, Douglas: 37, 273; entered in primary for delegates, 33-34; letter asking N. H. delegate-candidates to withdraw, 34; support for candidacy, 33-34, 78, 81, 269-70, 271; votes for at national convention, 275, 303

"MacArthur and McCarthy in 1952": 33

"MacArthur-for-President": 33

Maine: 6, 8-25, 27, 67, 254

Maryland: 6, 230-58

Massachusetts: 6, 27, 35, 70-99, 107, 108

Mayors for Stevenson: 95

Michigan: 275

Minnesota: 30, 35, 53, 81, 112, 202, 286, 327

Mississippi: 209, 210, 307, 333

Moody Resolution: see Loyalty oath

National committee members: *Democratic:* Conn., 143, 144, 145; Del., 225; D. C., 327, 329, 331, 332; Maine, 22, 23; Md., 253; N. H., 43, 49; N. J., 203, 206, 208; N. Y., 167, 169, 171, 173; Pa., 281, 283; P. R., 351; R. I., 116, 119; Vt., 63, 65; W. Va., 305, 307, 311; *Republican:* Conn., 128, 133, 135, 136; Del., 223, D. C., 325, 326; Maine, 13, 14, 19; Md., 241, 242, 243, 245; Mass., 78, 79, 87; N. J., 192, 200, 201; N. Y., 156, 157, 162; Pa., 269; P. R., 346, 349, 350; R. I., 111; Vt., 56, 60; W. Va., 294, 297-98, 301, 302, 303, 311

National convention votes, 1952: see "Key Facts" at beginning of each chapter

National presidential primary, favored by Truman: 44

Nebraska: 156, 310, 311

Negroes on delegations: 85, 162, 169, 171, 199, 207, 222, 242, 281, 306, 326, 333

Nevada: 67

New Hampshire: 6, 26-53, 67, 82, 89, 156, 164, 168, 212

New Jersey: 6, 82, 96, 186-214, 287, 291

New York: 6, 148-83, 286, 287, 288, 289, 290, 291, 310, 311

Occupations of delegates: see Composition of the delegation

Ohio: 213

Oregon: 31, 164

Organized labor: activities of, 9, 46, 88, 93, 94, 151, 188, 262, 263, 278, 284, 294, 328; representatives on delegations, 22, 38, 65, 92, 117, 143, 145, 207, 252, 281, 306, 333

Party membership, nature of: 29, 75-76, 130, 150-53, 154, 189-90, 263-64, 320, 329-30; see also Loyalty oath; Seating contests

Patronage in state government: 150, 155, 203, 263

Patronage problems after election: 87, 166, 245-46, 275, 294

THE NORTHEAST

CONGRESSIONAL DISTRICTS